VIRGINIA

BAPTIST MINISTERS.

BY

JAMES B. TAYLOR.

With an Introduction,

BY REV. J. B. JETER, D.D.

IN TWO SERIES.

SERIES I.

PHILADELPHIA:
J. B. LIPPINCOTT & CO.
T. J. STARKE, RICHMOND, VA.
J. F. WEISHAMPEL, JR., BALTIMORE.
1859.

PRINTED BY
LIPPINCOTT & CO.,
PHILADELPHIA.

PREFACE TO THE FIRST EDITION.

In the work of human redemption, the divine Being has given a sublimely glorious exhibition of his perfections. This display is made not only in the person and work of Christ, but by the Spirit's influence on the hearts and lives of men. Hence, the biography of the eminently pious may well be regarded with deep and lively interest. In every transgressor, converted from the error of his way, we behold a monument on which is inscribed the triumph of the gospel. Especially is this true in reference to those who, with becoming zeal, labor as the heralds of the cross. Not only will they shine as "the stars in the firmament" in a future state, but even in this world they reflect, with no common lustre, the glory of their divine Redeemer.

The author of the following pages has long believed that an essential service might be rendered to the cause of truth and righteousness, by preparing a judicious biography of prominent Virginia Baptist Ministers. To some extent, this work was executed by the venerated Semple, in an appendix to his History of Virginia Baptists. The publication of those sketches sufficiently indicated the utility of embracing in a separate volume a brief survey of the lives and labors of all those eminent Virginia Baptist preachers who have gone to their reward.

This work has been undertaken by the author with the earnest hope that some good might be effected. He has presented a collection of portraits, and, so far as opportunity has been furnished, he has faithfully sketched the intellectual and moral features of his brethren now no more. If, in any instance, he has failed, the failure has been unintentional. He has not wished to magnify or conceal defects, neither has he been willing to give a flattering exhibition of beauties which the original really possessed.

Some allowance must be made to the biographer, on account of the scanty materials from which a portion of this work has been executed. From various sources he has sought information; and, while he acknowledges with gratitude the valuable assistance furnished by several brethren, he regrets that, in many inquiries, he has been entirely disappointed. On this account, he has been reluctantly compelled to leave out of these sketches the names of several whose memory ought to be dear to all our churches. Some of Virginia's most able and useful Baptist ministers might be mentioned, whose character it would have been a grateful task to hold up for the imitation of others.

In giving the biographies of nearly one hundred ministers of the gospel, an opportunity has been furnished of making practical observations, both on the beauties and defects of which the Christian character is susceptible. This duty the author has not been willing to decline. He commits the work, as it is, to his brethren; and if the God of all grace shall make it a blessing to his fellow-men, the warmest wish of his heart will be gratified.

PREFACE TO THE SECOND EDITION.

In presenting the second edition of this work to the public, the author is happy to say that he has been able to furnish nearly forty additional memoirs of Virginia Baptist Ministers. There are still other brethren, who have ceased from their labors, concerning whom nothing has been said in this volume, because the needed information could not be obtained. As the memoir of Lott Cary has been published in a separate edition, it is omitted in this; the same may be said of the sketch of Abner W. Clopton.

PREFACE TO THE THIRD EDITION.

For some time past this work has been out of print, and the demand such, as to call for another edition. The present volumes or series contain an enlargement of the old sketches. Some of these have been rewritten, and all carefully revised. In addition, one hundred or more sketches have been prepared of those devoted men who more recently have passed to their reward. An earnest endeavor has been made to do ample justice to the memory of all. If any failure is found, it must be attributed to the want of definite information. Few can understand how difficult it has been to secure the necessary facts bearing on the history of some of our most valuable men. At some expense, and by patient toil, the author has been enabled to collect a mass of facts, which he believes will be of real and permanent value to the cause of truth.

This work now appears in two distinct volumes or series. The first contains most of the sketches heretofore published, in an improved form. The new sketches are contained in the second series. It has been deemed wise to publish these sketches in two series, so as to make each volume complete in itself. Many having supplied themselves with the old edition, will prefer to take only the second series; while perhaps much the larger number will desire both volumes.

The author has found the preparation of this work a truly pleasant task. His conviction of the soundness of our principles as a people has been increased as he has seen them working, by these noble instruments whom God has raised up. He has also found more deeply impressed upon his heart a grateful sense of the Divine power and mercy in our behalf. Not only has the Baptist ministry of Virginia made its mark upon the State in which it has so willingly labored, but in various other portions of our beloved country. The names of Toler, Shackleford, Hickman, Craig, Smith, and Thomas, are as dear to Kentucky as to the State that gave them birth. While the hills and vales of the Old Dominion, a century ago, resounded with the uplifted cry of Marshall, Taylor, and others, as they proclaimed the salvation of the Lord, distant regions were afterwards entered by them, and the same joyful announcements made. Where is the State, South or West, that has not been made a debtor to the ministry of Virginia? In every place their "faith toward God is made known:" the memorial of their deeds is recorded.

INTRODUCTION.

"THE RIGHTEOUS SHALL BE IN EVERLASTING REMEMBRANCE."

To record the labors, and cherish the memories of good men, is a sacred and delightful duty. To insure its performance God has made provision in the sympathies of our nature, and by the teaching of his Spirit. So long as men admire the self-sacrificing, the generous, the noble in human character, will the righteous, with their labors, sufferings, and successes, be kept in remembrance. Abel, by his "excellent sacrifice," though he has been dead thousands of years, yet speaks, and will speak to the end of time. Every pious man makes an impression for good on his generation. The world is better because he has lived in it. His humble deeds may not be engraved on marble, or inscribed on the historic page, but they are cherished in many a grateful heart, and their benign influence will be felt long after his head rests in the tomb. His abiding record is on high. The humblest works of faith and love have a place in the book of God's remembrance, and will meet a bright reward.

Rev. J. B. Taylor has performed a pious and most acceptable service in his efforts to rescue from oblivion the names, the virtues, and the works of the worthies who laid the foundation of our denominational prosperity in Virginia, or have contributed to increase it. It has been with him a labor of love, extending through many years, and involving considerable expense and most diligent and careful research. He has, by his timely and well-directed efforts, laid the friends of evangelical piety, and especially the Baptists, under lasting obligation.

The author selected for his cultivation a wide and interesting field. The early Baptist ministers of this State were a remarkable set of men. They were raised by Providence to accomplish a great work; were divinely girded for the severe and seemingly unequal conflict into which they entered. They were, with rare exceptions, men of moderate education, and taken from the medium walks of life. But they were of earnest piety, many of them endowed with good gifts for public speaking, and some of them eloquent and impressive preachers, who would do credit to any pulpit in any age. It is questionable whether Lunsford has now his equal in the State for commanding eloquence. No preacher has ever had greater power to command the attention and interest the feelings of an audience than the eccentric Leland. These holy men had to contend with a hierarchy, in which the spirit of piety, if it ever existed, had been succeeded by the spirit of bigotry and persecution. The established church was protected by intolerant laws, and was generally supported by the wealth, learning, and aristocracy of the colony. The clergy, inflamed by a desire to protect their stipends, and the rulers, invested with authority, combined to suppress the threatening heresy. Under these disadvantages our fathers maintained the combat. They preached the gospel without any hope of earthly reward. The scorn of the rich and great, the violence of mobs, fines, and imprisonment, awaited them wherever they went; but still they preached in private houses, in barns, in groves, and in prisons. These men deserve the commendation of mankind. They were unfaltering friends of civil and religious freedom. They were, and it must be universally admitted by candid minds, sound, earnest preachers of the gospel. They achieved a great work. Many causes, providentially, contributed to their success. The aggressions of the British government had awakened the spirit of inquiry and resistance in the colony. The public mind was stirred, and it was impossible to limit its investigations to secular matters. The aspiration after liberty, stimulated in the revolutionary times into a controlling passion, could not be satisfied until the religious shackles imposed by an arrogant hierarchy were broken off. Favored by these circumstances, our noble ancestors in the ministry continued the contest until the last vestige of the established church was erased from the statute-book, religious equality was secured for all the citizens and sojourners in the State, and broad and solid foundations were laid for the prosperity of the cause which they had so bravely supported.

But the fathers have passed away, and the fields which they brought into cultivation are being reaped by new men. A century has passed since the beginning of this great moral revolution. Several intervening generations have been swept away by the resistless current of time. Great changes have taken place in the Baptist ministry since the days of the "Apostle" Harris, and of the indefatigable Craigs. If the limits assigned to this introductory essay would permit, it might be interesting to compare the present with the early ministry of the Baptist denomination in this State, and to mark the changes which have taken place, and the various influences that have accelerated or retarded them. The reader may find ample materials for such a work in the volumes before him. We can now only glance at the subject. The ministers of the present day have more mental cultivation than the fathers had; but whether they have as strong faith and as fervent zeal may well be questioned. The pioneer preachers were fired with an inextinguishable ardor in preaching the gospel. They traveled extensively at their own charges, or with such occasional aid as was furnished them by their brethren. They inquired not for salaries, but for openings of usefulness; and though they erred in failing to inculcate on their brethren the duty of supporting the ministry, their error proclaimed their disinterestedness and zeal. Our modern preachers know more of books, and adopt sounder principles of biblical interpretration than did our early preachers; but probably they know less of the contents of the Bible. The fathers were men of one book. That they loved, and studied, and committed to memory; and to that they appealed in support of all their teaching. From it they derived their inspiration; from it they drew their armor; and from it beamed the light that guided them in their labors. We excel our fathers in combination, in liberal plans for the extension of Christ's kingdom; but they, in many cases, excelled us in individual and heroic exertions for the same cause. We have no reason to be ashamed of our ancestors; they were true, earnest, godly, useful men. We love to give them honor. Whether, if they could revisit the scenes of their devoted labors, they would be proud of their sons, is doubtful. They would have much to learn, and many prejudices to subdue, before they could appreciate the present order of things. Our plans for spreading the gospel, our colportage operations, our seminaries for the education of young ministers, and our Sunday-schools, would be to them new, and would not meet their approval without careful examination. The result of that inquiry is not doubtful.

Between the early ministers and ministers of the present time, several generations, as already noted, have passed away. Among these may be found some of the brightest ornaments of the Virginia pulpit; men well educated, if not eminent for learning; of fervent piety and commanding talents. With some of these it was the privilege of the author of the ensuing volumes, and of his cotemporaries, to be acquainted. They were noble men, and ennobled by grace. Where can we find the ministers of the present age who excel Clopton in deep and burning piety; Rice, in a masculine and controlling intellect; Semple, in clear, practical sense; Broaddus, in chaste and touching eloquence; Kerr, in vivid and overpowering declamation?—not to mention a host of worthies of various and precious gifts. Shall the memories of such men be permitted to perish? Not until a sad degeneracy shall take place in the churches which they planted, watered, and pruned.

I cannot close this hasty article without calling the attention of my brethren in the ministry to the weighty responsibility that rests upon us. Others have labored, and we have entered into their labors. We are called to reap the fields which others have sowed. The degree of prosperity enjoyed by our denomination in the State should fill us with gratitude to God, not self-confidence; with humility, not pride. If we contemplate the progress already made as an incentive to future exertion, we shall do well. Let us mark the means by which our success has been attained, that we may continue their diligent use. The history of our ministers and our churches will demonstrate that success has been due to an humble, affectionate, and faithful presentation of the gospel to perishing sinners. We have been in no measure indebted to worldly display or carnal policy for our denominational growth and strength; and far distant be the day when we shall resort to such influences for the promotion of our cause.

Much of our present prosperity is attributable to the disinterestedness of our ministers; to their freedom from jealousy and partyism. Without an ecclesiastical unity, our churches are remarkably united in views, spirit, aims, and labors. All desire, and pray for, and rejoice in, the success of all. Let us carefully guard against the demon of discord. Party leaders are a curse to the churches. Let not this language be misunderstood. Wisdom and experience should guide us in all our deliberations, and all our plans; but they should guide not as a matter of right, but of concession—not by the weight of authority, but by the force of argument and persuasion. But there are men in most religious communities who must rule or annoy; who are remarkable not for prudence, but self-will; who would rather head a party, however small and contemptible, than submit to the carefully considered decision of a majority; who, in short, prefer "to be judges among fools, rather than fools among judges." Such men do incalculable mischief. To our comparative freedom from such leaders may be ascribed much of the present harmony and efficiency of our denomination in Virginia.

It is hoped that the following volumes will do much to quicken, encourage, and establish our churches. With so many bright examples before us, we shall be most culpable if we do not conduct ourselves as "becometh the gospel of Christ." Let us, brethren, "be not slothful, but followers of them, who through faith and patience inherit the promises."

J. B. Jeter.

CONTENTS OF FIRST SERIES.

LIVES OF

VIRGINIA BAPTIST MINISTERS.

SHUBAEL STEARNS.

IN preserving the memory of those who have distinguished themselves among men, we are not to be confined to the learned and the brave. These may deserve a place in the grateful recollections of posterity, for discoveries in science, or achievements in war. But merit, exhibited in patient and laborious exertions for the spiritual improvement of man, deserves a much higher regard. When the records of eternity shall be unrolled, he will be esteemed truly great who has been wise to win souls to Christ, and who, counting not his life dear unto himself, has labored faithfully, "to testify the gospel of the grace of God."

Such was Shubael Stearns. He was one of the pioneers who led the way in promulging the glad tidings of salvation in Virginia. He was born in the City of Boston, in the year 1706. Concerning his early history, little or nothing is known. In giving a sketch of his life, the biographer must pass over many incidents, which, if known, might be interesting.

About the year 1740, a most extensive revival of religion was experienced in the New England States, through the instrumentality of the celebrated George Whitefield and others. In consequence of some peculiarities in the views and manner of the laborers in that work, they, with their followers, were called New Lights, and afterwards Separates. With this body of Christians Mr. Stearns connected himself, in the year 1745. Immediately after, his mind became impressed with the obligation to preach the gospel, and, accordingly, he entered upon this responsible work. He continued with the Pedobaptists until 1751, when, examining the word of God, he was convinced that, in reference to the ordinance of immersion, he had neglected a most important command of the Redeemer. The futility of infant baptism was also discovered, and he determined to take up his cross, be baptized, and unite himself with the Baptists. He was immersed by Elder Wait Palmer, at Tolland, Connecticut, and on the twentieth of May in the same year, was ordained to the work of the ministry.

Mr. Stearns continued to labor in the New England States two or three years, but he soon became restless in contemplating other portions of our country, which were more destitute of the preached word. He panted to carry the news of redeeming mercy where they had been as yet but partially proclaimed, and cherished a solemn impression that it was his duty to travel more extensively. Accordingly, he left his native State, and pursued his course in a southwesterly direction, accompanied by some Christian brethren. He concluded to remain awhile in Virginia, preaching in the Counties of Berkeley and Hampshire. There seems to have been a number of the friends of the Redeemer in this region, who gave him a hearty welcome, and encouraged him in his labors. Before his arrival, a Baptist church had been constituted on Opeckon Creek, Berkeley County, and among them Mr. Stearns was eminently useful.

The next field occupied by this man of God was in Guilford County, North Carolina. Here he permanently settled. The great spiritual destitution which prevailed seems to have induced his removal to that region. Such was the anxiety to hear the gospel preached, that the people would frequently travel a day's journey to attend a religious meeting. This afforded an extensive range for the benevolent spirit of Stearns. He commenced his labors with building a house of worship, and constituting a church of sixteen persons. The following notice from Semple's History, will furnish an encouraging statement of the success of his ministry among this people:—

"The inhabitants about this little colony of Baptists, although brought up in the Christian religion, were grossly ignorant of its essential principles. Having the form of godliness, they knew nothing of its power. Stearns and his party, of course, brought strange things to their ears. To be born again appeared to them as absurd as it did to the Jewish doctor, when he asked if he must enter the second time into his mother's womb and be born. Having always supposed that religion consisted in nothing more than the practice of its outward duties, they could not comprehend how it should be necessary to feel conviction and conversion; and to be able to ascertain the time and place of one's conversion was, in their estimation, wonderful indeed. These points were all strenuously contended for by the new preachers. But their manner of preaching was, if possible, much more novel than their doctrines. The Separates in New England had acquired a very warm and pathetic address, accompanied by strong gestures and a singular tone of voice. Being often deeply affected themselves when preaching, correspondent affections were felt by their pious hearers, which were frequently expressed by tears, trembling, screams, and acclamations of grief and joy. All these they brought with them into their new habitation, at which the people were greatly astonished, having never seen things on this wise before. Many mocked; but the power of God attending them, many also trembled. In process of time, some of the inhabitants became converts, and bowed in obedience to the Redeemer's sceptre. These, uniting their labors with the others, a powerful and extensive work commenced, and Sandy Creek Church soon swelled from sixteen to six hundred and six members."

In the midst of this church Mr. Stearns closed his valuable life. He had traveled extensively in North Carolina and Virginia, and been instrumental in doing much good, when his Master called him to his reward in heaven. When first confined to his bed, his mind was depressed, but the darkness was of short duration. He was made to suffer much, and protractedly, in body, but his soul was joyful in the God of his salvation. Having preached to others the Saviour of sinners, he found him in the trying hour precious to his soul. On the 20th of November, 1771, his happy spirit was dismissed, to take its place among the holy and good in a better world. His body was interred near the meeting-house in which he had so often spoken the word of God.

At this distant period, it is not possible to present a distinct portraiture of his character as a minister of the gospel. Mr. Morgan Edwards* has, in his own peculiar style, furnished a few interesting facts, which are annexed, and with which we close the biography of one of the most useful ministers of the eighteenth century :—

"Mr. Stearns was a man of small stature, but of good natural parts and sound judgment. Of learning he had but a little share, yet was pretty well acquainted with books. His voice was musical and strong, which he managed in such a manner, as one while to make soft impressions on the heart and fetch tears from the eyes in a mechanical way; and anon, to shake the very nerves, and throw the animal system into tumults and perturbations. All the Separate Baptists copied after him in tones of voice and actions of body; and some few exceeded him. His character was indisputably good, both as a man, a Christian, and a preacher. In his eyes was something very penetrating—there seemed to be a meaning in every glance. Many stories have been told respecting the enchantments of his eyes and voice, but the two following examples we give with the more confidence, because the subjects of them, viz., Tidence Lane and Elnathan Davis, were men of sense and reputation, and afterwards became distinguished ministers of the Baptist Society.

"'When the fame of Mr. Stearns's preaching,' said Mr. Lane, 'had reached the Yadkin, where I lived, I felt a curiosity to go and hear him. Upon my arrival, I saw a venerable old man sitting under a peach-tree, with a book in his hand, and the people gathering about him. He fixed his eyes upon me immediately, which made me feel in such a manner as I never had felt before. I turned to quit the place, but could not proceed far. I walked about, sometimes catching his eyes as I walked. My uneasiness increased, and became intolerable. I went up to him, thinking that a salutation and shaking hands would relieve me; but it

---

* Morgan Edwards was an eminent Welsh minister, and pastor of the First Baptist Church in Philadelphia for ten years subsequent to 1761. From his unpublished writings Mr. Benedict has drawn largely in his History of the Baptists.

happened otherwise. I began to think that he had an evil eye, and ought to be shunned; but shunning him I could no more effect than a bird can shun the rattlesnake when it fixes its eyes upon it. When he began to preach, my perturbations increased, so that nature could no longer support them, and I sunk to the ground.'

"Mr. Lane afterwards became a very useful Baptist minister, and was one of the first of the denomination who removed to Tennessee, where he administered, until his death, with reputation and success.

"Elnathan Davis had heard that one John Steward was to be baptized such a day by Mr. Stearns. Now this Steward being a very large man, and Stearns of small stature, he concluded there would be some diversion, if not drowning; therefore, he gathered about eight or ten of his companions in wickedness, and went to the spot. Mr. Stearns came, and began to preach. Elnathan went to hear him, while his companions stood at a distance. He was no sooner among the crowd than he perceived some of the people tremble, as if in a fit of the ague; he felt and examined them, in order to find if it were not a dissimulation; meanwhile one man leaned on his shoulder, weeping bitterly; Elnathan, perceiving he had wet his new white coat, pushed him off and ran to his companions, who were sitting on a log at a distance. When he came, one said, 'Well, Elnathan, what do you think now of these people?' affixing to them a profane and reproachful epithet. He replied, 'There is a trembling and crying spirit among them, but whether it be the Spirit of God or the devil, I don't know; if it be the devil, the devil go with them, for I will never more venture myself among them.' He stood awhile in that resolution; but the enchantment of Stearns's voice drew him to the crowd once more. He had not been long there before the trembling seized him also; he attempted to withdraw, but his strength failing, and his understanding being confounded, he, with many others, sunk to the ground. When he came to himself, he found nothing in him but dread and anxiety, bordering on horror. He continued in this situation some days, and then found relief by faith in Christ. Immediately he began to preach conversion work, raw as he was, and scanty as his knowledge must have been.

Mr. Davis was born in Baltimore County, Maryland, 1735; was bred a Seventh-day Baptist; went to Slow River, North Carolina, in 1757; was baptized by Shubael Stearns at Sandy Creek, and ordained by Samuel Harriss, in 1764; continued in North Carolina until 1798, when he removed to South Carolina, and settled in the bounds of the Saluda Association."

DANIEL MARSHALL.

The conspicuous part which Daniel Marshall took in the early history of Virginia Baptists will make a brief notice of his life acceptable to our churches. He was instrumental in the conversion of many sinners, and the organization of several churches in the southern part of the State. The notice which follows was prepared by his son, Elder Abraham Marshall, and originally published in the "Georgia Analytical Repository" of the year 1802:—

"In giving a biographical sketch of my honored father, we must look back to the distance of almost a century. His birth was in the year of our Lord 1706, in Windsor, a town in Connecticut. He was religiously educated by respectable and pious parents, and being hopefully converted at twenty years of age, joined the then standing order of Presbyterians in his native place. The natural ardor of his mind soon kindled into the fire of holy zeal; and, without the advantage of a liberal education, raised him so high in the esteem of his brethren, that they called him to the office of a deacon. In the exemplary discharge of his duty in this capacity he continued nearly twenty years. During this time he married; and lost a wife, by whom he had a son, named after himself, Daniel, who is still a useful member of society. At the age of thirty-eight years, our worthy parent was one of the thousands in New England who heard that son of thunder, Rev. George Whitefield, and caught his seraphic fire. Firmly believing in the near approach of the 'latter-day glory,' when the Jews, with the fullness of the Gentiles, shall hail their Redeemer, and bow to his gentle sceptre, a number of worthy characters ran to and fro through the Eastern States, warmly exhorting to the prompt adoption of every measure tending to hasten that blissful period. Others sold, gave away, or left their possessions, as the powerful impulse of the moment determined; and, without scrip or purse, rushed up to the head of the Susquehanna, to convert the heathens, and settled in a town called Onnaquaggy, among the Mohawk Indians. One, and not the least sanguine, of these pious missionaries, was my venerable father. Great must have been his faith! great his zeal! when, without the least prospect of a temporal reward, with a much-beloved wife and three children, he exchanged his commodious buildings for a miserable hut; his fruitful fields and loaded orchards for barren deserts; the luxuries of a well-furnished table for coarse and scanty fare; and numerous civilized friends for rude savages! He had the happiness, however, to teach and exhort for eighteen months in this place, with considerable success. A number of the Indians were, in some degree, impressed with eternal concerns, and several became cordially obedient to the gospel. But just as the seeds of heavenly truth, sown with tears in this unpromising soil, began to appear in their first fruits, the breaking out of war among the savage tribes occasioned his reluctant removal to Connogogig, in Pennsylvania. From thence, after finding it much more difficult to benefit Scribes and Pharisees than Publicans and sinners, he removed to a place near Winchester, in Virginia.

"Here he became acquainted with a Baptist church belonging to the Philadelphia Association; and as the result of a close, impartial examination of their faith and order, he and my dear mother were baptized by immersion, in the forty-eighth year of his life. He was now called, as a licensed preacher, to the unrestrained exercise of his gifts; and though they were by no means above mediocrity, he was instrumental in awakening attention, in many of his hearers, to the interest of their souls.

"Under the influence of an anxious desire to be extensively useful, he proceeded from Virginia to Hugwarry, in North Carolina, where his faithful and incessant labors proved the happy means of arousing and converting numbers. Being evidently and eminently useful, as an itinerant preacher, he continued his peregrination to Abbott's Creek, in the same State, where he was the instrument of planting a church; of which he was ordained pastor, in the fifty-second year of his age, by his brothers-in-law, Rev. Messrs. Henry Ledbetter and Shubael Stearns. Soon after receiving this honor, my reverend father, traveling at different times into Virginia, baptized Colonel Samuel Harriss, with whom he immediately afterwards made several tours, and preached, and planted the gospel in various places, as far as James River. It was but a few years after his ordination, before, induced by appearances of increasing usefulness, he took an affectionate leave of his beloved charge, and settled on Beaver Creek, in South Carolina.

"In this place, likewise, a church was raised under his ministry; and until brought to a good degree of maturity in divine things, was an object of his tender and unremitted care and solicitude. At the direction of divine Providence, as he conceived, and as subsequent events have proved, his next removal was to Horse Creek, about fifteen miles north of Augusta.

"The fruits of his labors in this place remain in a respectable church, some of whose sons, raised up under his care, have successfully diffused the light of divine truth through various benighted regions. From Horse Creek my aged father made his first visits to this State. On the second or third of these, while in prayer, he was seized, in the presence of his audience, for preaching in the Parish of St. Paul, and made to give security for his appearance in Augusta, on the following Monday, to answer this charge. Accordingly, he stood a trial, and after his meekness and patience were sufficiently exercised, he was ordered to come, as a preacher, no more into Georgia.

"In the words of an Apostle, similarly circumstanced, he replied, 'Whether it be right to obey God, or man, judge ye.' Consistently with this just and spirited replication, he pursued his luminous course; and on the 1st of January, 1771, came with his family, and took up his final earthly residence at the Kioke. The following spring the church here was formed, and it is famous for having furnished materials for several other churches. For this purpose many common members have been dismissed, and several ministers ordained. Among these are Rev. Messrs.

Saunders Walker, Samuel Newton, Loveless Savage, Alexander Scott, and the writer of this article. Through God's blessing on the ministry of her indefatigable founder and pastor, this church continued to lengthen her cords and strengthen her stakes, breaking forth on the right hand and on the left, until our beloved country was unhappily involved in the horrors of war. No scenes, however, from the commencement to the termination of hostilities, were so gloomy and alarming as to deter my inestimable father from discharging the duties of his station. Neither reproaches nor threatenings could excite in him the least appearance of timidity, or anything inconsistent with Christian and ministerial heroism. As a friend to the American cause, he was once made a prisoner, and put under a strong guard. But, obtaining leave of the officers, he commenced and supported so heavy a charge of exhortation and prayer, that, like Daniel of old, while his enemies stood amazed and confounded, he was safely and honorably delivered from this den of lions. Even the infirmities of old age, and the evident approach of the king of terrors, were not sufficient to shake his faith or hope, nor in the least perceivable degree to abate his zeal.

"A few months previous to his decease, rising in his pulpit, which he had frequently besprinkled with his tears, and from which he had as often descended to weep over a carelesss auditory, he said, 'I address you, my dear hearers, with a diffidence that arises from a failure of memory and a general weakness of body and mind, common to my years. But I recollect, "he that holds out to the end shall be saved;" and I am resolved to finish my course in the cause of God.'

"Accordingly, he attended public worship regularly, even through his lingering mortal illness, until the last Sabbath but one before his dissolution. In his family he invariably performed his usual round of holy duties, until the morning immediately preceding his happy change. Fully apprised of this, as at hand, and perfectly in his senses, he expressed, distinctly and emphatically, his steady and increasing confidence of future bliss.

"The following, taken by me in the presence of a few deeply affected friends and relatives, as he delivered them, were his last words :—

"'Dear brethren and sisters, I am just gone. This night I shall, probably, expire. But I have nothing to fear. I have fought a good fight; I have finished my course; I have kept the faith. And henceforth there is laid up for me a crown of righteousness. God has shown me that he is my God; that I am his son; and that an eternal weight of glory is mine!'

"The venerable partner of his cares, and, I may add, faithful assistant in all his labors, sitting bedewed with tears, by his side, he proceeded:—

"'Go on, my dear wife, to serve the Lord. Hold out to the end. Eternal glory is before us!'

"After a silence of some minutes, he called me, and said, 'My breath is almost gone. I have been praying that I may go home to-night. I had great happiness in our worship this morning, particularly in singing, which will make a part of my exercises in a blessed eternity.'

"Now, gently closing his eyes, he cheerfully gave up his soul to God, with whom, I doubt not, he walks, 'high in salvation and the climes of bliss.'

"This solemn event took place at the dawn of the second day of November, 1784, in the seventy-eighth year of his age.

"A suitable discourse to his memory was delivered from the above-mentioned passage of holy writ, by the late Rev. Charles Buffey.

"Whatever infirmities might appear in my certainly eminently pious and extensively useful father, it would not become me to bring them into view, except it were to show, as might easily be done, that 'e'en his failings leaned to virtue's side.' And I handle too feeble a pen to delineate the various excellent qualities and graces which adorned him in every relation he sustained through life. I will only say—

"'Tho' no proud pile, learn'd pen, nor letter'd stone
His virtues rare, to late posterity reveals;
He'll ever shine, and waxingly has shone,
Through rolling years, in ministerial seals.'"

It may be proper to add, that Mr. Marshall was twice married. Concerning his first wife nothing is known. We copy a few lines from editorial remarks of the "Repository," in which, besides a reference to his family, there is found a eulogy, which is believed to be merited:—

"In 1748 Mr. Marshall married his second and last wife, Miss Martha Stearns, sister to Rev. Shubael Stearns. Mr. Marshall had the rare felicity of finding in this lady a Priscilla, a helper in the gospel. In fact, it should not be concealed that his extraordinary success in the ministry is ascribable, in no small degree, to Mrs. Marshall's unwearied and zealous co-operation. Without the shadow of a usurped authority over the other sex, Mrs. Marshall, being a lady of good sense, singular piety, and surprising elocution, has, in countless instances, melted a whole concourse into tears by her prayers and exhortations.

"Another cause to which Mr. Marshall's distinguished utility is attributable, in a great measure, was his bold and independent method of procedure. With a soul expanded by contemplations on august objects, a boundless ambition directed to a correspondent prize, and the world completely under his feet, he was capable of the most difficult and arduous enterprises, and could be dismayed by no dangers. Superior to local attachments, he went from place to place, instructing, exhorting, and praying for individuals, families, and congregations, whether at a muster, a race, a public market, the open field, an army, or a house of worship; wherever he was able to command attention.

"Such conduct was, indeed, and may still, by many, be considered irregular, and little less than as savoring of insanity. But if he acted in some of these instances as if he were beside himself, it was for the sake of precious souls; and the fruits of his astonishing exertions have abundantly shown that he was constrained by the love of Christ.

"It may possibly be thought that Mr. Marshall was the subject of delusive hope; that he was culpably enthusiastic, when he left New England, with a family, to roam under the rising beams of the latter-day glory, as he supposed, for the conversion of souls. But let this matter be fairly considered, and it will appear that his most sanguine expectations must have so far been fully realized. Since the period at which Mr. Marshall commenced his career, many burning and shining lights have aroused a slumbering world, and liberally shed the lustre of truth in its darkest recesses; thousands of able and evangelical writers and preachers have been raised up, and as many gospel churches formed; a revolution in America has bestowed religious liberty on one quarter of the globe; the system of the man of sin has been almost demolished; liberty of conscience has made rapid advances in Europe; the shouts of all truly religious denominations have been mingled at the funeral of bigotry; the Scriptures have been translated into several barbarous languages; missionaries have gone out, literally, into all the world; and sinners of all descriptions have fallen, by thousands, beneath the sword of the Spirit, which is the word of God.

"Now, can it be reasonably presumed, that when Mr. Marshall, in the fervor of his piety, exchanged New England for the Mohawk nation, he expected, that by this time the kingdom of Christ would be more triumphant than the present advanced state of religion throughout the world fully justifies?

"As to any special confidence that Mr. Marshall might have had in God, as engaged to preserve and prosper a family devoted to His service, the reader will probably be of opinion that it could not have been stronger than it ought to have been, in view of the promises on which it was based."

JOHN ALDERSON, SEN.

No man of his day was more distinguished among the Baptists, than he whose name precedes this sketch. He was one of the earliest evangelical preachers of Western Virginia. To him are many of the churches indebted under God for their existence and growth. He was born in Yorkshire, England, and came to this country when quite young. The circumstances under which he left his native land were peculiar. His father, a minister of useful talents and respectable character, opposed, with considerable violence, a matrimonial connection he was about to form. To divert the attention of his son from this alliance, he prevailed on him to travel, and furnished him with a horse and the requisite funds. In a short time these means were exhausted, and the prodigal was at length bound on board a vessel, which brought him, without the consent or knowledge of his parents, to America. On arriving in this country, he was hired by the captain, for his passage money, to a respectable farmer of New Jersey by the name of Curtis. His conduct during his term of labor was such as to gain the esteem of Mr. Curtis. He afterwards married his daughter, and was highly respected by all with whom he became acquainted.

A short period subsequent to his marriage, the subduing grace of God arrested him. He became a believer in Christ Jesus, and was baptized in his name. With his characteristic energy, he at once began to recommend the Saviour to others. Having removed to Germantown, Pennsylvania, he continued in that vicinity to preach the gospel until the year 1755, when he removed to the County of Rockingham, Virginia. Upon his settlement in this State, he applied himself to the work of the ministry, and within twelve months a Baptist church was constituted, called Smith's and Lynville Creek Church, in the County of Rockingham. He became the pastor. This connection was retained about sixteen years, when he removed to the County of Botetourt.

In the year 1781, about nine years after his removal, he was called to the rest of heaven.

JOHN GARRARD.

THE subject of this memoir was among the earliest and most successful Baptist ministers of Virginia. Nothing is known of his parentage, the circumstance of his conversion, or his entrance into the ministry. He migrated from the State of Pennsylvania to the County of Berkeley, Virginia, in the year 1754, and there labored for some time as a preacher of the gospel. That part of the country was then sparsely inhabited, and subject to the assaults of the Indians. Having been frequently annoyed by them, most of the Church, with Mr. Garrard, removed below the Blue-ridge, and settled for awhile in the County of Loudon. During his stay there, he was instrumental in the conversion of many sinners. From house to house he went, warning men to flee the wrath to come, and preaching Christ, and him crucified.

Thus, what seemed at the time a heavy trial, was made to eventuate in good. Such was his success that it was deemed expedient to constitute another church, which was called Ketockton. When the Ketockton Association was formed, consisting only of four churches, he was one of the delegates, and assisted in the deliberations of the meeting. This was after his return to the County of Berkeley. He continued to serve the Mill Creek Church until his death. For some time he was also employed in supplying Buck Marsh Church, in the County of Frederick. In addition to these efforts in his own immediate vicinity, he delighted to spend as much time as possible in carrying abroad the blessed gospel. Like the Apostle of the Gentiles, he cherished a holy ambition to preach Christ where he had not been named. In the journeys of that devoted man, David Thomas, he was frequently accompanied by Elder Garrard, and proved a most faithful and successful coadjutor.

His talents were by no means inconsiderable. Such was the estimation in which he was held by his brethren, that for several years in succession he was chosen Moderator of the Association. He was a speaker of lively address. In his whole ministerial course, he was distinguished by a glowing and persevering zeal. He continued to vindicate his Master's cause, until, at an advanced age, he was called to give account of his stewardship.

JAMES READ.

VERY little is known concerning the history of James Read, before his conversion to God. According to his own account, he was in very early life the subject of much alarm, under the consciousness of his guilt, as a transgressor of the Divine law. He seems, however, to have entertained, on the subject of religion generally, very incorrect ideas. It was not until 1756, he being then about thirty years old, that he submitted to the sway of the Prince of peace. His conversion took place in North Carolina, under the ministry of Elder Daniel Marshall. Up to this period, his opportunities for mental improvement were quite limited, insomuch that, at the time he entered the ministry, he could neither read nor write. Under the tuition of his wife, he was soon able to peruse the pages of unerring truth.

Although he was in many respects unqualified to instruct in spiritual things, as an evangelist he was successful in winning souls to Christ. His spirit was stirred within him, when he beheld the thousands around him exposed to ruin; and he lifted up his voice in simplicity and godly sincerity, declaring the gospel of Christ. He traveled extensively both in North Carolina and Virginia. Indeed his talent seems to have been peculiarly suited to itinerant labor. In company with Samuel Harriss in one of his journeys, seventy-five, and in another more than two hundred, were buried with Christ in baptism.

It is painful to be compelled to state, that for some impropriety of conduct, he was excluded from the fellowship of his Christian brethren. After the lapse of two or three years, when satisfactory evidence had been afforded to the church of his repentance, he was restored to their affections, and to the full exercise of his ministerial functions. To the end of his course he exhibited a blameless life, and was made of God useful in his cause.

Notwithstanding the piety and success of this man of God, he was evidently in some things enthusiastic. He was too much inclined to regard his impressions as immediately from heaven. To this he was subject from childhood. It is partly to be accounted for from the fact, that he was almost altogether uncultivated, and that the early part of his life was passed in a time of comparative ignorance.

His death took place in 1798, in the seventy-second year of his age, having been more than forty years engaged in the ministry. His end is said to have been most triumphant. He was willing to leave the world, because he expected to be with Christ. In taking his departure, he said to a friend: "Do you not see the angels waiting to convey my soul to glory?"

WILLIAM MURPHY.

Although Elder William Murphy finished his course in one of the Western States, a brief reference to his life and labors deserves a place in this work. Under the ministry of Elder Shubael Stearns, he was awakened and led to Christ, and by him he was baptized. He began to proclaim the gospel at a very early period of our denominational history, and occupied quite a conspicuous station in the ministry. His labors were mostly performed in the southwestern parts of the State,—the region now occupied by the Roanoke and Strawberry Associations. He preached much also in the State of North Carolina.

His exertions were attended with success. As his natural powers of mind were good, his addresses attracted considerable attention, and many were brought to a knowledge of the truth. The Lord honored him with being the principal instrument in the conversion of Samuel Harriss, whose usefulness in the church was afterwards so extensive.

His discourses were of a doctrinal cast. About the year 1775, a very considerable discussion took place among the churches, on the extent of the atonement. In this controversy, Elder Murphy took an active part. It is believed, however, that he was more ambitious to become the instrument of glorifying the Saviour in the salvation of souls, than to distinguish himself as an able polemic.

JOSEPH MURPHY.

This laborer in the vineyard of Christ was a brother to William Murphy. He was baptized by Elder Shubael Stearns. He did not, when young, enjoy very favorable opportunities for the cultivation of his mental powers. But when born of God, and called to labor in word and doctrine, he assiduously applied himself to study, and became considerably improved. He was possessed of a fearless temper, and was thus qualified to stem the torrent of persecution, which in his day rolled in upon the church. He and his brother were reproachfully called "the Murphy boys," in allusion to their youth. But this he regarded not. He was not easily daunted by the opposition of his foes. When, on a certain occasion, he was apprehended and tried for daring to preach without a warrant from the establishment, he defended himself in the most manly and Christian-like style. Such was the impression produced on the minds of those who heard him, that he was at once acquitted and set at liberty.

After laboring successfully many years in the State of Virginia, he removed to North Carolina, and became pastor of a church on Deep Creek, in the County of Surry. In that region, he was eminently useful. It is said by Mr. Benedict, that he was considered the most distinguished minister of the Yadkin Association. His influence was also considerably felt in the State of South Carolina. In the year 1766, he assisted in the constitution of the Congaree Church, which has since then much prospered.

The particulars of Mr. Murphy's last days are not known. He was living in the year 1803, being then more than eighty years of age. He was characterized for his peculiar cheerfulness, and was much respected by all who knew him.

DUTTON LANE.*

Dutton Lane was born November 7th, 1732, near the City of Baltimore. At what time he became a resident of Virginia, is not known; but he was baptized by Shubael Stearns, in 1758. He was ordained to the ministry, and, probably, to the care of Dan River Church, October 22d, 1764, having commenced public speaking immediately after he was baptized. Mr. Lane was not a man of much learning; but, having a strong constitution, a commanding voice, and fervent spirit, he did great things in his Master's service.

Unenlightened as the Virginians were, at that time, it was not to be expected that he would be allowed to go in peace. His

* Prepared by Elder R. B. Semple.

own father was among the first to set his face against the Baptists generally, and against his own son Dutton in particular. He once pursued him with an instrument of death. It fell out, however, that instead of killing his son, he was himself slain by the sword of the Spirit, from which he soon after revived with a hope of eternal life, and was baptized by that very son whom he would have slain.

Mr. Lane was once preaching at a place called Meherrin, in Lunenburg County, where a Mr. Joseph Williams, a magistrate, charged him, before the whole congregation, not to come there to preach again. Mr. Lane mildly replied, that as there were many other places where he could preach without interruption, he did not know that he should come there again shortly. After wishing peace to the rest of the company, he gravely addressed Mr. Williams, and said, "Little, sir, as you now think it, my impressions tell me that you will become a Baptist, a warm espouser of that cause which you now persecute." This prediction came to pass; for, in about twelve years, Williams embraced religion, was baptized, and became a zealous member and useful deacon in the church that was afterwards formed at that place.

Once he was preaching against drunkenness, and exposing the vileness and danger of the practice, when one John Giles stood up, saying, angrily, "I know who you mean," and with a blasphemous oath declared, "I'll demolish you." But this self-condemned sot was prevented from doing any harm.

One William Cocker had conceived such malignity against the Baptists, that he was accustomed to say, that he would rather go to hell than heaven, if going to heaven required him to be a Baptist. But falling in, accidentally, where Mr. Lane preached, he was struck with deep conviction; and being delivered by converting grace, he became a pious Baptist.

Mr. Lane continued preaching till his death; but the latter part of his life was somewhat obscured by his adopting and maintaining certain strange opinions. By diving into subjects not revealed, and rather neglecting those which were obvious and more important, he was much less regarded. He lived and died a pious man, however, in the estimation of those who knew him well.

SAMUEL HARRISS.

FROM the few reminiscences which remain of the life and labors of Samuel Harriss, he may be recognized as one of the most laborious and useful ministers of the last century. He was born January 12th, 1724, in the County of Hanover, Virginia, but in early life settled in Pittsylvania. Before his conversion to God, he not only maintained a reputable character, but occupied several prominent stations in society—such as "church warden, sheriff, justice of the peace, burgess for the county, colonel of the militia, captain of Mayo Fort, and commissary for the fort and army." To fill these offices he was, without doubt, well qualified, not only by the kindness of his heart and his engaging manners, but by the possession of a vigorous and cultivated mind.

It was not until he had reached his thirty-fourth year that he became the subject of the Redeemer's kingdom. His serious impressions seem to have been occasioned by mingling with the pious, and reading the sacred Scriptures. He had not been accustomed to hear the gospel preached by the Baptists, a sect of people who for some time had been exciting much attention by the simplicity and zeal with which they recommended the truth of God. In the perplexity and distress of his mind, Mr. Harriss determined to be present at some of their meetings. It is said that when engaged in the army, in the discharge of his official duties, he providentially found an opportunity of hearing the gospel by Joseph and William Murphy, who had appointed a meeting at a house near Allen's Creek, on the road leading from Booker's Ferry, on Staunton, to Pittsylvania Court-house. As the people were collecting, Colonel Harriss rode up, splendidly attired in his military habit. What is to be done here, gentlemen? said Harriss. Preaching, colonel. Who is to preach? The Murphy boys, sir. I believe I will stop and hear them. He dismounted. The house was small, and in one corner stood a loom, behind which the colonel seated himself. The Lord's eye was upon him, and the truth became effectual in deepening his convictions. Such was his agony of mind, that at the close of the meeting his sword and other parts of his regimentals were found scattered around him.

Some time after this, he was introduced into the liberty of the children of God. His joy in realizing deliverance from the kingdom of darkness was of the most rapturous kind; and a fixed determination was formed to consecrate himself to the service of "Him who died for him, and rose again." Although, in view of the persecutions with which the Baptists were assailed, and his own elevation in society, there was strong temptation to neglect his duty, he nevertheless chose to suffer affliction with this despised people, and was, in 1758, baptized by Elder Daniel Marshall.

He commenced his ministerial course during the year succeeding his connection with the church. It was evident from the time of his conversion, that the Lord designed to make him extensively useful in building up his cause in Virginia. He made a relinquishment of his worldly honors, and gave himself wholly to the work of preaching the gospel. For seven or eight years his labors were mostly confined to Pittsylvania and the neighboring counties. It is remarkable that during this time he had not been authorized by the church, of which he was a member, to administer the ordinances, although he filled the office of a ruling elder. Some peculiarity of sentiment relative to the ministerial office, was most probably the occasion of this delay, for while he preached the word and exercised the pastoral rule, he did not officiate in baptism and the Lord's supper.

In 1769 he was ordained, and began to administer the ordinances. Mr. James Ireland, who was afterwards so distinguished in the Baptist ministry of Virginia, was the first individual he baptized. Mr. Ireland thus refers to this circumstance:—"He was a great favorite of the ministers in Virginia, and they had planned it among them that I should be the first person he baptized. He was considered a great man in the things of time and sense, but he shone more conspicuously as a luminary of the church. He was like another Paul among the churches. No man was like-minded with him. As the sun in his strength, he passed through the State, displaying the glory of his adorable Master, and spreading his light and heat to the consolation of thousands."

The following extract, from the pen of Elder John Leland, will not here be out of place. At that time Mr. Leland lived in Virginia: "In August, 1786, I attended a meeting of the General Committee at Buckingham; after which I traveled southward to Pittsylvania, to visit that great man of God, Rev. Samuel Harriss. I had met Mr. Harriss before on the banks of James River, and accompanied him at his meetings through Goochland, Fluvanna, and Louisa, to Orange. At a meeting in Goochland, after preaching was over, Mr. Harriss went into the yard, and sat down in the shade, while the people were weeping in the meeting-house, and telling what God had done for them, in order to be baptized. A gentlewoman addressed Mr. Harriss as follows: 'Mr. Harriss, what do you think all this weeping is for? are not all those tears like the tears of a crocodile? I believe I could cry as well as any of them, if I chose to act the hypocrite.' On this address, Mr. Harriss drew a dollar out of his pocket, and replied, 'Good woman, I will give you this dollar for a tear, and repeat it ten times;' but the woman shed no tears. In 1787 Colonel Harriss made me a visit, whose coming called out a vast crowd of ministers and people. His eyes—his every motion was preaching; but after he had read his text, his mind was so dark that he could not preach; and of course the lot fell on me. From my house he went down to Spottsylvania, where the work of the Lord, like a mighty torrent, broke out under his ministry."

At this period he had become well known throughout Virginia. His journeyings had extended to the more eastern and northern portions of the State; and wherever he went, the truth, in its simplicity, was dispensed. His success as an evangelist was most astonishing. The gospel, preached by him, was attended by the Spirit of God, and made effectual in the conversion of many souls. It is said that he had been allowed, with tokens of the Divine blessing, to preach Christ crucified in almost every part of Virginia, and in many parts of North Carolina. The estimation in which he was universally held, may be ascertained from the fact, that when the General Association decided that the apostolic office was designed by the head of the church to be perpetual, he was unanimously chosen to fill this office. This unscriptural decision was made, and the appointment conferred in the year 1774. The office was retained by him but a few months. This circumstance is referred to simply for the purpose of showing how far, by his labors of love, he had gained the affections and confidence of his brethren.

Perhaps few men of the eighteenth century contributed more to extend the truth and ordinances of the New Testament than Samuel Harriss. He was in almost all respects well qualified to secure the attention of those who heard him. "His manners," says Mr. Semple, "were of the most winning sort. He scarcely ever went into a house without exhorting and praying for those he met there. As a doctrinal preacher, his talents were rather below mediocrity; unless at those times when he was highly favored from above, then he would sometimes display considerable ingenuity. His excellency consisted chiefly in addressing the heart; and perhaps even Whitefield did not surpass him in this respect. When animated himself, he seldom failed to animate his auditory."

The fact has been already alluded to, that his influence among the Baptists of Virginia was deservedly extensive. He was called to preside at most of the associations, and other meetings for business which he attended. In the struggles that took place between the Baptists and the established church, he was also honored to take a very prominent part. He was not, however, required by his Master to sustain the same fiery persecutions which were endured by some of his brethren. His influence in society previously to his conversion, as well as his naturally fearless spirit, contributed much to his advantage.

It is not intimated that no trials were suffered, or sacrifices made, by this man of God. He gave up all for Christ. "Being in easy circumstances," says Mr. Semple, "when he become religious he devoted not only himself, but almost all his property, to religious objects. He had begun a large new dwelling-house, suitable to his former dignity, which, as soon as it was finished, he appropriated to the use of public worship, continuing to live in the old one. After maintaining his family in a very frugal manner, he distributed his surplus income to charitable purposes." Persecutions also were suffered. Among other things mentioned by Mr. Semple, he states, "that he was once arrested and carried into court as a disturber of the peace. In court, a Captain Williams vehemently accused him as a vagabond, a heretic, and a mover of sedition everywhere. Mr. Harriss made his defence. But the court ordered that he should not preach in the county again for the space of twelve months, or be committed to prison. The colonel told him that he lived two hundred miles from thence, and that it was not likely he should disturb them again in the course of one year. Upon this he was dismissed. From Culpepper he went into Fauquier, and preached at Carter's Run. From thence he crossed the Blue-ridge, and preached in Shenandoah. On his return, he called at Captain Thomas Clanahan's, in the County of Culpepper, where there was a meeting. While certain young ministers were preaching, the word of God began to burn in Colonel Harriss's heart. When they finished, he arose and addressed the congregation: 'I partly promised the devil, a few days past, at the court-house, that I would not preach in this county again in the term of a year. But the devil is a perfidious wretch, and covenants with him are not to be kept; and therefore I will preach.' He preached a lively, animating sermon. The court disturbed him no more.

"On one occasion, in Orange County, he was pulled down as he was preaching, and dragged about by the hair of the head, and sometimes by the leg. His friends rescued him. On another time, he was knocked down by a rude fellow while he was preaching. But he was not dismayed by these, or any other difficulties. To obtain his own consent to undertake a laudable enterprise, it was sufficient for him to know that it was possible. His faith was sufficient to throw mountains into the sea, if they stood in the way. He seems also never to have been appalled by the fear or the shame of man. He could confront the stoutest son of pride."

The views of Elder Harriss underwent a very material change in the latter part of his ministry, with reference to the obligation of the churches to support those who employ their time in preaching the gospel. For many years he not only entertained, but taught the sentiment, that no pastor or evangelist should expect remuneration for his services. This course was pursued in opposing the support of the established church by legal taxation. But he lived to deplore the extreme to which he had allowed himself to go; an extreme as opposed to justice as it is to revelation. The following well-authenticated anecdotes exhibit most interestingly his change of opinion on this subject:—*

"He, with several others, officiated in the ordination of a young man living near the City of Richmond. This young man had a wife and two or three children dependent on his efforts for support; he was in moderate circumstances, but industrious and economical, and they were comfortable and happy. In the charge which was delivered by Elder Harriss, he took occasion to refer to the salaries of ministers, in allusion to the recent circumstances of the established religion in Virginia, and adjured the young brother to give his life to the work, trust to the Lord for support, but never to receive a cent for preaching; no, never! The services closed, and the brethren separated. Some five or six years after this event, Elder Harriss and another brother, passing late in the evening through this neighborhood, remembered the affectionate and talented young minister, wished to know how he did, and determined to spend the night at his house. They rode up to his residence, but as they approached, they observed that his fields were but half tilled, his fences dilapidated, and his farm nearly destroyed by the stock. His house and yard were in keeping with his other affairs. Everything had the appearance of neglect, and evidently all was hastening to ruin. They called. His wife came to the door. How changed! She did not now wear her former rosy and contented appearance, but was emaciated, pale, and care-worn. Brother —— was not at home; he was absent on a tour of preaching, and, said his companion, he is scarcely ever with us. They told her they had come to spend the night with the family. She remarked that nothing could give her greater pleasure than their company and conversation, but she had not in the house a meal to place before them. Well, said they, never mind that, feed our horses, we are not hungry; we can wait until morning, and stop for breakfast on our way. I am sorry, said

---

* Extracted from "The Baptist," published in Tennessee, Elder R. B. C Howell, editor.

she, we have nothing on the farm we can give your horses, unless we cut down some green corn. How is this, said the venerable minister, does not Brother —— provide for his family? He cannot do it, said his wife, weeping—he preaches constantly, and you know when he was ordained you charged him never to receive anything for preaching; to which advice he has always strictly adhered. The ministers bade her farewell, and turned away from this scene of suffering and poverty with aching hearts. The teachings of the word of God rushed powerfully upon the mind of Elder Harriss, and he was oppressed with a view of the consequences of his unfaithfulness. The next day he met the congregation; he could no longer forbear, but nobly confessed his error before the assembled multitude; he that day preached on the duty of ministerial support, relating this event, and reminding them of the ease with which many of them who were living in affluence could relieve this distress."

On another occasion, when traveling in company with a brother in the ministry, the conversation was directed to this subject. He confessed the error he had indulged in the early part of his ministry, at the same time deploring the influence he had exerted on his brethren who labored in word and doctrine, and especially on the churches; an influence which he saw was likely to be most injurious to the interests of religion. Such was the anguish of his mind, in reviewing his course, that he insisted on retiring to the forest and making it a subject of special prayer. There, with strong crying and tears, he *lifted up* his confessions and petitions in the name of his ascended Redeemer.

Respecting the last moments of this servant of Jesus Christ but little is known. For some time before his death he was seized with an attack of paralysis, from which he never entirely recovered. Though on this account his labors were much interrupted, he still continued, to the extent of his ability, to recommend to all around him the service of his Master. He was not willing to be an idler in the vineyard of the Lord. At length, after having seen more than threescore years and ten, he took his departure from this scene of toil and pain, to receive a crown of life.

This sketch will be closed by one or two anecdotes, related by Elder Semple, with a few reflections from his pen:—

"When he first began to preach, his soul was so absorbed in the work, that it was difficult for him to attend to the duties of this life. A man owed him a sum of money, which he actually stood in need of, to defray the expenses of his family. He went to the man, and told him he would be very glad if he would discharge the debt he owed him. To which the man replied, he could not pay him the money. Harriss said, 'I want the money to buy wheat for my family. You have a good crop by you—I had rather have wheat than money.' The man answered, 'I have other uses for my wheat.' 'How, then,' said Mr. H., 'do you intend to pay me?' 'I never intend to pay you until you sue me,' replied the debtor.' Mr. Harriss left him, meditating, good God, said he to himself, what shall I do? Must I leave preaching to attend to a lawsuit? Perhaps a thousand souls will perish in the mean time for the want of hearing of Jesus. No! I will not! Well, what will you do for yourself? What? I will sue him at the court of heaven.

"Having resolved what to do, he turned aside into a wood, and fell upon his knees, and thus began his suit: 'O blessed Jesus! thou eternal God, thou knowest that I need the money which the man owes me, to supply the wants of my family; but he will not pay me without a lawsuit. Dear Jesus, shall I quit thy cause, and leave the souls of men to perish? Or wilt thou, in mercy, open some other way of relief?' In this prayer, Mr. H. found such tokens of Divine goodness, that, to use his own words, Jesus said unto him: 'Harriss! keep on preaching, and I will become security for the payment.'

"Mr. H. having his debt thus secured, thought it most proper to give the debtor a discharge. Accordingly, he shortly after, passing by to a meeting, carried a receipt in full to the man's house, and gave it to his servant, desiring him to give it to his master. On his return by the house, after meeting, the man hailed him at his gate, and said, 'Mr. H. what did you mean by the receipt you sent this morning?' Mr. H. replied, 'I meant just as I wrote.' 'Well, but I have not paid you,' answered the debtor. Harriss said, 'True; and I know, also, that you said you never would, unless the money came at the end of an execution; but, sir, I sued you in the court of heaven, and Jesus has agreed to pay me. I have therefore given you a discharge!' This operated so effectually upon the man's conscience, that in a few days he prepared and sent to Mr. H. wheat enough to discharge the debt.

"Some of the Christian worldlings of the present day will say: Aye! but this will not do often. We answer: The principle is correct at all times, viz., to commit our grievances to our heavenly Father, and trust him for a full recompense. How differently do those brethren act, who, for the mere pelf of this world, not only go to law with the wicked, but with their own brethren! And sometimes, in order to gain their point, will strive to blast their reputation in open court! For the honor of religion, it must here be added, that these things have seldom (we wish we could say never) occurred among the Baptists.

"A criminal, who had been just pardoned at the gallows, once met him on the road and showed him his reprieve. Well, said he, and have you shown it to Jesus? No, Mr. Harriss, I want you to do that for me. The old man immediately descended from his horse in the road, and making the man also alight, they both kneeled down. Mr. H. put one hand on the man's head, and with the other held open the pardon. And thus, in behalf of the criminal, returned thanks for his reprieve, and prayed for him to obtain God's pardon also.

"A volume might be filled with entertaining anecdotes respecting this venerable man."

DANIEL FRISTOE.

Elder Daniel Fristoe was born in the County of Stafford, December 7th, 1739. His parents were in comfortable circumstances, but the advantages of even a liberal English education were not enjoyed. Some attention was given to his morals, for, in childhood and youth, though of sprightly disposition and fond of gay society, he was never known to indulge in the grosser vices of the age. Up to the time of his conversion, he was accustomed to attend the Episcopal Church, as his father's family were of that order.

Nothing further can be gleaned concerning him until the grace of God became magnified in the renovation of his heart. Elder David Thomas seems to have been the honored instrument of leading him to the Saviour, in the twenty-third year of his age. The following circumstance, which is related by Fristoe in his History of the Ketockton Association, resulted in the production of serious concern on the subject of his soul's salvation. He was induced, probably by motives of curiosity, to ride several miles to hear a Baptist minister preach. His horse having escaped and left him, he was compelled to remain all night with the family at whose house the meeting was held, and who were members of the Baptist church. In the evening, several, who a short time previous had tasted and felt that the Lord was gracious, visited the family, and soon entered into conversation on subjects pertaining to the kingdom of God. How much good might be effected, if the moments were generally thus spent by those who fear the Lord, when they meet together in the social circle! They would not only promote each other's growth in knowledge and holiness, but a spirit of inquiry might be awakened among those present who knew not God. Thus it was in relation to Daniel Fristoe. He had heard without emotion the discourse which was preached in the course of the day, while the free interchange of sentiment which was indulged among the disciples, led to the discovery of his lost estate. He retired under the affecting consciousness that he was destitute of the pearl of great price. He beheld himself to be justly exposed to wrath, and began to seek the way of salvation. Under the ministry of Elder Thomas, he became acquainted with the way of life, and joyfully walked therein. "Jesus Christ, and him crucified," became the foundation of his trust and the joy of his heart. He delayed not to make known the happy change he had realized. Immediately he was baptized by David Thomas, and "went on his way rejoicing."

He did not engage in the work of the ministry until several years after his conversion. The Lord's cause, however, was not forgotten by him during this interval. At social prayer-meetings he was quite useful as a leader, frequently exercising his talent in exhortation. The church of which he was a member, at length encouraged him to devote himself fully to the work of the ministry.

His own mind became satisfied that it was his duty to do so, and subsequent events proved that the Lord was with him and blessed his labors. His journeys were frequent and extensive, during which he made it his chief object to spread the news of salvation through Jesus Christ.

When Brent Town Church was constituted, Elder Fristoe was called to preside over them. This took place in the year 1773. His labors having been successful in the State of Maryland, and a church raised up, he also became their pastor. In conjunction with Elder William Fristoe, he traveled regularly to the County of Frederick, a distance of seventy miles, preaching the gospel, and was instrumental in originating Buck Marsh Church. Indeed, wherever he went, many through his ministry were converted to God.

His discourses were mostly of the hortatory character. By his brother, Elder William Fristoe, he is represented as having been qualified to awaken attention by his warm and impassioned manner. There does not seem to have been much depth of thought exhibited, and his style was far from being accurate or beautiful. But he loved the souls of men, and sought to persuade them to turn from their sins to God. He was also very deeply concerned to promote the harmony and purity of the churches.

"An anecdote, related by William Fristoe, who served his brother Daniel many years, shows the sources of ingenuity possessed by the latter, whose ministerial career, though short, was remarkably successful. The surviving brother, being himself a careful and sound interpreter of the Scriptures, though he related the anecdote with much pleasure, by no means recommended a licentious freedom in spiritualizing the Divine Word. During a public meeting, two preachers were appointed to preach to the same congregation on the same evening, the last of whom was Daniel Fristoe. It so happened that the first preacher delivered a tedious and uninteresting discourse. Daniel perceived that the congregation were weary, and was sensible that his labor would be in a great measure lost, unless he could, by some expedient, rouse and fix their attention. He therefore, upon rising, proposed to dismiss the congregation, that the weary might retire, suggesting, at the same time, that if there were any who felt themselves sufficiently free from fatigue to remain, he would address them after the others had withdrawn. He moreover proposed, for the satisfaction of those who might go, to tell them the text from which he designed to speak; and, accordingly, opening the book of Judges, he read a portion respecting Sampson and the foxes. He then paused for the congregation to retire, but in vain, for the hearers were riveted to their seats, and were all attentive to hear what could be said about Sampson and the foxes. A rigid expounder of Scripture, such as William Fristoe was, would have perceived very little gospel in this historical narrative; but the inventive genius of Daniel was at no loss to find occasion for discourse concerning his Saviour. Under the figure of Sampson the strong, he exhibited Him who is the power of God; and he pointed out parallel circumstances in their birth, their exploits, and their victories at death. Under the figure of the foxes, he portrayed the ministers of the gospel, wild by nature, but tamed and brought into the service of the Redeemer by his invincible power, and sent forth, two and two, with the craftiness of foxes, though with the harmlessness of doves. From the tying of the foxes to each other, he inferred the agreement and affection that should subsist between gospel ministers. The fire-brands between their tails, the burnt harvest of the Philistines, and their consequent starving poverty, were, to the lively imagination of the preacher, instructive emblems of the terrors of the law, with which Christ's ministers are armed, the destruction of a sinner's self-righteous hopes, and the miserable poverty to which he is reduced, when he is brought at length to lie a helpless suppliant at the Redeemer's feet. This exposition was followed by a most animated exhortation. No man slept; but the hearts of many were moved, and God blessed the truth which was brought to view in this extraordinary and ingenious discourse."

His ministerial career was brief. Having been appointed a messenger from Ketockton to the Philadelphia Association, he was, while in the last-named city, seized with the smallpox, from which he partially recovered; but before he could return home, a relapse terminated his existence. He died at Marcus Hook, in the thirty-fifth year of his age. His remains were taken back to Philadelphia, and interred in the burial-ground of the Baptist Church. He left to mourn his loss, a wife and seven children, while his churches were deprived of a faithful and laborious pastor.

DAVID THOMAS.

ELDER DAVID THOMAS was born at London Tract, Pennsylvania, August 16th, 1732. What the circumstances of his parents were, is not known; though it is ascertained that when a youth, he enjoyed facilities for the cultivation of his intellectual powers. He was educated at Hopewell, New Jersey, under the direction of the distinguished Isaac Eaton. Such were his literary attainments, that the Rhode Island College (now Brown University) conferred on him the degree of Master of Arts.

No particulars have been obtained respecting the conversion of Mr. Thomas, or his entrance into the work of preaching the gospel. He seems to have commenced his labors as a minister when quite young. Several excursions to the State of Virginia were made by him before his removal thither, which took place in the twenty-eighth year of his age.

About a year previous, he married Mrs. Shreve, of Maryland, the widow of Mr. William Shreve, whose descendants were afterwards prominent in the history of Kentucky. This lady shared with him in his toils and sorrows as a minister of Christ. Having determined to devote himself, as a self-appointed missionary, in the then sparsely settled portions of Virginia, he spent eighteen months or more in the County of Berkeley. In the year 1762, he visited Fauquier County, became instrumental in originating Broad Run Church, and afterwards, on invitation, became their pastor.

"The origin of the Broad Run Church, and the manner in which Mr. Thomas was introduced among them, is thus related. A short time previous to his removal to Virginia, two men in this region, without any public preaching, became much concerned about their souls; were convinced of the reality of vital religion, and that they were destitute of it. While laboring under these convictions, they heard of the Baptists (New Lights, as some called them,) in Berkeley County, and traveled about sixty miles over a mountainous way, in search of them. By the preaching and conversation they were much enlightened and comforted, and were so happy as to find what had hitherto been to them mysterious, how a weary and heavy-laden sinner might have rest. The name of one of these men was Peter Cornwell, who afterwards lived to a good old age, and was so eminent for his piety as to receive from his neighbors and acquaintance the title of 'St. Peter.' It is related by Mr. Edwards, 'that this Peter Cornwell induced Edmund Hays (the same man who removed from Maryland to Virginia in 1743) to remove and settle near him, and that interviews between the families of these two men were frequent, and their conversation religious and devout; insomuch that it soon began to be talked of abroad as a very strange thing. Many came to see them, to whom they related what God had done for their souls. They exhorted, prayed, read the Bible and other good books, to the spreading of seriousness through the whole neighborhood. Cornwell and his companion (whose name is not mentioned) in a short time made a second visit to Berkeley, and were baptized; and Divine Providence had so ordered matters, that in this visit they met with Mr. Thomas, whom they invited to go down and preach among them. He accepted the invitation, and settled with them as before related, and soon became the instrument of diffusing gospel light in Fauquier and the adjoining counties, where ignorance and superstition had long prevailed.

"Mr. Thomas is said to have been a minister of great distinction in his day. Besides the natural endowments of a vigorous mind, and the advantage of a classical and refined education, he had a melodious and piercing voice, a pathetic address, expressive action, and, above all, a heart filled with love to God and his fellow-men. During a few of the first years of his ministry in Virginia, he met with much persecution, being frequently assaulted both by individuals and mobs. Once he was pulled down while he was preaching, and dragged out of the house in a barbarous manner. At another time, a malevolent individual attempted to shoot him, but a by-stander wrenched the gun from him, and thereby prevented the execution of his wicked purpose. The slanders and revilings he met with, says Mr. Edwards, were innumerable; and if we may judge of a man's prevalency against the devil, by the rage of the devil's children, Thomas prevailed like a prince. But the gospel had free course; and Broad Run Church, of which he was pastor, within six or eight years from its establishment, branched out and became the mother of five or six others. The Chappawamsick Church was constituted from Broad Run in 1766.

"Elder Thomas traveled much, and the fame of his preaching drew the attention of the people throughout an extensive circle, so that, in many instances, they came fifty and sixty miles to hear him. It is remarkable, that about this time there were multiplied instances in different parts of Virginia, of persons who had never heard anything like evangelical preaching, but who were brought, through Divine grace, to see and feel their want of vital godliness. Many of these persons, when they heard of Mr. Thomas and other Baptist preachers, would travel great distances to hear them, and to procure their services, as ministers of the gospel. By this means the gospel was first carried into the County of Culpepper. Mr. Allen Wyley, a man of respectable standing in that county, had been thus turned to God, and not knowing of any preacher in whom he had confidence, he had sometimes gathered his neighbors, read the Scriptures, and exhorted them to repentance; but being informed of Mr. Thomas, he, with some of his friends, traveled to Fauquier to hear him. As soon as he heard, he knew the joyful sound, submitted to baptism, and invited him to preach at his house. He also preached in the County of Orange, and, in company with Elder Garrard, carried the word of life through all the upper counties of the Northern Neck."*

Elder Thomas ultimately removed to Kentucky, when nearly threescore and ten years old. It was a sublime spectacle to see this aged veteran leaving the home which had become endeared to him by a thousand painful and pleasant recollections, to enter upon an untried field, and this, too, at a period of life when most

* Extracted, with some alterations, from Semple and Benedict.

men would deem it a duty to retire from active pursuits. He removed to Kentucky, too, it is said, when the religious aspect of things was far from encouraging. He entered at once into the work of the ministry, and accepted the pastorate of the Washington Church. It is said, that at the meeting of the Elkhorn Association, which met at the Great Crossing, shortly after, being surrounded by multitudes, whose fathers had heard him in the Old Dominion, his peculiarly musical, sonorous voice sounded out its inspiring tones, rousing and encouraging his brethren to hope for a special blessing from the Lord. And so it was. The following was one of the most noted years in the history of Kentucky Baptists. A glorious revival ensued, and many trophies of the Redeemer's power were seen.

As age increased his sight failed, and before his death he was nearly blind. But even then, he ceased not his loved work. Led into the place he had been accustomed to fill, he continued to hold up the Almighty Saviour as the one, only source of hope to the guilty. The following beautiful reference to a scene which transpired just before his death, is eloquently pictured by Rev. S. H. Ford, the gifted editor of the "Christian Repository," of Louisville, Kentucky:—

"Early in the present century, a young man, of powerful frame and noble figure, with face glowing with new-found hope, crossed the Kentucky River, near where Boone once encamped alone, through the winter, and following the windings of Hickman Creek, he urged his horse along the narrow, broken path. He was then some twenty-six years of age. He had just beheld, by faith's pure vision, God's harvest-field on earth; and his great heart thrilled to the deep tones of Christ's commission—'Go ye into all the world and preach the gospel.'

"The youth was Jeremiah Vardeman. Down in his soul were great, solemn thoughts; over that soul rolled glorious visions. In enthusiastic fervor he was making a kind of pilgrimage to a lone hermit, one of the last, and holiest, and greatest of an age of trial and of triumphant heroism.

"Near the close of the day, as the autumn evening with its solemn splendors breathed its voiceless hymn of praise, the youth, with his soul filled with unutterable thoughts, sat by the open window in an old log-house, beside an aged man. He was past his fourscore years, and had long been entirely blind. He had preached the Sabbath just preceding, and had risen feebly from his pallet to welcome the stranger who had called on him. Let us look at the old man a moment. In youth he must have been over medium height. He now bends, yet gracefully, beneath the weight of years. His brow is broad and contemplative. His mouth is large, but beautifully chiseled. The rest of his features are open and full of character; while his whole face has the mild, sweet aspect of a loving heart; and age, with its defacings, leaves no tracks of storm-passions or harrowing remorse. Intelligence still beams out, though the windows of the soul are closed. The scholar, the thinker, the man of energy and of power, are seen still in their partial eclipse. The light of a soul full of deathless faith and mantled in holy love, lingers there with a radiance more soft and beautiful than that autumn twilight. And the long, gray locks, which fell disparting from his temples down upon his shoulders, seemed to crown him with a halo of patriarchal glory. This was David Thomas, a Christian hero, whose memory will live forever. The meeting of two such men, and the object of it, are worth the record, are worth the thinking of. They were neither of them ordinary spirits. Both men of strong *faith*—that essential element of all greatness. The one was on the threshold of his life-battle, in youth's strong vigor, ardent, intent; ready for the onset, conscious of strength divine, and certain of victory—a real man, who believed the gospel had power in it. The other retired from the battle-field, his fight finished; whose life had been one of dauntless, aggressive, uncompromising valor; who had fought the good fight, not of shows, and management, and respectability, and popularity, but the fight of *faith*—and had been blessed, oh! as few men living had been.

"They met in the old log house for the first time. The old man spoke little of himself or his labors. The future of the youth was the theme. The hour of parting came. Vardeman knelt beside the old man's chair, while the patriarch prayed. 'Such a prayer,' has Vardeman often said, 'I never heard from mortal lips!—"God bless him, and may he be blessed,"' and his trembling hand was laid on the bowed head of the youth. The young man went on in his glorious work. His life has been given."

It will not be doing full justice to the memory of this great and good man, if we omit to name the fact that, during the struggle for religious liberty through which the Baptists passed in their earlier history, David Thomas exercised a most commanding influence. He wrote, and plead in his numerous appeals to listening crowds, for a total non-interference by government with religious matters. One of his pleas for liberty was written in poetry. The following is a quotation :—

"'Tis all one voice, they all agree,
'God made us, and we must be free.'
Freedom we crave, with every breath,
An equal freedom, or a death.
The heav'nly blessing freely give,
Or make an act we shall not live.
Tax all things: water, air, and light,
If need there be; yea, tax the *night;*
But let our brave, heroic minds
Move freely as celestial winds.
Make vice and folly feel your rod,
But leave our consciences to God."

Elder Thomas was suddenly called to his heavenly home. He had sought a brief repose upon his couch, and gently sinking into a soft, sweet slumber, he woke no more on earth. Blessed rest! The rest of the holy is his.

JOSEPH ANTHONY.

THIS laborer in the Lord's vineyard was among the early fruits of the preaching of Elders Reed and Harriss, in the County of Goochland. He was baptized by J. Waller, in one of his journeys through that region, and united with the Dover Church. He had previously improved every opportunity of exhorting his fellow-men, and immediately on his connection with the church, he devoted himself to the work of preaching the gospel. Nor was his labor vain. Wherever he went, the Lord was with him, giving him many seals to his ministry. For a time he was actively engaged with Mr. Webber in the County of Chesterfield; and was successful in the constitution of two or three churches. Afterwards he became an associate with Elder Elijah Baker, in the counties between Richmond and Hampton. He finally removed to the western part of this State, and became the pastor of Otter and Burton's Creek Churches, in the Strawberry Association. In these churches he was useful. Many were, through his means, introduced into the kingdom of Christ. After his settlement in the County of Henry, his efforts were more confined than formerly, but he was not less diligent. In the Strawberry Association, he was always considered a judicious and active man. When the Mayo Association was formed, he was chosen their Moderator, and continued in this office until his death.

In the early part of his ministry, he suffered much from the opposition of the enemies of the cross of Christ. He was among those who were immured in the jail of Chesterfield in 1770–71. He however maintained his steadfastness, and continued, with all boldness, to declare the whole council of God. Such was the power of his ministry while in jail, as he lifted up his voice and proclaimed Christ to the crowds without, that it was judged the best policy to dismiss him. The jailor was directed to shut the door of his cell, but to leave it unlocked, that it might be reported he had fled from prison. Mr. Anthony chose to continue. The door was then left open—still he remained. He was then persuaded, with his fellow-prisoner, to escape. But he replied, "they have taken us openly, uncondemned, and have cast us into prison; and now, do they cast us out privily? Nay, verily; but let them come themselves and fetch us out."

Mr. Anthony's talents were not above mediocrity. Few, however, of all who have labored in the vineyard of the Lord, in Virginia, have been more unwearied than he, or more successful. What tended more than all to his usefulness, was his fervid piety. He loved his Master, and cheerfully counted all things but loss, that he might extend his kingdom and glory. In all his intercourse with his fellow-men, he manifested a lively concern for their salvation, and it is said that he almost invariably made it a practice to converse affectionately with them, warning them to escape the wrath to come.

JOHN WEATHERFORD.

Although this servant of the Redeemer has but recently gone the way of all the earth, he was born nearly a century ago, perhaps about the year 1740. The place of his nativity was Charlotte County. His parents were poor, though respectable. They were both members of the Presbyterian denomination, his father sustaining the office of Elder in the Church over which Mr. David Rice, a distinguished Presbyterian minister, presided. Nothing worthy of notice occurred in his childish years, except that he was remarkable for the sprightliness of his disposition.

He does not appear to have been attentive to his soul's interests, until he was awakened by hearing a discourse delivered by Elder S. Harriss. This produced serious reflection. The more he prosecuted his inquiries, the more numerous and aggravated his sins appeared. He represents himself as having long struggled against the New Testament plan of salvation. He sought, by good works, to recommend himself to God, but all his efforts failed. He found himself, on every hand, defective, and pursued by a fiery law which cried for vengeance. Strange it is that men, whose whole lives have been a series of rebellion against the Divine Majesty, and who, in their best attempts at reformation, are still unholy, should so strongly incline to seek justification by their own merits. But thus it is. The enmity of the carnal heart exhibits itself by continual endeavors to palliate sin, and to resist the righteousness of God. The subject of this memoir persisted in exertions to make himself worthy, until, in despair, he fled to Christ. Here he found relief. His burden was removed. The eyes of his understanding being enlightened, he saw that God could be just, and yet justify the sinner who believes in Jesus. Now there was peace with God through a Mediator. He could *now* glory only in the cross.

It has been stated, that his seriousness was occasioned by hearing a sermon from Elder Harriss. At this time the Baptists had not excited much attention. Indeed they were but little known. When Mr. W. became a converted man, he had not thought of the distinction which existed between the Presbyterians and the Baptists. In reading the New Testament he was surprised to find so many passages apparently favoring the practice of the latter. As he himself said, he was almost ready to think he had found a spurious copy. He endeavored, however, to satisfy himself by banishing the subject from his mind; but it was all in vain. He then sought from his father such an explanation as might enable him to join the Presbyterian Church. Here also he failed. With the confidence of having his scruples removed, as his last alternative, he sought an interview with Mr. Rice. This conversation proved more satisfactory. But in re-perusing the Scriptures, all his difficulties returned. A second time he conversed with the minister, but without being convinced of the exclusive scriptural propriety of believers' baptism. Finding his young friend rather disposed to contest the subject, Mr. Rice said to him, "I perceive you will be a Baptist; go, and the Lord be with you." His sincerity was now brought to the test. He had been taught to regard the practice of the Pedobaptists as correct. His family and friends belonged to that party. The Baptists were few, poor, and despised. They were suffering much on account of their distinctive tenets. If he should unite with them, he must expect to pass through fiery tribulation. But no conference was held with flesh and blood. As soon as he became thoroughly convinced of his duty, he at once obeyed his Lord, by being buried with him in baptism. This was before he had reached his twentieth year.

From the time of his conversion, he manifested a peculiar concern for the welfare of immortal souls. Though young, he determined to commence a prayer-meeting in the vicinity of his father's residence. This he conducted with much propriety and success. The neighbors were astonished at the holy boldness of this young disciple; and believing he was influenced by benevolent motives, encouraged him to persevere. He soon began to preach. It is worthy of remark that he received much approbation in his labors from other denominations, although he was himself a warm and decided Baptist.

The entrance of Elder W. into the ministry must have occurred about the year 1761. He became at once a zealous and successful herald of the cross. He not only preached in his native county, but traveled much, especially in the southern part of the State. As he was among the earliest Baptist ministers of Virginia, it was his honor to suffer persecution for the sake of Christ. Naturally, he was a man of courage, but it was the promise, "Lo, I am with you alway," that enabled him to meet the coming storm. Trusting in the Lord, he feared no evil. Neither stripes nor imprisonment deterred him from the performance of duty. The rulers of the Episcopal Church were much vexed at the success of Mr. W. Wherever he went, his ministry was attended by crowds, and many were converted through his instrumentality. It was a source of great mortification that a plain man, without any pretensions to learning, should so far obtain the confidence of the people. Various measures were adopted to silence him and his fellow-laborers. But they preferred obedience to God rather than man, even at the expense of liberty and life. Having gone down as far as Chesterfield, preaching the good news of salvation, he was arrested by Col. Cary, and thrown into prison. He was in confinement five months. During this incarceration, he enjoyed much of the Divine presence. And, as it was with the Apostle, his trials only promoted the furtherance of the gospel. He continued to exercise a powerful influence in the county. Says the brother who communicated these facts: "His courage forsook him not. The love of Christ constrained him. He preached at the door of the prison as long as allowed the privilege; when refused that, he preached through the grates of the window. But such determined opposition did he meet, that an effort was made by his enemies to put a stop to that also. For this purpose they built an outer wall, or fence, above the grate; but Weatherford devised means to overcome the obstacle. A handkerchief, by the congregation, was to be raised on a pole, above the wall, as a signal that the people were ready to hear. His voice being very strong, he could throw it beyond these impediments, and convey the words of life and salvation to the listening crowd. Before his release, some souls were blessed, and he was owned as the honored instrument in their conversion. During this imprisonment a circumstance occurred, which we beg leave to record. Of those who felt that they had experienced the renovating influence of Divine grace, nine wished to follow their Master, by being *buried* in baptism. He sent to his native county for Elder Williams to come down to perform the ordinance, but he shrunk from the dangerous undertaking. He then remembered that Elder Chastain, of Buckingham, was, as he thought, of a *truer* stamp, and sent for him. He came, and in the night, or perhaps about twilight, these persons were baptized.

"By the kindness of Patrick Henry (of whom he never spoke but with a glow of affection) he obtained the prison bounds, and by his further aid, was ultimately liberated."

This imprisonment of Elder W. occurred in the year 1773. After his liberation he returned home, to labor with still greater efficiency in his Master's cause. The vindictive spirit manifested by the enemies of the cross only served to increase, in his own heart, the impression of responsibility to Christ. There was felt, too, more deeply, the necessity of bringing gospel influences to bear upon the depraved passions of men. He saw that submission to the peaceful reign of Messiah alone would control these passions and make the world what it ought to be. And especially was it known by him that this gospel was the power of God, and the wisdom of God unto salvation. He could not, therefore, but speak the truth. The unsearchable riches of Christ must be declared.

How far he was successful in the constitution of new churches, is not known by the biographer. Nor has it been ascertained whether, in the early part of his ministry, he presided over any of the churches. He was then mostly engaged as an evangelist. Near the close of the last century, he became pastor of Cub Creek Church, in Charlotte, and Lower Fallings, of Campbell County. Mr. Semple states, in his history, that these churches prospered under his ministry.

In 1813, he removed to the County of Halifax, and in 1823 to Pittsylvania, where he closed his days. For several years before his death, he became too infirm to travel far from home, but frequently preached in his own neighborhood. His interest in Divine things never diminished. The great truths on which, during a long ministry, he delighted to dwell, were still the joy of his heart. During his last sickness, he frequently referred to the astonishing love of God to poor sinners. Every day he requested the beautiful lines of Newton to be sung :—

"Amazing grace, how sweet the sound," etc.

Those present would be called to his bedside, that he might speak to them of the loving kindness of the Lord. Sometimes he would shout the Divine praises aloud. His faith, to the last, was unwavering. He died at the house of Mr. Nowlen, on the 23d of January, 1833, being more than ninety years of age.

This venerable servant of Jesus Christ was distinguished for the length of time he was employed in his Master's cause. Between seventy and eighty years did he preach a crucified Saviour, and recommend him to the lost and guilty. He was willing to suffer, and he did suffer much, for the sake of Christ. His temporal circumstances were far from being comfortable. With a large family, having had fifteen children, twelve of whom were daughters, he often found it difficult to obtain for them the necessaries of life. He is another of those painful instances of laborious effort in preaching the gospel without receiving a competent support. With many of his brethren, he had labored to pull down a religious establishment, which had been sustained by a graceless and salaried ministry. But while the churches rejoiced in the demolition of a system so pernicious, they allowed themselves to build up another, equally abhorrent and dangerous. They saw men making the ministerial office a mere sinecure, and loudly condemned; but they forgot that the faithful laborer is worthy of his hire. The delusion of those they opposed did not consist in liberally supporting their ministers, but in obtaining the support by compulsory measures. While they should have resisted all civil or national interference in religious matters, attention ought to have been paid to the maintenance of their pastors, by liberal voluntary contributions. In consequence of this omission, Elder W. was often compelled either to neglect the ministry and labor on his farm, or allow his family to suffer.

"He was himself a man of generous heart, and sometimes suffered temporarily by excessive liberality. Though he was of large, majestic stature, he was remarkable for the tenderness of his spirit. He possessed the softness of a little child. He was true to his trust, which he ever kept inviolate, though sometimes at a heavy loss. These last remarks may be illustrated by the following circumstance, which he would relate with the most grateful acknowledgment of the kindness of his benefactors. There lived by him a man in embarrassed circumstances, whose wagon and team, his main support, were stopped by the sheriff, just starting to Richmond. Though Weatherford had no confidence in the man, yet sympathy for the family prompted him to be bail. The man failed to fulfill his engagements, upon which Weatherford's only horse was taken, in a busy season, and left with him to produce on the day of sale. He carried it, knowing his crop must be lost, if his horse was sold. But on his arrival, and the case being known, Colonel Watkins, a county man, but not a neighbor, addressed the company: 'Gentlemen, this worthy and industrious minister must not lose his horse by the treachery of one whom he relieved. We should not suffer it. Come to this table, and show your sympathy for suffering innocence.' So saying, he put down a five-dollar bill on the table, and called on the company to follow. The amount was soon made up, and Mr. Weatherford rode home to finish his crop."

In the pulpit, Elder Weatherford's manner was interesting. Though he did not exhibit the attractive graces of oratory, he commended the truth, in its simplicity, to the consciences of men. He was a diligent reader of the Scriptures, and an able expositor. "Sometimes," says one who knew him well, "he would almost electrify his congregations by the originality and ingenuity of his thoughts. On a certain occasion he was proving that Christ was the Messiah, and remarked, 'Even the devils knew him, but he suffered them not to testify; they shall not be witnesses now; as my Lord would not allow them then, I will pass them by as He did, but tell you as I pass, why he did not admit their testimony. It makes against any man's cause to produce questionable evidence, and these were perjured witnesses.'"

In sentiment he was Calvinistic. He heartily approved of all efforts which were likely to be productive of good. He was heard to say, "although I believe in salvation by grace, yet antinomianism, the perversion of this precious truth, which leads to fold hands and wait God's time, comes directly from the infernal pit, and will carry you there." "His soul would kindle with holy joy," says a Christian brother, "when in his sickness I would read of Judson, and other missionaries; the effects of Sabbath-schools, of Bible and tract societies. He was in favor of any plan that might spread the savor of the Redeemer's name, and meliorate the condition of his fellow-creatures.

REUBEN FORD.

For half a century, Elder Reuben Ford was known as an active and useful minister of the gospel among the Baptists of Virginia. He commenced his labors in those times which "tried men's souls," and then he was an able and fearless defender of the truth, as it is in Jesus. He was allowed also to reach that period when the fires of persecution had ceased to burn, and to behold the Redeemer's empire extending itself throughout the whole State of Virginia.

Elder Ford was born about the year 1742. No information has been obtained concerning his early history. In the twentieth year of his age, under the preaching of George Whitefield, he became convinced of his lost condition as a sinner, and fled for refuge, to lay hold of the hope set before him in the gospel. He was not baptized until about seven years after, when, having heard Elders Read and Harriss preach, he publicly put on the Lord Jesus, and became attached to the Baptist Church. Previously, however, he had frequently addressed his fellow-men, calling on them to escape the wrath to come. After his baptism, having been ordained to the work of the ministry, he became a most active laborer, in declaring the unsearchable riches of Christ. In the County of Goochland, especially, were his efforts successful. A large number were introduced into the liberty of the children of God; and in the year 1771, the Goochland Church was constituted, with about seventy-five members. This was among the earliest Baptist churches of the State of Virginia. Elder Ford became their pastor. Such was the success of his ministrations, that this church greatly increased in numbers and efficiency. In the year 1799, a season of refreshing, from the presence of the Lord, was enjoyed, during which one hundred and twenty were added. Another revival, confined mostly in its effects to the colored people, was realized in 1806. Thus, from time to time, did the Lord attend his efforts with tokens of approbation. In 1773, several members were, by letter, dismissed from the Goochland Church, for the purpose of forming another in an adjoining neighborhood, which was called by the name of Dover. At several periods other colonies were sent out, viz., Chicahominy, in 1776; Licking Hole, in the same year; and Hopeful, in 1807. Many ministers, also, were called out into the field, from the Goochland Church.

During a great part of his ministry, Elder Ford had the charge of three or four churches; in addition to this, he frequently extended his labors into other neighborhoods. He took a leading part in all the efforts of the denomination. For more than thirty years, in succession, he was appointed clerk of the Dover Association. On various occasions he belonged to important committees, whose duty it was to present to the legislature the views of the Baptists concerning the grievances which, for a series of years, had been imposed by the establishment.

Perhaps no man was more universally respected and beloved. Though his talents, as a preacher, were not brilliant, yet his simplicity, affection, and faithfulness, obtained the attention of all who heard him. The blamelessness of his life tended much to increase his usefulness, and throughout all the circle of his influence he enjoyed, in no common degree, the confidence of the people. All believed him to be a Christian, because they saw in the uniformity of his life the fruits of the Spirit. The following testimony, from Semple's History of the Virginia Baptists, is now valuable, although it may be doubted whether it is most judicious so highly to eulogize any living minister; it was written several year before Elder Ford's death.

"Mr. Ford is now about sixty-eight years of age, and is a venerable man indeed. Few men ever deceived less by their physiognomy than Elder Ford. No man sees him who does not view him with reverence at his first appearance, and no man ever was dissappointed in him. Grave, without the least moroseness; cheerful, without a symptom of levity; modest, gentle, and affectionate in his manners, yet firm in his purposes; he has everything, out of the pulpit, which might serve as a model of a gospel minister; his life is truly spotless; his talents are of the useful kind; in his doctrine he is somewhat tinctured with Arminianism."

A very strong attachment to the subject of this memoir was cherished by the churches over which he presided. It could not be otherwise. As their bishop, he manifested peculiar tenderness and concern for their spiritual prosperity. He was not satisfied, unless their fruitfulness abounded.

"Purity, in principles and practice, (he at one time remarks,) renders a church amiable in the sight of God, and comely in the sight of the world; thereby is God glorified, and by this heavenly light are sinners brought over and made to embrace the holy gospel of the blessed Jesus. As sound principles and a wholesome discipline reflect honor upon the holy author of our religion, they have also a tendency to promote the peace of the churches."

Respecting the duty of the pastor and deacon, he thus speaks: "A gospel church, suitably organized, will have its minister and deacons. There are relative duties these owe to each other, which are too much neglected. It is the minister's duty diligently to preach the word, administer the ordinances of Christ, to take care of, watch over, and feed the flock of God. The deacon's duty is to serve the church in temporal matters, providing the elements for the Lord's table, and to stir up the members of the church to their duty, in making contribution for all necessary expenses, particularly for the relief of the poor members and the support of their minister."

Some years previous to the death of this venerable servant of the Redeemer, considerable efforts were made by the Baptists to spread among the heathen the unsearchable riches of Christ. To some extent, these efforts were opposed by him. But their results excited his surprise, and for several months before he left this world he professed to be thoroughly convinced of their propriety. A worthy deacon of one of his churches, now living, has frequently heard him express his deep regret at the unfounded prejudices he indulged against the missionary cause. He even went so far as to say, that he believed the Lord had afflicted him on account of the opposition he had manifested.

For many months he was confined to his house most of the time. The infirmities of age continuing to increase, he was at length unable to ride, as usual, to the house of God. He would then frequently prevail on his friends to take him thither, and, supported in the pulpit by his brethren, he would, to the extent of his ability, exhort the church to continue in well-doing. Thus he closed his life.

RICHARD MAJOR.

ACCORDING to the testimony afforded by Elder William Fristoe, in his history of the Ketockton Association, RICHARD MAJOR was a most excellent and useful minister of the last century. He was born near Pennsbury, Pennyslvania, in the year 1722, and was educated under the influence of the Presbyterian Church. When quite a youth, his mind was frequently disturbed by painful apprehensions of the wrath to come. The gayeties of life were sought as a refuge to shield him from the remonstrances of conscience and the denunciations of the Divine Word. No permanent satisfaction, from this source, was obtained, for the consciousness of guilt and danger still oppressed him. Afterwards, he endeavored to satisfy himself by the indulgence of skeptical views. Serious doubts concerning the plan of mercy revealed in the gospel were entertained. The sport of conflicting thoughts and emotions, he was driven from one source to another, until every unrighteous hope failed, and he fled to the cross of Christ for consolation. Here relief was found. The clamors of conscience were hushed to silence ; all perplexing doubts and fears were removed, and his soul made happy in believing. For some time after his conversion, he was a regular communicant of the Presbyterian Church. He, however, became convinced of his guilt, in neglecting the important institution of baptism, and determined to take up his cross and follow his Master into the watery tomb. He was baptized by Elder Isaac Steele, of New

Jersey, in the year 1764. Two years after his immersion, he removed to the State of Virginia, and settled in the County of Loudon. The circumstances which led to the devotion of his life to the ministry were peculiar. Having been called to lead in social meetings, he adopted the plan of reading printed sermons to the people ; serious impressions were, in this way, made on the minds of many, and they were induced to procure the books and read for themselves. While engaged in reading, he would frequently leave the author, and break out in most earnest and affectionate exhortations. By degrees he laid aside the printed sermons, and with the Bible as his text-book, began to teach his fellow-men the way of salvation. His example, in this respect, is worthy of imitation. How much good might be effected, if deacons and private members of our churches were more active in conducting prayer-meetings, and reading well-selected discourses, or the Word of God, to the people ! There is scarcely a congregation of believers in which some individuals may not be found who are qualified for services of this kind. Indeed, there is reason to believe, that there are many in our land remaining inactive, whose duty it is to go forth as the heralds of salvation. The course now suggested would afford an opportunity for the development of those dormant gifts which a church may possess, and result in vast good to the people at large.

In 1768, he was ordained as the pastor of Little River Church. Reference to his success, while he sustained this relation, is found in Semple's History of the Virginia Baptists. It is there stated that Little River Church was formed of individuals who had been converted under the ministry of D. Thomas. It is then added, "In this work, however, he was powerfully aided by Rev. Richard Major, their first pastor; for although the first seed was sown by Mr. Thomas, yet Mr. Major watered and nourished the plants, until he brought them to perfection. So rapidly did the gospel spread, in this church, that just two years after they were constituted, they were the most numerous church in the association, having two hundred and seventy-two members. Her branches, however, extended into the neighboring parts. When any of these branches became sufficiently numerous, they were constituted into new churches, by which the mother church was reduced in numbers. During Mr. Major's life, they were a happy and united people, greatly attached to their minister. After his death, they were without any regular pastor for some years."

In regard to his influence in another church, called Bull Run, Elder Semple states, "When the gospel was carried here by the amiable Richard Major, a great revival of religion arose, so that in a little time a church was constituted, having one hundred and twenty-six members. From the constitution of new churches, etc. their number had become somewhat reduced, until, about 1792, they had the smiles of heaven, and large additions were made. Not many less than a hundred were baptized; by which this church rose to higher prosperity than she had ever previously enjoyed." In addition to his pastoral labor, he performed much in the work of the Lord as an itinerant. Six or eight churches were originated principally through his instrumentality.

There were two particulars in which this man of God excelled —an affectionate spirit, and habits of indefatigable industry. Such was the urbanity of his manners, that all who knew were compelled to love him. In this consisted much of the secret of his usefulness. The law of love being deeply impressed upon his heart, he was kind in all his reproofs and warnings, and with peculiar earnestness recommended to his dying fellow-men, Christ, as able and willing to save to the uttermost all that came to him. In this respect, he closely imitated his Lord and Master. Wherever he went, he seemed intent on doing good. He was most assiduous in performing what he knew to be duty. With an iron constitution, he was able to endure the severest hardships, and always seemed most happy when he could be useful to his fellow-men. His journeys were frequent and extensive. His vigorous powers of mind and body were thus faithfully devoted to Him whom his soul loved. "So much was he esteemed in the latter part of his life, that he had serious apprehensions that he must be too much at ease for a gospel minister; or, in other words, it seemed as if the expression, '*woe be unto you when all men speak well of you,*' applied to his case. In the midst of these thoughts, he accidentally heard a man lay to his charge one of the most abominable crimes. At first he felt irritated; but, re-collecting his previous reflections, he was soon reconciled."

Elder Major did not pass through his ministerial career without suffering some of the persecutions which, in his time, were heaped upon the lovers of Jesus. From Edwards and Semple the following paragraphs are selected, in which a few particulars are given respecting the rude treatment he received from the enemies of the cross of Christ. "In Fauquier County, the officer with a warrant from Capt. Scott, attempted to take him, but providentially failed. At Bull Run there were warrants against him, and a mob, with clubs, rose to assist the execution of them; but here again they failed of their design, chiefly by means of the Davises, usually called the *giants;* those stout brothers had been prevailed on to oppose him; but after they had heard him preach, they became well affected toward him, and threatened to chatise any that should disturb him. In Fauquier, the mob were very outrageous, but did no mischief, though his friends feared they would have pulled him to pieces.

"A certain man, whose wife had been baptized by Mr. Major, determined to kill him on sight, and went to meeting for that purpose. He sat down in hearing, intending to catch at some obnoxious expression which might fall from the preacher, and under that pretence, to attack him. But God produced a different result; for the man, instead of executing his design, became so convicted that he could not keep on his feet; and was afterwards baptized by the man he intended to murder. Another actually attacked him with a club, in a violent manner. Mr. Major, being remarkable for great presence of mind, turned to him, and, in a solemn manner, said, 'Satan, I command thee to come out of the man.' His club immediately began to fall, and the lion became as quiet as a lamb. These are a few of the many occurrences of this kind, that took place in the long life of this valuable man."

Concerning the close of his highly useful life, Elder Semple thus writes: "For ten or twelve years before his death, his sturdy constitution began to fail. He was attacked by a very painful disease, and, to gain relief, he went to the medicinal springs. From the water he could get no relief, but, by apparent accident, was informed of a remedy, which, upon trial, he found very effectual. This gave him respite for several years. But, being attacked by the same disease again, after a tedious and painful illness he finished his course, at about fourscore years of age. He has doubtless found a bright mansion in his Father's kingdom."

JOHN MEGLAMARE.

As it is nearly forty years since the subject of this biography was removed from his earthly labors, but few persons are to be found who have any distinct recollection of facts, such as would furnish an extended record of his life. In justice, however, to him and the cause of Christ, it would not be proper to allow such memorials as do exist, to perish. He was born on the 7th of June, 1730, in one of the Northern States. It is not known whether he was under the tuition of pious parents, or how far the circumstances of his early life were favorable to the origiuation of serious thought. Be this as it may, it is ascertained that he was not altogether unconcerned on the subject of religion, when quite a youth. Previous to his conversion, he had removed to Halifax County, North Carolina. Here he became acquainted with God's method of salvation, and joined the Kehukee Church, under the care of Elder Thomas Pope. This was in the thirty-fourth year of his age.

His labors in the ministry commenced shortly after his connection with the church. While engaged in preaching the gospel in his own county, the Lord was pleased to afflict the church, of which he was a member, by the removal of their pastor. Elder Meglamare was called to succeed him, and continued to fill the pastoral office in the Kehukee Church until the year 1772. The following were the circumstances which led to his resignation :—

In 1770, during one of his preaching excursions in Sussex County, Virginia, such indications of Divine approbation were given, that he was encouraged to make stated appointments ; and for several months continued to visit that people, preaching mostly in private houses. A most interesting state of religious feeling throughout the neighborhood was the result. Many became the subjects of the Prince of peace, and were baptized by Elder Meglamare, among whom was Mr. James Bell, a man of much influence in the county, and afterwards a useful minister of the gospel. Under these circumstances, the subject of this memoir yielded to the solicitations of the people, and removed to Sussex. Shortly after, a church, consisting of eighty-seven members, was constituted on Raccoon Swamp, and he was chosen to be their under-shepherd. In this station he was eminently useful. The Lord added to the church daily such as should be saved. He was not, however, satisfied with feeding the flock of God, but traveled extensively through the adjacent counties. The churches of Mill Swamp, Black Creek, Seacock, and High Hills, were brought into existence chiefly through his instrumentality. Until a short time previous to his death, he continued a most diligent and persevering laborer in the work of the Lord. When, in consequence of age and enfeebled health, he found himself unable to prosecute the duties of his office, he resigned the care of Raccoon Swamp Church to Elder Browne, who was unanimously chosen his successor.

During the whole of his ministry, Elder Meglamare was held in high reputation. This is indicated by the fact, that for more than twenty years before the division of the Kehukee Association, he was invariably called to the chair at their annual meetings. He was one of those who assisted in the formation of that body, and contributed not a little in stemming the tide of error which, in that early day, was beginning to flow in upon the churches. By his wisdom and firmness, in a great degree, were the disciples brought into harmonious co-operation. In the year 1791, the Portsmouth Association was formed. As long as he lived, and was able to attend the yearly meetings, he was always elected to preside over its deliberations. As a disciplinarian in the church, and a guide in associational bodies, he was very useful.

It has been stated that some time before his death he was compelled to relinquish his pastoral relation. This was occasioned by the most distressing asthmatic complaint, which continued until December 13th, 1799, when his Master dismissed him from the toils of this life, in the seventieth year of his age. "Precious in the sight of the Lord is the death of his saints."

ELIJAH CRAIG.

THE earliest information which has been obtained respecting Elijah Craig, is connected with his conversion, about the year 1764. Having heard Elder David Thomas preach, he was arrested in his indifference to Divine things, and, for a length of time, was much alarmed, in the consciousness of his fallen and helpless condition. At length his mind became somewhat relieved, though not satisfied. In 1765, he found an opportunity of hearing Samuel Harriss, and such was the coincidence between his own views and feelings and the delineation of gospel truth drawn by Elder Harriss, that he became perfectly satisfied, and rejoiced in the freedom wherewith Christ had made him free. He began, at once, to exhort his fellow-men, whenever he could collect them in his neighborhood. Says Mr. Semple: "His tobacco-house was their chapel. Being most of them laboring men, they used to labor all day, and hold meetings almost every night at each other's houses, and on Sundays at the above-mentioned tobacco-house. By these little prayer and exhortation meetings, great numbers were awakened, and several converted."

In a short time he began, amid much persecution, to extend his exertions, and to preach wherever he went, that the blood of Jesus Christ cleanseth from all sin. In these exercises he was accompanied by several others, who were of a kindred spirit. The Lord wrought by them, and attended their efforts, by his signal smile. In the County of Culpepper, he met with much opposition. One of the exhibitions of violence, on the part of his enemies, is thus referred to by Elder Semple. "They sent the sheriff and posse after him, when at his plough. He was taken and carried before three magistrates of Culpepper. They, without hearing arguments, pro or con., ordered him to jail. At court, he, with others, was arraigned. One of the lawyers told the court they had better discharge them; for that oppressing them would rather advance than retard them. He said they were like a bed of camomile, the more they were trodden, the more they would spread. The court thought otherwise, and determined to imprison them. Some of the court were of opinion that they ought to be confined in a close dungeon, but the majority were for giving them the bounds. Mr. Craig says 'they were fed on rye bread and water, to the injury of their health.' After staying there one month, preaching to all who came, he gave bond for good behavior, and came out. He was also confined in Orange jail, at another time."

Mr. Craig was considered a man of considerable talent. No doubt can be entertained that what he did possess, he employed well. With a zeal which the floods of persecution could not quench, he prosecuted his Master's work, and was made a blessing to many. In his labors, as pastor of Blue Run Church, he was very successful. It became a large and flourishing body.

In the year 1786, he removed to Kentucky. There he unhappily became implicated in some personal altercation, which resulted in his exclusion from the church. He was, however, restored, and continued in fellowship until his death, which occurred in the year 1808. He seemed, by this and other circumstances, to have given away, in his declining age, to a censorious temper. It is said by Mr. Semple, that "in a pamphlet he published, he undertakes to prove that stationed preachers, or pastors of churches, are precluded by the Scriptures from receiving any compensation for their services. In this pamphlet, he takes so many opportunities to condemn preachers for being money seekers, that it would seem the main design of the publication was to indulge a fault-finding temper."

The following testimony by one who knew him well will close this article: "Elijah Craig was considered the greatest preacher of the three brothers; and in a very large association in Virginia, Elijah Craig was among the most popular for a number of years. His preaching was of the most solemn style—his appearance as a man who had just come from the dead, of a delicate habit, a thin visage, large eyes and mouth, of great readiness of speech, the sweet melody of his voice, both to preach and sing, bore all down before it; and when his voice was extended it was like the loud sound of a trumpet. The great fervor of his preaching commonly brought many tears from the hearers, and many no doubt were turned to the Lord by his preaching. He was several times a prisoner of the Lord for preaching. He moved to Kentucky at a later date than his brothers; his turn for speculation did him harm every way; he was not as great a peacemaker in the church as his brother Lewis, and that brought trouble on him: but from all his troubles he was relieved by death, when perhaps he did not much exceed sixty years of age, after serving in the ministry, say forty years."

JOHN PICKET.*

MR. PICKET was born in King George County, January 14th 1744, of respectable parentage. He had, when grown to the years of maturity, a very strong propensity to gaming, and sports of every kind. He followed the business of a dancing-master; and probably, with a view to obtain employment, as well as to indulge his propensity for sport, he went, about the year 1764, or 1765, to Pee Dee, in North Carolina. God intended this tour for a very different purpose. While there, he attended a meeting of Joseph Murphy's, one of the earliest Baptist preachers in those parts. Murphy spoke a word, in season, to this prodigal. He came to himself. He began to loathe the sports and pleasures to which he had been devoted. He went to his Father, and was feasted with the fatted calf and clothed with the best robe. He was baptized by J. Murphy in 1766. Soon as he felt the smiles of his Heavenly Father, he wrote to his earthly parents, in Fauquier, informing them of this marvelous change. To them, it was strange indeed, that this, their lost son, should become so fervently pious, while their other sons, that they had always with them, continued to be the same. This letter produced great alarm in the family, and some good effects. Mr. Picket continued in North Carolina for some time, being unwilling to leave the society of those to whom he was united by ties stronger than death. He did not return to Fauquier until after the death of his father, in 1767. When he came, finding his friends and

* By Elder R. B. Semple.

neighbors irreligious, he began to warn them, commencing first with private conversation and exhortation, then with family worship. Those exertions being crowned with success, many being convicted and some converted, he began to preach. Mr. Picket then procured a visit from Mr. Murphy, who came to Fauquier, and baptized a few. The work spread far and near. Mr. Picket being fervent in spirit and thus encouraged, held not his peace day nor night, but proclaimed boldly the things of God. In the fall of 1768, Messrs. Harriss and Read came and baptized thirty-seven more, and constituted them into a church, November 12th, 1768, under the name of Carter's Run. Mr. Picket was ordained, and took the care of this church, May 27th, 1772. His zeal and activity could not pass unnoticed by the enemies of the cross. The mob broke into the meeting-house and split to pieces the pulpit and table, while the magistrates issued their warrant, and, seizing Mr. Picket, thrust him into Fauquier prison. There he continued for about three months, preaching through the grates, and admonishing as many as came to him, to repent and turn to God The Word of God was not bound. Great numbers were awakened under his prison labors. This took place about 1760. When he was turned out of prison he increased his zeal, and extended his labors to Culpepper and over the Blue Ridge, where he was so successful that, on the first baptizing that was supposed ever to have taken place in Shenandoah, as many as fifty were baptized. He was never wearied in well-doing, but continued steadfast to the end. We will now close our account of him in the words of the manuscript, furnished by one of the members of his own church:—

"He was sound in faith, calling on sinners to repent, not sparing himself, but giving his labors to the Lord, and to his fellow-men. Toward his latter days, his zeal for the good of souls seemed to increase. About June, 1803, he told his wife that his work was finished, tenderly beseeching her and his children to serve the Lord, and so fell asleep."

Well might the unrighteous, but enlightened prophet, wish to die the death of the righteous!

WILLIAM FRISTOE.

BEING one of those who stood up in defence of the truth, amid fiery persecutions, the subject of this memoir was, while he lived, the object of veneration and regard among his brethren in Christ. It is due to him, and the cause he advocated, to preserve a memorial of his character, sufferings, and toils. As far as he followed his Master, others may be stimulated, by his example, to do good, and glorify God. Such records may not only prove an incentive to practical holiness, but teach many valuable lessons concerning the Divine government, both in providence and redemption. In the history of the church, the arm of the Lord is revealed; we behold its power in defending those who put their trust in him. Though the wicked may rage, taking counsel together against the Lord and his anointed, yet we see their purposes frustrated, and all their plans overturned. He who sitteth in the heavens, laughs at them; the Lord holds them in derision.

William Fristoe was a native of Stafford County, Virginia. By one of his surviving and most intimate friends, he is said to have been born in the year 1742. His parents were respectable, but in moderate circumstances. His education was limited, he being, when grown, only able to read and write. He grew up without the opportunity of hearing the gospel, as it was seldom, if ever, in its purity preached in his native county. His parents belonged to the established church, though they do not seem to have been pious persons. He has said, that when five years old, he was sensible that he was a sinner against God; and his greatest concern was how he should obtain forgiveness and meet with acceptance. In his fourteenth or fifteenth year he was watching with a sick and dying man, in company with one who was raised a Scotch Presbyterian. In the course of the night, this person, having allusion to the sick man, cried out, "God be merciful to him for Christ's sake." Elder Fristoe was sensibly struck with the expression, as being something which he had never heard before mentioned; and the constant inquiry with him, from that time, was, how God could, consistently with his justice and the purity of his nature, have mercy on a sinner for the sake of, or on account of, another? He continued in this distressed situation, until he heard the gospel preached by what was called the New Lights, when his mind became relieved and happy in Christ Jesus. Not long after, he made an open profession, and was baptized by Elder David Thomas, who had been instrumental in raising up and constituting Chapawamsick Church. This took place when he was about twenty or twenty-one years of age. The church soon discovered that he possessed promising gifts, and requested him to preach. The performance was so pleasing to the brethren, that it was not very long before he was ordained, and obtained a license from the then legal authority, the Episcopal bishop, and was called to the pastoral care of the church.

In his twenty-first year he entered upon this responsible work with a zeal and perseverance becoming its vast importance. Having felt the value of atoning blood, he everywhere made known its efficacy, and recommended it to the guilty. The Lord was with him, giving seals to his ministry. In conjunction with two or three other laborers, he was the honored means of leading into the church, with which he was united, a large number of believers. But he did not confine his ministry to this part of the Lord's vineyard. He traveled extensively, and was instrumental in forming several new churches. Some of these were regularly attended by him, though at great inconvenience to himself. He was in the habit, with his brother Elder Daniel Fristoe, of attending every month the Buckmarsh Church, Frederick County, a distance of seventy miles from his own residence. He also regularly visited a church in Fauquier, called Thumb Run, about forty miles distant. In referring to these heavy labors, he remarks, "Neither winter's frost nor summer's heat is to be dreaded; the frowns of men and rage of devils must be borne when the object is the winning a bride for and the espousing of souls to Christ."

Besides traveling extensively, Elder Fristoe at different times supplied several churches regularly; among others, Chapawamsick, Brentown, Hartwood, Grove, and Rockhill. In January, 1787, he took charge of Broad Run Church, Fauquier County. When he removed to the County of Shenandoah he resigned them all, excepting Broad Run, which he attended until the year before his death. After his settlement in Shenandoah, he took charge of Ebenezer, Buckmarsh, Bethel, Zion, and Salem, in their destitution, and gave them up one after another as soon as pastors could be obtained. To the end of life he was animated by the noble resolution to spread the gospel of Jesus Christ, even amid contempt and persecution. Although he was poor, and had an expensive family dependent on him for support, he still gave himself to this great work. He has been known, on returning from a tour of preaching, to work for several days, and most of the night by fire-light, in mauling rails and preparing his ground for receiving the crop.

The church called Chapawamsick, in Stafford, with which Elder Fristoe first connected himself, was one of the oldest of the Ketockton Association. In reference to the additions this church received and their subsequent history, Mr. Semple thus speaks: "So rapidly did the word increase among them, that in 1770, three years after their constitution, they had one hundred and seventy-six members. And the following year, after dismissing thirty-six members to form the Potomac Church, they had remaining two hundred and twelve. The next year, dismissing ninety-seven at once to form Brentown Church, they were reduced to one hundred and sixteen. From this period, Chapawamsick gradually declined for many years. William Fristoe had fallen into Potomac and Daniel into Brentown, so that the mother church was rather destitute. About 1786, William Fristoe returned and continued among them for many years. In the great revival about 1791 and 1792, this church arose from the dust and put on her garments of praise. Her number, from being very small, increased to nearly a hundred."

The Ketockton Association was the first formed in Virginia. The following incident, referred to by Mr Fristoe, and, after his death, narrated by a Christian brother, will illustrate the humble piety and fervent zeal of those times. The narrator states:—

"In the year 1766, when the first association in Virginia was organized, among the persons assembled on the occasion were the Fristoes, Daniel and William, who afterwards made so distinguished a figure in the history of the Virginia Baptists, and who were at that time young disciples. William Fristoe, who entered into his rest but a few months ago, relates an anecdote that illustrates the spirit of those times. The meeting above mentioned was held at Ketockton Meeting-house, Loudon County, about sixty miles from Chapawamsick, the residence of the Fristoes. Notwithstanding this distance, they remained at the meeting until the afternoon of the day preceding that on which they judged it necessary for them to be at home. To reconcile the claims of business with those of religion, they resolved to travel the whole of the intervening night; and, accordingly, a company of them set out, cheering the darkness and wearisomeness of the way with animated talk of the love of Jesus. About the middle of the night, when they were also near the middle of their journey, one of their number, older than the rest, was about to be parted from them because his home lay in a different direction. At his proposal they alighted from their horses, and having tied them to the boughs of the trees, they gathered into a group in the midst of the spreading forest; and kneeling upon the ground they poured forth the overflowings of their hearts in devout prayer to Him who saw and heard amidst the shades of night and the solitude of the wood. When at the call of the aged disciple they had all prayed in succession, he arose and laid his hands upon their heads, encouraged them, gave them his parting blessing, and bade them press on in the ways of the Lord. Having received his benediction, the young disciples pursued their journey and reached their homes just as the sun had commenced his way through the sky."

The subject of this memoir soon after his ordination occupied an extensive influence among the churches. Elder Semple states that some of the most eminent preachers in Virginia owned him as their spiritual father. Lunsford, Mason, and Hickerson, with several others, received the tidings of peace from his lips. It was thus natural that he should enjoy the affections of many. But the high stand which he occupied in an early period of his ministerial career was principally gained by his intelligence and discretion. For his prudence, he was remarkable. At the meeting of the Ketockton Association in 1774, when a number of senior ministers were present, and he only in the twenty-sixth year of his age, he was elected to preside over their deliberations. The chair was most generally occupied by him, especially in the latter part of his life.

Some allusion has been made to his success in winning souls to Christ, in the early part of his ministry. It may be remarked, that nature had furnished him with powers to command attention as a speaker. "In the pulpit," says Mr. Semple, though not versed in the learning of the schools, he displayed abilities which many doctors of divinity have not attained. His language, though plain, was strong and nervous. His manner was solemn, as one having authority." His talents and addresses were highly polemical, and at times there was an apparent severity in his allusions to the sentiments of others. As a disputant he was able—few being qualified to compete with him in argument. His religious views were strongly Calvinistic. There was probably too much disposition in all his discourses to dwell on what are called the higher doctrines of the gospel. Human nature is prone to extremes. While good works are essential as evidences of Christian character, it is possible they may be allowed to occupy an improper place in the system of religious truth; men may place an undue reliance on them, and thus fail to give God all the glory of their salvation. Or, not attributing any merit to their own works, they may fail sufficiently to hold up Christ, and Him crucified, as the way to heaven. Practical religion is often urged by the preacher without due reference to doctrinal truth. And so with regard to the opposite extreme. God's eternal and discriminating love is clearly revealed in the Bible, and constitutes one of its most precious doctrines. Salvation is of grace. From first to last, in the great scheme of redemption, God alone is entitled to praise. But the grace of God may be turned into licentiousness. And even among godly men, who would spurn the idea of encouraging laxity of morals, there is danger of harping too much on doctrinal sentiments. An undue prominence may be given to a few truths, to the comparative neglect of others equally important. This, there is reason to believe, was a defect in the preaching of Elder Fristoe. Notwithstanding, he was an able minister of the New Testament. Though with characteristic tenacity he clung to the glorious doctrine of Divine sovereignty and its kindred truths, so as to render him somewhat suspicious of those who did not reach his standard of sentiment, he was, nevertheless, a valuable and useful laborer in the Lord's vineyard.

The subject of this sketch was not a man of education. He did not, however, despise it. "Learning," said he, "is highly esteemed among the Baptists, and many who have been called to and exercised public offices, have very sensibly felt the inconvenience they had to labor under for the want of it. But it is not considered essentially necessary to a gospel minister. Where the Author of nature has endued a person with strong intellect, capable of taking in high and sublime ideas, and prying into mysterious and intricate subjects, and given him to know his dear Son, whom to know is life eternal, the ministry may be entered even without learning. For a person of this description forever to remain in silence, merely for the want of education, would be like a beautiful flower blooming in a desert, unnoticed by few, and enjoyed by none."

Though Elder F. had not the advantage of an improved mind, he endeavored, by reading as much as possible, to make up this deficiency. A reference to this subject is made by Elder Cumberland George in the following interesting facts: "In relation to the early advantages of Elder Fristoe," says Mr. George, "I will relate one particular which I obtained from his own lips. A certain Mr. Morson of Falmouth, Stafford County, becoming acquainted with Elder Fristoe, was strongly attached to him, and being a gentleman of considerable wealth, invited him to remove to a farm some few miles above Falmouth, where there were not only comfortable buildings, but furniture and provisions for the use and comfort of his family, together with an extensive and valuable library, to which unrestricted admission was given him. Here Mr. Fristoe remained for nearly two years, and through the kindness of his friend, was enabled to give himself almost entirely to reading and to the ministry of the Word. Mr. Fristoe always regarded this a signal interposition of the hand of God in his favor. Nor was he idle while God's providence seemed to say 'Work.' Those two years of devotion to study enabled him to acquire such a stock of knowledge as essentially to assist him in his ministry through life."

Mr. Fristoe was in the habit of devoting much time to the perusal of the sacred Scriptures. To the law and testimony he professed to look for authority in religious faith and practice. A few remarks on the subject of baptism from his pen will show how far he considered the neglect of this duty sinful, as also his views on the impropriety of admitting infants to the ordinance. "It is readily granted, Paul's epistles were addressed to the churches, and not to the world; and it will not be denied by us that there were parents and children both members in the churches, but they were such children as could read Paul's address to them, or hear it read; could understand the contents of those epistles and form their conduct according to the instructions given therein, and of course capable of believing in the Lord Jesus, and acting as worthy members of the church, to the duties enjoined on them in those epistles. It is well known the obligation children are under toward a parent is never removed; had these been of the infant tribe they would not have had understanding sufficient to obey their parents, and therefore can have no allusion to them.

"The jailor and his household, Lydia and her household, have been often brought, with the assurance that the Baptists would agree there were infants among them, and that inasmuch as the household was baptized, it furnishes a presumptive proof at least in favor of infant baptism—to which we answer:—

"As to the jailor, we have a plain statement, that he believed in God with all his house; rejoiced in God with all his house; and he and all his were baptized straightway; so, then, from the accounts given, they were all of understanding to receive the word delivered by the apostles, all capacitated to act faith in Christ, all rejoiced having a saving knowledge of God, and all submitted to the sacred ordinance of baptism. As for Lydia we have no account that she had husband or children; the account is, that she worshiped God, that she heard Paul preach, that her heart was opened, and she and her household were baptized; the natural inference is, that she had servants or assistants, in carrying on her trade, and that they believed and were baptized.

"As we cannot, consistently with the Scriptures, admit any to church communion without being baptized on the profession of their faith, we are often asked, if we think there are not Christians among other denominations as well as among the Baptists; and if so, it is very wrong to disown or reject such. We have never called in question that there are Christians in other sects; it is not their Christianity we scrutinize, but the support of the institutions of the gospel in their purity. Those of our neighbors who are privy to our conduct, know full well we purchase books written by eminent and spiritual divines belonging to other denominations. But, provided a person possessed with grace should be guilty of a wrong course, does grace in his heart make his conduct right? By no means! For, could that be supported, there would never be a wrong done by a Christian. Suppose a gracious man was seduced and led away to worship an idol, could that worship be acceptable to God because he professed grace? By no means! It is so far from lessening the crime or making it no crime, that it is greatly heightened and aggravated; so, when persons are enlightened from above, and enjoy the teaching of the spirit of grace, and then live in the willful neglect of a known duty, it is dishonorable to God, and unbecoming their high calling.

"We are acquainted with none of the Pedobaptists but what acknowledge that in the apostolic day baptism was by immersion, and the subjects were believers; but while that is allowed by them, it is thought unreasonable the Baptists should not be equally liberal in allowing the sprinkling of infants to be right likewise. Here our suit has been long, and continues still at issue. It is out of the question for both to be right, because there is but one rule laid down in Holy Writ for Christ's followers, as it respects baptism; and that is, 'He that believeth, and is baptized'—'Repent and be baptized'—'If thou believest with all thy heart thou mayest' be baptized. And 'they believed and were baptized;' and 'who can forbid water, that these should not be baptized?' This appears to be the uniform language of the New Testament, being consistent with the command of the great Lawgiver.

"When we make search for infant sprinkling, and open our ears to hear what the Scripture reports, a dead silence takes place, and we go off without any information about it. We read of a prostitute church in the revelation of John the divine, a church which had departed from the true worship of God and addicted herself to superstitious, idolatrous worship. What says the voice of God in this case? 'Come out of her, my people, and be not partaker of her crimes, that ye perish not in her plagues.' From this it appears that God had a people in that corrupt, apostate church, but it was no reason, because they had grace, that they should stay there, but quite the reverse.

"From all that has been said, we see no cause for retraction or a change of our custom; we feel it obligatory on us to contend for the faith once delivered to the saints, and maintain the ordinances in their purity as delivered by Christ and his apostles. Viewing it as a dreadful sin to change God's ordinances, being forewarned to touch not, handle not, which all are to perish with the using after the commandments and doctrines of men, our Lord informs us, he that breaks the least of His commands, and teaches men so to do, shall be called least in the kingdom of God."

An aged brother now living, and who was familiar with his opinions and habits for many years, states that "he promoted collections at different associations, for foreign and domestic missions." It was doubtless his desire, that the gospel of the kingdom should be preached to all nations, and he was too well acquainted with the word of God not to know that the designs of infinite mercy were to be effected through the instrumentality of means. He well knew that while all success is from God, and that to him all the glory will be due, there is much for the church to do as instruments in the glorious work of evangelizing the nations. It is strange that any brethren should object to the operations or designs of missionary and other benevolent associations. But this hostility is every day becoming less inveterate. For this the Lord be praised.

Concerning the deportment of Elder Fristoe, it may be said, he had a good report of those who are without. His life gave practical evidence that he loved holiness, and desired to promote the Divine glory. He was an example to the believers, and thus adorned the doctrine of God his Saviour.

In the year 1809, he published a work of which he was the author, entitled "The History of the Ketockton Baptist Association." For any inaccuracies of style, he thus apologizes to the reader in his preface: "Should defects appear in the following work, it need not be wondered at, for the author is no scholar, nor affects learning, and in the course of his life never made any notes, nor kept any journal, neither has he been supplied from any other hand, only the little aid from our associational record. The production has been principally written from recollection and the little strength of his own judgment."

This work is not altogether confined to the Ketockton Association. It refers to the history of the Baptist denomination throughout Virginia; especially to the persecutions they suffered and the sentiments for which they were distinguished. Many interesting facts are recorded.

Mr. Fristoe lived to see a good old age. He died after a short illness at his own residence in Shenandoah County, on the 14th of August, 1828, having reached his eighty-sixth year. He had been for more than sixty years a defender of the truth, and one of the pillars of the church in the upper country. In giving notice of his death, a brother observes, "he was, perhaps, excelled by no man in the State in point of biblical knowledge, and for his pious walk and unblemished character; but his character and standing were so well known in this and the adjoining States, that any remarks from me upon this subject would seem to be unnecessary. Suffice it to say, that truly a great man has fallen in Israel."

JOHN WALLER.*

JOHN WALLER was born December 23d, 1741, in Spottsylvania County, and was a descendant of the honorable family of Wallers, in England. At a very early period he manifested a great talent for satire. This determined his uncle, who was his guardian, to

---

* By Elder Semple, with additions.

educate him for the law. He was put to a grammar school, and made encouraging advancement in the dead languages. His uncle's death and his father's narrow resources, added to his own unbridled inclinations to vice, prevented him from finishing even his classical education. He now began indeed to study, not the laws of the land, but those of the gaming table. Giving loose to every species of wickedness and profanity, he quickly acquired for himself the infamous appellation of *Swearing Jack Waller*, by which he was distinguished from others of the same name. So far did he indulge his mischievous temper, that he once had three warrants served on him at the same time on account of one uproar. It was frequently remarked by the common people, "that there could be no deviltry among the people unless Swearing Jack was at the head of it." He was sometimes called *the Devil's Adjutant* to muster his troops. To these may be added his fury against the Baptists. He was one of the grand jury who presented L. Craig for preaching. This happily terminated in his good. Mr. Craig, in order to turn their mischievous intentions into something beneficial, watched the dismission of the jury, and having gained their attention, thus addressed them: "I thank you, gentlemen of the grand jury, for the honor you have done me. While I was wicked and injurious, you took no notice of me, but since I have altered my course of life and endeavored to reform my neighbors, you concern yourselves much about me. I shall take the spoiling of my goods joyfully." When Mr. W. heard him speak in that manner, and observed the meekness of his spirit, he was convinced that Craig was possessed of something that he had never seen in man before. He thought within himself that he should be happy if he could be of the same religion with Mr. Craig. From this time he began to attend their meetings, and was found of the Holy Spirit. The commandment came, and he died. He saw and felt himself a sinner. He now for the first time, except in blaspheming, began to call upon the name of the Lord. His convictions were deep and pungent. He ate no pleasant bread and drank no pleasant water for seven or eight months. He was almost in despair. He relates his exercises in the following words:—

"I had long felt the greatest abhorrence of myself, and began almost to despair of the mercy of God. However, I determined never to rest until it pleased God to show mercy or cut me off. Under these impressions I was at a certain place, sitting under preaching. On a sudden, a man exclaimed that he had found mercy and began to praise God. No mortal can describe the horror with which I was seized at that instant. I began to conclude my damnation was certain. Leaving the meeting, I hastened into a neighboring wood and dropped on my knees before God to beg for mercy. In an instant I felt my heart melt, and a sweet application of the Redeemer's love to my poor soul. The calm was great but short."

From this time he felt some increase of strength, yet sometimes the enemy broke in upon him like a flood and he would be almost ready to give up his hope. But the application of these words gave him great comfort: "Who is among you that feareth the Lord; that walketh in darkness and hath no light; let him trust in the name of the Lord, and stay upon his God." Isaiah i. 10. And again: "By this we know that we have passed from death unto life, because we love the brethren."

By the time Messrs. Harriss and Read came on their next tour he felt sufficiently confident to become a candidate for baptism, and going up into Orange County was there baptized by Mr. Read, in the year 1767. Baptism was to him as it has been to thousands, a sanctified ordinance. His soul received great accession of strength and comfort. Having contracted debts by dissipation, he sold property to pay them. He conferred not with flesh and blood, but began to preach that men ought everywhere to repent. It was not long before his labors became effectual, at least in one way. That arch-enemy of souls, whom he had served so faithfully before, now began to rage, and succeeded in raising a powerful opposition.

At length it was thought proper to constitute a church in Mr. Waller's neighborhood. He was ordained their pastor, June 20th, 1770. He now began to extend his labors. Bending his course to Lower Virginia, he baptized Rev. William Webber, being the first he did baptize. Accompanied by J. Burrus he traveled as far as Middlesex, and wherever he went he was attended by a Divine power, turning many to righteousness. His name sounded far and wide. By the ungodly he was considered as a bold, inexorable fanatic, that would do much mischief unless restrained. The Baptists and their adherents looked upon him as set for the defence of their cause, and with much confidence rallied him as their leader. His persecutions in several counties were of the most painful character. The following letter, written by him during an imprisonment of forty-six days in the County of Middlesex, will exhibit something of the severe trials to which he and his associates were subjected in making known the truth as it is in Jesus. It is dated

URBANNA PRISON, MIDDLESEX COUNTY,
August 12, 1771.

DEAR BROTHER IN THE LORD:

At a meeting which was held at Brother McCain's, in this county, last Saturday, while Brother William Webber was addressing the congregation from James ii. 18, there came running toward him, in a most furious rage, Captain James Montague, a magistrate of the county, followed by the parson of the parish and several others who seemed greatly exasperated. The magistrate and another took hold of Brother Webber, and dragging him from the stage, delivered him, with Brethren Wafford, Robert Ware, Richard Falkner, James Greenwood, and myself, into custody, and commanded that we should be brought before him for trial. Brother Wafford was severely scourged, and Brother Henry Street received one lash from one of the persecutors, who was prevented from proceeding to further violence by his companions; to be short, I may inform you that we were carried before the above-mentioned magistrate, who, with the parson and some others, carried us one by one into a room and examined our pockets and wallets for fire-arms, etc., charging us with carrying on a mutiny against the authority of the land. Finding none, we were asked if we had license to preach in this county; and, learning we had not, it was required of us to give bond and security not to preach any more in the county, which we modestly refused to do, whereupon, after dismissing Brother Wafford, with a charge to make his escape out of the county by twelve o'clock the next day on pain of imprisonment, and dismissing Brother Falkner, the rest of us were delivered to the sheriff and sent to close jail, with a charge not to allow us to walk in the air until court day. Blessed be God, the sheriff and jailor have treated us with as much kindness as could have been expected from strangers. May the Lord reward them for it! Yesterday we had a large number of people to hear us preach; and, among others, many of the great ones of the land, who behaved well while one of us discoursed on the new birth. We find the Lord gracious and kind to us beyond expression in our afflictions. We cannot tell how long we shall be kept in bonds; we therefore beseech, dear brother, that you and the church supplicate night and day for us, our benefactors, and our persecutors.

I have also to inform you that six of our brethren are confined in Caroline jail, viz., Brethren Lewis Craig, John Burrus, John Young, Edward Herndon, James Goodrick, and Bartholomew Cheming. The most dreadful threatenings are raised in the neighboring counties against the Lord's faithful and humble followers. Excuse haste. Adieu.

JOHN WALLER.

In this bright and burning way, Waller continued until 1775 or 1776, when he formed an acquaintance with one Williams, a preacher of some talents, apparent piety, and in Mr. Wesley's connection, consequently an Arminian: this man, by his conversation and books, so wrought upon Mr. Waller's mind as to bring him over to believe the Arminian system. Knowing this to be contrary to the opinions of his brethren, he resolved to make a bold effort to preach and argue his principles at the next association, and thereby convince his brethren; or, failing in this, to submit to be cut off from them. Accordingly, he took his text, 1 Cor. xiii. 11. In his exordium he stated, that when young and inexperienced in religion he had fallen in with the Calvinistic plan; but that becoming more expert in doctrine, or, in the language of his text, when he became a man he put away these childish notions. He then went lengthily into the argument. For want of truth or talents he made few, if any converts to his opinions; and, of course, had to confront the whole host of preachers and members now assembled. Mr. Waller, foreseeing his fate, took the shorter and more reputable course. Instead of awaiting a fair trial, he proclaimed himself an independent Baptist preacher. This step was probably resorted to by Waller under an expectation that his popularity was so great that he should be able to bring over many of the churches to his party. Be this as it may, he immediately commenced his operations on an extensive plan. On his return from the association he used his utmost endeavor to form a strong party. He preached from house to house over a large field of ministerial labor; ordained lay elders in every neighborhood, to prevent inroads; and also several helps in the ministry. He also established what he called camp-meetings, in which they continued together several days under certain written regulations.

The novelty of these meetings excited the attention of the people in such a manner that great multitudes crowded after him. By these means his party gained strength daily. Few men possessed greater talents for leading a party of this description than Mr. Waller. The only thing in which he was deficient was, that he could not be happy while separated from his brethren. He used to say, that in the midst of apparent prosperity and the caresses of his friends, he still yearned after the people of God from whom he had withdrawn. Some years after his restoration, he said to a young preacher who was dissatisfied and talked of dissenting, "If you could have a distant view of my suffering and leanness of soul while a dissenter from my brethren, you would never again indulge such a thought." He was again fully reinstated in connection with his brethren in 1787.

A very great revival commenced under Mr. Waller's ministry in 1787. This continued for several years, and spread through all his places of preaching. In this revival he was greatly engaged, and baptized from first to last many hundreds. Early in this revival Mr. A. Waller, son of his brother Benjamin, was brought in, and in some few years began to preach. Mr. Waller immediately recognized him as his successor, and declared that he believed his work in that part of the earth was finished. Accordingly, November 7th, 1793, after taking the most affectionate farewell of the churches, he removed to Abbeville in the State of South Carolina. This removal was said to have arisen, partly from economical considerations, and partly from a strong desire with himself and wife to live near a beloved daughter, who had some time previously married Rev. Abraham Marshall of Georgia. Perhaps there might be other causes. His labors in his new residence were also blessed, but not to a great extent. He remained, however, faithful in the cause until his death, which took place July 4th, 1802.

His death was, as might have been expected, truly glorious. His eldest son describes it in the following words: "His conflict with death, as it respected bodily affliction, was truly hard; but his soul appeared to be happy indeed! Never did I witness such resignation and Christian fortitude before! He was reduced to a perfect skeleton, and in several places the skin was rubbed off his bones. His pains were excruciating; but no murmur was heard from his lips. On the contrary, he would often say, 'I have a good Master, who does not give me one stroke too hard or one too many.'

"The last sermon he preached was on the death of a young man. The text on which he preached was Zechariah ii. 4. 'Run, speak to this young man.' He addressed himself chiefly to youth, in feeble, but animating strains; observing that he counted upon its being the last sermon he should ever preach: and fervently prayed that, Sampson like, he might slay more at his death than he had done in his life. He continued speaking until his strength failed him, and with reeling steps he advanced to a bed, where we thought he would have expired. Thence he was removed home in a carriage for the last time. He said, as to his soul, he was under no concern, he had given that to Jesus long since, and he was under no doubt his Master would provide a mansion for it. Just before his departure he summoned all his family, black and white, around him, and told them he was anxious to be gone, and to be present with Christ, and then warned them to walk in the fear of God, cordially shook hands with all, and soon after, with a pleasant countenance, breathed his last, and fell asleep in Jesus." I looked on the corpse with these words fresh in my mind:—

"O lovely appearance of death."

Thus this great man of God conquered the last enemy, and ascended to *that rest that remaineth for the people of God.* He died in the sixty-second year of his age, having been a minister of God's word for about thirty-five years, and in that time had lain in four different jails one hundred and thirteen days, besides receiving reproachings, buffetings, stripes, etc. Nor was his labor in vain in the Lord. While in Virginia he baptized more than two thousand persons, assisted in the ordination of twenty-seven ministers, and in the constitution of eighteen churches. For many years he had the ministerial care of five churches, for which he preached statedly. As a preacher his talents were not above mediocrity, but he was certainly a man of very strong mind. His talent for intrigue was equaled by few. This he exercised, sometimes beyond the innocence of the dove. He was, perhaps, too emulous to carry his favorite points, especially in associations, yet it must be owned that such influence as he acquired in this way, he always endeavored to turn to the glory of God.

LEWIS CRAIG.

This is a name well known in Virginia. It is interwoven in the history of many of her churches, and will continue to live in the memory of the pious, while time endures. To Lewis Craig, and his brother Elijah, may we look as among the principal instruments of introducing the gospel in the eastern part of our State.

The family with whom they were connected are said to have been eminently pious. The parents, and all their children, seven sons and four daughters, were all members of the Baptist Church. Lewis is said to have been first awakened under the preaching of Samuel Harriss, and to have remained for some time in deep distress. In following the preacher from place to place he would sometimes break out in solemn exhortation to others, while he confessed that he was himself without hope. He ultimately rejoiced in Christ, and in 1767, when about twenty-seven years of age, was baptized, and began to preach. He was far from possessing a cultivated mind, but being a sensible man, and having a very musical voice, with agreeable manners, and, especially, going forth under the constraining influence of the love of Christ, he excited much interest among the people he addressed. He traveled almost constantly, and the large congregations which everywhere attended his ministry were entreated to escape the Divine wrath, with the most impassioned earnestness. Nothing could exceed the burning zeal with which he persuaded men to be reconciled to God. His sermons consisted in a plain pungent exhibition of the evil of sin, and its ruinous consequences, with the glad tidings of redeeming love through a Saviour. Hundreds of his hearers found in these announcements the means of salvation. The gospel came to them not in word only, but in power, in the Holy Ghost, and in much assurance.

These successful results were principally manifested in the Counties of Orange and Spottsylvania. The first Baptist church organized, between the James and Rappahannock Rivers, called Lower Spottsylvania, afterwards Craig's, was the fruit of his efforts. This church was constituted in 1767. Three years after this period he received and accepted an invitation to preside over them as their pastor. Additions were regularly made to their number; but in 1767 an extensive revival was enjoyed, when more than one hundred were baptized. The church continued to prosper until 1781, when their pastor removed to the western country; a large number of the members of the church left the State with him, and a serious decline was experienced.

Before Elder Craig's departure to the West, he was counted worthy of his Master to suffer painful trials in the discharge of his ministerial duties. Various means were employed to alarm and cause him to give up his practice of preaching the gospel. He thought of the Saviour's dying love, and determined to go forward even at the expense of life. At length he was arrested by the sheriff of Spottsylvania, and brought before three magistrates, in the yard of the meeting-house, who bound him, with others, in the penalty of two thousand pounds, to appear at court two days after. They attended, and were arraigned as disturbers of the peace. The prosecuting attorney represented them to be a great annoyance to the county by their zeal as preachers.

"May it please your worship," said he, "they cannot meet a man upon the road but they must ram a text of Scripture down his throat." After hearing their defence, the court determined that they should be liberated, provided they would give security no more to preach in the county within twelve months. To this condition Elder C. and his companions refused to yield. They were then sentenced to close confinement in the jail. As they passed on to prison through the streets of Fredericksburg, they united in singing the lines—

"Broad is the road that leads to death."

They remained in prison one month, and were then released. Elder Craig then visited Williamsburg, to obtain relief for his brethren. The following letter was conveyed by him from the deputy governor to the king's attorney :—

"SIR : I lately received a letter signed by a good number of worthy gentlemen, who are not here, complaining of the Baptists; the particulars of their misbehavior are not told, any further than their running into private houses, and making dissensions. Mr. Craig and Mr. Benjamin Waller are now with me, and deny the charge : they tell me they are willing to take the oaths, as others have. I told them I had consulted the attorney-general, who is of opinion that the general court only have a right to grant licenses, and therefore I referred them to the court; but, on their application to the attorney-general, they brought me his letter, advising me to write to you. Their petition was a matter of right, and you ought not to molest these conscientious people, so long as they behave themselves in a manner becoming pious Christians, and in obedience to the laws—till the court, when they intend to apply for license, and when the gentlemen, who complain, may make their objéctions, and be heard. The act of toleration (it being found by experience that persecuting dissenters increases their numbers) has given them a right to apply, in a proper manner, for licensed houses, for the worship of God, according to their consciences ; and I persuade myself, the gentlemen will quietly overlook their meetings, till the court. I am told, they administer the sacrament of the Lord's Supper near the manner we do, and differ in nothing from our church but in that of baptism, and their renewing the ancient discipline; by which they have reformed some sinners, and brought them to be truly penitent: nay, if a man of theirs is idle, and neglects to labor, and provide for his family as he ought, he incurs their censures, which have had good effects. If this be their behavior, it were to be wished we had some of it among us. But, at least, I hope all may remain quiet till the court.

"I am, with great respects to the gentlemen, sir,

"Your humble servant,

"JOHN BLAIR.

"WILLIAMSBURG, July 16, 1768."

The prisoners were, after a short time, released. During their confinement, Elder C. preached through the gates to large crowds, and was the means of doing much good. When he was permitted to go at large, he went forth with renewed spiritual strength, defending the truth as it is in Jesus. He was enabled to thank God that he was permitted to suffer shame for the name of Christ. Day and night in his neighborhood and in all the surrounding country he ceased not to teach and to preach the gospel.

In 1771, about three years after this, he was again imprisoned, in the County of Caroline. He had several times preached there, and was quite successful. Says Mr. Semple, in referring to this circumstance, "Mr. Craig continued to visit this place, and to cultivate the seed sown. Believers were added from time to time. Satan took the alarm, and stirred up opposition to Mr. Craig. A warrant was issued, and Mr. Craig was carried before a magistrate, to whom he gave bond not to preach in the county within a certain number of days; but feeling himself hampered by this measure, he thought it best to incur the penalty; and accordingly preached some little time after, at one Reuben Catlet's plantation, and was taken up by virtue of a warrant and committed to prison, where he staid three months."

With undiminished ardor and success Mr. Craig continued to preach after his liberation. It is stated in Semple's History, that Tuckahoe, Upper King and Queen, and Upper Essex Churches, in the Dover Association, were planted under his ministry. As long as he remained in Virginia he was eminently useful. It has been already stated that in 1781 he removed to the West. He settled on Gilbert's Creek, Lincoln County, and immediately formed a church of those who had been dismissed with him, from Craig's, in his native State. In about two years after he again removed within six miles of Lexington, and built up the first Baptist church in that part of Kentucky, called South Elkhorn. Here he was drawn into the whirlpool of speculation, and suffered many losses. His peace of mind also was much disturbed. Still he retained an untarnished reputation, and continued to preach, while the church was greatly multiplied under his ministry. In 1795 he settled in Bracken County, where also the Lord made him greatly successful, as a large church was built up under his care.

There is reason to believe that no man in Kentucky exercised a more wide-spread and commanding influence for good than Lewis Craig. In removing from Virginia he had taken with him most of the members of the Upper Spottsylvania, since called Craig's Church. This was the oldest and most flourishing body of baptized believers between James and Rappahannock Rivers. He had been their successful pastor, loved and honored by them for ten or twelve years, and when his purpose was formed to migrate to the then far off western wilderness, they almost unanimously resolved to share in the perils and discomforts of his exile. Such was the enthusiasm awakened in this band of disciples, that of this large church a sufficient nnmber did not remain to continue the organization. It was necessary to disband, and not until several years after was the church re-established.

The pastor and flock, numbering about two hundred members, and called by John Taylor "the traveling church," commenced their long, toilsome journey. The whole, embracing children and servants, numbered nearly four hundred. It was a sublime spectacle! Onward they marched, over an almost trackless wilderness, Jehovah their guide and defence. Unharmed by beasts of prey, or the savage red man, they were permitted to reach the home they sought. We may well imagine how these pilgrims often lifted up holy hands, without wrath and doubting. They found many a Bethel in which to draw near to God, and oft, to them, it was the very gate of heaven. As they passed over mountain and valley the stillness of ages was broken by their songs of praise. The wilderness and the solitary place were indeed made glad, for never before had hymns of thanksgiving by human voices reverberated among those trees of the forest.

The church thus borne on to their destined home continued under the care of Lewis Craig. Settling awhile on Gilbert's Creek, they afterwards removed to South Elkhorn, as already stated. Here Mr. Craig purchased land. The first grist-mill in Kentucky was built by him. The above facts have been mainly received from John Taylor. He says, "South Elkhorn was eight miles from where I lived. I seldom went there but at monthly meetings. I now became more acquainted with that old successful man in the ministry, Lewis Craig. His orthodoxy mainly lay in salvation through Christ, by unmerited grace, and urging repentance on all to whom he preached. He had the most striking gift of exhortation that was perhaps in use in Kentucky; while with him in South Elkhorn, he treated me as a father would a son."

On another occasion, referring to Craig, he says, "There was but one church on the north side of Kentucky, and this was South Elkhorn, where Lewis Craig was pastor. Perhaps in the month of August, 1784, I became a member of that church, and thus I was brought under his pastoral care. He was then in the prime of his life, as to the gospel ministry—of the age between forty and fifty. Mr. Craig is yet living, and about eighty-three years old: he is one of the old gospel veterans in Virginia, where he often suffered imprisonment for the crime of preaching repentance to sinners."

Writing afterwards respecting the expediency of forming a new church at Clear Creek, he says, "We held a council on the subject of a constitution, but we found a difficulty, in this way: a number of the members had been in the church, with Lewis Craig, in Virginia, and in the traveling church through the wilderness, and its establishment in Kentucky, and, above all, if we had a new church, we might lose Lewis Craig as our pastor. Though we had four ordained preachers, all of us did not make *one* Lewis Craig."

He lived to advanced age. His last days were distinguished by increased spirituality of mind. His conversation was mostly on heavenly topics, and it was frequently said that he seemed to enjoy much of heaven in his soul. His trials had been greatly sanctified to his good, and, like a little child, he yielded quietly to the will of his Father. He died, after a short illness, in the eighty-seventh year of his age.

His sermons were remarkable for their evangelic and practical character. He possessed an easy address, his language was simple and flowing, and in exhortation excelled most of his contemporaries. Very often, when several sermons had been preached, without producing, apparently, any effect upon the people, he would follow, and by his pathetic appeals produce almost universal feeling in the congregation. He was always very industrious in his habits, and strictly temperate. Endowed with a natural sweetness of temper, and being much under the influence of the gospel, he was greatly beloved by all classes of men.

John Taylor says respecting him, "Perhaps there was never found in all Kentucky such a gift of exhortation as in Lewis Craig. The sound of his voice would make men tremble and rejoice. The first time I heard him preach, I seemed to *hear* the sound of his voice for many months. He was of middle stature, rather round-shouldered; his hair black, thick-set, and somewhat curled; a pleasant countenance; free spoken; and his company very interesting. He was a great peace-maker among contending parties."

JOSEPH CRAIG.

THOUGH not distinguished for those peculiarities which elevated to a high place, in the affections of Virginia Baptists, the two brothers Lewis and Elijah Craig, it will not be proper altogether to pass over the name of Joseph, another of the Craig family. He does not appear to have risen high as an expounder of the Scriptures, or even as a preacher. Much itinerant labor, however, was performed by him, and not without success. After preaching for some years in Virginia, he settled with his brothers in Kentucky, and continued there to exercise his ministerial functions. He is said to have been at times very eccentric. On one occasion, at Guinea's Bridge, while preaching, he was apprehended, and an attempt made to carry him before a magistrate. Mr. Semple says, "Thinking it no dishonor to cheat the devil, as he termed it, he slipped off the horse, and took to the bushes. They hunted him with dogs, but, Asahel like, being light of foot, he made good his retreat."

Another case is mentioned by John Taylor. He is represented to have been pursued by his persecutors, and climbing into a tree, he was shaken down, his hands tied, and an attempt made to carry him to court. He said, "If you put Joseph Craig in prison, I will have no hand in it." He would neither walk nor ride, and they were compelled to liberate him. Walking along the streets of Lexington, some young men resolved to indulge in sport at his expense, by asking curious questions. His only reply was, "Get thee behind me, Satan;" thus turning the ridicule of all beholders on them.

Crossing a ferry, one day, when he offered to pay, the ferryman declined receiving it, saying, "Mr. Craig, you may pray for me." Reaching the opposite side of the stream, Mr. Craig called the man to him, that he might pray for him. He said, "Not now, Mr. Craig." But the preacher said, "I will not go away in your debt." The ferryman disliked it much, but was compelled to submit, and Mr. Craig prayed most earnestly for his deliverance from the captivity of sin.

Says John Taylor, "By vigorous industry and care of his property, Mr. Craig made a good estate. He reared many children, sons and daughters, and taught them all habits of industry. Find his children where you may, they are surrounded with affluence, and of respectable standing among men. Nearly all of them also have a place in the church of Christ. Mr. Craig was small of stature, stooping shoulders, of a hardy complexion, active in business, persevering as a traveling preacher, or rather exhorter, for in that lay his greatest gift. He died of a lingering complaint, after laboring in the ministry, say fifty-nine years. His age was nearly eighty."

WILLIAM BASKETT.*

ELDER WILLIAM BASKETT was born in Goochland County, October, 1741. Having descended from parents who were poor, and not being favored with the means of education, but little is known of him until his twentieth year, about which time he was married to Miss Mary Pace, who was also a native of Goochland. In this, his only matrimonial connection, he was blessed with thirteen children, eight sons and five daughters.

From his earliest years he had been impressed with ideas of the value and necessity of religion; had regularly attended public worship; and had even received, as he advanced in age, the Lord's supper. After his marriage he established in his family morning and evening service, in which he read prayers. This he did for seven years, while yet he had not, as he afterwards discovered, known or felt the nature and effects of gospel truth.

About this period his neighborhood began to be visited by Baptist preachers. Of them and their doctrines, numerous and different reports were in circulation. The first of these, an opportunity to hear whom presented itself, was Brother Corbley. He went, moved partly by curiosity and partly with a desire to be profited. This was the first preacher not of the established church that he had ever heard. On his return home at a late hour he found Mrs. Baskett waiting patiently to be informed concerning the new preacher and his tenets, of which he gave a description before he received any refreshment. Soon afterwards they both had an opportunity of hearing Brother Corbley, and of seeing him administer the ordinance of baptism. The minds of both became now so much concerned, that Mr. Baskett, to use his own words, "was scarcely able to follow his plough;" and when he returned from the field he frequently found his wife engaged in prayer.

While filled with anxiety as to what they should do to be saved, they walked on a dark and rainy night three miles to hear

* By Elder Robert Lilly.

a preacher of the established church. Mr. Baskett asked the preacher if there was such a thing to be entertained as a hope of personal interest in the merits of Christ; a knowledge of acceptance with God? The preacher replied, that for his own part, he felt a comfortable hope while he kept the commandments, and at no other time. The continued distress and further inquiries of Mr. and Mrs. Baskett subjected them to the charge on the part of the preacher of being *deranged.* The circumstances under which he obtained comfort are found in the following extract from a letter written by himself a little before his death :—

"In childhood and youth, I often promised God I would serve him, if spared to be a man. From my marriage, in my twentieth, until my twenty-seventh year, I attended scrupulously to secret and public prayer and worship, and to the ordinance of the supper. But, now, I saw myself a guilty, undone sinner; and, during eight months, was without comfort. At length, one night at midnight, on my bended knees, imploring Divine mercy through Christ, and throwing myself at the disposal of sovereign grace, my mind was turned to the words, 'He that trusts in the Lord shall never be confounded.' I saw that 'God was, in Christ, reconciling the world unto himself, not imputing their trespasses unto them.' For several days my heart was filled with joy. Since, my life has been a constant warfare. I am sensible of much remaining imperfection, but cannot fear death or judgment. The judge is himself my friend. Nor do I apprehend destruction by my spiritual foes or my trials. It is God who worketh in us both to will and to do. In six troubles he is with us, and doth not forsake us in the seventh. If we pass through waters, they cannot overflow us; if through fires, they cannot burn us. I believe all this in my heart. If my conduct does not agree with this, place no confidence in me or what I say. My desire is to glorify God through the remainder of my life. The tree is best known by its fruits. Please to send me an account of your own religious experience."

Not long afterwards Mr. and Mrs. Baskett were baptized, together with two other neighbors, by Elder Elijah Craig. These first Baptists of that vicinity frequently visited each other for conversation and social prayer. Brother B. thought himself far inferior to the rest of this little company in scriptural knowledge; but they always urged him forward, and he was soon employed in the exhortation of his neighbors, who attended these meetings for the purpose of hearing. Others made a profession of faith under his labors; and in the year 1774 a church was constituted, called Lisles, consisting of eighteen male members and thirty-two white female members. This church was served by Elder Webber as pastor, until 1787, under whose ministry, in the course of two years, many souls were added. In the toils of this revival Mr. Baskett shared largely, and in 1789 he was ordained to the work of an evangelist. Five years afterwards Elder Webber removed to Kentucky, when Elder Baskett was called to the pastoral office.

From this time until the year 1815, he was blessed in his family and church. His faithfulness and zeal as a pastor, and all his conduct in his domestic affairs, were exemplary. He lived to see all his children married and settled, and himself possessed of extensive property which had gradually increased upon his hands. On the 21st of April his aged consort, after a few days' indisposition, fell asleep in death. The next Sabbath he preached his last, and those present said his best sermon, from the words, "We have no continuing city, but seek one to come." On the 30th of the same month, his own tranquil spirit escaped this state of trial, and went to the enjoyment of rest. In his illness he consented to receive medical aid, he said, merely to gratify his friends. He knew he was about to depart, and found his soul supported by the consolations of the gospel, and cheered and sustained by its gracious promises.

The removal of these two faithful servants was improved on the 24th of June ensuing, by Elders Purrington and Hiter. Elder Hiter preached from Phil. i. 21: "For me to live, is Christ; to die, is gain." Elder Purrington from 2 Kings, ii. 12: "My Father, my Father, the chariot of Israel, and the horsemen thereof." The large concourse which assembled, and the feelings they manifested, bespoke the excellence of those pious souls, and the high veneration and affection with which they were regarded. "The memory of the just is blessed."

JOHN COURTNEY.*

THE REV. JOHN COURTNEY was born in the County of King and Queen, about the year 1744. His parents were members of the Protestant Episcopal Church, in which, of course, he was himself educated. His eldest brother as well as his father were conspicuous and influential members of that church.

Of the early history of this sincerely loved and justly venerated man, scarcely anything is known. Although he was in after life found possessed of a mind and heart excellent, in no ordinary degree; and although his labors were useful to an extent reached by few whose names have been echoed far and wide, yet, in the midst of his toils, fatigues, and success, his acquaintance was almost confined to his native State. It has sometimes happened that men of superior virtues have been unknown in the world, as mines of inconceivable value lie hid in the bowels of the earth. The history of the acts of the Apostles is for the most part limited to narrations concerning two of them, Paul and Barnabas, who were themselves not of the twelve. Enoch was doubtless a man of distinguished merit; yet with the exception of his age and the mention of the fact that he had descendants, his biography by Moses is contained in these few words, "And Enoch walked with God; and he was not; for God took him." Nor had we been favored with any further information of his character, if, after a lapse of thousands of years, it had not been apparently by accident recorded, "Enoch also, the seventh from Adam, prophesied of these, saying, 'Behold the Lord cometh with ten thousands of his saints, to execute judgment upon all.'"

The decease of his father left him an orphan when young, and the possession of the estate according to law devolving on the oldest son, it was determined, as soon as his age would allow it, that John should be bound apprentice to the business of carpenter. No more is now heard of him until having arrived at years of maturity he makes his appearance abroad. Thus it

* Prepared by Elder Henry Keeling.

had been with Him, whom Elder Courtney delighted to honor and serve, the glorious Redeemer. From the age of twelve to thirty years nothing is said of *Him*.

Mr. Courtney as a man possessed a generous, frank, and nobly independent spirit. And these dispositions were remarkably to be observed in his subsequent character, as a Christian and a minister of the gospel. This coincidence is, no doubt, common. Enterprise, decision, perseverance, and boldness, were characteristics of the Apostle Paul, both before and after his conversion to the faith of Christ; but the objects toward which they were directed were changed by his conversion.

At what period of life he entered the matrimonial relationship is rather uncertain, but it is known to have been previous to his making a profession of religion. His conversion is dated at the great revival of religion which, under the preaching of John Waller, Lewis Craig, James Childs, John Shackleford, Robert Ware, Iverson Lewis, and others, secured persecution, even to blows, stripes, and imprisonments. After the example of Moses, who "chose rather to suffer affliction with the people of God, than to enjoy the pleasures of sin for a season," he joined himself to the persecuted, and with them identified his religious interests, in which all others were involved to a much greater extent than now, when liberty is enjoyed.

Having experienced the efficacy of gospel truth in his own heart, he soon began to persuade others to repent, and in his turn suffered the frowns and wrath to which his companions had been and were exposed. At about this time the Revolution was maturing its plans, and within a few years the independence of the United States was declared. Repeatedly were the services of this man of God required, both in the camp and in the field; since, although considered by his own denomination entitled to preach and administer church ordinances, not having been ordained according to the usages of the Church of England, he was not recognized by the law as a minister of Christ. But probably if the law had not compelled him, his patriotism and valor, and love of liberty, civil and religious, would have taken him to the field.

After the close of the Revolution he removed to the City of Richmond. Here, in addition to his pastoral labors, he "wrought with his own hands, ministering to his necessities," and to those of such as were "with him." During a period of more than forty years, he served the Baptist Church in this city either as their *exclusive* or *senior* pastor. Faithfulness, affection, disinterestedness and zeal, marked his whole career. He could with propriety adopt the language: "Therefore, remember, that I ceased not to warn every one night and day with tears. I have coveted no man's silver, or gold, or apparel. I have showed you all things, how, that so laboring, ye ought to support the weak; and to remember the words of the Lord Jesus, how he said, 'It is more blessed to give than to receive.'"

Elder Courtney did not enjoy the advantage of education. It is well known that in his early days these were confined to the opulent and great. In this Colony only one college existed, William and Mary in Williamsburg; and all the Colonies besides could number only four. Had the means of learning been as abundant then as now, his aspiring mind had elevated itself to the rank of any of his contemporaries. It was, indeed, among the endeavors of those who were in power, to prevent the progress of letters and the diffusion of knowledge.

But how much even the *want* of learning may have been instrumental in contributing to the excellency of this distinguished man, it is not possible to imagine. Want of learning is a *great disadvantage* and *misfortune*. Yet it is as easy to conceive that even this may be made conducive to a man's virtue and usefulness, as it is to conceive that the barrenness of a soil may promote the wealth of its inhabitants, by creating enterprise, industry, and economy.

It is truly desirable that ministers of the gospel be *well* educated men. But this should *never* form the base of their qualifications. And who will assume the responsibility of saying that none but classical and scientific men shall preach? or who will name the attainments requisite to be made? Education is important in an orator or statesman; yet with such a one as could not be called classical, Patrick Henry inspired and roused into effort a nation, and the immortal Washington conducted it to freedom. And an Apostle declares, "I, brethren, come not unto you with excellency of speech, or of man's wisdom, declaring unto you the testimony of God; but was with you in weakness, and fear, and much trembling." But he was a man of strong and rational powers, candor, godly sincerity, knowledge of things and men, acquaintance with the Word of God, ardent devotion, and exemplary life. He did not direct others to the path of life, and himself wander in the road to death. More than half a century proves the genuineness of a profession which he had made when it was unfashionable and hazardous.

In the performance of pastoral duty, assistance was found necessary, during the last fourteen years of his life. Of these, he was aided nine years by the Rev. John Brice; one by the Rev. Andrew Broaddus; and three by the Rev. Henry Keeling.

For four years previous to his death, he seldom, if ever, attempted to preach; but was nevertheless employed in the work of his Lord and Master. Long will his faithful visits be remembered. Even when debility prevented him from being able to dismount from his horse, he rode from door to door, to encourage, counsel, and exhort. As the termination of his days approached, his decline was evident. It was the privilege of the writer of this sketch to be frequently with him. The lessons of patience, gratitude, and heavenly-mindedness, which his appearance and conversation inculcated, will never be forgotten. In the deepest affliction he not only did *not* complain, but rendered thanks to God.

On the 18th of December, 1824, this servant of God went to receive his reward. Having lived the life of the righteous, he died his death. With a "hope, full of immortality," he fell asleep in Jesus. In few instances can the declaration of Paul the Apostle have been more appropriate: "I have fought a good fight, I have finished my course, I have kept the faith; henceforth there is laid up for me a crown of righteousness, which the Lord, the righteous Judge, will give unto me at that day, and not unto me only, but unto all them that love his appearing." Sixteen years before him, the partner of his youth and riper years entered that "rest which remaineth for the people of God."

JOHN KOONTZ.

It is a pleasing task to review the lives of those who have been leaders in promoting any important reformation among their fellow-men. Especially does such a review become interesting, if numerous and severe trials have been cheerfully sustained for the sake of Christ and his kingdom. Who does not find a melancholy delight in perusing the brief narrative which the sacred historian gives of the first martyr's zeal and sufferings? How nobly does he plead for God, and how faithfully does he expose the evil and danger of sin! With what constancy and meekness does he fall beneath the shower of stones with which his bloody persecutors assailed him! Numerous instances of the sacrifice of life or of worldly enjoyment for Christ's sake have occurred since the days of Stephen, all of which furnish indubitable evidence of the divinity of the gospel.

Among those who suffered for the name of Christ among the early Virginia Baptists, was Elder John Koontz. He was, by extraction and birth, a German. At the time of his conversion, he resided in Frederick, near Front Royal. In that county he was baptized, December, 1768. Shortly after he was called to the work of the ministry. For several months his efforts were confined to the vicinity of his residence. But in the latter part of 1770 he visited his brother, then residing in Shenandoah, and finding the people generally ignorant of those things which belonged to their peace, he began to exhort them to escape the wrath to come. The sentiments he advanced, and the benevolent zeal with which he inculcated them, excited universal attention. Vast crowds attended his ministrations; nor did they hear in vain. The Lord opened their hearts to receive the word, and caused the truth to be mighty in their deliverance from the kingdom of darkness. As the excitement increased, and many found redemption in Christ, several other Baptist ministers visited the county, and assisted this young laborer in gathering the harvest. At that time he was not ordained. Those who believed in Christ, were baptized by Elder Samuel Harriss, while Mr. Koontz continued to lift up his voice like a trumpet, to cry aloud and spare not. With unwearied assiduity he availed himself of all facilities to preach a crucified Saviour. In that settlement there were many Germans, to whom his ministry was much blessed. Frequently to the same congregation he would preach, first in Dutch, and then in English.

These efforts, in connection with the labors of Elder John Picket and others, resulted in the constitution of Whitehouse, since called Mill Creek Church, in 1772. At this time there were two members who employed their talents in preaching the gospel, and in making choice of one of these to be their pastor, some difference of sentiment existed, by which they remained a short period unsupplied. But ultimately, having prevailed on Mr. Koontz to remove from Frederick and settle among them, they unanimously elected him to that office. This occurred in 1776, when he was ordained.

During the first years of Elder Koontz's ministerial labor in the vicinity of Mill Creek, his progress was much impeded by the opposition of some German Menonists, a sect which prevailed in that region. Several of these heard and received the truth. A very considerable excitement was produced in consequence of this circumstance, and as Elder Koontz was the principal instrument in the revival, they directed their shafts against him. Mr. Semple thus describes this event: "In order to overturn the works of Satan, as they called it, they sent for preachers from Pennsylvania. In some short time four or five Pennsylvania Menonist preachers came. They labored much to prevent the work then going on. They conceived, as he could preach in Dutch, that John Koontz was the chief cause of this disturbance, and thought if he could be convinced, or by any means checked, there would be no more of it. To this end the preachers came to his house, and labored much to convince him. They contended that Christians ought not to hold with going to war, with slavery, or taking legal oaths; that these were fundamental points. To this Mr. Koontz replied, that the Baptists upon these points left every man at his own discretion, wishing each to follow the dictates of his own conscience. He then questioned them as to the reason of their hope in Christ, whether they had felt the power of godliness in their hearts, or whether they relied upon their nursery faith. He found them entire strangers to vital godliness, denying the existence thereof. They left him, and held meetings in the neighborhood two days, striving publicly and privately against the revival then happily progressing. Their labor was in vain; God still added to his people such as should be saved."

Perhaps no Baptist in the United States has suffered more at the hands of opposers than did this servant of the Lord. Various means were employed to deter him from speaking in the name of Christ. Like his Master he was treated with contumely and scorn. They threatened him with imprisonment and stripes. But, sustained by an Almighty arm, he continued steadfast to his purpose. To please God, rather than man, was the desire of his soul. Conscious of the rectitude of his heart, and the scriptural character of the principles he inculcated, he was ready, with Paul, not to be bound only, but also to die for the name of the Lord Jesus. His firmness in passing through the furnace will be evinced in referring to an extract from the history of the Virginia Baptists. "Once Mr. Koontz was met on the road and beaten. On another occasion, he attended a meeting toward Smith's Creek. When he arrived at the place he was met by a set of ruffians, who forbade his preaching. One Captain Leahorn, a respectable man, interfered and insisted he should preach, and prevailed. The persecutors, however, threw out heavy threats, that if he ever came that way upon that errand again they would beat him severely. Mr. K. could not be deterred from coming, and they kept their word. He went not long after. His enemies had thrown in money and hired a son of darkness to beat him. Accordingly, as soon as he arrived, the miscreant began to strike him with the butt end of a large cane—requiring him to promise never to come there again. This Mr. K. refused to do. The fellow continued beating until he had almost disabled him. Then he left him. While thus suffering Mr. K. felt nothing more than a firm determination not to yield. But the savage had left him but a few steps before he felt his soul exceedingly comforted. He could then thank God that he was counted worthy to suffer persecution for the name of Christ.

"Some time after this he and Martin Kaufman went to a place

about six or seven miles from thence, and while they were preparing to preach he heard a man in a room adjoining that in which he and Mr. Kaufman were sitting, inquire for Mr. Koontz. When he heard the inquiry he immediately suspected that some mischief was in agitation, and stepped into a third room, out of sight. The man, who had probably been instigated by some other persons, did not know either Koontz or Kaufman. When he came into the room he supposed Martin Kaufman to be John Koontz, and without asking any questions fell upon him with a stick, or something of the kind. It was not until he had received many blows that he could convince the persecutor that he was not named Koontz. In the mean time the man's wrath was satisfied, and he went off without finding Mr. Koontz.

"On another occasion he attended an appointment, but before he had begun to preach they took him off and said they would carry him to prison. At a small distance from the place they met a man coming to meeting; he said he had come to hear Mr. K. preach; that they should not carry him any farther, and attempted to rescue him. But the persecutors beat him off. When they had carried him a small distance farther he said to them, 'Take heed what you do; if I am a man of God, you fight against God.' One of the party was immediately alarmed. The warning dropped was owned of God, working in him a repentance not to be repented of. They had proceeded but a little way before the whole company began to relent, and agreed to let him go. The man who first took the alarm, and two or three more of the company, afterwards became Baptists."

The valuable labors of this devoted man were not circumscribed by the county in which he lived. They were extended to the adjacent Counties of Culpepper, Rockingham, Hardy, etc. etc. He was the chief means of the formation of Lunie's Creek Church. Several years after their constitution, when in quite a declining state, they succeeded in obtaining a supply of ministerial labor from him, although he was compelled to ride about seventy miles. Lost River Church also enjoyed the benefit of his direct influence for some time.

Speaking of Elder Koontz, in 1809, (several years before his death,) Mr. Semple says: "From the time of his initiation into the ministry until this day, he has continued faithfully to declare the counsel of God. Among the Baptists there have been many active and laborious preachers, whose souls have glowed with seraphic ardor: leaning upon the sacred promises, they were willing to suffer with Christ here that they might reign with him hereafter. But considering Mr. Koontz's unwearied labors in the ministry; the length of time in which he has been engaged, (about forty years;) considering that he has a constitution that has seldom or never failed him, requiring short and few intervals of rest, it may be fairly stated that few, if any, in the State have surpassed him as to the amount of service devoted to his Lord's vineyard. He has been a laborer indeed, and will no doubt receive his full wages whenever the Lord of the vineyard shall reckon with his servants."

The same honorable testimony to his fidelity in the work of the ministry is borne by those who knew him to the end of life. His views on the subject of believers' baptism were of the most uncompromising kind. The same may be said respecting the doctrinal truths of the gospel. In his defence of what he believed to be the counsel of God he was faithful. When he was called from his earthly labors he was between eighty and ninety years of age.

JOHN MUNROE, M.D.

Born in 1749. In his twenty-first year he became pious and entered the ministry. He was also a practitioner of medicine. He is represented in Semple's History as having been very useful for many years in the County of Fauquier. "In the pulpit," says the historian, "he is a man of solemn dignity, warm address, and speaks as one having authority. He frequently takes up contested subjects, and his opponents sometimes complain that at such seasons he administers very strong corrosives. The Doctor, however, independent of this, preaches the gospel of peace in power and demonstration of the spirit."

Before he removed to Hampshire County he was instrumental

in founding several churches, particularly Upper Carter's Run and Long Branch. After his removal also, the Lord made his efforts a blessing to his cause. He became the pastor of New River and Crooked Run Churches in Hampshire, and afterwards of Buckmarsh, Frederick.

His demise occurred at his residence, on Big Capon, Virginia, on the 17th of August, 1824. In noticing this event, a Christian brother remarks: "Few men have been instrumental in doing more good. He was a warm, experimental, and practical preacher of righteousness. The last sermon he ever preached was on a day of fasting, humiliation, and prayer, solemnly set apart by the church at Buckmarsh, (of which he was pastor,) on account of the dreadful disease which was spreading through the neighborhood. On that occasion he was warmer than we ever saw him before; his whole soul seemed engaged. His text was Joel, ii. 1. 'Blow ye the trumpet in Zion, and sound an alarm in my holy mountain: let all the inhabitants of the land tremble, for the day of the Lord cometh, for it is nigh at hand.'

'He preached as though he ne'er should preach again,
And as a dying man to dying men.'"

On the succeeding Sunday his aged wife followed him to the grave. She had for many years been a pious and exemplary member of the Baptist church. "Blessed are the dead which die in the Lord; from henceforth, yea saith the spirit, they rest from their labors, and their works do follow them."

WILLIAM MARSHALL.

William Marshall was born in the Northern Neck, 1735. His connections were highly respectable, he being an uncle of Chief Justice Marshall. In early life he was remarkable for his devotion to the fashionable amusements of the day. His tall, graceful form, dark piercing eye, and engaging manners, rendered him the pride of the circle in which he moved. Until he reached years of maturity he continued a neglecter of God and his salvation, having had very few opportunities of hearing the gospel in its purity proclaimed. In the year 1768, he was providentially brought under the ministry of those who were then called New Lights, and became the subject of deep concern. So great was his distress, that for a time he despaired of salvation. But the Lord in mercy relieved his painful anxiety. This occurred in the County of Fauquier. He soon joined the Baptists, and entered the field of ministerial labor.

The conversion of this votary of fashion excited the surprise of many. Especially were they amazed, that an individual of so much distinction should have united with a sect everywhere spoken against. His ministry was attended by crowds. Most of his auditors were prompted by curiosity, desiring to hear what the convert would say respecting the change he had experienced; others went, supposing him to be deranged; and a few to mock and oppose him. He, however, was undaunted:

> " His tongue broke out in unknown strains,
> And sung surprising grace."

The word preached was not in vain, but was attended with the Holy Ghost sent down from heaven. One of the most remarkable seasons of ingathering which Virginia has ever known resulted from his labors. The enemies of the truth were much enraged, and determined, if possible, to arrest the march of this new doctrine; they seized Mr. M. and attempted to put him in prison, but his brother, Col. Thomas Marshall, interfered, and succeeded in obtaining his release. He continued to preach in the County of Fauquier with unabated zeal and success. Among the seals to his ministry were John Taylor and Joseph Redding, who afterwards became popular and useful laborers in the Lord's vineyard. He subsequently visited the County of Shenandoah and there preached with equal success. Thousands came to see and hear him. It is said that large congregations would stand in deep snow with the utmost patience, while he declared to them the unsearchable riches of Christ. The first baptism in the waters of the Shenandoah was performed by Elder Samuel Harriss in 1770. At this time, as the result principally of Marshall's labors, fifty-three went down into the liquid grave, and were thus buried with their adorable Lord in that ordinance.

For several years he continued his itinerant labors. Indeed, at that time he was scarcely qualified for any other than the work of an evangelist. The burden of his discourses was "repent and believe the gospel." Surrounded by a moral wilderness, he saw the necessity of clearing the ground before it could become a fruitful field. There had not been time to investigate the mysteries of the gospel or to prepare himself for expounding the word of God. His chief object was to warn men of the danger of living and dying in sin, and the necessity of turning to the Lord through Jesus Christ. He was one of the most faithful and energetic preachers who ever raised their voices in Virginia. He afterwards became the pastor of Happy Creek Church. This station he occupied but a short time. In 1780 he removed to Kentucky, and settled in what is now called Shelby County. Shortly after this, by a fall from his horse, he was so disabled as to disqualify him for preaching. During this confinement he found leisure for reading and meditation, and when he recovered he was much more doctrinal and systematic in his pulpit efforts. His broken bones were imperfectly united, and in consequence he suffered much pain. Notwithstanding this he traveled extensively, and preached with his wonted zeal. "It was," says a cotemporary preacher, "interesting to see this old man assisted to the stand and propped up by his friends, and to hear him pour forth the most delightful strains of gospel truth. His strong mind, deep research, and prayerful spirit, well qualified him to clear the subjects he discussed of all ambiguity. He was rather inclined to consider the command to wash the disciples' feet, etc., as obligatory on all Christians."

He was a man of much prayer; when traveling in company with his brethren he was fond of alighting from his horse and with them presenting supplications to the mercy-seat. As he advanced to the close of life he grew in grace, and became more conformed to the Divine image. He died in 1808, in the seventy-third year of his age and in the hope of immortal life.

JOHN CORBLEY.*

JOHN CORBLEY was born in Great Britain in 1733, and while a boy agreed to serve four years for his passage to Pennsylvania. When his time expired he removed to Winchester, Virginia, and ultimately to Berkeley County: here, in a conversation with Elder Garrard, he was awakened to a sense of his lost condition. He was baptized by Mr. Garrard, and began to preach. Becoming conspicuous as a leader among the Baptists, the enemies of religion considered him worthy of a prison. He was accordingly put into Culpepper jail, where he stayed a considerable time. Here he was exceedingly useful. He was regularly in the habit of preaching, from the windows of his prison, the gospel of peace. After his liberation he suffered in various methods, being often threatened with death. Not unfrequently was he taken from the pulpit and cruelly beaten, after having been dragged from place to place. The exact year in which he was imprisoned is not known, but it was probably previous to 1770, for in 1769 he was a delegate from Mountain Run Church, in Culpepper, to the Ketockton Association, and acted as their clerk. His name does not appear on the minutes again until 1775, when he comes as the representative of a church called Goshen, in Redstone Settlement, Pennsylvania. It appears that he had moved there several years previous to this, and in conjunction with Isaac Sutton, had planted the first three or four churches in the Redstone Settlement.

His first wife was of the Quaker persuasion, and was married to him previous to his profession of religion. She proved a thorn in his side during her life. She died, and he married a most amiable woman, by whom he had several children. But how delusory is all earthly bliss! The Indians, for many years, were exceedingly troublesome in the Redstone country. Mr. Corbley and his wife and children, on a Sunday morning, started to walk to the meeting-house, less than half a mile from his house. After going a short distance, it was found that his Bible, which he had

* By R. B. Semple, with alterations.

given his wife to carry, had been forgotten. He went back after it. On his return to overtake his family he saw two Indians running, one of whom made a direful yell. He suspected an attack, and ran to a fort about half a mile off and obtained assistance. When they came to the place, he found his wife killed with a tomahawk, and the infant which she had in her arms thrown across her breast, with its brains dashed out against a tree. Three of the other children were killed, and two scalped and wounded that afterwards recovered. Only one, a little boy, escaped unhurt. He was attacked, but a dog seized the Indian that was pursuing him, by which he got into the bushes and hid himself. The feelings of Mr. Corbley on this afflicting occasion are beyond description. He fell into a melancholy state of mind, during which he was scarcely able to preach. Reflecting, at length, that the hand of Providence was visible in the preservation of his own life, he took courage and recommenced his labors In that country, though thinly settled, his ministry was very effectual, three or four hundred having been baptized by him. He was a man of eminent gifts, and esteemed by most a very pious Christian. His success drew upon him the resentment of the wicked, which they vented in a very diabolical manner. A base woman accused him of making frequent criminal proposals to her, and offered to confirm it by a solemn oath. Although he knew it to be false, and the church did not believe it, yet he thought it best to remain silent, and not preach until it could by some means be cleared up. The woman was cited to appear before a magistrate, in order to swear her to what she affirmed, and in the mean time the church earnestly engaged in prayer. When she came before the magistrate she was taken with a trembling, and for some time remained speechless. Some wished to excuse her and let it pass off; but Mr. Corbley insisted on her swearing, which she did, and expressly declared his innocence, and said it was a plot laid by certain persons whom she named.

He was sick but a short time previous to his decease. On the 9th of June, 1803, the day of his death, he had an appointment to preach; but being ill, his brethren and friends met at his dwelling, when, as well as he could, he addressed them. A few minutes previous to his departure he asked for his hymn-book, read, and sung a few lines. Thus this man of God ended his ministerial labors, leaving this world in the triumphs of faith. A large connection of relations and brethren in Christ survived to lament their loss,—but their loss was his gain. His funeral sermon was preached by Elder David Phillips, from Rev. xiv. 13: "Blessed are the dead which die in the Lord from henceforth; yea, saith the spirit, that they may rest from their labors, and their works do follow them." He was buried with the following inscription on his tombstone:—

Death, thou hast conquered me;
I by thy dart am slain;
But Jesus Christ shall conquer thee,
And I shall rise again.

In the course of his ministry he had two public debates on the subject of baptism, one with a Methodist minister by the name of Cook, and the other with a Mr. John Armstrong, a Presbyterian. In both cases he ably defended the views of the Baptists, greatly to the satisfaction of the Baptist churches, and to the advantage of the cause of truth. Subsequently he wrote an able defence of believers' baptism in a pamphlet of some size, in answer to the above-named Mr. Cook.

Mr. Corbley, though a good preacher, was thought to do more good out of the pulpit than in it. He generally after preaching mingled with the congregation, and, by singing and exhortation, made very serious impressions. He was greatly beloved as a Christian and minister. His sentiments were Calvinistic, being opposed alike to Arminianism and fatalism. Among the churches formed through his instrumentality two or more are in Virginia.

ELIJAH BAKER.

THE biography of ELIJAH BAKER will, no doubt, be read with special interest in many portions of our State, on account of the wide range he was allowed to take in preaching the gospel of Christ. A brief review of his life may be profitable to *all*. in illustrating how much may be done by one man, who, with singleness of purpose and energy of action, consecrates his talents to the good of his fellow-men.

Elder Baker was born in Lunenburg County, in 1742. That no flesh may glory in His presence, God often selects the weak things of the world to confound the things that are mighty. His purposes are not unfrequently effected by instruments comparatively insignificant. The subject of this sketch was born of humble parentage, and the earlier years of his life were spent in obscurity. He very soon exhibited an ardent temperament, which led him into the indulgence of many popular vices. He was a lover of pleasure more than a lover of God. But *He* who is rich in mercy checked him in his course of sensuality, and gave a new direction to his desires. He became at first the subject of partial reformation and an attentive hearer of the gospel. Though convinced of his guilt and danger, the struggle between his own heart and the humbling requisitions of the Divine Word was long and desperate. Determinations were frequently formed to abandon forever his sinful pursuits, but as often were they broken. Increasing anguish of mind was the result. He was at length as an humble, dependent rebel, brought to the feet of Christ. There he found relief. Thenceforward he contemplated himself as a recovered sinner, and, constrained by the love of a Saviour, began to speak his praise. His perceptions of the plan of salvation were at first obscure, in consequence of which he suffered much depression. But as he became acquainted with Christ, and him crucified, his reliance was more simple and consoling.

Having found the Redeemer precious to his heart he could not be satisfied until he had publicly made known what the Lord had done for him. He was baptized by Elder Harriss, in 1769, and united with the Meherrin Church, in the County of Lunenburg.

Immediately after his baptism he began to recommend Him in whom he had found so much consolation. His talents were not of the most promising character, and yet he could not be repressed in directing others to the foundation in Zion. There was soon developed such a spirit, and his gifts so far improved by exercise, as to warrant the church to set him apart to the work of the ministry. He was soon invited to take charge of Malones

Church, Mecklenburg County, which invitation he accepted. The pastoral connection was retained about twelve months, when he relinquished this field of labor and became an itinerant. He gave himself wholly to the work of publishing salvation for several years, during which time he traveled extensively throughout Eastern Virginia. It is doubtful whether any other man in the State has been as successful within the same length of time. Through his instrumentality all the churches between Hampton and Richmond City were originated, and several on the Eastern Shore. His efforts in the Counties of Henrico, New Kent, etc. down to Warwick, were of the most indefatigable kind. In this region he spent the year 1773, and the two following years. He labored also in the County of Gloucester.

As he was afterwards permanently settled on the Eastern Shore, it will be interesting to notice his early efforts among the people of that region. He was invited thither by a Mr. Elliot of Gloucester, who having, under the influence of Elder Baker's preaching, been brought to a knowledge of the truth, was deeply anxious that those among whom he formerly lived should be partakers of the gospel hope.

It was his privilege to be the first Baptist preacher who had visited that shore. Much attention was excited in all the neighborhoods he visited, as both the manner and matter of his addresses were novel. The first discourse he delivered seems to have been productive of much good. He attended, on Easter Sunday, one of the established churches as a hearer. The Episcopal minister failed to attend. He then informed the congregation that if they would allow him he would address them himself. They consented. Finding a slight elevation near the road, he preached in the open air with great warmth, a plain gospel sermon. Considerable excitement was the result. Some were offended with the faithfulness of the new preacher; others expressed astonishment at the unction with which he delivered his message; and some returned deeply affected. Such was the interest produced in all that region, that when a few weeks after he made another visit, the parson had given notice he would prove the Baptist to be in error. Elder Baker was one of his hearers, and afterwards day and night, for more than a week, he continued to preach the gospel of Christ. His ministry was attended by listening crowds, many of whom were baptized by him. Such were the indications of the Divine blessings, that Elder Baker concluded it was his duty to accept the pressing invitation he received to settle among this people. A short time previous he was united in marriage with Sarah Copeland, a lady of respectable connections. He became a resident of Northampton County, and in 1778 took charge of the Lower Northampton Church. He continued his exertions on the Eastern Shore both of Maryland and Virginia, and was the principal instrument in building up several churches, and of bringing into the work of the ministry several who had united with the people of God. It was at length thought proper to organize a new association, and, in 1782, the messengers of the churches having assembled at Salisbury, they formed themselves into the Salisbury Association. In 1808 a division took place for the sake of convenience, and the churches on the Virginia side of the Eastern Shore were constituted into what is called the Accomac Association.

It might be expected that such a course of successful labor would meet with opposition. At one period the hostility which the servants of Jesus experienced was of the most determined character. Elder Baker was counted worthy to share in this hostility. He realized the most cruel treatment. For several days he was confined in the Accomac jail. None of these things moved him. He not only maintained his steadfastness, but increased in activity and boldness, in preaching Christ and him crucified.

The following fact stated by Elder Semple deserves a place here—showing, as it does, the recklessness of that enmity which was cherished against him, and the spirit he exhibited in securing every opportunity of doing good to the souls of men: "The most atrocious attempt to persecute was that of seizing him by a lawless power, and carrying him on board a vessel in the adjacent waters, where they left him—having contracted with the captain to make him work his passage over the seas, and then leave him in some of the countries in Europe, alleging *that he was a disturber of the peace.* This took place on Saturday night. He was immediately put to work and kept at it until late at night.

The next day being Sunday, he asked and obtained leave of the captain to sing and pray among the crew. The captain attended, and was convinced that he was a good man. Without delay he set him on shore. In the mean time his friends had dispatched a messenger to the governor, to obtain authority to prevent his being carried forcibly away. This they obtained; but Mr. B. was discharged before his return."

Mr. Leland, in a letter to Robert B. Semple, thus alludes to the history of this man of God: "Is it possible for you to get the biography of Elijah Baker? He began his career in Mecklenburg, or near that place; was cotemporary with John Williams, and first ordained in a church of that county; then came to Boar Swamp, and, with J. Anthony, planted that church; then to Charles City, James City, and York, where he also planted churches; thence he crossed the Mockjack Bay and did the like in a part of Gloucester called Guina; thence over the Bay to the Eastern Shore of Virginia and Maryland, where he constituted the first ten Baptist churches in those parts. He was a man of humble parentage, small learning, and confined abilities. But with one talent he did more than many do with five. If justice could be done his memory the detail would make a rich page in your intended history. At the last Salisbury Association which he attended, when nearly worn out with disease, at the close of the meeting he addressed the audience in a manner as if heaven and earth were coming together; then, returning to Mr. Lemon's, soon died."

Elder Baker did not live to an advanced age. For many months his health was extremely feeble, preventing him in a great measure from the pursuance of his ministerial labor. To the close of life, however, he was employed to the utmost of his ability. He had attained a high elevation of Christian character; and his path, like the shining light, continued to shine more and more unto the perfect day. The state of his mind a few weeks before his death will be evinced in the following brief extract of a letter, written by him to his brother Elder Leonard Baker, who was then pastor of Musterfield Church, Halifax County. "And now, brother, are you struggling through the trials of this life, leaning upon your beloved? Are you laboring and waiting for the coming of the Lord Jesus, who shall change our vile bodies and fashion them according to his glorious body? Or have you sunk into a lukewarm state? which I fear has been the fact with some. Dear brother, some of my complaints are such that I do not expect to continue long in this world. However, I leave that to my dear Redeemer, who has the power of life and death in his own hands. In all probability I shall never be able to go out as far as your house again; yet I should be very glad to see you if you could make it convenient to come over once more while I live I will pay all your expenses. If our dear mother is yet alive, I can send out some relief to her. As to religion, thanks be to God, there is some little stir among us! I have baptized eight lately."

His brother had the privilege of reaching the Eastern Shore before his dismission from earth. His death was peaceful; it took place November 6, 1798, in the fifty-sixth year of his age. The following testimony, given by Dr. Lemon, at whose house he died, deserves to be recorded: "In Mr. Baker I found the Israelite indeed, the humble Christian, the preacher of the gospel in the simplicity of it, and the triumphant saint in his last moments. In his preaching he was very plain, and generally experimental; always very express on the doctrine of regeneration; never entering upon the doctrines by which he conceived he should give offence to one or another. In his last illness I attended his bedside, day and night, for three weeks, and had many most agreeable conversations with him on the glorious things of the kingdom of Christ. He retained his senses to the last minute, and seemed rather translated than to suffer pain in his dissolution. Death was to him as familiar in his conversation as if he talked of an absent friend from whom he expected a visit."

JAMES IRELAND.

James Ireland was born in the City of Edinburgh, in 1748. He was early sent to school by his father, who intended to give him a thorough education. Considerable proficiency was made in the Latin language and other branches of learning, but before he had completed his course he contracted a strong prejudice against study, which retarded his progress and rendered his education defective. Being rather inclined to a romantic temper, after he left school his father decided on sending him to sea, with the hope that this propensity would be cured and that he might be induced to turn his attention steadily to business. Several voyages to the northern seas were taken, during which he was exposed to imminent perils. Frequently he experienced such marked providential interferences as were well suited to awaken grateful emotions toward his Almighty Deliverer, but his heart remained callous. After his return from these voyages, in consequence of some indiscretion, he left his father's house, and embarked for America. With regard to this he says, "I consider my removal as the most auspicious epoch of my life. It pleased my great Deliverer to bring good out of evil. True it is, on my first arrival in Virginia, and for a few years after, this now happy country groaned under the tyranny of a rigorous religious intolerance; but it soon pleased the Giver of all good, through the instrumentality of the Revolution, to burst asunder the bands of oppression."

On his arrival in America, he took charge of a school in the northern part of Virginia. At this time he had not the fear of God before his eyes. In the new settlements where he lived, as he states, "there was not the least respect for the Sabbath, except among a few Quakers, who, on that day, would meet at a certain house and pursue their mode of worship." Their practice had some effect on his mind, and brought to his recollection the scenes of his childhood, when, under the direction of his parents, he was taught to venerate the Lord's day and to believe in the necessity of conversion. In thinking of the past, he would sometimes weep, and pray to God to have mercy on him. But these impressions were of short duration. "I could soon," he says, "join in the wicked amusements of those around me without remorse, and being of an aspiring disposition, it did not suit my taste to be a common accomplice with them, but an active leader in all their practices of wickedness, so that it might be said of me, as in Isaiah, 'I drew iniquity with the cords of vanity, and sin, as it were, with a cart-rope.' During the year that I resided in those parts, I cannot recollect that ever I experienced any remorse of conscience except in one instance, so wretched and hardened had I become. I possessed certain qualifications by which I could accommodate myself to every company: with the religious I could moralize a little, with the well-bred I could be polite, with the merry I could be antic, and with the obscene I could be profane. I may say, with great propriety, that I was engaged to treasure up unto myself wrath against the day of wrath and revelation of the righteous judgment of God to come. The god of this world had so blinded my understanding that, comparing my pleasures in sin with my confused ideas of the happiness of heaven, I often thought I would not have desired the happiness of the saints above if God would have allowed me to enjoy it. I was not only willing to be wicked, but studied to be so. Profane jest-books I procured to improve me in vice, and never could I hear a pertinent answer, as would nonplus an opponent in folly, without studying a variety of answers."

Such, according to his own language, was the deplorable condition of this youth. But God, who is rich in mercy, had determined to pluck him as a brand from the burning. He had been accustomed, for the gratification of those around him, to indulge a poetic talent which it was thought he possessed. A pious young man, who had before evinced some desire to be of spiritual advantage to him, presented a request that he would compose a few lines on a religious subject. Having complied, his second composition, on "the natural man's dependence for heaven," was the means of his own conviction. He became deeply concerned about the salvation of his soul, having perceived that all his former dependences for heaven were untenable. For some time he continued in an unhappy state of mind. Referring to his feelings, he remarks: "The deep impression upon my soul had a very considerable influence upon my exterior appearance; that wild vivacity that flashed in my eyes, and natural cheerfulness that appeared in my countenance, were entirely gone; my flesh began to pine away, my ruddy cheeks had vanished, and all that remained was a solemn, gloomy paleness; while my head was often hanging down like a bulrush, under the internal pressure of my guilty state."

After many painful apprehensions, and much reading of the Word of God, he was at length brought to behold the beauty and sufficiency of Christ. "My head," he observed, "was like a well of water, while the tears ran down for several hours without intermission; and, of all the tears I ever shed, these were the sweetest. My hard heart was melted into contrition, while I was laid low in the dust before God, under the sweet impression of his goodness to me."

The change which took place in his feelings and life was blessed of the Lord to the turning of others. During this time they had not enjoyed the privilege of hearing the gospel preached. Shortly after, Elder John Picket, being informed of these instances of conversion, rode sixty miles to visit the neighborhood and dispense to them the Word of Life. He remained two days, preaching at the house of Mr. Ireland, and to him it was indeed the sincere milk of the Word. He divulged his feelings freely to Elder Picket, and received from him advice suited to his circumstances.

On leaving, Elder Picket promised again to visit and preach to them. When the time of the next appointment arrived, he was prevented by unavoidable circumstances from complying with his engagement. The congregation having met, a consultation was held among the few pious persons who were present, and it was determined that Mr. Ireland should address the people. He thus describes his first attempt: "About twelve o'clock a tolerably large congregation were met. In dependence on God, and in fear and much trembling, I went forward. Worship was introduced by singing the hymn, 'Let me but hear my Saviour say.' The hymn was expressive of the real exercises of my heart. After prayer, I addressed the people from John, iii. 3. My heart was greatly enlarged, my zeal inflamed, and my desires ran out for the salvation of souls in such a manner that I have often thought, could I have had twenty tongues to employ that day, there would have been matter for them all. I dare not say but I had some sweet thoughts that God would bring me into the ministry, but against them I struggled, and would not give them entertainment in my heart, under the apprehension that they were the production of pride. However, it was a day full of comfort to us who were banded together in love, and also of deep humility to myself."

He continued to speak in public, as opportunity allowed, for some time before he united with any church. Indeed there was no church within his reach. Those who, with him, had been brought to a knowledge of the truth, were accustomed regularly to meet and receive instruction at his hands, although they had not submitted to the ordinances. But when they understood "the way of God more perfectly," they determined to follow Christ in baptism, and be regularly constituted into a church.

Having been educated a Presbyterian, Mr. Ireland was not easily convinced of the obligation to be baptized. In his own words, the manner in which he was led to discover his duty is thus described: "A circumstance among our little society on Smith's Creek produced a degree of anxiety for a short time, but happily terminated to our satisfaction. The circumstance related to myself. The work of God through the Colony was at that time principally carried on under the ministry of the Baptists, then distinguished by the appellation of Regulars and Separates. Both parties were Calvinistic in their sentiments, and our little body was disposed to join them by submitting to the rules of their society. We were fully persuaded that their baptism was right, according to the example of Jesus Christ and the practice of his Apostles.

"In this point they were all of one heart and one mind, myself only excepted. I was still tenacious of the old mode of sprinkling, according to the Presbyterian plan. They apprehended that if ever any minister was raised among them, I would be the individual, and if I continued under that persuasion it would create a difficulty. This, no doubt, occasioned many prayers to be sent up to the throne of grace, that I might be convinced of my error in this respect. Discovering the uneasiness that existed among them, I was led to search the Scriptures impartially, and in a short time it pleased God to remove the scales from my eyes, and give me to see that I must be a partaker of the grace of faith in Christ before I could be qualified to obey the ordinance of his institution. The application was very powerful, so that nothing could erase it from my heart. I determined at once to obey Christ by following him into the water, and thus put him on professionally. All being now united together in one mind and one judgment, and possessing a warm zeal for the glory of our Redeemer, we wished to know which of the two bodies, Regulars or Separates, had the warmest preachers and the most fire among them. We determined in favor of the latter, although the ministers of both were zealous men."

With the advice of his brethren, he attended the meeting of the Separate Baptist Association, which was held at Sandy Creek, North Carolina, in 1769, for the purpose of receiving baptism and ordination. At this meeting, Elder Samuel Harriss, who previously had refused ordination, was regularly set apart to the ministry, and authorized to administer the ordinances. It was proposed that he should baptize Mr. Ireland, and for this purpose a meeting was appointed to be held in Pittsylvania. Mr. Ireland thus refers to this interesting circumstance: "Three days and the greater part of the nights were employed in preaching to the people, at Mr. Harriss's, many of the hearers having come great distances. The third day the whole body of the church went into their meeting-house, according to their rule, to hear experience and receive subjects for baptism. I endeavored to make them acquainted with what the Lord had done for my soul, and with my desires for submitting to an institution of God's own appointment.

"After short interrogations, only for the satisfaction and edification of the church, they gave me the right hand of fellowship, and declared me to be a proper subject for baptism. Next day, in the afternoon, was appointed for the administration thereof; it being Sunday, we were to meet very early in the morning for preaching. There were eleven ministers present. Considering the distance I lived, it was proposed among them, and acceded to, that I should preach my trial sermon, and obtain credentials. Worship being over, we repaired to the water for the administration of baptism. Mr. Garrard was to speak on the nature and design of the ordinance, and Mr. Harriss was to administer it, which accordingly was done, in the presence of a large and solemn audience. Next morning I had to take leave of that church.

My credentials were signed by eleven ministers, that I might go forward, as an itinerant preacher, without any hesitation."

Immediately after his baptism he returned home, and in the spirit and power of his Master devoted himself to the great work of preaching the gospel. The Lord added many seals to his ministry. But he soon found that bonds and imprisonment awaited him. His growing popularity and success excited the indignation of the rulers of the established church, and brought down upon his head fierce persecution. "At one time," he says, "preaching being over, and concluding with prayer, I heard a rustling noise in the woods, and before I opened my eyes to see what it was, I was seized by the collar by two men while standing on the table. Stepping down and beholding a number of others walking up, it produced a momentary confusion in me. The magistrates instantaneously demanded of me what I was doing there with such a conventicle of people. I replied, that I was preaching the gospel of Christ to them; they asked, who gave me authority so to do. I answered, He that was the author of the gospel had a right to send forth whom He had qualified to dispense it. They retorted upon me with abusive epithets, and then inquired if I had any authority from man to preach. I produced my credentials, but these would avail nothing, not being sanctioned and commissioned by the bishop. They told me that I must give security not to teach, preach, or exhort, for twelve months and a day, or go to jail. I chose the latter alternative." This occurred in Culpepper. He was accompanied to prison amid the abuses of his persecutors, and while incarcerated in his cell not only suffered by the extreme inclemency of the weather, but by the personal maltreatment of his foes. They attempted to blow him up with gunpowder, but the quantity obtained was only sufficient to force up some of the flooring of his prison. The individual who led in this infamous conduct was, shortly after, in a hunting excursion, and while asleep in the woods, bitten by a mad wolf, of which wound he died in the most excruciating pain. There was also an attempt made by Elder Ireland's enemies to suffocate him, by burning brimstone, etc. at the door and window of his prison. A scheme was also formed to poison him. But the mercy of God prevented. He states, that he might speak of a hundred instances of cruelty which were practiced. "I expected," says he "every court, to be brought out to the whipping-post before the gazing multitude; I sat down and counted the cost, and believed, through Christ strengthening me, I could suffer all things for his sake. It appeared that their power did not reach so far, or it would have been executed. At this period I received letters from the ministers of our persuasion, and from a variety of churches with whom I was connected. From these churches I received general information, how singularly letters I wrote, were, under God, blessed to the conversion of numbers, who were anxiously led to inquire into the cause for which I suffered, as well as the grounds of that fortitude which bore me up under these sufferings. My prison, then, was a place in which I enjoyed much of the Divine presence; a day seldom passed without some signal token of the Divine goodness toward me, which generally led me to subscribe my letters in these words, 'From my palace in Culpepper.'" As a specimen of the letters written to him, a few of the closing lines of one from Elder David Thomas will not be uninteresting: "O brother, if you can, by bearing the charming, lovely cross of Jesus Christ, win one of the strongest of Satan's strongholds, no matter then how soon you die; and if you thus die for Him, how would the glorious armies of the martyrs above shout, to see Ireland coming from a prison to reign with them in glory!"

It is painful to record, that this unholy opposition was mainly the result of clerical influence. The ministers of the established church were generally found most active in those imprisonments which were experienced by Baptist ministers in Virginia. Mr. Ireland states that, at his trial, "the county parson was very officious in giving his assistance to the bench in the dilemma they were in. I applied to Mr. Bullet to move the court to give the parson and me leave to argue the point in hand, before them, and if I did not confute him, I would go to prison as a volunteer! He, with a smile, replied, the word of God does not pass current in this house; I answered, it appears so, or they would not imprison those who preach it."

To expose the oppressions of his day, another extract from Elder Ireland's pen will be introduced, by which it will be perceived that a man of reputable character, of good talents, and aiming to promote the well-being of society, was not allowed, by the consent of his church, to speak in public, or to build a house of worship, without special consent from the governor. It was necessary to travel down from Culpepper to Williamsburg, that this privilege might, in person, be obtained, and then, not without examination by some Episcopal minister. The following is the extract:—"I went up to Frederick County, drew up a petition addressed to Lord Botetourt, the then Governor of Virginia, praying him to grant me the privilege of having a meeting-house built in Culpepper County, to be occupied without molestation, on condition of my conforming to the rules prescribed for Protestant Dissenters. To this I obtained the signature of a number of respectable inhabitants, both of Frederick and Culpepper Counties, and repaired to the capital, at Williamsburg. The governor, I understood, was a religious man; and his universal conduct was stamped with the approbation of all, both within and without his capital. Whether he possessed vital religion or not I will not presume to determine, but he received my petition with all the graces of a gentleman, and gave me direction what measure to pursue, antecedent to granting the privileges I requested. I found the clergy in the city of quite a different character from the governor; they appeared obstinately determined not to give me the requisite examination: every one shifted it upon another, till at last I obtained it from a country parson, living eight miles from the capital, and presented it to the governor and council, who granted me a license for those things petitioned."

It was Elder Ireland's portion to suffer many other painful trials, but his ministry was increasingly successful. He was instrumental in forming several churches of the Ketockton Association, and for many years filled the pastoral office with two or three of those in the Counties of Frederick and Shenandoah. Several hundreds were by him led into the watery tomb, expressive of their death unto sin. In 1802 he baptized, in one of his churches, ninety-three persons, fifty-two of whom were received in one day.

In consequence of injuries sustained by a fall from his horse, and afterwards by the overthrowing of his carriage, he was in the early part of 1806 confined to his bed. He soon became much afflicted with the dropsy, and suffered the most excruciating pains. Notwithstanding his extreme illness he did not neglect family worship, even after he became so weak that he could not sit up; then he would lead in prayer, and seem to enjoy it while in a recumbent posture. He gradually declined, until May 5th, 1806, when his spirit fled to mansions on high. The following notice of his character and labors is taken from the Winchester Gazette :—

"Elder James Ireland was pastor of the Baptist congregations at Buckmarsh, Happy Creek, and Water Lick, in Frederick and Shenandoah Counties, Virginia. He had labored nearly forty years in his Lord's vineyard, and during a great part of the time through much infirmity of body. He was always distinguished as an able minister of the New Testament, rightly divining the Word of Truth, giving to saint and sinner their portion in due season. During his last illness, which confined him to his bed about three months, his mind was tranquil and serene. Fully sensible of his approaching dissolution, and perfectly resigned to the will of God, he endured all things, as seeing Him who is invisible; and having an eye to the recompense of reward, patiently waited for the manifestations of the sons of God. On Sunday, the first instant, a suitable and affecting discourse was delivered at Buckmarsh Meeting-house, the place of his interment, to a numerous and weeping audience, by Elder William Mason, from 2 Tim. iv. 7, 8: 'I have fought a good fight, I have finished my course,' etc.

"Mr. Ireland was a man of common stature, a handsome face, piercing eye, and pleasant countenance. In his youth he was spare, but he became by degrees quite corpulent, so that not long after his second marriage he wanted but nineteen pounds of weighing three hundred."

This sketch will be closed by the introduction of two or three stanzas composed by him shortly after the Declaration of Independence. They furnish a specimen of his talent for poetry :—

I.

America! exult in God
With joyful acclamation;
Who has, through scenes of war and blood,
Displayed to thee salvation.

When armed hosts,
With warlike boasts,
Did threaten thy destruction,
And crossed the main,
With martial train,
To compass thy subjection;
Thy sole resource was God alone,
Who heard thy cries before his throne,
Beheld with hate their schemes of blood
Impending o'er thee like a flood,
And made them know it was in vain
To make thee longer drag their chain;
That thou shouldst be
A nation free
From their unjust oppression.

II.

Hail! now ye sons of liberty,
Behold thy constitution!
Despotic power and tyranny
Have seen their dissolution.
No clattering arms,
No war's alarms,
Nor threats of royal vengeance;
Thy hostile foes
Have left off those;
Now own thy Independence.
Replete with peace, valiant we stand,
Freedom the basis of our land;
Blest with the beams of gospel light,
Our souls emerge from sable night;
Jehovah's heralds loud proclaim
Eternal life through Jesus' name,
Point out his blood
The way to God,
For our complete salvation.

III.

Amid the blessings we enjoy
From God the gracious giver,
Let gratitude our hearts employ,
To praise his name forever;
Beware of pride,
Lest, like a tide,

It flows and gains possession;
'Mongst empires all,
Both great and small,
Pride always brought oppression;
Pride finds the way to rule and reign,
And forges the despotic chain;
Denies we should enjoy or have
The right that God in nature gave.
Against this baleful evil fight—
Resist its force with all your might,
And join as one,
Before the throne,
That God would keep us humble.

IV.

Most gracious God, thee we adore,
Whose mercy faileth never;
Thy guardian care we now implore,—
Be thou our king forever;
May gospel rays
Divinely blaze
With an immortal lustre,
And teach us how
Our hearts to bow
To the Redeemer's sceptre!
Oh may the silver trump of peace
Within our empire never cease,
Until the ransomed, holy race,
Are called in by sovereign grace.
Then may the conflagration come,
And sinners rise to hear their doom!
Thy chosen ones,
In endless songs,
Will shout forth hallelujahs!

JAMES GREENWOOD.

The biographer regrets that but few facts connected with the life of James Greenwood have been obtained, notwithstanding frequent inquiries made in the region where he spent his days.

He was born about 1749, in the lower part of Virginia, and in his twentieth year became a Baptist and a workman in the Lord's service. Few ministers have pursued a more unexceptionable course. A blameless life is one of the most important qualifications which the Scriptures require in him who fills the office of a bishop. Without this, the most splendid talents will only prove a curse to the interests of religion. This will enable a man of comparatively weak capacity to do good, where one of strong intellect but equivocal piety will be utterly useless. This was the most striking peculiarity in reference to Elder Greenwood. His daily deportment uttered a language more powerfully persuasive than all the sermons he ever delivered. All who knew him confided in his piety, and found in his life an evidence of the purifying influence of the gospel While he was universally beloved by others, there was at all times entertained by *him* a deep sense of personal unworthiness. He was truly an humble man.

Elder Greenwood was quite useful in the vineyard of Christ. At the constitution of Piscataway Church, Essex County, he was induced to become their pastor, and continued to sustain that relation for nearly forty years. "The church," says Mr. Semple, "under his care has prospered without intermission. In 1788 and 1804 there were precious revivals, in each of which years a respectable number was added; but it is worthy of note that, even in the coldest season, this church gradually gained strength, enjoying uniform serenity and peace." In addition to efforts in Piscataway he traveled much in the lower counties, and was the honored instrument of saving many souls from death.

Notwithstanding the lovely character sustained by this servant of the Redeemer, he did not escape the rage of those who, in his day, persecuted the church of God and wasted it. Indeed it was not to be expected. If the Lamb of God was led to the slaughter his servants may well calculate on unkind treatment. Elder Greenwood was apprehended while actually engaged in proclaiming the gospel of peace. He was standing not far from the place now occupied by Bruington Meeting-house, King and Queen County, when he was rudely seized and forced to prison. But he was not without consolation. The Lord was with him in his dungeon and lightened his chain. Nor was the time in his

Master's service lost, for while in prison he lifted up his voice and proclaimed liberty to the captives of sin. As the sound of salvation was heard from the grated windows of his cell the multitudes without wept, and many believed unto eternal life. Such was the effect of his ministrations that his foes judged it most politic to open the prison doors and let him go free.

JOHN WILLIAMS.

It is regretted that the materials which once existed, and which would have essentially contributed to complete this sketch, are not now to be obtained. Those which *have* escaped the ravages of time will tend to show that Elder Williams was among the most eminent servants of God in our own or any other denomination.

He was born in Hanover County in 1747. His parents, though not wealthy, were in comfortable circumstances, and availed themselves of the opportunities they enjoyed, to give their son a liberal education. At what time he left Hanover is not known, but in 1769 he was engaged in the capacity of sheriff in Lunenburg County. About this period the right hand of the Lord was gloriously displayed in various parts of Virginia, and many yielded to his sway. The counties in the southern part of the State shared largely in these triumphs. Elder Samuel Harriss, with others, were the instruments of awakening this interest in spiritual things. It was at this time that Elder Williams's attention was first directed to the subject of religion. Having been brought to the feet of Christ and realized the efficacy of the blood of the atonement, he began at once to tell others of the value of a Saviour. He was extensively acquainted in the county in fulfilling the duties of the sheriffality, and was allowed a favorable opportunity of doing good to others. Nor did he neglect it. He warned his fellow-men to turn from sin's deceitful ways, although he had not as yet fulfilled the command of the Redeemer by being buried with him in baptism, or united with any Christian church. He was not immersed until 1770, six months after his conversion.

He continued to prosecute the work of the ministry as a licentiate with the diligence and perseverance of one who knew the value of the gospel, and who earnestly desired the salvation of sinners. Within three years the number of disciples had so far increased, that it was thought expedient to form a new church in the County of Lunenburg, to be known by the name of Meherrin. They were constituted November 27th, 1771, and after being supplied a short time by Elder Jeremiah Walker, they invited the subject of this memoir to become their pastor, which invitation he accepted. It was at this period, December, 1772, he was publicly set apart by imposition of hands. He appears, while laboring for this church, to have been eminently useful. At the Association, in 1774, it was ascertained from the report of the churches that the church at Meherrin had received during the previous year a larger number than any other represented at that meeting. Such was the increase during his administration that five or six churches were originated from the Meherrin Church, in the Counties of Lunenburg, Mecklenburg, and Charlotte. In 1785 he removed his membership to Sandy Creek Church, Charlotte, and became their pastor. This relation he sustained as long as he lived. He consented also, in 1786, to serve the Blue-stone Church, Mecklenburg County. They were supplied by him about eight years, until the removal of Elder William Richards into their immediate vicinity, when he tendered his resignation. It ought here to be mentioned, that immediately after Elder Williams's conversion to God he began to preach in a destitute neighborhood of Mecklenburg County, and was successful in the formation of a church called Allen's Creek. Here, for twenty years, as frequently as possible and with much success, he preached the gospel. Many colored persons were brought to a knowledge of the truth and added to this church.

The influence of this servant of Christ was not to be confined within these limits. He early distinguished himself as one who felt deeply for the general interests of the Redeemer's kingdom. He was a regular attendant at the meetings of the General Association, which continued in existence until 1783, and afterwards, when the General Committee was organized, he never failed to be present. Many of the most important subjects were discussed at these meetings, and there is satisfactory evidence that he was one of the leading spirits in those deliberations. To some of the good objects to which he turned his attention, and in the prosecution of which he faithfully toiled, it may not be uninteresting to invite the attention of the reader. By this reference it will be seen that he possessed a spirit of enlarged benevolence as well as a vigorous and cultivated mind. Any scheme which promised to promote the welfare of man he was not only willing to approve, but to aid in its accomplishment. Among those important measures which engaged his attention will be mentioned:—

1. The cause of religious liberty. When he entered the ministry the Church of England was established by law, and dissenters were deprived of many privileges enjoyed by Episcopalians. As non-conformists they were liable to the loss of personal liberty and to the experience of many painful sufferings. The Baptists, in their enlightened and honest zeal to spread the influence of a Saviour's love, felt most sorely these grievances. Elder Williams was, in the meetings of the General Association and General Committee, one of the most unbending champions in opposing these proscriptions, and employed his influence to encourage his brethren to resist, by all scriptural means, these unhallowed though legalized oppressions. At the meeting of the General Association in 1775, a resolution was adopted authorizing memorials to be prepared and circulated throughout the State, praying the General Assembly of Virginia that the church establishment might be abolished and that religion might be allowed to stand upon its own basis. Elder Williams, with two others, were deputed to wait on the legislature with these petitions. At several other times was he appointed on a mission of this kind. Nor were his efforts with those of his brethren vain. He lived to see one of the warmest wishes of his heart gratified; the entire prostration of ecclesiastical tyranny. The following extract expresses in his own forcible language his high sense of the value of those civil and religious privileges which had been conferred on our nation.

"We live in an extraordinary day—under the benign influence

of the gospel sun, that seems to be rising to his meridian height; no nation or people, since government was first introduced into the world, ever enjoyed equal privileges with us. We boast not merely the enjoyment of civil, but of religious liberty, without any check or control from the hand of oppression. How ought every one to praise the Lord for his goodness and wonderful works to the children of men! How ought we to wrestle with God in prayer for grace equal to the day, that we may not, like Jeshurun, grow wanton and abuse these glorious privileges!"

2. The interests of education found in him an efficient patron. He was not in the habit of indulging an idea that the cultivation of intellect was necessarily unfriendly to the exercise of fervent piety. The subject of education, it is well known, was favorably received, and plans adopted for its promotion by the Baptists of the last century. In 1793 it was committed by the General Committee to John Williams and Thomas Read, who reported the following plan:—That fourteen trustees be appointed, all of whom shall be Baptists; that these, at their first meeting, appoint seven from the other denominations, and that the whole twenty-one then form a plan and make arrangements for executing it. Why this scheme failed is not distinctly known; but it is evident that the brethren of that day not only contemplated the institution of a seminary of learning, but actually adopted the incipient measures for carrying their wishes into execution. An extract is here presented from a paper prepared by Elder Williams, which indicates his own feelings and the progress which had been made in the cause of education. "Two seminaries of learning are proposed in our State, one on each side of James River. We have sufficient encouragement from our learned brethren in the North that we shall not want for able, skillful teachers. *This will also require very diligent efforts and liberal contributions.* And if we in this, as we ought in everything, do it with a single eye to the glory of God and the advancement of the Redeemer's interest, then shall we have sufficient grounds to hope we shall meet with the approbation of heaven." In these lines, we may observe that he not only felt a lively interest in educational operations, but indulged fervent devotion to God and a desire

that all the plans he fostered might advance the Redeemer's kingdom.

3. Another subject in which Elder Williams felt a deep and lively interest was the preparation of a history of the Virginia Baptist Churches. The reference of this *work* to his hands is thus alluded to by Elder Semple :—"The compilation of a history of the Virginia Baptists having been committed wholly to the hands of Mr. Williams after Mr. Leland's removal, he had made no inconsiderable progress in collecting documents, when, in consequence of the decline of his health, he found himself under the necessity of resigning his trust. This he did in a letter to the General Committee in 1794. The committee received his resignation and resolved to decline it for the present." A few years previous he himself thus refers to this subject: "It is thought very expedient to form or compile a history of the baptized churches in Virginia, their rise, progress, hindrances, remarkable events and occurrences, chief instruments, present condition, etc. Our General Committee have taken up the matter and appointed ministers in the various districts to collect materials, who find it very necessary to claim the exertions and assistance of the several churches, ministers, and other individuals. We desire every circumstance to be presented as clearly as possible, and with candor and truth."

It has been already stated that Elder Williams was highly distinguished as a minister of reconciliation. He was a man of no ordinary strength of intellect. This is indicated by such written documents as were left by him and the concurrent testimony of those who knew and now survive him. He was much devoted to reading, and his attainments were by no means inconsiderable. Especially on theological subjects was his knowledge enlarged and profound. It is much to be regretted that many who undertake the important work of instructing others are themselves destitute of information. The subject of this biography did not belong to this class; he was a workman who needed not to be ashamed, rightly dividing the word of truth. As a public speaker he is thus described by Elder Semple: "His talents if not equal to any were certainly very little inferior to those of the first grade. His appearance in the pulpit was noble and majestic, yet humble and affectionate. In the beginning of his discourses he was doctrinal and somewhat methodical; often very deep, even to the astonishment of his hearers; toward the close, and indeed sometimes throughout his sermon, he was exceedingly animated. His exhortations were often incomparable."

From the minutes of Associations to which he belonged, and other sources, it appears that in his religious sentiments he was a moderate Calvinist. He delighted to dwell on those doctrines which tend to humble the sinner and exalt Christ. It is intimated by some who knew him that he was favorable to open communion. If this was his sentiment it was not carried into practice. Nor did he fail on all suitable occasions to vindicate the exclusive propriety of believers' baptism. Mr. Patilloe, a Presbyterian minister of some celebrity, having preached in his vicinity a discourse on the subject of baptism, a reply of considerable merit was prepared by Mr. Williams. This reply he intended to put to press, had the discourse itself been published. A brief extract from the preface will indicate the spirit with which the work was undertaken: "I hope I have sufficiently demonstrated to my countrymen, for a series of years, that I am not overbearing on others, or bigoted to those of my principles which are not essential to salvation: I have universally endeavored to promote a catholic spirit, with peace and concord in the Israel of God. But nevertheless I am set for the defence of the gospel; and as such, circumstances often occur that require me to contend for the faith and order of Christ's church."

This leads to a notice of one of the most prominent features in the character of John Williams. He was, to use his own phrase, a man of catholic spirit. In this respect he exhibited a pattern of loveliness which every minister should imitate. Some men seem to enjoy themselves only in the atmosphere of controversy. They prefer to occupy their time, not in acts of benevolence, but in finding fault with those around them. Though immovably firm in maintaining the truth, Elder Williams was a lover of peace. He regarded all who loved our Lord Jesus Christ, although there might exist some difference of opinion on religious subjects. He was in the habit of associating with the Presbyterians, some of whom were residents in his neighborhood.

But especially in his own denomination was he solicitous to have the unity of the spirit increased and perpetuated. A most interesting letter written by him to Dr. Rippon of London, in 1792, will here be introduced. No one can transport himself back to the period when it was penned and call up to his imagination the events which had transpired, without having awakened in his bosom the most thrilling emotions.

"CHARLOTTE COUNTY, VIRGINIA.

"Long have I been desirous a door of correspondence might be opened between the ministers and churches of Christ, of the Baptist denomination in Europe, especially in your kingdom and those of North America, etc. For, notwithstanding we are at a distance of three thousand miles, yet we are born of the same spirit and pursuing the same glorious object. The convulsions and fluctuations of the times, with other circumstances, have hitherto prevented my making an attempt; but considering the desirableness of Christian acquaintance, the unity of the spirit, and the fellowship of the churches, I have ventured to *draw a bow* and leave the event to Divine Providence. Though I am not an old man, I have seen Virginia as dark as midnight—touching spiritual things—except in a few instances. But, glory be to God, *we that sat in darkness have seen a great light!* The Sun of righteousness, with divinely illuminating and cheering rays, seems to be rising to his meridian splendor in our hemisphere. Jesus is going forth with a bow and a crown, conquering and to conquer, and we, the despised Baptists, have become a numerous, and, blessed be God, a united people. Could you be wafted across the Atlantic upon the wings of an angel and sit down among us, your soul would triumph, and you would stretch forth your hands to enable your little sister in the wilderness to make advances. If God should bless the design and a door of correspondence be opened and maintained, I shall in future give you a more circumstantial account of our churches, etc. At present, it will be sufficient to say, we became so numerous and so extensive that we could not with propriety associate at one place and time; therefore, divided into various convenient districts, each district to send delegates annually to meet in General

Committee, by which union and harmony are maintained. There were from our beginning bars of distinction kept up, and we lived under the titles of *Regulars* and *Separates;* but the Lord, in his wonder-working goodness, has caused this unhappiness to be removed, and we have become a united people, and are now distinguished by the title of '*The United Baptist Churches in Virginia;*' the blessed and happy effects of which it is out of my power minutely to describe. We had before (but particularly at the time of the union's taking place) adopted in a soft, general manner, what is called with us 'The Philadelphia Confession of Faith,' and which is better known with you by the title of 'A Confession of Faith, set forth by upwards of a hundred congregations in England and Wales, in the year 1689.' I mention this to give you a general idea of our principles.

"Before the American Revolution the Baptists upon this continent had a very superficial knowledge of each other out of their own Colonies; but since then a universal acquaintance and harmony seem to be taking place, much to the glory of God and the advancement of the Redeemer's interests. *New England* was more out of our idea than Old England; but now, blessed be God, not only an epistolary correspondence is kept up, but personal visits have actually taken place, at least from them to us; the salutary effects of which we are daily experiencing. These things prompt me to be more determined (I hope with an eye to the glory of God) to extend the correspondence to our brethren and fathers in the kingdom of Great Britain. Much in favor to us may be expected therefrom."*

This sketch would not be complete if we should fail to mark another resemblance which existed between Mr. Williams and his Divine Master. He loved the souls of men. Their salvation was ardently desired by him. He was himself active and laborious in pointing to the Lamb of God, that taketh away the sins

* This letter contains an educational plan, which, when realized, will probably be of considerable service to the interests of religion. It was forwarded by way of Providence, accompanied with a polite epistle from President Manning, expressive of his approbation of the general design; a design which by this time may be more matured, and I think needs only to be known in order to be executed.—*Note by Rippon.*

of the world. Immediately previous to the Declaration of Independence, while the American army were encamped in the lower part of Virginia, permission to preach to the soldiers was obtained from the legislature, and he gladly engaged in the work. Had he lived in the present day, none can question that he would heartily unite in those efforts which are intended to send among the nations the unsearchable riches of Christ. In allusion to the success of the gospel in our land he thus writes: "We have had agreeable accounts from the churches touching the advancement of Emanuel's interest;" and then he breaks out in the following prayer: "May the Divine effusion become general! may the blessed Jesus go forth conquering and to conquer, until his name and praise be one in all the earth!" This prayer expresses the spontaneous wish of a heart in which had been shed abroad the love of Christ. In proportion as the evil of sin is known and salvation is prized, will be the fervency of desire to send the gospel to every creature.

While the discourses of this man of God were highly doctrinal, there was no undue stress laid on one portion of the Divine Word to the exclusion of another. Partial exhibitions were not given for the sake of sustaining a favorite theory. He understood the art of giving to each his portion of meat in due season. The precepts, as well as the promises of the Bible, were urged on the attention of the churches. A good specimen of his views and his method of recommending moral obligation will be furnished in the extract which follows: "Notwithstanding all that Jehovah is doing for our American lands, what crowds of thoughtless, ungrateful men and women are to be found; the major part of our neighbors and families, perhaps careless in sin, or reveling in vice and luxury. The inestimable worth of souls, the cause of God in general, and our numerous civil privileges, combine to call upon us, in the most serious and pointed terms, to stand fast in the liberty wherewith Christ hath made us free. Every circumstance points out to us the importance and necessity of holy living, pious deportment, a well-educated offspring, and proper family government. Heads of families may do much, *yea, very much* is expected and required from them. Of what avail will be the best laws and well-ordered civil government, the most virtuous rulers and warm pathetic addresses from the pulpit, if religious domestic government is not supported. What very great discouragement must faithful ministers of the gospel be under when professors do not aid them by their pious exertions; therefore, dear brethren, be exhorted to strengthen their hands by walking and steadily persevering in every practical part of Christianity. In fine, let us all, to the utmost of our power, stand up firm for the cause of virtue and religion; let us bear open and practical testimony against the dissipations and extravagancies which, in their very nature, awfully threaten the interests of liberty, learning, morality, and religion."

A brief reference will now be made to the close of his valuable life. He was not permitted to see an old age. A quotation from Elder Semple will give all the particulars, which may be interesting, respecting the latter part of his days: "Being very corpulent, at an Association in the year 1793 he accidentally fell by the turning of a step as he was passing out of a door, and became for a year or two a cripple, being under the necessity of going on crutches. Notwithstanding, he would still go in a carriage to the meetings, and preach, sitting in a chair in the pulpit. During several of the last years of his life he was afflicted with a very painful disease. Under his severe suffering he was not only patient, but when he could have any mitigation of his pain he was also cheerful. About ten days before his death he was attacked by a pleurisy from which no medicine could give him relief. His work was finished; and April 30th, 1795, he fell asleep."

Nothing very remarkable transpired at his death. He was pensive and silent. He told his wife, that to live or to die was to him indifferent: he had committed this to God, who, he knew, would do right. He said he felt some anxiety for his numerous family, but that these also he was willing to trust in the hands of a gracious Providence.

LEWIS LUNSFORD.

EARLY HISTORY AND CONVERSION TO GOD.

Lewis Lunsford may be enumerated among the most distinguished names which have adorned the history of the Baptist denomination. He was born in the County of Stafford, Virginia, about the year 1753. In raising up instruments to accomplish his all-wise purposes, the Lord is often pleased to pour contempt on wealth and station in society, and to make his selections from the obscure walks of life. The weak things of the world are chosen to confound the things that are mighty, that no flesh may glory in his presence.

The parents of Elder Lunsford were poor, and from earliest infancy he was accustomed to the hardships peculiar to his condition in life. Though possessing a mind of superior order, the ample stores of knowledge were not in childhood placed within his reach. But for the grace of God, which plucked him as a brand from the burning, and brought him into the ministry, his splendid talents might have remained undeveloped.

"Full many a gem of purest ray serene,
The dark unfathomed caves of ocean bear;
Full many a flower is born to blush unseen,
And waste its *sweetness on the desert air.*"

He was destined, however, to shine pre-eminently, and, with his powers consecrated to the cause of Christ, to be the instrument of extensive good to his fellow-men. At what time his conversion took place cannot, with precision, be now determined. It must have occurred at an early period, as there is reason to believe he was employed in preaching the gospel to others when not more than seventeen years old. The instrumentality of his turning to God is attributed to Elder William Fristoe, and by him he was baptized.

Entrance into the Ministry.

He united himself with the Potomac Church, now called Hartwood, and began immediately to proclaim salvation through the blood of atonement. He was discovered by all to possess remarkable talents, and crowds attended his ministry from every direction. His extreme youth, united with the fluency and pungency of his address, excited astonishment. He was familiarly called "the wonderful boy." It is justly a matter of surprise, amid the admiration and flattering attentions he received, that he was not ruined. There were indicated, by his stability, not only native greatness of mind, but the guidance and sustentation of an Almighty arm. He was intent on pursuing the great object of extending the Redeemer's glory in the salvation of men. Having been taught in the school of Christ the value of the soul, and the immensity of that price which has been paid for its redemption, all personal considerations were lost sight of, if by any means he might save some.

Extent of Labor, Settlement, etc. etc.

A few years after his entrance into the ministry, he left his native county, and extended his influence through all the counties of the Northern Neck of Virginia. In Westmoreland, Northumberland, and Lancaster, especially, did the Lord make his ministrations effectual, and believers were daily added to the church. Several churches were gathered as the fruit of his toils; the most prominent of which are, Nomini, Moratico, and Wicomico. When the Moratico Church was constituted, in the year 1778, he was unanimously chosen to be their pastor. This relation he sustained as long as he lived. It is proper here to state that he was never ordained by the imposition of hands, as he entertained the sentiment that there was nothing necessary to constitute a valid ordination but the call of some church to the work of a pastor or an evangelist. Many of his brethren at that time considered his course objectionable in reference to this subject; they were, however, disposed to make it a matter of forbearance; they loved him still, and co-operated with him in every good work.

Of him it might be truly said, "in labors more abundant." His was a heart overflowing with sympathy for the wretched, and he was ready to disregard his own comfort and advantage to administer to their spiritual advantage. If a stream was to be crossed, even at personal peril, and though he must work the boat himself, no hesitation was allowed. Over one of the large water-courses of the lower country, three miles wide, he once paddled a small canoe with a garden pale, rather than allow himself to fail in reaching his appointment.

Said one who knew him well: "My dear departed brother's zeal in the Redeemer's cause has been to me among the most pleasing qualities I saw in him; and the more so, as in a good degree it abounded while he was among mortals. His Lord well knew what had been given him to do, and seemed, out of peculiar love, to hasten him in his work, quickly to ripen him for heavenly rest. Being thus quickened, he spared no pains in seeking the salvation of souls, and the prosperity of the churches, laboring more abundantly with the people, at all seasons, not in a confined set of forms, but accommodating his seasons and places of meeting, his subjects and methods; he thus hoisted and managed his sails, so as to receive the advantage from any heavenly wind that blew. One evening, preaching from the text, 'As for me, God forbid that I should sin in ceasing to pray for you; but I will teach you the good and the right way;' he said, 'he was at a loss to know whether to preach or pray, and wished the people to signify which they chose. A number of weeping souls were soon on their knees, and he turned his preaching into praying.'

"Once when he had preached an evening sermon," continues Mr. Toler, "in a barn, many having eaten the spices of the garden of the Lord, they seemed unwilling to close the service. After they had remained awhile longer there, and it was concluded they must part, they commenced singing in a body, in the yard of the dwelling-house. When Mr. Lunsford was on the steps, going into the house, he discovered the people stood still in the yard, unwilling to depart, and turning, addressed them once more, by the light of the candle; and, as rain falls freely in a wet season, so from this after-cloud showers soon fell, not only of grace, but of tears. He said, 'I must confess, this is more like enthusiasm than anything I have lately seen, but whether we be beside ourselves it is to God, or whether we be sober, it is for your cause.'"

"The zeal of mine house hath eaten me up." This language of the Psalmist, and quoted by the Saviour as applicable to him, might well be used in reference to Lunsford. "He bore not, however," said the above-named writer, "the name of an enthusiast, nor did he deserve it. He acted upon deliberate thought, and was governed by principle. He was highly pleased to see celestial fire among the people, if even there should be a little wildfire with it, rather than the appearance of lukewarmness. And what pious heart would not? The exquisite transports experienced by some, in religious exercises, are only known by those who feel them."

As illustrative of the quenchless ardor of his zeal, it is said that, attending a night-meeting, Mr. William Bledsoe preached, but he was seriously indisposed, and compelled to lie down during the sermon. He became much interested, and after the preacher closed, arose and addressed the people with unusual power. It was a season of deep solemnity.

Perhaps no man in our State preached more frequently, or gave himself more entirely to the care of the churches—always appearing as messenger to the Association, and as a delegate to the meeting of the General Committee. Every Lord's day was given to some special monthly appointment, besides which, an average of three or four times every week he was required to preach in the adjacent neighborhood. Extensive tours in other regions were also taken. Says Mr. Toler: "He journeyed much to preach the gospel in this State, and his rides were very lengthy. I have known him ride one hundred and twenty miles, in fifty successive hours, to reach his meetings. He seemed to be an 'angel flying in the midst of heaven, having the everlasting gospel to preach unto them that dwell in the earth.' He used to say, his life was a continual chase through the world; and so it was." Day by day, and often late at night, he was found in his journeys—exposed to the most inclement season, that he might prosecute his loved employ. Once he is represented as traveling on a tour of preaching to the Valley of Virginia. When he left home the rain was falling, but he hesitated not, pressing on until, drenched and cold, he was compelled to stop for a season. Having warmed himself by the fire, he continued until night, when he commenced preaching services; but during prayer it became necessary to desist and retire to bed, overcome by the exposures of the day. Another minister present attempted the service, and having preached, Mr. Lunsford then arose and delivered an animated discourse. The weather still inclement, the next day he urged his way, preaching day and night through the tour. Crowds attended his ministry. Much excitement in spiritual things was awakened, "the people," says Mr. Toler, "wondering at the gracious words that proceeded from his mouth." Tours of this kind, in the same region of country, were repeated, and with marked success. In a single neighborhood several were baptized, and a flourishing church was built up.

It is said his journeys extended to the State of Kentucky three different times. While thus distant from his home, he employed his time in the proclamation of the glad tidings, passing to and fro, in the sparsely peopled settlements, that he might confirm the saints and warn sinners. Writing to a brother, after his return from Kentucky, under date of March 11, 1793, he says :—

"I sit down to answer your friendly letter, which brings the agreeable news of the visit of our brethren, (Andrew and Richard Broaddus,) as also to give information of Mr. Lyle's visit to you. The state of things with regard to religion is somewhat distressing in Kentucky. What with the doctrine of restoration, and some sharp contentions between ——— and ———, which have divided the ——— Church, and involved the principal members of the whole Association on the north side, the appearance is gloomy, and there is no knowing where these things will end. Notwithstanding all this, there are many precious ministers, and precious people, too, in that country, who have a high regard for the gospel of Jesus, and are fond of good preaching and good preachers.

"The emigration to that country is incredible. Its fruitful soil yielding the most luxuriant abundance to all those who cultivate it; inviting the poor and the wretched from the barren wastes of this continent, and elsewhere, to fly to her fertile arms, that she may fill their mouths with good and their hearts with gladness.

"I am happy to hear of your journey up to Berkeley. I intended to be up this spring, but your going will supersede the use of my visit at this time. I hope, however, to go up some time hence.

Pray, present my most affectionate love to the brethren, sisters, and friends in those parts. Assure them of my warmest desire for their prosperity. Accept my thanks for your kindness in visiting this destitute place in my absence. I wish to visit your parts as soon as I can make it convenient."

The following has reference to a visit from Rev. Isaac Backus. Writing to a Christian brother, he says: "Nothing could have been more welcome than your messenger, who arrived last night with the agreeable news of the arrival of Mr. Backus in this part of the world. I am now filled with strong assurance of what I never even hoped for—the sight and conversation of the man whose name has long been venerable in my esteem. I hope you will accompany him down. I am sorry the time is so short to give notice. I shall endeavor, however, to do the best I can."

Habits of Study, Talents, etc.

It has been already stated that the subject of this sketch was, by nature, highly gifted. He did not satisfy himself with these endowments. He was diligent as a student, and acquired a large fund of useful knowledge. In the early part of his ministry, when compelled to labor during the week, while he preached on Lord's day, he was accustomed to occupy a large portion of the night in reading by firelight. When he settled in the Northern Neck, he supplied himself with a small but valuable collection of books, and employed all the time he could abstract from active ministerial labor in the cultivation of his intellectual powers. His memory was most retentive. The stores of knowledge which he had accumulated were always at hand, and so well arranged that, when necessary, he could bring them forth and use them to the instruction of his auditors. In ability to make extensive and accurate quotations from good authors few, if any, excelled him. Among other things, he possessed a very considerable taste for the study of medicine, and read the most approved works on that subject. His medical attainments were so considerable that his services as a physician were frequently solicited by families residing at a distance. The following reference to his talents as a minister is furnished by Elder J. B. Jeter, pastor of the First Baptist

Church, Richmond, and for several years pastor of the Moratico and Wicomico Churches in the Northern Neck:—

"Lunsford was unquestionably endued with superior genius. Destitute of literary acquirements, residing in an isolated and obscure part of the country, having access to few books and few enlightened ministers, he rose, by native vigor of intellect and dint of application, to real distinction. For this distinction he was not indebted to the gloom by which he was surrounded. He would have been distinguished in any age or any country. I have conversed with several intelligent gentlemen who were intimately acquainted with him, and who concur in the opinion that his pulpit talents were of the first order. His conceptions were clear, quick, and sublime; his style, though negligent and unpolished, was plain, copious, and strong; and his gestures were natural and impassioned."

The following anecdote was related by a living clergyman of high standing, who belongs to a different denomination of Christians from that to which Lunsford belonged. Dr. S. S. Smith, of Princeton, New Jersey, had engaged to preach in the neighborhood of his appointment; through courtesy to Dr. S., Lunsford declined preaching, and repaired with all his congregation to hear the Doctor's sermon. Dr. S. having heard the fame of Lunsford, earnestly pressed him to preach. Lunsford, yielding to his importunity, preached after Smith had delivered his discourse Dr. Smith afterwards remarked: "I had heard much of Lunsford's preaching, and was prepared to hear a great sermon, but the one-half was never told me."

Testimony equally creditable to Elder Lunsford, as a man of talents and an able speaker, is given by Mr. Semple in the following language: "During several of the last years of his life he was much caressed, and his preaching more valued than that of any other man who ever resided in Virginia. Lunsford was a sure preacher. He seldom failed to rise pretty high. In his best strains he was more like an angel than a man. His countenance, lighted up by an inward flame, seemed to shed beams of light wherever he turned. His voice, always harmonious, often seemed to be tuned by descending seraphs. His style and his manner were so sublime and so energetic that he was indeed like an ambassador of the skies, sent down to command all men everywhere to repent. He was truly a messenger of peace, and by him the tidings of peace were communicated to multitudes. So highly was he esteemed among his own people, that but few preachers visited them to whom they would willingly listen, even for once, in preference to their beloved pastor. He was also clever in conversation, having a considerable share of wit, which, in his cheerful moments, he would use in an innocent but entertaining manner. In argument he inclined somewhat to be satirical, and by this means sometimes gave offence to those who did not know him well. It was, however, perfectly clear that he did not design to sport with the feelings of any. Probably no man of his popularity ever had fewer enemies."

Usefulness, Character, etc.

Although this distinguished man was taken from the field of labor in the vigor of his days, but few have accomplished more than he did for the extension of the Redeemer's kingdom. He was in various respects useful. As a pastor he was affectionate and faithful. He delighted to contribute to the relief of those who were in suffering circumstances. Being qualified to administer in sickness, he attended the calls of distress which met his ear, and uniformly without compensation. In regard to the spiritual interests of his charge, he watched for souls as one who was to give account. Mr. Semple says of him: "From the time he settled in the Northern Neck, and indeed from the time he began to preach there, he gradually increased in favor with the people. It is hardly probable that any man ever was more beloved by a people when living, or more lamented when dead. He had two remarkable revivals of religion in the bounds of his church; the one about the time of the constitution of the church, and the other commenced in the year 1788, and had scarcely subsided at his death, in 1793. During these revivals he was uncommonly lively and engaged. He preached almost incessantly; and, by his acquaintances, after the last revival, it was thought that he made a rapid advance both in wisdom and warmth, especially the latter, from which he never receded during his residence on earth."

A brief extract from the communication of Elder J. B. Jeter will, in this place, be furnished, as it refers to the character and usefulness of Elder Lunsford: "Lunsford wielded a powerful influence in the Northern Neck. His amiable disposition, his affable manners, his sprightly conversation, and, above all, his unaffected piety, gained him the esteem of all good men; and his power of reasoning, the keenness of his sarcasm, and his undaunted spirit, made him a terror to the wicked. An aged man, now living, states that he usually dined at the tavern at Lancaster Court-house on court days, and that the promiscuous crowd gathering around the table would wait with profound respect for this man of God to render thanks for the refreshment. He was eminently useful. A few are now living to testify the efficiency of his ministrations. The churches which he founded have enjoyed a large measure of prosperity. They evidently bear, in the present day, the impress which they received from his labors.

"If Lunsford were now living, he would be an advocate for the benevolent institutions by which the age is distinguished. The Moratico Church-book contains an order, made during his pastorate, and doubtless by his influence, for making collections to aid the college in Providence, Rhode Island, now Brown University. He was a man of enlarged views and feelings. He corresponded with Isaac Backus, of New England, and Dr. Rippon, of London. With the Presbyterian ministers of his neighborhood he maintained the most intimate and friendly intercourse. He appears to have possessed a catholic spirit toward all Christian denominations."

Respecting his views of truth, and sympathy for whatever promised to diffuse it, Mr. Toler, one of his intimate associates, testifies in substance: "In preaching, he was accustomed to dwell on the miserable state of fallen men, and the glorious scheme of redemption through the Lord Jesus. The thunders of Sinai did not so much mingle with what he said as the cries of Calvary: Jesus as *the Christ*, his obedience to justify, his blood to atone, the work of the Holy Spirit in the heart of the sinner, the force of evangelical faith, the spread of Emanuel's kingdom,—these were some of his favorite themes. He seemed to anticipate a glorious future, when the kingdoms of this world shall become the kingdoms of our Lord and his Christ. With what pungency did he preach the Word, what energy clothed his expressions, what arguments flowed from his lips, what earnestness streamed from his eyes, what music dwelt upon his tongue, while to surrounding multitudes

'He preached as if he ne'er should preach again,
And as a dying man to dying men!'"

Lunsford was a man of weighty influence. His appearance and manners were suited to impress favorably. In form erect and well proportioned, with auburn hair, light complexion, and blue eyes, in all his apparel neat and becoming, it is said he always inspired with respect those with whom he was thrown into society. To quote Mr. Toler again: "His discreet behavior entitled him to that freedom and esteem among his aquaintances necessary to a minister's usefulness. Even his reproofs were so ingenious as to procure for him more friendship than ill-will. Though he could easily be severe, he sometimes by gentleness gave weight to his remarks. The more he was known the better he was loved.

"Some persons were once hauling the seine near where he was, and he walked toward them. A gentleman present swore profanely. Mr. Lunsford gently tapped him, repeating an old proverb—'if you swear, you will catch no fish.' The gentleman has often said the manner of the reproof obliged him to like it. Some time after this he was a constant hearer of Mr. Lunsford, became a member of his church, a deacon, and one of his most intimate friends.

"Being, with others, at the house of a respectable gentleman of the bar, the dog came in; and after speaking of his great age and how much he valued him, the lawyer said, 'I have thought, when he died, to have him buried in a Christian-like manner; but I suppose I could hardly get a parson to officiate!' 'I should think,' Mr. Lunsford very gravely replied, 'a lawyer might suffice for a dog.'

"I recollect to have heard it said, that while Mr. Lunsford was a youth, he heard some people talking about him, in an assembly at a stage where he had come to preach, when one remarked, 'Is that beardless fellow going to preach for us?' While on the stage he took occasion to say, 'If religion consisted in beards, the goats would have had it before now.'"

PERSECUTIONS.

The early part of Lunsford's ministry was in the midst of perilous times. No power of mind or education, no piety, zeal, or faithfulness, was sufficient to shield from the assaults of persecution. It was the portion of him whose biography is now under consideration, to suffer, at different times, for the name of Christ. The most prominent particulars, relative to this part of his life, cannot be better related than in the words of Elder Semple. Referring to his early visits to the Northern Neck, he says: "Here, as in most other places where the Baptists preached, they cried out that some new doctrine was started, that the church was in danger. Mr. L. was accounted worthy to share a part of this opposition. A clergyman appointed a day to preach against the Anabaptists. Crowds attended to hear him. He told stories about Jack of Leyden and Cromwell's roundheads; but he could not, by such tales, stop the gospel current now swelling to a torrent. When Mr. L. preached again in those parts, they attacked him by more weighty arguments. A constable was sent with a warrant to arrest him. The constable, with more politeness than is usual on such occasions, waited until Mr. Lunsford had preached. His fascinating powers palsied the constable's hand. He would not, he said, serve a warrant on so good a man. Another man took it, went tremblingly and served it. Mr. Lunsford attended the summons, and appeared before a magistrate. He was held in a recognizance to appear at court. The court determined that he had been guilty of a breach of good behavior, and that he must give security or go to prison. He was advised to give security, under the expectation of obtaining license to preach. He tried but could not. He often regretted that he had taken this step, and was sorry he had not gone to prison. This took place in Richmond County.

"After the repeal of the law for establishing one sect to the exclusion of the rest, a banditti attended Mr. Lunsford's meeting, with sticks and staves to attack him. Just as he was about to begin to preach they approached him for the attack. His irreligious friends, contrary to his wish, determined to defend him.

This produced a great uproar, and some skirmishes. Mr. Lunsford retired to a house. The persecutors pursued him. He shut himself up, and they were not hardy enough to break in to him. One of them desired to have the privilege of conversing with Mr. L. with a view of convincing him. He was let in, and did converse. When he came out he wore a new face. His party asked him the result. You had better, said he, converse with him yourselves."

Sickness, Death, etc.

The following quotations from Elder Semple, referring to his last hours, will close this biography: "This great, this good, this almost inimitable man, died when only about forty years of age. He lived in a sickly climate, and had frequent bilious attacks. These were sometimes very severe. For two or three years before his death he labored under repeated indispositions, even when traveling about. His manly soul would never permit him to shrink from the work so long as he had strength to lift up his voice. Sometimes, after going to bed as being too ill to preach, prompted by his seraphic spirit, he would rise again, after some other person had preached, and deal out the bread of life to the hungry sons and daughters of Zion.

"The Dover Association, for the year 1793, was held at Glebe Landing Meeting-house, in Middlesex County. This was nearly opposite to Mr. Lunsford's, and, the river excepted, not more than fifteen or eighteen miles from his house. Although just rising from a bilious attack, he would not stay from a place where his heart delighted to be, and where he had the best ground to believe he could do good. He went, and appeared so much better that he made extensive appointments to preach in the lower parts of Virginia. He was chosen to preach on Sunday, and he did preach indeed. On Tuesday he came up to King and Queen, and preached at Bruington Meeting-house, from these words: 'Therefore, let us not sleep, as do others, but let us watch and be sober.' It was an awakening discourse, worthy of this masterly workman. On that day he took cold, and grew worse. He, however, preached his last sermon the next day evening, observing, when he began, 'It may be improper for me to attempt to preach at this time, but as long as I have any strength remaining I wish to preach the gospel of Christ; and I will very gladly spend and be spent for you.' He then preached his last sermon, from—'Therefore, being justified by faith, we have peace with God through our Lord Jesus Christ.' He continued to grow worse, until, having arrived at Mr. Gregory's, in Essex, he took his bed, from whence he was carried to the grave. In his sickness he was remarkably silent, having very little to say which he could avoid. He was fond of joining in prayer, and sometimes exerted his now relaxed mind in making remarks worthy of such a man. He expressed some anxiety at the thought of leaving his helpless family, but appeared quite resigned to the will of Heaven. On the 26th of October, 1793, he fell asleep in the arms of Jesus, aged about forty years."

Rev. Henry Toler preached two funeral sermons for him: one at the place of his death, another at Mr. Lunsford's Meeting-house in Lancaster County, called Kilmarnock. These two sermons were printed in a pamphlet, and annexed to them were two handsome elegies, written by ladies of his church. It seemed to be a mystery to many why God should have called home so great, so useful a man, in the bloom of life. Those who thought proper to explain the ways of Providence generally agreed that Mr. Lunsford's popularity as a preacher had risen too high; the people, wherever he was, or where he was expected, seemed to have lost all relish for any other man's preaching; that God, knowing the capacity of most of his servants, was unwilling that the lesser lights should be so much swallowed up by the greater. Perhaps the better way is to form no conjecture about it; but rest persuaded that the ways of God are always wise, however unaccountable to man.

"He was twice married. He had by his first wife one surviving child; by his second he left three children."

It will not be inappropriate to present a few lines from one of two poetic effusions, occasioned by the death of Mr. Lunsford. The elegy from which the following quotation is taken was written by Miss Clarissa Pollard, afterwards Mrs. Hall, and mother of Rev. Addison Hall. It was addressed to Rev. Henry Toler:—

Dear honored friend, forgive my daring muse,
If at this time so bold a theme she choose;
An abler pen this subject might demand—
How then shall I direct this trembling hand?
Can Lunsford's fame be heightened by my pen,
Or made to shine among the sons of men?
Ah, no! as soon might twinkling stars give light,
When yon bright orb dispels the gloom of night.

But shall I then forbear? must friendship lie
Buried in woe and deep obscurity?
While others spread their woes abroad, can she,
Who knew his friendship, sad and silent be?
What though unskilled in art's sublimer rules,
Untaught in all the doctrines of the schools,
Of birth obscure, can she her muse restrain?
Because not eloquent, is friendship vain?

My pen, forbid this deep desponding sigh:
Fresh courage take; submissive be, while I
In faltering tone thy feeble aid command,
To mourn a great reformer of our land,
Who, zealous for his country and his God,
Proclaimed the joyful news of peace abroad,—
True gospel peace, through Christ's atoning blood;
Great advocate for Zion, Lunsford stood.

In youth he rushes forth; wonderful boy!
The sinner's terror, and the Christian's joy.
"Go, herald, go," the Great Emanuel cries;
Forthwith with speed the obedient stripling flies.
"I go, Great God, but trust thy grace alone;
Thou seest me weak, do thou my message own,
Attend the truths that I proclaim abroad,
And let the nations know thou art the Lord."

His prayers are heard—through Heaven the echo rings:
"I'll own thy message," saith the King of kings;
"Thine eyes shall see a numerous crowd ascend
From nature's night, and then thy days shall end,—
Thy days of grief, which thou on earth shall see,
Shall soon be o'er; soon shall thou rest with me.
Be patient then, and learn to kiss the rod;
'Tis thus I wean the purchase of my blood
From earthly joys, that they may seek in me
Unbounded bliss and pure felicity."

Encouraged by his God, he ventures through
A dreary world, with these great ends in view:
The good of souls, the glory of his King,
These fire his heart, and tune his lips to sing.
Unawed by wicked men, forward he moves,
Bold in the Saviour, who his zeal approves;
With rapid flight he hastens to the field,
Resolved, through Christ, the Spirit's sword to wield;
Foremost he comes, in front of battle stands,
And Moses-like, rears his extended hands.
Israel prevails; the foes of Zion flee;
His eyes behold the promised company.

His work now done: "Go, Gabriel," Jesus cries,
"And bring my servant to these upper skies.
I know his zeal, his prayers, his groans, and tears,
His deep distresses, and heart-rendering cries.
I'll set him free from bondage, pain and woe."

WILLIAM WEBBER.

To the subject of this sketch are the Baptists of Virginia indebted, in no ordinary degree, for the diffusion of the pure gospel and the origination of many of their churches. As far as the path he trod may not be obliterated by time, it will be a grateful task to trace his steps, and to review the dealings of the Lord as they were exhibited in his history.

ELDER WILLIAM WEBBER was born August 15th, 1747, of respectable parentage. Although in comfortable circumstances, his father did not afford him a liberal education. This was the privilege of few in those days. At the age of sixteen he left his father's house and was apprenticed to a house-joiner. There do not seem to have been any peculiar indications of seriousness until his twenty-third year, when he heard some of the Baptist preachers, and became concerned about his soul's interests. He found joy and peace in Christ Jesus, and was baptized by Elder John Waller. At that period not one of the churches now in the Dover Association had been constituted, and he united with the Lower Spottsylvania Church, that being most contiguous to his residence. A short period subsequent to his connection with the church he was ordained. Several years after his entrance into the ministry he was almost exclusively engaged in itinerant labor. In the counties south of James River he traveled extensively. In Lower Virginia also, he was most indefatigably employed in pointing sinners to the Lamb of God. In 1774 he was invited to the pastorate of the Dover Church, from which the Dover Association took its name. This invitation he accepted, and continued to sustain the relation as long as he lived.

The seals to Elder Webber's ministry were numerous. He whom he served had made him wise to win souls. Churches in various places sprang up as the result of his self-denying toils. And when the pressure of domestic duties and the maintenance of a growing family necessarily abridged his labors, he was still useful in his own neighborhood. The general influence he possessed qualified him to do good on an extensive scale. He was a member of the first meeting of the General Association, in 1771. With but few exceptions, he was called to preside over the deliberations of this body, as well as the meeting of the General Convention of Virginia Baptists. After the organization of the Dover Association he was for fourteen years, in succession, elected to fill the chair. For this office he seems, in many respects, to have been well qualified; not, indeed, by elegance of manners, but by an unostentatious simplicity. He was, in the true sense of the word, dignified in his address, and commanded the respect of all.

It will be expected that something be said concerning his talents. In the pulpit he was distinguished by the plain, artless manner in which he exhibited the truth. There was not indicated in his public addresses more than ordinary depth of mind. It is said, however, that in the social circle he displayed much mental vigor. Mr. Semple remarks, that "he was a man of sound and correct judgment, well acquainted with mankind, well versed in the Scriptures, sound in the principles of the gospel, and ingenious in defending them." As he commenced his ministry in those times when a corrupt establishment prevailed, it could not be expected that he would escape the indignation of the dominant party. By their unholy persecutions he suffered much in a very early part of his career, as a preacher of righteousness. It has been already said that his labors in the counties south of James River were extensively useful. A few months after his ordination he, with Joseph Anthony, was arrested in the County of Chesterfield, and, in the midst of winter, committed to prison. He might have been released immediately after his apprehension, had he been willing to give bond and security that he would no more speak in the name of Christ. This he refused to do. He remained in confinement three months. During this period he was not unemployed, nor useless. Such was the interest which had been excited in the county by his previous labors, that crowds frequently assembled around the jail, and from the grates they heard, with joyful hearts, the message of a Saviour's love. The wicked designs of his persecutors were utterly defeated; for the word of the Lord mightily prevailed. Many believed the gospel, and acknowledged the Lord Jesus as their Redeemer and King. Perhaps in no portion of his life did Elder Webber prosecute more successfully his labors of love.

This was not the only trial of this kind to which he was subjected. The very next year, while on a tour of preaching, in company with Elder John Waller, through some of the lower counties, he was again seized by the enemies of the truth. This occurred in the County of Middlesex, on the 10th of August, 1771, while he was addressing the congregation from the words, "Show me thy faith without thy works, and I will show thee my faith by my works." He was assailed by a magistrate, who, with a club, endeavored to strike him to the earth. In this he was prevented by those who were present. Having, however, a warrant to apprehend all who preached, he, in company with the parson of the parish and a sheriff, proceeded to take Mr. Webber, with several others. Their saddle-bags were searched; and, finding nothing which might afford a pretext for the charge of treason, they were required, on pain of imprisonment, to promise they would not preach again in that county. To obey God, rather than man, they preferred—even at the peril of liberty or life. They were committed to prison and closely confined in cells of the most disagreeable character. The subject of this sketch felt happy in being counted worthy thus to suffer for the name of

Christ. On the next court day, he and his fellow-prisoners were attended by a guard to the court-house for trial. Not being willing to yield his right to preach the gospel, as the terms of release, he was remanded to prison. His sufferings were extreme. He was allowed by the court nothing but bread and water. This, with confinement in a close and offensive room, produced sickness. In his affliction he experienced the sympathies of many in the county; and such was the influence of patient endurance of these sufferings, on the public mind, that his persecutors were willing, at length, to liberate him and his companions. He was more than six weeks in their hands, four of which were spent in close confinement.

The severe trials endured by him prove the malignity of that hatred with which the enemies of the Cross opposed the servants of Jesus. It might be supposed he was, of all men, least likely to suffer at the hands of the wicked, as he possessed the most lamb-like disposition. They hated him, however, on account of the truth which he vindicated. His was persecution "for righteousness' sake."

In the neighborhood where mostly, in the latter part of his life, he preached the gospel, the most marked respect was shown him by all classes. The churches for which he labored were much attached to him. How could it be otherwise? In all his intercourse with the world he maintained a spotless character. Affectionate in his disposition, those with whom he was more intimate most ardently loved him. He was a cheerful, interesting companion. What served, most of all, to throw a lustre over his whole character, was his unaffected and habitual devotion to the service of the Redeemer. He seemed to aim, in mingling with others, to do good and to exalt the Saviour. To speak of Christ was his delight. The art of giving a profitable direction to conversation was possessed by him in no small degree.

He lived to the age of sixty-two years. For seven or eight years before his death his health was exceedingly feeble. His last illness was of long continuance, during which he gave pleasing evidence of the consoling and supporting influence of that gospel which he had so long and so faithfully preached to others. He who had been with him in the dungeon and enabled him to sing praises amid insult and suffering, was now near to illume his way as he passed through the dark valley of the shadow of death. A short time previous to his death he was visited by Elder Benjamin Watkins, of Powhatan, who found him in a most rapturous state of mind. "Brother Watkins," said he, "I never had such glorious manifestations of the love of God as I have enjoyed since my sickness. Oh, the love of God!" Thus, with heaven in view and heaven in his soul, he left the earth on February 29th, in the year 1808.

JOHN ALDERSON, Jr.

John Alderson was the son of Elder John Alderson, Sen., and was born in New Jersey, March 5th, 1738, O. S. In his seventeenth year his father settled in Rockingham County, Virginia, and took charge of the Lynnville Creek Church. At that time Western Virginia was comparatively a wilderness, having but few inhabitants. Shortly after the removal of his father he took an extensive tour for the purpose of exploring the country. During this journey the burning spring near Charleston was discovered, which produced considerable alarm among their company.

In his twenty-first year he was married to Miss Mary Carroll. He continued, several years after this event, wedded to the world and negligent of eternal things, although he was often the subject of partial concern. It was not until he had reached the meridian of life that his heart was surrendered to the Prince of peace. Having suffered severe affliction in the loss of an only daughter, whom he dearly loved, and in the experience of severe illness himself, he began to think; some remarks of his father also were carried with power to his heart, and he awoke to the consciousness of his lost condition. The following is his own account of his conversion: "My father being much from home, and I being the oldest son, much dependence was placed on me to take care of the farm, so that I had very little opportunity to learn. The chief books I read were the Bible and the Baptist Catechism; which last I memorized, and not only said it over at school, but also in the public congregations on Sundays after sermon. By these means I was kept from all gross immoralities. By an expression dropped from my father after I had recovered from a very severe sickness, my mind was solemnly impressed. After passing through a painful and tedious law-work, in which I would make resolutions and then break them, I became more deeply concerned. I sought the Lord with my whole heart, and ultimately obtained comfort, great comfort, by reflection on these words: 'Ye are built upon the foundation of the apostles and prophets, Jesus Christ himself being the chief corner-stone.'"

It must have been pleasing to his venerable father to baptize this son. He had himself been toiling almost alone amid trials and dangers, and now he enjoyed the prospect of assistance in the person of his own son. He was not long without this assistance. After much anxiety of mind on the question of duty, he was at length, by the great Master, thrust into the vineyard. Respecting this matter he says: "After many doubts as to my conversion, I began at last to be exercised about preaching. At first I thought it imposssible that so weak a creature as I could be called to preach; but being persuaded, at last, by many Divine tokens, that it was the will of God, I entered upon the solemn work."

His father having about this time removed to Botetourt County, he was ordained and took charge of the Lynnville Creek Church, October, 1775. He did not remain in Rockingham more than two years. Having two or three times visited Greenbrier, the indications of Providence were such that, in 1777, he conceived it his duty to settle in that county. The account of his removal and subsequent labors are thus referred to by one of his descendants:

"In the year 1777 he removed to Monroe, (at that time Greenbrier County,) and settled on Greenbrier River. The few inhabitants that were then to be found in this region of country were not unfrequently harassed by the inroads of frontier Indians. The object of Mr. Alderson's removal was to extend the Christian religion among this people. Until he came among them they had been entirely destitute of preaching. When unmolested by the savages, he preached to the people assembled in such places as were most convenient; when they were necessitated to shut themselves up in their forts, he traveled from one garrison to another to preach, sometimes defended by a small guard ; at other times his only defence was the arms which he bore. He frequently met with opposition. On one occasion the occupants of a fort refused his entrance. They at length permitted him to preach. Seven years he labored in this field without seeing a single Baptist minister. In the mean time he had the pleasure of baptizing a few individuals. Others who belonged to the church of which he was formerly pastor had removed to this settlement. Of these, making in all twelve persons, he succeeded in forming the Greenbrier Church, November 24th, 1781. This was the first Baptist Church that was planted in Western Virginia. But very few were added to the original number until the year 1785. In the fall of this year a revival commenced which continued until 1791. Though our forefathers termed this a revival, during the whole period above mentioned only twenty-four persons were baptized. The excitement that was produced had a very powerful effect upon the whole region of country. The mouths of opposers were stopped, and the popular sentiment in regard to religion was much changed. The bounds of the Greenbrier Church included all that district that now composes the Greenbrier Association. The influence of the revival was of course extensive."

As the truth continued to spread, other churches were constituted, the principal of which were Indian Creek and Big Levels. For many years he was the pastor of Indian Creek, and was in the habit of riding the distance of eighteen miles regularly to preach for them. In the midst of his heavy labors and trials in the ministry, he was compelled with his own hands to support a growing family. Notwithstanding this, he was remarkable for his punctuality in fulfilling his preaching engagements. He never failed to attend the meetings of the Association, and was usually chosen to occupy the chair. As a disciplinarian he was so distinguished that he was frequently consulted in matters of difficulty both between individual members and churches. It was his heart's delight to respond to the calls of duty.

During the year 1805 his bosom companion, who was a member of the same church with himself and who had shared largely with him in all his trials, was removed from his embraces. This he considered the severest affliction he had ever realized. For some time he was exceedingly depressed, but ultimately found the trial eminently sanctified to his spiritual good and promotive of his usefulness. He determined to give up his worldly pursuits and consecrate his time more exclusively to the work of preaching the gospel. To this purpose he adhered, and with apostolic zeal employed his talents for the good of the churches. As he advanced in age his labors were more circumscribed; but still, in his own immediate vicinity, he was constantly engaged.

Two years previous to his decease his physical powers in a great measure failed, so that he was unable to travel or preach. For his accommodation several sessions of the Greenbrier Association were held at the Greenbrier Meeting-house. On one of these occasions a gentleman, who regarded him as the instrument of his conversion and who had for many years been connected with the Methodist Church, presented himself as a candidate for baptism. In relating the exercises of his mind to the church Elder Alderson, seated in his arm-chair, became so overcome by the ecstasy of his feelings that he broke out in a most impassioned exhortation, at the same time expressing his gratitude to God for the distinguished favors he had received. The effect was electrical. The whole congregation was deeply affected. This was the last time he ever appeared in public. Having made a disposition of his property, a portion of which he directed to be appropriated to benevolent purposes, several of the last months of his life were spent with his son, Joseph Alderson. Excepting great feebleness, he enjoyed good health, and possessed, in vigorous exercise, his mental powers. Especially was this the fact in reference to the things of the kingdom. He delighted to converse on heavenly subjects, and exhibited the spectacle of an aged veteran who was ready to be offered and the time of whose departure was at hand. He had fought a good fight, he had finished his course, he had kept the faith. It was his privilege to enjoy the well-grounded assurance of receiving a crown of life. He still, more than ever, manifested an anxiety for the prosperity of the churches and the dissemination of the gospel.

In January, 1821, he was suddenly attacked with illness while standing on his feet, and by some of his family was caught and laid upon his bed, from which he never again rose. He lingered for several weeks, and at length expired, March 5th, 1821. His remains were deposited in the burial-ground of Greenbrier Church, there to rest peacefully until the resurrection morn.

Two or three additional allusions to this servant of God will close the sketch. He was a man of fervent piety and unblemished life. He possessed the confidence and respect of all. With plain, unostentatious demeanor, and a zeal according to knowledge, he proved that he was "honest in a sacred cause." Such practical marks of adherence to the will of God are more effectual in winning men from the path of death than the most talented and eloquent discourses.

Elder Alderson possessed an intellect naturally vigorous. Had he passed his early days in a region and time in which the opportunity of obtaining education was enjoyed, he would doubtless have shone among the most distinguished of his age. But living in a region comparatively uncultivated, and being accustomed from a child to labor for a maintenance, such advantages were denied. He was, however, not negligent in the improvement of his talents. As far as he was permitted, by the claims of a dependent family and the loud call for labor in the vineyard of the Lord, he applied himself to reading, and was, to a considerable extent, successful in the cultivation of his mind. His preaching was of a doctrinal cast, yet highly practical He delighted to dwell on the atonement of Christ and to recommend him to the attention of men.

He was, without doubt, one of the most prominent men of the Baptist denomination in Western Virginia, and it may be doubted whether in any part of the State one more self-denying and devoted could have been found. Many souls, at the last great day, will hail him as the instrument of recovery from the yawning pit. No higher distinction need be sought in this world, than that to which he aspired. To do good was his beloved employ. He now rests from his labors, and his works do follow him.

DAVID BARROW.

IN noting the history of this eminent minister of Jesus, it becomes an occasion of devout thanksgiving, that in the early endeavors of Virginia Baptists so many men of gifted minds were raised up to officiate among them as evangelists and pastors. They were in few instances scholastically educated, but they were endowed with all the elements of greatness, in their strong, good sense, unwearied industry, intimate knowledge of the Scriptures, earnest manner, and deep-toned piety. God made them what they were, and raised them up for the noble purpose of sustaining and spreading widely the truths and ordinances of the New Testament.

DAVID BARROW was one of these men. He was the son of William Barrow, of Brunswick County. His mother was Amy Lee, daughter of William Lee, of the same county. David, their second son, was born October 30, 1753. His early life having been spent in industrial pursuits on his father's farm, he acquired those habits of self-reliance and energy which in all future life distinguished him. In the seventeenth year of his age deep religious impressions operated in leading his mind to build a hope of eternal life on the Son of God. In the same year he joined the Baptist Church, being baptized, as is supposed, by Elder Zechariah Thompson; and before he was eighteen years of age had begun to proclaim the salvation in which his own heart rejoiced. His gift, as a licentiate, was exercised for about three years, during which time he was a diligent student.

Every available means for intellectual cultivation were eagerly sought. Day and night he might be seen poring over books—and thus he made himself, what he afterwards was, a scribe well instructed in the things of the kingdom. Not only the word of God, but the whole range of knowledge was surveyed, so far as the opportunities and facilities furnished would allow. He became a good English scholar. None of the errorists in his vicinity, however learned or gifted, were able to grapple with him. It was necessary, even in his early ministry, to contend earnestly for the faith delivered to the saints, and he proved himself worthy of the cause he plead. The noble stand he took, as hereafter to be noticed, arrested the march of pernicious sentiments which even then had begun to prevail.

In his nineteenth year Mr. Barrow married Miss Sarah Gilliam, daughter of Hinchey Gilliam, of Sussex County, by whom he had twelve children. His first pastorate was with the Mill Swamp Church, Isle of Wight County, which had been a little before originated under the efficient labors of Elder J. Meglamare. He was called by this body of Baptists to assume their spiritual oversight, and in January, 1774, removed and settled among them. The June following, by the imposition of hands he was solemnly ordained to the full work of the ministry. He was afterwards called also to the care of South Quay and Black Creek Churches, in Southampton County. An effectual door of usefulness now being opened, he entered it, and labored not in vain. The Lord wrought with and through him, many scoffers were led to Christ, and the churches were greatly increased in numbers and efficiency. He became eminently popular in the pulpit as well as the social circle. His manners, general information, fearlessness in the defence of truth, and spotless life, all contributed to swell the tide of beneficial influence.

The labors of Mr. Barrow were not confined to the churches he served. In Lower Virginia and North Carolina he traveled much, and everywhere exercised a commanding sway. But it was principally with the Mill Swamp Church he found his ministry most favored. It became one of the largest churches of the Kehukee Association, with whom it was then identified.

The year after his ordination and settlement with this church, trials of a very serious character were realized by the brethren of the Kehukee Association, in consequence of unscriptural sentiments and practices, which had begun to prevail to a considerable extent. In the language of one of their historians, "Several of those churches, that at first belonged to the Kehukee Association, were gathered by the Free-Will Baptists, and, as their custom was to baptize any persons who were willing whether they had an experience of grace or not, they had many members and ministers in their churches who were baptized before they were converted; and after they were brought to a knowledge of the truth, and joined the Regulars, openly confessed they were baptized before they believed. Some of them said they supposed they should reach heaven by it. Several of their ministers confessed they had preached and administered the ordinance of baptism to others before they were themselves converted; and so zealous were they for baptism, that one of their preachers confessed, if he could find any willing to be baptized, and it was in the night, he would immerse them by *firelight*, lest they should determine otherwise before the next morning."

Against this system of baptismal regeneration a few bold spirits maintained a firm and persevering opposition. Among those who contended earnestly for the faith as it was once delivered to the saints, the subject of this sketch was, perhaps, the most intelligent and unyielding. He insisted that men were to be baptized, not to make them in heart Christians, but because they were already such, and because this institution was designed to be the significant mode by which forgiven believers were publicly to profess allegiance to the King of Zion. Other unscriptural views, also, he opposed. There is reason to believe that his influence was greatly blessed, in arresting the tide of error which was beginning to set in upon the churches.

As Mr. Barrow lived in a day when the contest was going on between the friends and foes of religious liberty, he became one of the principal leaders of reform, and employed his talents and influence to obtain a change in many of the then existing and oppressive laws of Virginia. At the meetings of the Association he most eloquently vindicated the right of all men to worship God according to their wishes, and urged his brethren to maintain a united and immovable stand against those enactments which took away this right. Nor was he unsuccessful. A strong public sentiment was created in Lower Virginia, which assisted to bring about a repeal of laws as injurious in their influence as they were unjust in themselves.

Elder Barrow had himself smarted beneath the severe hand of persecution. Several times it was attempted to prevent him from filling his appointments. His sufferings were frequently painful. "In 1778 he received an invitation to preach at the house of a gentleman who lived on Nansemond River, near the mouth of James River. A ministering brother accompanied him. They were informed, on their arrival, that they might expect rough usage; and it so happened. As soon as the hymn was given out, a gang of well-dressed men came up to the stage, which had been erected under some trees, and sung one of their obscene songs. They then undertook to plunge both of the preachers. They plunged Mr. Barrow twice, pressing him into the mud, and, holding him down, nearly succeeded in drowning him. In the midst of their mocking they asked him if he believed, and throughout treated him with the most barbarous insolence and outrage. His companion they plunged but once. The whole assembly was shocked, the women shrieked; but no one durst interfere, for about twenty stout fellows were engaged in this horrid measure. They insulted and abused the gentleman who had invited them to preach, and every one who spoke a word in their favor. Before these persecuted men could change their clothes they were dragged from the house, and driven off by these enraged churchmen. But three or four of them died in a few weeks, in a distracted manner, and one of them wished himself in hell before he had joined the company," etc.

Among other important matters, to which the attention of the churches was called by Elder Barrow, was the subject of domestic missions. This he urged at various meetings of the Association, and, to some extent, succeeded in obtaining the consent of his Kehukee brethren to supply the destitution within their own limits. He was also active in the inculcation of a duty which had been much neglected by the churches, viz. the support of the ministry. It is to be lamented that the extortions of the Episcopal clergy should have driven our brethren to the other extreme; many not only failed to teach and enforce the obligation of the churches to provide for the maintenance of their pastors, but declaimed and wrote against it. Elder Barrow, however, took a scriptural view of this subject, and was not unwilling to disclose it.

Elder Barrow continued with the Kehukee Association until the Portsmouth Association was formed. This occurred in 1791, when the churches in Kehukee were forty-two in number, while the new body contained nineteen churches. These last were all in Virginia. During his continuance with the parent association Mr. Barrow was one of her most efficient sons. He was always found taking an enlightened and dignified course, in the deliberations of her annual meetings. And when the new association was organized, he remained the same active and judicious friend of every good word and work. During his short connection with them he was several times called to occupy the chair. In 1797 he removed to Kentucky, much to the regret of many friends of enlightened piety in Virginia.

From Mr. Barrow's pen a small pamphlet was published, containing a sort of farewell address to his brethren, upon his departure to the western country. He dwells with deep feeling on the separation, seeming to break away from his loved associations here as by constraint—a constraint imposed by the parsimony of his churches. They had not suitably administered to his necessities. It was accordant with the spirit of the times to make little or no systematic arrangements for the support of the ministry. The churches had suffered so sorely under a hireling priesthood in connection with the establishment, that their pastors were themselves accustomed to preach against the payment of salaries, many of them absolutely suffering for the want of competent support. In common with many of his brethren, Elder Barrow found it necessary to seek a new home in the more newly settled and fruitful lands of Kentucky. As explanatory of his reasons for removal, and of his sentiments toward the brethren from whom he was to be sundered, he says :—

"On long and very serious deliberation, I have determined, under Divine Providence, to move my residence from this country to the State of Kentucky. As I have been for many years exercising my feeble talents in the sacred work of the ministry, which has been the means of procuring many respectable acquaintances, most of whom I have no opportunity of seeing before my removal; and, as a memorial of my unabated affection for my friends, and to stop the mouths of some few enemies, who, in my absence, may say ungenerous things concerning the motives of removal and the doctrines I have preached, I think it best thus to express my sentiments before I leave this part of the country.

First, I will give the reasons for moving; second, exhibit a summary of my creed; and third, express my parting wishes and prayers.

"First. The reasons of my removal—*Negatively.* It is not from any personal prejudice against any man, woman, child, or party, under heaven. Nor is it to accumulate stores of wealth for my children. For we are informed by the lips of inspiration 'that they who will be rich, fall into temptation and a snare, and into many foolish and hurtful habits, which drown men in destruction and perdition.' Nor is it on account of the present deadness and coldness of religion, for I am well convinced God will revive his work in these parts. Nor is it to get rid of temptations and trials, for we learn that affliction cometh not forth of the dust, neither doth trouble spring out of the ground; yet, man is born unto trouble as the sparks fly upward.

"*Affirmatively.*—1. I find by long experience and constant efforts I cannot comfortably support my family, educate my children, and attend to public calls, as I have done, without falling into the line of speculation. To let my family suffer is inconsistent with Scripture and reason. 'If any provide not for his own, and especially for them of his own household, hath denied the faith, and is worse than an infidel.' The business of speculation I think incompatible with the work of the ministry, or, at any rate, it is a difficult thing to attend to both. * * * And, if I must turn into the business of agriculture, which I think a safe and honorable employment, common sense dictates it would be most advisable in a country where the God of nature has been most liberal with respect to soil.

"Second. Another reason is, that by the sale of my property I may pay my just debts, which I have been obliged to contract for the support of my family, while I have been otherwise employed.

"Third. That I may, with the blessing of God, be able, moderately, to educate my children.

"Fourth. One distinguishing trait in the ministerial character is, that he should be given to hospitality; whereas, in my situation, with my income, I cannot exercise that disposition as duty calls for, without severely feeling it afterwards. For these reasons, I leave this country and remove to one where Nature has been more bountiful."

Mr. Barrow then proceeds to give his religious and political creed. It will be interesting to note by this document, written more than sixty years ago, what would seem to have been the theological views of many of the fathers in the Virginia ministry. We present a part of the pamphlet. He says :—

"1. I believe in only one indivisible, eternal, all-wise, all-powerful, all-holy, all-just, all-good, self-existing, self-governed, omniscient, omnipresent God; and that in Deity there are three Divine Personalities different in character and office, but strictly One in design, nature, and essence, the Father, the Son, and the Holy Ghost.

"2. I believe the inspiration and infallibility of the holy Scriptures, as contained in the Old and New Testaments.

"3. I believe the existence of an everlasting covenant between the Father and Son, to secure the salvation of God's elect.

"4. I believe the decrees of God are eternal, consistent, wise, and immutable, and that they extend to all matters and things in the universe; yet, not so as to exclude the use of means, but rather that certain and proper means are decreed, to bring about certain and fixed ends in his universal government.

"5. That God elected or chose his people in Christ before all worlds, as a sovereign act of his own good pleasure, without any good or evil thing foreseen in them, as moving him thereto or preventing him therefrom.

"6. That man was created in a state of innocency, but through the seduction of Satan, being left to his own natural powers, fell into transgression by eating the forbidden fruit, by which he became an enemy to God. The whole fountain of nature being defiled, so that, by this single act of disobedience, the whole race of human creatures justly fell under condemnation, and are born into this world in a state of darkness, corruption, slavery to Satan, and a whole train of lawless passions, lusts, and appetites, without either inclination or power to will or do the mind of God, till influenced thereto by the powerful operations of the Divine Spirit.

"7. That it is God's prerogative, and that it is consistent with his law and sacred perfections, to justify the ungodly through Christ's engagement, or by imputing his righteousness to them.

"8. I believe the Incarnation of the Son, or *Word* of God.

"9. I believe the all-sufficiency of Christ's atonement, for the pardon of all those whom he represented.

"10. I believe the absolute necessity of conversion, regeneration, in a work of sanctification on the souls of fallen creatures; not to justify them, but to fit or make them meet for eternal glory.

"11. That good works naturally result from sanctification, and should be zealously maintained by all Christians *for necessary uses. For these things are good and profitable to men.*

"12. I believe the safety, final security, and certain salvation of all those whom Christ represents; for as much as they are justified of God, called and sanctified by the Holy Ghost.

"13. That Christ did constitute a church, the foundation, plan, and government of which is plainly to be found in the New Testament; and that professing and orderly believers only have a right to membership.

"14. That the ordinances in the church are two, Baptism and the Supper. And that Baptism is only rightly administered when it is performed by a properly qualified person on an orderly professing believer, by dipping or plunging the whole body in water, in the name of the Father, Son, and Holy Ghost. And that the Supper is only properly administered and received, when it is handed out and partaken of by such persons as the Scripture directs, and eaten and drunk in a loving and discerning manner, the laity with the clergy having a right to the wine, as well as bread.

"15. That there will be a resurrection of the just and unjust; also, that the righteous shall enjoy eternal happiness, and that the wicked shall suffer everlasting damnation

"A Summary of my Political Creed.

"1. I believe the natural equality of man, except in some monstrous cases.

"2. I believe that liberty, with a right to a good character, of acquiring and possessing property, with the enjoyment of life and members, and the means of defending them, is the unalienable privilege of all men who have not forfeited those blessings by their own personal misdemeanors.

"3. I believe that government is an evil, as it cannot be supported without making considerable sacrifices of natural liberty; but, in our present state of depravity, it is to be preferred to a state of nature.

"4. That government is a civil compact of a people emerging from a state of nature, contrived by themselves for their own security, and is subject to the control, and is liable to alteration, when thought proper by a majority of such community.

"5. That no man can be bound in person or property but by laws of his own making, or that of his representatives, fairly chosen.

"6. That all natural-born citizens, arriving at an age, the community may have a call for their services; and all emigrants, having conformed to the rules of naturalization, are entitled to the right of suffrage.

"7. That no description of men, having gained such confidence of their fellow-citizens as to have a majority of suffrages in fair and free elections, can be excluded the office of judge, representative, etc.

"8. That representatives and judges are trustees and servants of the people, and are constantly accountable to them.

"9. That it would be good for a community that no man exercise more than one office under government, at the same time, of any kind whatsoever.

"10. That the military ought to be under strict subordination to the civil power.

"11. That representatives should be chosen annually.

"12. That all officers or servants of the people should have moderate, but sufficient salaries, fixed by law.

"13. That all religious tests and ecclesiastical establishments are oppresive, and infringing the rights of conscience.

"14. That civil rulers have nothing more to do with religion in their public capacities than private men, save only that they should protect its professors in the uninterrupted enjoyment of it, with life, property, character, in common with other good citizens.

"15. That no man, or set of men, in a community, are entitled to exclusive privileges.

"16. That the liberty of the press, and the people's right to express their grievances, cannot be restrained, but by tyrannical governments.

"17. That a well-regulated militia is the best natural defence of a free government.

"18. I believe, in a situation like ours, that an indissolvable union and well-planned confederation of the States are essentially necessary to their safety and well-being.

"19. That trial by jury, though liable to some exceptions, is most to be depended on.

"20. That unreasonable or excessive bail should never be required of any man.

"21. That tortures, to force confession of suspected crimes, are cruel and heathenish.

"22. That long and unnecessary imprisonment is tyrannical.

"23. That general warrants to search suspected places should never be granted, but on probable evidence.

"24. I believe, as no individual has a right to take his own life on any supposed dissatisfaction, or deprive another of his species of existence, except in self-defence, consequently no community can delegate a power to their representatives to do that they themselves have not a right to do, either separately or collectively, only as above stated. *This may show the necessity of proportioning punishments to crimes, and the utility of pentitentiary houses.*

"25. That no community can long enjoy tranquillity but by strict adherence to virtue and frequent recourse to fundamental principles.

"26. Lastly. That honesty forever was, and forever will be, the best policy.

"III. Express my parting prayers and ardent wishes.

"I most heartily pray for, and with the prosperity of the true Church of Jesus Christ, in general! That she may *keep the ordinances as they were delivered to her at the first.* That she may maintain a regular and gospel discipline. That she may shortly experience a glorious revival and numberless additions, and *arise and shake herself from the dust, and appear the beauty of the whole earth.* I wish all false doctrines and heretical principles may clearly be discovered, and sink into darkness, where they belong; and that 'Heaven-born truth' may universally prevail. I most ardently wish that all those unhappy divi sions, animosities, janglings, groundless criticisms, heart-burnings, evil-speaking, love of pre-eminence, and persecution, which have so long torn the Church of Christ, may happily and entirely subside. That all party names may be lost in oblivion, and that an indissolvable union may take place among all true Christians, upon the old apostolic plan."

After Mr. Barrow's removal to Kentucky he continued to pursue his ministerial work with diligence and success. While he lived, he was a useful minister of the gospel, although some difficulty was created by his peculiar views on the subject of slavery. His death occurred about the year 1814, having reached a good old age, and spent by far the greater part of his life in preaching the gospel of the blessed God. His age, at the time of his dismissal from the earth, was about seventy-five years.

Elder Barrow possessed a discriminating mind. His talents were of a high order. It is much to be questioned whether, as a speaker, he has ever been excelled by any Baptist minister of Virginia or Kentucky. He rarely attended an Association, when he was not chosen to occupy the pulpit on Lord's day. His discourses were expressed with clearness and furnished with the happiest illustrations. He was a man of peace, of uncommon meekness; and but few holier men have been found in the gospel ministry in modern times. Religion was the general topic of conversation wherever he went; and into whatever society he might enter, by godly conversation and fervent prayer he would be known as a minister of the Lord Jesus. "He magnified his office;" and while his sermons were argumentative and doctrinal, he was regarded as a "son of consolation," confirming the souls of the disciples wherever he preached.

As a pastor, he was much beloved and highly useful. He presided in this capacity over the churches of South Quay, Mill Swamp, and Black Creek, in Virginia, and over others after he removed to Kentucky. Many, through his instrumentality, were brought to a knowledge of the truth, and instructed in the things of the kingdom.

JAMES BELL.

Elder James Bell was born in Sussex County in 1745. His parents were connected with the Episcopal church, and conformed to all its externals, while it seems they did not make any pretensions to renewal of heart. Their children being educated to regard the forms of Episcopacy, the subject of this sketch continued his adherence until his conversion to God.

Of his earlier years but little is known, excepting that in childhood he gave indications of a mind highly gifted by nature. When he arrived at manhood and a full development of his talents was made, he became the subject of much admiration and esteem. He was invited to several important offices in Sussex County, which he accepted and filled to the satisfaction of all. Having been urged to become a candidate for the General Assembly of Virginia, he was elected by a large majority. The county was represented by him for many years, during which time he became increasingly popular, and enjoyed the respect not only of his own county men but of many of the surrounding counties.

In the midst of this prosperity he lived without God. How strangely does the perverseness of the human heart exhibit itself, by a proud neglect of the Bible and its requirements, in proportion to the number and variety of earthly blessings enjoyed! Especially when elevation in official dignity is attained, are men prone to look down with contempt on those obligations imposed by the God of heaven. It is esteemed a meanness to embrace the doctrines and obey the precepts of Him who died on the cross. Thus it was with Mr. Bell. But God, who is rich in mercy, subdued the enmity of his heart and led him into the path of life. Thoughtfulness on Divine things was at first occasioned by a visit of his brother Benjamin, who for some years had resided at the South, and who had become a member of the Baptist church. The relation his brother gave of the change he had experienced, and the affectionate concern which was manifested for his welfare, affected him deeply. His eyes were opened to discover his own miserable condition, and in the anguish of his soul he began to inquire for the way of salvation. He was brought into a new world. Christ became the foundation of his hopes and exceedingly precious to his heart. The whole current of his desires and habits now received a new direction. He renounced his worldly honors, not because he esteemed the occupancy of honorable stations in civil life inconsistent with his relation to Christ, but because he felt it his duty to spend his days in preaching the gospel. Accordingly, having been baptized by Elder John Meglamare, he began to recommend the service of his new Master to all around him.

The baptism of Elder Bell occurr in 1770. He attached himself to the church called Raccoon Swamp, and continued among them until within a short time previous to his death, when he joined Sappony Church. After laboring for some time as an itinerant, he was called to take the pastoral care of Sappony Church. He was instrumental in winning many souls to God and building up the churches. He was zealous in the performance of his work, and his zeal was according to knowledge. The unblemished character which he sustained did much to make his ministry useful. All respected him as a consistent follower of the Redeemer. The ministerial career of this servant of God was short. His death occurred in September, 1778, about eight years after his connection with the church, and in his forty-third year. Some time before his departure he desired that all his family might be collected together, that he might give his dying advice. It was an affecting scene. The man of God just on the verge of heaven, and leaving behind him many who would be exposed to the corrupting influence of this world, could not be satisfied without giving once more the voice of affectionate warning. He exhorted his children and all who were present to make preparation for another world. In the most distinct terms he referred to his own prospects, declaring that Christ, and Christ alone, was the foundation of his hope. Elder Burkitt being present, was requested to preach his funeral sermon from the words of Paul, "It is a faithful saying," etc. Thus was God pleased in his inscrutable wisdom to deprive the church at Sappony of her beloved pastor, and the cause at large of an efficient helper. "How unsearchable are his judgments, and his ways past finding out!"

JAMES GARNETT.*

ELDER JAMES GARNETT, SEN., was born in Culpepper County in November, 1743. His father, Captain Anthony Garnett, was a man of respectable standing in civil society, but made no profession of religion. His mother was a very pious member of the Methodist church, and manifested a deep interest in the spiritual welfare of her children. The Lord, whose "eyes are over the righteous," heard her supplications, and brought many of her children to a knowledge of the truth; among the number was the subject of this brief memoir. During his youth and early manhood he was very wild and thoughtless. He was a strong, active man, and took much pleasure in feats of agility, particularly in foot-racing, in which he greatly excelled. Thus he continued walking according to the course of this world, and giving no evidence of any particular concern about the welfare of his soul, until he was nearly thirty years old. But the Lord had mercy in store for him. About 1770, under the ministry of Elder Elijah Craig, he received religious impressions, which continued many months before he obtained a hope. His convictions were unusually severe, and sometimes the agony of his soul was overpowering. On arriving, on a Lord's day, in sight of Blue Run Meeting-house, he heard the saints singing the well-known hymn of Dr. Watts,

"Lord, what a wretched land is this!"

It made such an impression on his mind that, before he reached the house, he fell to the ground, unable to proceed farther. He felt the full force of those words; to him this was a "wretched land," and the world could give no relief to his distressed mind. No cheering fruits, no wholesome trees, nor streams of living joy were to be found. Thus guilty, condemned, and almost in despair, he lay until the singers reached the words of the same hymn,

"But Judah's lion guards the way,
And guides the strangers home."

At this moment his mind was relieved, and he found peace from

---

* By James Slaughter.

a view of the fullness, in Jesus Christ, the "Lion of the tribe of Judah," who has promised to guide the strangers and pilgrims home to eternal rest.

He was baptized shortly afterwards by Elder Elijah Craig, and became a member of Blue Run Church, in Orange County. It was soon apparent that he felt more than ordinary concern for the salvation of perishing sinners around him; and though he had been favored with a very limited education and was sensible of the greatness of the work before him, yet he conferred not with flesh and blood, but, urged on by a sense of duty and an ardent love for the souls of men, zealously engaged in the work of the ministry. Nor did he labor in vain. The Lord blessed his efforts to the awakening of many.

When Crooked Run Church was constituted, which was soon after the baptism of Elder Garnett, he became a member of that body, and in about two years was called to the pastoral care of that church. This office he filled until a short time before his death, in 1830, a period of more than fifty-five years. He resigned the office at last solely because his bodily infirmities prevented him from rendering efficient service. Under his pastoral care the church at Crooked Run generally enjoyed much peace and harmony, and was blessed with many refreshing seasons, when large additions were made to her numbers.

In point of morality and correct Christian deportment few have surpassed Elder Garnett. He was a pattern to all who knew him. Such was "the even tenor of his way," that his presence produced impressions of awe and veneration upon the minds of the irreligious. A near neighbor of his, a professed infidel, has been frequently heard to declare that he had often been checked, and constrained to desist from his evil practices, by the sight and Christian deportment of Elder Garnett. At home or abroad, in public or private, he was always the same. Religion was his constant theme, and he never heard of the prosperity of Zion or revivals of the Lord's work, either far or near, but it seemed to put new life into him and call forth expressions of gratitude to God for his goodness to men.

For nearly sixty years he was an active laborer in the vineyard of the Lord, feeding the flock and winning souls to Christ.

Although he had a call to take charge of some other churches, he declined all, and confined his ministrations mostly to Crooked Run Church, where he generally worshiped every Lord's day. But for eight or ten years before his death he was greatly afflicted with the asthma, which circumscribed his labors and prevented his preaching beyond the limits of his immediate neighborhood. It was, for a considerable time, with great difficulty that he could get to the house of worship on Lord's days. But such was his love for the sanctuary, that if he was able only to sit up he would have his family convey him to the house of God, and, being unable to stand, he would sit in his chair and pray, preach, and exhort, until his bodily strength was almost exhausted. The last Sabbath he spent on earth he passed the hours of worship with the church and congregation at Crooked Run; when with more than ordinary feeling and many tears he exhorted his brethren to love and good works, and warned sinners, in view of a coming judgment, to flee from the wrath to come. That day will long be remembered by many who were present. Much that he said gave evidence that he had some presentiment of the fact that the time of his "departure was at hand." He in effect took leave of his brethren, saying, "If I never see you again in this world, from my heart I wish you well, and I hope to meet you in a better world; if I have ever said anything to wound the character or feelings of any of you, I now ask to be forgiven." He was then apparently in the enjoyment of as good health as he had been for several years. But the Lord had ordained that he should spend the next Sabbath in that region where the weary pilgrim is at rest. Accordingly, two or three days after, on the 16th of April, 1830, he suddenly expired, having only time to take an affectionate leave of his family. He breathed his last, in the eighty-sixth year of his age, with a pleasing smile and countenance, indicative of assurance that heaven was his home and that angels were ready to convey his spirit there. He often said he could not feel afraid of death, and so it seemed to be when the messenger came.

His funeral sermon was preached, the day after his decease, by his grandson, Elder James Garnett, Jr., (who succeeded him in the pastoral charge at Crooked Run,) from 2 Timothy, iv. 7:

"I have fought a good fight," etc. The services were closed by singing a favorite hymn of the deceased,—

"Jerusalem, my happy home!"

It was a solemn and melting time. Doubtless many present remembered, with hearts flowing with gratitude, love, and veneration, the delightful seasons they had enjoyed with this aged, devoted servant of God. How beautifully verified are the words of the Psalmist in the case of the deceased: "Mark the perfect man, and behold the upright, for the end of that man is peace." Precious in the sight of the Lord is the death of his saints.

Elder Garnett was twice married. He raised fourteen children, all of whom have been hopefully brought to a knowledge of the truth, and have become members of the Baptist church, a wonderful instance of the blessing of God on obedience to the injunction to Christian parents to bring up their children in the nurture and admonition of the Lord. Two of his sons, Robert and John Garnett, have for many years been engaged in the work of the ministry.

Elder Garnett's preaching talents were not of a high order, but the purity of his life, and the fervor of his appeals to the unconverted manifesting the most constant love for the souls of men, made a deep impression on those who heard him. His preaching was blessed to the conversion of many. His name and character are held in esteem and veneration by the whole circle of his acquaintance. It was said that he was never known to converse on any other subject than religion while going to the house of worship on Lord's day. In conversation with a brother in the ministry, upon the subject of a careless life and light-mindedness in some professing religion, Elder Garnett expressed his fears that many such were deceived. The brother reminded him of Peter's fall, and urged that such an example ought to induce the exercise of much charity to such professors. "Ah," said Elder Garnett, "I have no idea of feeding Christians on Peter's sins." This sentiment is worthy of being remembered; it may serve as a reproof to some who, instead of taking shame to themselves for giving so little evidence of the life and power of religion in their general deportment, take consolation and encouragement from the occasional stumblings and misdoings of others.

GEORGE LAYFIELD.

It is to be lamented that the memory of a man who was so much and so deservedly regarded as Elder George Layfield should have been allowed, in a measure, to perish. His parents, George and Elizabeth Layfield, were residents of Maryland, in which State he was born, October 27th, 1749. He became a professor of religion in early life, and for several years was connected with the Presbyterian church. He seems to have paid no attention to the subject of infant sprinkling, or even indulged a suspicion that it was unauthorized by the Word of God, until he was allowed an opportunity of hearing a Baptist preach. A severe and protracted contest was carried on in his own mind when he had gained his consent to give it a thorough examination. The regard he felt for the brethren of his own persuasion, and the pride of consistency, prevented him for a time from yielding to the sway of truth. He at length submitted, and was baptized into Jesus Christ and connected himself with the Baptist church.

A short time after this change of sentiment he entered upon the work of proclaiming to others the great salvation. Having removed to the Eastern Shore of Virginia, a wide and effectual door was opened, and he became a most active and successful laborer throughout that peninsula. It was his privilege for several years to be associated with that eminently devoted man, Elijah Baker. Conjointly they were the instruments of originating the church called Pungoteage. Some time after their constitution they gave to Elder Layfield an invitation to become their pastor, which he accepted. This relation he sustained to the close of life. At various periods, also, he statedly served the churches of Matompkin, Masongo, and Chingoteage.

Respecting his character as a Christian and minister it would be difficult to exaggerate. He was remarkable for consistency of deportment. With him the discharge of duty was the result of principle, and it was therefore habitual. In his intercourse with others he was grave yet cheerful. He was universally respected as a man of genuine piety, not being willing to hide his light under a bushel; he was careful to let it shine before others, that they might glorify his Father in heaven. The pastoral office was filled by him with much faithfulness. His brethren, to whom he dispensed the word and ordinances, looked up to him as children to a father. He possessed to the end of his earthly course their confidence and affection; and was regarded by all the surrounding churches as an Israelite indeed in whom was no guile.

As a public speaker his talents were above mediocrity, though his opportunities for early improvement were scanty. By personal application he had succeeded, to some extent, in the cultivation of his mind. He is said to have been studious. He did not aim, in his address, at greatness, but usefulness. The truth was declared in simplicity and godly sincerity. He universally directed his remarks to the hearts and consciences of his hearers. His preaching was generally characterized rather by the exhibition of evangelic, fundamental truths, than the more mysterious and abstract doctrines of the gospel. Toward those who did not agree with him in opinion he maintained a kind and conciliatory spirit, and seemed more anxious to win an opponent to the consideration of truth than to manifest a cold reserve or dogmatic pertinacity. From the best information which can be obtained, his death occurred about the year 1814. He was four times married. His widow and several children still survive him.

JOHN YOUNG.

ALTHOUGH very few particulars respecting the life and labors of ELDER JOHN YOUNG can be obtained, it would not be proper in a work of this kind wholly to overlook him. He deserves a place among those who have followed the Lamb whithersoever he went.

Elder Young was a native of Caroline County. He was born January 11th, 1739. His education was limited, having been confined from childhood to the occupation of farming. About 1770 he was introduced into the liberty of the children of God, baptized by Elder J. Read, and soon commenced the great work of preaching the gospel. He was ordained in 1773, at which time the church called Read's, in his native county, was constituted. The pastoral care of this church was accepted by him. He continued to preach in that vicinity twenty-five years The word of salvation was for the first time carried by him to several parts of Lower Virginia. Nor was his ministry vain. In one year alone sixty or seventy were added to Read's Church through his instrumentality.

In 1799 he removed to Amherst, and the following year became pastor of Buffaloe Church, now called Mount Moriah. Here also his labors were owned with a blessing, and many rejoiced in the God of salvation. Nearly one hundred persons were baptized by him in 1803.

During the early part of his ministerial career he was one of those who passed through great tribulation for Christ's sake. He was arrested in one of his preaching excursions and committed to prison. For the space of six months he remained in close confinement in Caroline jail, until by a writ of habeas corpus he was taken to Williamsburg. In other instances this inoffensive, meek, and pious man became the subject of unholy opposition, because he chose to obey God rather than man, and to preach Christ and him crucified to the people. None of these things deterred him from the pursuance of this great object. To the end of life (which was protracted to old age) he continued a faithful servant of his Master. He was not only instrumental in the conversion of hundreds of souls, but in bringing forward into the ministry many of the most useful preachers of Virginia, who were baptized by him.

Elder Young was not remarkable for brilliancy of talents; few, however, were his superiors in good sense. His gifts were of the useful rather than the showy kind. When he stood up to commend the character and service of his Master, his style was plain but pointed, and his manner unaffectedly simple. Many of those speakers who attract the wondering gaze of the multitude, and are much applauded for their eloquence, present little that is substantial in their addresses. They are more distinguished for noise and show than valuable heart-stirring thoughts. But the subject of this memoir was rather intent to convince his auditors of the evil of sin and persuade them to be reconciled to God, than to display himself.

What gave great efficacy to his influence was the blamelessness of his life. Holiness to the Lord might be seen inscribed on all his actions. Not to himself did he live, but to Christ. In his intercourse with his brethren, and his appeals from the pulpit, he uniformly insisted on the necessity of a holy character to qualify for the kingdom of heaven. And he was not willing to recommend to others what he practiced not himself.

There was one subject which occasioned him much solicitude and compelled him to wet his pillow with many a tear; none of his children, during his lifetime, became the followers of Christ. Nor was he deficient in family government, but sought to instruct his children, and to lead them in the paths of righteousness. The following extract from a discourse delivered by Elder William Duncan, in 1827, will be deeply interesting, referring as it does to the subject of this sketch:—

"In the early part of my ministry," said Mr. Duncan, "I traveled and preached much with a venerable servant of God who has now entered into his rest. He devoted himself wholly to the promotion of evangelical truth, sustaining hunger and thirst, cold and heat, for the love of souls. He once said to me, 'My brother, though I love to preach the gospel, and often feel its refreshing influence, yet one circumstance sometimes creates doubt in my mind. I have seven children for whom I have long been praying, and yet *not one* of them is a Christian. If I were a righteous man, surely my prayers would prevail; but believing God can answer the requests of his people after their death, *I am determined to persist as long as I live.*' What think you of my feelings to-day, when, on my arrival, I was informed that two of this very man's sons had been lately baptized, making, of the seven children, four who had been added to the church since his death? And what, think you, were the joys of this redeemed spirit contemplating such an event? Or, if this joy is reserved for another period, what will be his emotions when he shall embrace them all, in the city of God, and with them swell the eternal song of praise to his Redeemer?—Wait on the Lord: be of good courage, and he shall strengthen thine heart: wait, I say, on the Lord."

A short time after this discourse was preached another of his sons, Mr. William Young, residing near Richmond, was brought to a knowledge of the truth, and became a member of the Second Baptist Church of that city. Thus it may be that he who toiled and prayed and wept for the salvation of his children, may meet them all in heaven as the redeemed of the Lord. What encouragement have parents to persevere in the arduous yet delightful work of bringing up their children in the fear of God! They shall reap if they faint not. God will honor them that honor him.

Mr. Young continued his pastoral relation until he was disqualified for its duties by the infirmities of age. He then resigned his charge, and was succeeded by Elder William Duncan. Still, however, he preached frequently, as his strength would allow. Though worn out in the service of his Redeemer, he was not weary of it. When the period of his death drew near he maintained unshaken confidence in God, and rejoiced with unutterable joy. The family were called around his bed and exhorted to prepare for a better world. "Weep not for me," said the dying saint, "I shall soon be released from this dull clog of mortality. Then shall I be saved from temptation and sin. I know in whom I have believed; I have fought a good fight, I have finished my course, I have kept the faith. Let no pomp be connected with my funeral. Nor is it necessary to wear the customary badges of mourning on my account. I shall soon receive the crown of glory. Will you not all prepare to meet God? I wish to see you in heaven." He requested that Elder John Courtney, of Richmond, should preach his funeral sermon. At the time he died he was perfectly rational, and enjoyed heaven in his soul. The rapturous state of his mind was indicated by his countenance. With a smile of delight and his eyes directed to heaven he breathed his last, April 16, 1817.

Thus was this preacher of righteousness allowed to reach his seventy-ninth year. He had been familiar with scenes of trial and persecution in the early part of his ministry, but lived to see the chains of ecclesiastical oppression broken to pieces, and the cause of truth triumphant. And, in the language of the devout Simeon, he might say, "Lord, now lettest thou thy servant depart in peace, for mine eyes have seen thy salvation."

REUBEN PICKET.

REUBEN PICKET was a native of Fauquier. He was born in 1752. In his seventeenth year his attention was directed to eternal things, and, after suffering much inquietude of mind, he joyfully submitted to the righteousness of God. A short time after his conversion, he was baptized by Samuel Harriss, in the County of Orange. His earliest efforts as a public teacher were made when he was not more than eighteen years of age. It might justly be regretted that the stores of knowledge were not then within his reach, and that his mind was not placed under a suitable training. Such advantages, there is reason to believe, would have been gladly improved by him; but at that early period the facilities for obtaining education were exceedingly limited.

With such opportunities as he did possess, he sought to qualify himself for usefulness. Such was his desire to do good, that through many difficulties he urged his way to testify to his fellow-men the gospel of the grace of God. He found an opportunity of exercising his gift in exhortation during a visit to the County of Shenandoah. In this county a very considerable excitement prevailed on the subject of religion, which allowed him a wide scope for public addresses, while the natural fervor of his own heart was called into exercise. Shortly after his visit to Shenandoah he began to preach. An acquaintance was formed with Elder Koontz, who a short time before had become an efficient Baptist minister. In each other's company, they passed from place to place, declaring the unsearchable riches of Christ; Koontz preached in Dutch, and Picket in English; both were eminently successful in turning men to God.

His labors, at this early period, are thus referred to by Elder Semple: "Mr. Samuel Harriss coming to preach in his vicinity, he felt a great desire to travel with him; but knowing he was not rich, and that his embarrassment would be great unless he followed some calling for a livelihood, he was very unhappy for some time. Spreading his case, however, before his Invisible Instructor, this text came forcibly to his mind: 'Go ye and preach the gospel: and, Lo I am with you alway.' He immediately forsook all earthly employment, and traveled with Elder Harriss, expecting to visit an Association in South Carolina. He was, however, detained by severe illness, and left by his brethren in a strange part of the world. His sufferings, both of mind and body, were extremely severe; but it was only the refiner's fire purging off the dross, and leaving Mr. Picket, like tried gold, to shine with sevenfold splendor. After his recovery, he felt the smiles of God in a more abundant manner than he had ever done. He then commenced his ministerial travels in North Carolina and Virginia, disseminating evangelical truth in various directions. He was still only about twenty years of age. Young as he was, his talents were extensively useful. Many acknowledged him as the messenger of peace to their souls, and several churches were constituted through his instrumentality."

In 1772 he was ordained. He had been the means of originating a church called Reedy Bottom, which was afterwards merged in Mayo, in Halifax County, to whose oversight he was called at his ordination. He continued their pastor as long as he lived, and in this relation was characterized by his activity and faithfulness. He was, however, not confined in his efforts to this congregation. Other churches were frequently visited, especially in seasons of difficulty and trial. He possessed a peculiar talent for binding together the hearts of his brethren, and preserving peace in the church. Among the Baptists he was universally beloved. No man in the Roanoke Association possessed such influence, and no one deserved it more. For many years in succession he occupied the chair at their annual meetings, and always presided with dignity and to the satisfaction of all. As an indication of the esteem in which he was held, the following minute from the record of the Roanoke Association is inserted. This was the session of 1822, the last he ever attended: "Brother Reuben Picket being present, (but from severe bodily affliction not being able to attend to the business of the Association,) in consideration of his great services, and the sincere love the brethren of this Association have for him, he is invited to a seat among us as an honorary member."

As has been already mentioned, his piety and affectionate manners constituted the secret of his influence among the churches. His talents were not of the highest order, but they were of the useful kind. He addressed the heart, and sought to reach the conscience of the hearer. While he was not accustomed to astonish by the brilliancy of his thoughts, he rarely failed to produce a very deep and solemn effect. His appearance and manners were highly impressive. Such are the men who are needed, in this guilty and miserable world, to be, in the most emphatic sense, the "messengers of peace."

Elder Picket was sometimes subject to great depression of mind, arising from derangement of the nervous system. A correspondent, in reference to this subject, states: "In his old age he had his shoulder broken by being overturned in a gig. From this accident he suffered very much, and, being confined at home for a long time, was greatly depressed. Some endeavored to jest him out of this state; but he grew worse. Being visited by a minister, he told him all his sorrows. He, entering into Picket's feelings, reproved those who had ridiculed him, told them that he was really afflicted, and then, addressing himself to Picket, expressed great commiseration for his condition, told him God alone could help him, and proposed that they should unite in prayer. During this exercise his soul was lifted up, his gloomy feelings left him, and he was filled with joy, which continued till death, which took place October 19th, 1823. 'Blessed are the dead that die in the Lord.'" The memory of this man of God is embalmed in the hearts of hundreds of the lovers of truth.

LEWIS CONNER.

Elder Lewis Conner was born November, 1745, in Culpepper, then Orange County, of respectable parentage. His father, John Conner, was a man of the most amiable character, esteemed by all who knew him for his upright conduct, gentleness of manners, and social virtues. He, it is believed, never made a public profession of religion; though some others of his family, besides Lewis, were Baptists. His circumstances in life were moderate, perhaps below mediocrity, and he had a numerous family of children. He was of Irish descent, and his wife, the mother of Lewis, was the daughter of Mr. Charles Kavenaugh, who emigrated from Ireland to Virginia when very young, and by industry and enterprise provided well for his offspring.

As there were in those days but few facilities for cultivating the youthful mind, Lewis received very little education. Naturally possessed of a strong and discriminating mind, if he had enjoyed the advantage of literary cultivation, he would, no doubt, have ranked high in the world of letters. Indeed, without the aid of literature, he arose to a highly respectable standing, and was justly considered one of the ablest divines in the upper part of Virginia. He commenced the world pennyless. Having a mechanical genius, he worked as a carpenter with an older brother, and also for a time with a wagon-maker. When twenty-one years of age he commenced on his own account, and was employed in both trades by a gentleman in the neighborhood in which Blue Run Church was afterwards constituted. In this situation he continued for some time, receiving the most affectionate attentions of his employer and his lady, persons of distinction in their neighborhood. Here those qualities of the head and heart which distinguished him through life more fully developed themselves, and he became a general favorite among his acquaintances. When the term of his engagement with this gentleman expired, he returned to the neighborhood of his father, and soon after married Mrs. Davis, the widow of Benjamin Davis. This occurred in 1768.

About this time a merciful God was pleased to extend the ministerial labors of Elder David Thomas to this county. And here, history informs us, he and Samuel Harriss were instrumental in the conviction and conversion of very many precious souls. Among the converts was Elder Conner. Although before this he had lived without reproach, even more than most of his age, yet, when by the light of Divine grace he saw the exceeding sinfulness of sin, and then the adaptedness of the Saviour in his different offices to the wants of sinners, he was induced to give up all for Christ's sake, and acknowledge Him as his only hope of salvation. He made a public profession of the religion of Jesus, and was baptized, with many others, by Elder Thomas, in the Rapid Ann River. Mrs. Conner, his consort, it is thought, was baptized about this time, but whether on the same day is not known.

Elder Conner at this time resided near the Raccoon Ford on the Orange side, and, soon after his baptism, began to exercise his gift publicly in singing, prayer, and exhortation. In these exercises he was associated with other young converts, particularly Lewis Craig.

They had no meeting-house, but held their meetings from house to house in the neighborhood. The spirit of the Lord, however, being strong in their hearts, their minds were soon drawn to the propriety of building a house of worship. Accordingly, Elder Conner and Lewis or Elijah Craig undertook and built a meeting-house of tolerable dimensions on the land of Uriel Mallory, on Mountain River, Orange County. Such was their zeal that, others perhaps finding nails, they erected and completed the building for the small sum of five pounds. Here a church was constituted, but the writer of this does not know who was the pastor, but supposes it was Lewis Craig. This church maintained her visibility till about the commencement of the Revolution, the effects of which, and removals, caused its extinction.

Among those that removed was Elder Conner, who settled on Cedar Run, in Culpepper, and shortly after on Robinson River, now Madison County. Soon after his removal to Madison he was called to perform a tour of militia duty, and his zeal for the cause of American independence impelled him on to North Carolina, where he served a long time under General Green as commander-in-chief. Shortly after his return from the southern tour he was again called into military service, and was in the siege which ended with the surrender of Cornwallis, at York. It is not our intention to speak particularly of his military career, but enough is known on that subject to show, that whatever he thought it is duty to undertake, was to be done. Peace being restored to his happy country, Elder Conner returned home to provide for the wants of his family. If he had not taken membership at Crooked Run, during his residence on Cedar Run, he probably did so soon after his removal to Robinson River.

During the great revival of religion in 1788, Elder Conner was greatly aroused, and a new impulse was given to the exercise of his gifts in preaching, which had not been so frequent after the dissolution of the church on Mountain Run.

He not only attended with Elder I. Garnett at Crooked Run, but traveled with Elder William Mason to Robinson Church (under Mason's pastoral care) and other places, at which he preached. In these tours an attachment was formed between these two old servants that was never lost.

About the year 1790, Elder Conner again removed, and settled on a farm he had purchased, near where the village of Woodville now stands, Elder William Mason being then the pastor of Ragged Mountain Church, now F T. Elder Conner frequently attended with him at that place. After a short time, Elder Mason being called to the care of Gourdvine Church, then newly constituted, prevailed on Conner to take his place as pastor of F T. The church unanimously chose him to that office, and he was ordained for the purpose, and entered upon its duties in the year 1793, preaching statedly twice a month. This church was greatly blessed under his ministry, and has always been respectable for its intelligence, its numbers, and the piety and fellowship of its members.

Some twelve or fifteen years after this period the church at Thornton's Gap invited him to become their spiritual shepherd, which he finally agreed to do, the church at F T reluctantly agreeing to give up one of its meetings in each month, that their brethren of Thornton's Gap might be accommodated. Soon after this he was called to the care of Battle Run Church, so that now he had the pastoral superintendence of three churches; and, besides, he preached statedly for some time at Salem Meeting-house, where a church was constituted a year or two after his death, under the care of Elder C. C. Conner, his grandson, now removed to Tennessee. Thus was his time fully occupied, and, it may be said with truth, profitably employed. If it can be said of any man ever known, that every one in his churches and congregations loved and venerated him, it is true of Elder Conner.

His opinion was always acknowledged as conclusive on any subject of difference among his brethren; and such was the respect in which his judgment and integrity were held by all in his neighborhood, that disputes on other subjects were frequently left to him, both parties choosing him, and agreeing to be satisfied with his decision.

In June, 1815, his earthly companion was removed from him, in her seventy-ninth year, after a tedious and painful illness. It is confidently hoped, by her surviving relations and friends, that she was prepared to enter into that rest which remains for the people of God. Some time in the ensuing year, all his children having left him to make settlements of their own, Elder Conner married the widow Farrow, and removed to her residence near Battle Run Meeting-house, where he continued to reside till his death. This lady had been a member of Battle Run Church for many years, and was to him an affectionate wife.

Several years before his death, becoming more infirm and residing more than twenty miles from F T Church, at his request, Elder William F. Broaddus was associated with him in the pastoral office of that church, and, after a year or two, growing more infirm still, he prevailed on the church entirely to release him. Not long after he resigned, also, and for the same reason, the care of Thornton's Gap, retaining only Battle Run, which was very near him.

At the time of his death he was but the nominal pastor of Battle Run, the church having, at his request, a short time before, associated with him Elder Thomas Buck, Jr., as assistant. Here he preached his last sermon; and some who heard it considered it inferior to none they had ever heard from him. He lived but a few weeks after, retaining his consciousness to the very last hour, and assuring those around him that he was about to take possession of the inheritance he had so long sought. His death occurred June, 1832, in the eighty-seventh year of his age.

Elder Conner's preaching talents were of no ordinary grade. He was not inclined to meddle with abstruse subjects, particularly in the pulpit. Redemption was the theme on which he delighted most of all to dwell. The sufficiency of the work of Christ to save all that believe on him was the grand topic of his pulpit exhibitions; and so filled was he with this subject that he rarely failed to become very eloquent while recommending Christ to his dying fellow-men. His language was strong, and, notwithstanding his deficiency in point of education, remarkably correct; his voice unusually musical, especially when animated by his own interest in the subject discussed; and, although it is probable he scarcely ever paid the slightest attention to any written laws in his gesticulation, yet his whole manner in the pulpit was highly graceful and commanding. He never preached long sermons, being satisfied, as he used to say, "to reap the *wheat,* without stopping to reap the stubble also." He rarely exceeded forty-five minutes, during which time he would say more than many would say in two hours.

Elder Conner might be considered a modern Calvinist. The writer of this article has heard him preach a great number of sermons without ever hearing him introduce any one of the "*five points*" for special discussion. It would be difficult to say whether or not he was a doctrinal preacher. If he introduced the doctrine of "*election*" it was with a view to exhort the brethren to "give all diligence to make their calling and election sure." If he spoke of "*total depravity,*" it was to urge men to go to Christ for cleansing. If he alluded to the "final perseverance of the saints," it was with a view to exhort the disciples to persevere. He used frequently to remark, "the best proof of the perseverance of the saints is, that they *do persevere.*" In short, whatever doctrine he introduced was presented in a manner so decidedly practical that no sinner could ever leave the sound of his voice without feeling that his duty had been affectionately urged upon him. Next to the Bible, he preferred the writings of President Edwards; and with such light as Edwards supplied him he was in no danger of Antinomian abstractions.

Elder Conner never entered into the spirit of modern missionary efforts. Indeed, his influence was exerted against the mission cause; and, being very considerable in the Shiloh Association, it no doubt proved a powerful means of preventing that body from enlisting in the missionary cause. This opposition may very readily be accounted for, without supposing that he entertained sentiments unfriendly to the spread of the gospel in heathen lands.

The truth is, he was not informed on this subject. He was an aged man when the mission influence commenced in this country. He was alarmed by the novelty of the scheme, and his fears of innovation upon long established Baptist customs deterred him from examining the subject. It is confidently believed by many who knew him well, that if he had witnessed the success that has attended the labors of our missionaries among the heathen, he would have entered heartily into the measure. Elder Luther Rice, who spent many a night under his hospitable roof, used to say, "Father Conner's *heart* is in favor of missions, though he does not see into our present operations." It was apparent to his intimate friends that toward the close of his life he was more inclined to favor this cause than he had been; and the idea is here repeated, that if he had seen what many others have seen of the success of this heaven-inspired enterprise, he would have advocated it with all his heart. Shortly before his death an extensive revival took place in Culpepper County; and while some who now wish to identify themselves with him were crying out "wildfire!" "enthusiasm!" etc. etc., he was rejoicing with the angels over repenting sinners. "Oh!" said he, to a young minister who had been telling him of the displays of God's grace recently witnessed in a revival, "how glad I should be to unite in such scenes; but my day has gone by. Go on, my brother, and the Lord make you instrumental of turning many to righteousness." These remarks are made in order to disabuse the public mind of an impression sought to be made by some who are now opposing everything like efforts for the conversion of sinners, and pleading all the time the example of Elder Conner.

In civil affairs, Elder Conner acted a very conspicuous part. He had given close attention to the progress of those political events which resulted in the present happy form of government, under which the people of the United States have become the admiration of the whole earth. His political opinions were eagerly sought after, and listened to with profound attention by the youth who were growing up around him, while aspirants to office in the county in which he resided never failed to feel themselves much surer of success, if they found the weight of his name and opinions in their scale. Perhaps it may be set down as a misfortune, so far as his ministerial usefulness was concerned, that so much of his attention was given to politics. He lived, however, at a day when the number of men capable of exerting an active influence in political affairs, was comparatively small; and those who knew him will remember, that with all his political knowledge and zeal there was a native dignity about him which could never stoop to do the work of a mere *partisan* politician.

For many years he filled, with credit to himself and advantage to the community, the office of magistrate, and was rewarded for his services by being appointed to the sheriffalty. The duties pertaining to these stations he discharged in a manner highly creditable both to his talents and his integrity. Indeed, he filled all the stations he sustained with so great satisfaction to all interested, that if an attempt were made to fix *a single stain* upon his character it could not succeed. All who knew him will sustain this declaration, and it is a declaration which, alas! can be made to few whose lives have filled so many years.

Elder Conner was once urging in the pulpit the necessity of Divine influence, in order to rectify the human *will*. After the sermon, an individual came to him in a great passion, and alleged that he had preached false doctrine: "for," said he, "the human will needs no rectifying."

"Will you allow me," inquired Mr. Conner, "to ask you two questions?"

"Certainly, sir."

"Well, sir, in the first place, do you believe that it is the duty of every man to submit at once to God, and to take up the cross and follow Jesus Christ?"

"Yes, sir, most assuredly; and if a man does not thus act, he alone is to blame."

"One more question: have *you* submitted to God, and taken up the cross, to follow Christ?"

"No, sir, I cannot say I have."

"It would seem then," replied Mr. Conner, with a pleasant smile, "that your will at least needs rectifying."

Not many years before his death an attempt was made to raise a fund for the purpose of compensating ministers sent by the Shiloh Association as corresponding messengers to other Associations. Elder Conner warmly supported this measure, upon the ground that the "laborer is worthy of his hire." Many, however, feared that it was an entering wedge for increasing the salaries of ministers, and warmly opposed it as a *money-loving* scheme, originating, as some remarked in the Association, in the disposition of the *horse-leech*, which is always crying, "give! give!" The proposition was voted down; whereupon Elder Conner remarked, "You have gained the victory, brethren, but a few such victories will disgrace your body."

The writer of this article has often heard Elder Conner deplore the backwardness of the churches in supporting the ministry. He did not speak this because he was himself in want; for God had favored him with abundance of earthly substance. But he thought it a great reproach to the church, that a minister should be suffered to labor without adequate compensation. Once he was heard to say, when speaking on this subject, "How honest men, and especially Christian men, can get over paying just debts, I leave for wiser heads to find out."

It has been thought by some that his talent was not so great in gathering converts as in building up and comforting believers, in which certainly he was conspicuous. In times of revival, he was always zealous; and his sermons abounded with exhortations to sinners. In prayer he was often sublime, his mind seeming gently to rise from sublunary things to the very portals of heaven; his voice assuming a soft melody that was highly impressive. In singing his voice was remarkably soft and melodious.

In church government perhaps he had few superiors, never favoring one party, but always endeavoring to promote harmony, which he eminently enforced by his own example. In his churches his pastoral duties were performed with fidelity to the Master, though with tenderness to his brethren. There was a conciseness in what he said, on occasions of misconduct in members, that was pecularly efficient and productive of good. One instance the writer will mention which he saw and heard himself, perhaps twenty years ago. A brother, somewhat advanced in years, was called before the church to answer the charge of excessive drinking. He had more than once before been arraigned for the same offence, and his brethren had borne with and excused him. Upon his contrition and acknowledgment they were again willing to pass it over, but requested that the Moderator should admonish him. He addressed him as follows: "Brother, you have reason greatly to love and respect your brethren, for their forbearance toward you. They might well have cut you off from them, and you could not have thought hard of them." The old member observed, "I feel it, and I promise you, Brother Conner, to try not to drink too much any more." "Don't promise me, brother," said Conner, "promise the Lord you will never drink another drop; for so sure as you drink a drop of spirits you will be a drunkard." This was said in his own peculiar manner, and it is believed was completely effectual in reclaiming the old brother, as it is not known that he drank again.

Elder Conner was a constant attendant of the Shiloh Association, and always conspicuous in its business. For something like twenty years he acted as Moderator with no little distinction.

Elder Conner was in his person tall, full-chested, stooping somewhat in his shoulders, which, with the arms, were uncommonly muscular; body short relatively, high forehead, dark and thick-set hair, thin visage, rather prominent cheek-bones, blue and rather small eyes, beaming with the mildest lustre beneath their high-arched brows. Such was the exterior man. In his rational faculties he was highly gifted. Endowed by nature with a strong mind and quick discriminating judgment, lively imagination, retentive memory, mild and even-tempered in disposition, all regulated by the influence of Divine grace, as manifested in his love to God and his fellow-men. The poor, the widow, and the orphan, found in him a friend so far as his means or personal services would go. The children of his first wife by her former marriage (especially the younger, whom he raised,) always venerated him as a father. The young persons of his acquaintance as well as the old eagerly sought his company, delighted with his chaste and interesting conversation. The writer of this poor tribute to his memory can truly say, that he never was in his company an hour at a time without being edified; and if the subject was religious, as it was apt to be, without having his strength and hopes increased.

JOHN SORREL.

JOHN SORREL was among the diligent and faithful laborers in the gospel vineyard, during that period of our denominational history when bonds and afflictions awaited them. His parents were respectable, bringing up their children in habits of industry and frugality. He was born about the year 1754, in the County of Essex. His only surviving son supposes that he and his wife were baptized by Lewis Craig, at an early period of the revolutionary struggle, and that soon thereafter he entered the Christian ministry. His early labors were in connection with Tuckahoe Church, in the county of his birth. This church, in 1819, received a new name, and is now known as Upper Zion. Here the subject of this sketch, where he was best known, seems to have been most abundantly successful. During the great revival of 1788, he was, in company with Elder John Shackelford, engaged in unremitted efforts by night and day, and was much favored in leading his fellow-men to know Christ and his salvation. Upon the removal of Shackelford to Kentucky, in 1792, he was called upon to succeed him in the full duties of the pastorate, and here prosecuted his work with unwearied diligence until the infirmities of age compelled him to lay down the implements of labor. In connection with this church, many, we have reason to believe, will in the great day of decision recognize him as their spiritual father and guide.

In Salem Church also, he much and faithfully toiled. This is one of the best churches of the Dover Association. Upon the spot where its house of worship now stands, where spreading oaks afforded the needful shade, seats were provided, and for several successive summers the indefatigable Noel was accustomed to address immense throngs of people, and was in those early labors essentially aided by John Sorrel. Here, at length, in 1802, Salem Church was constituted. Several years after Elder Sorrel was invited to become its pastor, and continued in this relation for a series of years.

In 1811 a remarkable revival of religion occurred, in which the churches of Tuckahoe and Salem largely shared. The minutes of the Dover Association for 1813, state that "Elder Sorrel, under whose ministry, accompanied by others, this work progressed, says there were above seventy or eighty added to Salem. The revival at Tuckahoe opened a short time after it appeared in Salem. God sent the fire, and he sent his faithful servant, the pastor of the church, Elder Sorrel, to blow the coals. Although more than sixty years of age, he was not slack to do his Master's work. God owned his labor and bade him preach on. More than one hundred were added to the church. From this and Salem the work spread to Bethel and Liberty, which are churches belonging to Goshen Association."

Besides the above, the subject of this notice preached for years at Diamond Meeting house in Essex County. This stood about one mile north of Mount Zion, in that county. The house has been removed and is seen no more. Not so with the effects of his ministry. In all that region the fruit of his labors appears. He also preached at a meeting-house called Haynes, in Caroline County. At Liberty also, and Reeds, he performed much ministerial labor.

On the spot now occupied by Enon, he was for some time accustomed to preach under an arbor prepared for the purpose, after which the people built a house, which he, on account of its proximity to a suitable place for baptizing, called Enon. He continued to labor there until his death. There too he labored not in vain. In connection with those toils, he was permitted to baptize Dr. Alexander Somervail and John Micon, who became eminently useful preachers, with many others.

Mr. Sorrel seems also to have been the pioneer laborer in the building up of Providence Church, near Bowling Green, Caroline County. Here, also, he first preached under an arbor, and in view of the favoring circumstances, all of which were recognized as of God, he called the house Providence, as soon as it was completed. He continued laboring here up to the time of his death.

Besides these regular ministrations he frequently took long tours with his brethren in the region south of James River, preaching, as he delighted to do, the gospel in which he trusted.

Thus lived and labored this servant of the Redeemer. His toils and sacrifices were abundant. But little compensation was received for his services. Yet he worked on. The age in which he lived was unfavorable to proper views of ministerial support. In his own domestic affairs he was judicious, laboring with his own hands, and requiring all the members of his family to perform a share of needful toil to secure a maintenance. Often would he continue at his work on the farm until the time to leave for his appointment on Saturday morning, and return on Sunday night. He was called upon to baptize numerous persons in all the circumjacent country, and never suffered inclement weather to interfere with an engagement. Though the advantages of early education were denied him, he yet, by constant daily reading of the Scriptures, prepared himself for his work. That work was diligently performed.

The death of our aged brother occurred November 12th, 1814. For some time before this event he was afflicted with cancer immediately under his eye; it became much inflamed by irritation, and caused him painful suffering. This prolonged disease he bore with becoming patience. His Heavenly Father's hand was seen in the trial. He would often repeat the beautiful hymn of Dr. Watts—

"Not from the ground afflictions grow,
Nor troubles rise by chance."

His heart was specially cheered by the sentiment of the lines—

"Yet with my God I leave my cause,
And trust his promised grace;
He rules me by his well-known laws
Of love and righteousness."

He passed away in the fullness of the gospel, and now, we doubt not, inherits the kingdom prepared for him from the foundation of the world.

He was permitted to see his family of seven children reach mature years. His wife survived him several years, she having died April 23d, 1830. Their remains lie interred together in the grave-yard of the Broaddus family, not far from Salem Meeting-house. Having been intimate with this family in life, he specially desired to slumber with them in the grave.

WILLIAM MASON.

Elder William Mason was born in Stafford County. At an early period he was baptized, and became a member of the Church at Chappawamsick. Soon after the revolutionary war he married and settled in Culpepper County, and became a member of the Mount Pony Church, of which he continued a member until his death.

It is not known in what year he entered the ministry. It is said his commencement was unusually unpromising: so much so, that many of his most intimate friends attempted to dissuade him from it; and even the church of which he was a member was reluctant to encourage him. But, animated by the love of perishing souls, he persevered until he was one of the most popular ministers in all the region of his labors.

In 1788 he became pastor of Mount Pony Church, soon after which a revival of religion took place, in the progress of which two hundred were baptized. During the same year he succeeded Elder George Eve in the pastoral care of the church at F T. Here also the Lord abundantly blessed his labors, and very many were brought to a knowledge of the truth. Old brethren, in describing the progress of this revival, have often been heard to say, "The heavens seemed to rain righteousness." This revival is well known among the brethren of Culpepper and Fauquier Counties as the great revival of '98. Such a season had not been experienced among the churches in all this region until 1832–33, when the Lord poured out his spirit most wonderfully, and hundreds, including many of the descendants of those whom Elder Mason had baptized, were added to the church. The writer of this had never heard much of the revival of 1798 until, during the revival just mentioned, a brother of Culpepper County gave him a glowing description of the former, and represented the two revivals as being characterized by very similar influences and circumstances.

In 1790, the church at F T had become very large; and as many of the members lived at a remote distance from their house of worship, a new church was constituted in Madison County, called Robinson River, composed chiefly of members dismissed for that purpose from F T. Of this church Elder Mason was chosen pastor, and continued with considerable usefulness until compelled by his infirmities to resign, which he did in 1822.

In 1791, Gourdvine Church was constituted in Culpepper County, chiefly of members dismissed from Mount Pony. Of this church also Elder Mason was chosen pastor, and continued with great harmony and with extensive usefulness until 1822.

In 1803, the church at Mount Pony experienced another precious visitation from the Lord, and great numbers were added. The influence of this revival extended to a neighborhood ten miles distant, where many were baptized and constituted into a church called Bethel. In order to serve this church as pastor, Elder Mason was induced to resign his charge at F T to Elder Lewis Conner. He continued pastor of Bethel with great success, until, prevented by old age and infirmity from preaching any longer, he resigned in 1822.

About the year 1793 or 1794 the churches under his care purchased a farm of about two hundred acres, on which he resided until his death. His whole attention being given to the ministry, he accumulated but little property, and indeed found it difficult sometimes to live comfortably. Perhaps his churches supposed that by placing him on a farm they would enable him to support his family without much further aid from them; whereas, unless he had possessed the means of cultivating his farm, it was worth but little more to him than a house and garden. If churches intend to subtract any part of the price of land given their minister from his yearly support, the gift had better be withheld. They may deprive him of a support by *seeming* to do him a kindness.

No pastor was ever more popular with his churches, and with

the community generally, than Elder Mason. As a proof of this it may be mentioned that he filled the pastoral office at Mount Pony thirty-five years; at Robinson River thirty-three years; at Gourdvine thirty-two years; at Bethel twenty years; at F T fifteen years, continuing with the first four from their constitution until his death; and only resigning the last by mutual consent, when the good of the general cause rendered it expedient that he should accept the charge of Bethel. Indeed, his preaching talents were such as to command the respect of the most intelligent of the community, many of whom sat with delight, and listened to the blessed invitations of the gospel as they fell from his lips, and gave proof that their hearts were touched by obeying the commandments and walking in the truth. At a very early period he gave himself to the reading of the Scriptures, with Poole's annotations; and for his acquaintance with the Bible, as well as for his general correctness as an expositor, he might be classed with the first preachers of his age. Moreover, he was distinguished for urbanity, whether in the pulpit or in private circles, so that his preaching and his company were highly appreciated by all who knew him: his ardent and uniform piety meanwhile endearing him still the more to those who love the image of Jesus.

It is deemed proper to allude here to an instance of weakness which occurred toward the close of Elder Mason's life. It is no part of the writer's intention to conceal facts which may be useful as a warning to others. After having spent the prime of his life in active labors for the cause of God, without a shade ever passing over his character, he unfortunately, on one or two occasions in his old age, became intoxicated by the use of wine. He had for many years been very infirm, and had now become exceedingly weak, so that a very small quantity affected him, and he not being aware of the extent of his weakness, once or twice drank more than his constitution would bear. His acknowledgments on the subject, however, were such as to satisfy his brethren and the community around him, whose fellowship and confidence he continued to enjoy until his death. How important that ministers should practice total abstinence from all intoxicating drinks, lest through old age or infirmity they should one day be overcome, and bring reproach upon the cause of Christ!

Elder Mason was in his doctrine moderately Calvinistic. Indeed, some of his more *orthodox* brethren used laughingly to charge him with "wearing *too* large a cloak." But he had the good fortune to live at a day when among Baptists a difference of opinion upon abstract propositions did not interrupt Christian communion. He was greatly instrumental in breaking down the wall of partition which had so long divided Virginia Baptists into "Regulars" and "Separates." Would to God there were those among us now whom He would honor as instruments of accomplishing the same good end. For since the fathers Fristoe, Conner, Mason, and others, have gone to their reward, certain foreigners have come among us, and have built up this odious wall again. He was a warm advocate of the missionary cause from the time it began to be discussed in Virginia until his death; often meeting with Brother Rice and encouraging him to go on with his work.

BENJAMIN BURGHER.

AMONG the oldest and most useful ministers of the Albemarle Association may be named ELDER BENJAMIN BURGHER. The advantages of a scholastic education were not enjoyed by him, as his early life was almost wholly employed in manual labor. By trade he was a blacksmith, at which he continued until his entrance into the ministry.

At what time precisely he became a professor of religion is not known. His serious impressions commenced in early life, and he was brought, after much painful solicitude, to the knowledge of the truth as it is in Jesus. This was at a period when the influence of the Baptists had not been extensively felt in his native county, and hearing of an Association to be held at Grassy Creek Meeting-house, North Carolina, he determined to attend, though it was nearly two hundred miles from his residence. In examining the Scriptures he saw the obligation of believers' baptism, and felt desirous to be more intimately acquainted with those who, as a denomination, practiced it. Having ascertained more particularly their doctrinal sentiments, church government, etc., and believing them to be in accordance with the word of God, he conferred not with flesh and blood, but "put on Christ" in baptism.

When about thirty years of age, he commenced the ministry. His soul burned with holy ardor to tell his fellow-men the tidings of a Saviour's love. He did not long continue at his trade, but devoted most of his time to the labors of the ministry. The Lord wrought by him in the subversion of the powers of darkness and the conversion of sinners. Several churches, either wholly or in part, through his instrumentality, were gathered together. Among the rest, the church called Mount Ed may be particularly mentioned. It is located in Albemarle County, and was formerly known by the name of Whitesides. The name was changed in 1806, when a new brick place of worship was erected. To this church he himself belonged, and in the pastoral relation for a series of years he faithfully served them.

As a preacher, Elder Burgher occupied an eminent position. In his comments on the word of God he was thought to be clear and judicious. He usually inclined to dwell on the more doctrinal portions of Divine truth; and there was sometimes indulged a degree of severity in defending what are called Calvinistic sentiments. This, in a slight degree, was the result of a natural bluntness of manner for which he was distinguished. Sometimes he would fail in his pulpit efforts altogether, while at other times he was exceedingly happy, and would come from the pulpit with tears flowing down his cheeks, and shaking hands with all the congregation.

In referring to the soundness of his views it should be stated that he was a very studious man. According to the apostolic injunction, he gave himself to reading useful books, but especially the word of God. Being quite independent in his circumstances, and having no children, the larger portion of his time was occupied in this way. His taste for composition was remarkable for one whose mind in early life had been so much neglected. Nearly all the circular letters of the Albemarle Association, for a series of years, were prepared by him. Several poetic effusions from his pen, it is said, discovered some merit; none of them, however, have been seen by the author of this sketch.

Although he was highly Calvinistic in his sentiments, the extremes of Antinomianism were never indulged. It is a mortifying fact that, in some instances, the truth has been held in unrighteousness by those who profess entire dependence on the grace of God for salvation. They have practically said, let us sin, that grace may abound. But the true Christian will forever repudiate such a conclusion. While he may contemplate himself as "chosen in Christ from before the foundation of the world," he will rejoice in the assurance that it was designed he "should be holy and without blame before him in love." In addressing his brethren on this subject, Elder Burgher thus remarks: "We beg leave to recommend the reading of the Epistle of James, which seems to be intended to excite practical piety among believers, that they might thereby prove their faith to be sincere. True believers are called to holiness, glory, and virtue. Faith purifies the heart, and works by love; nor can it ever be said in truth that Christ is the minister of sin; although he pardons sinners, heals the backslidings of saints, and preserves his people from the damnation of hell, yet it is in a way of righteousness and true holiness, so as to manifest his glorious perfections, and the riches of Divine grace in their eternal salvation."

It would not be proper to omit the fact that this estimable man was a warm and decided friend of missions. Although he was advanced in years when the efforts to send the gospel to pagan lands was commenced in this country, he gave it his cordial support. Aged men are prone to look with suspicion on all new enterprises, being unwilling to leave the beaten track which has been pursued by them from earliest youth. This accounts for the fact, that some excellent brethren have not entered with zeal into the various plans of Christian benevolence which characterize the present day. Such brethren ought not to be treated with unkindness, much less ridiculed and contemned. If they are not to be convinced of the expediency of these measures, they should still be regarded as the children of God, their deportment being in other respects consistent. As already remarked, Elder Burgher did not yield to the prejudice that the mission cause was not tenable, because in Virginia no effort was made until 1814. In 1816, he thus pleads with his brethren: "Brother Judson and his wife are now at Rangoon, in the Burman Empire, learning the language, to enable him to preach to them. Another brother and his wife, with a Miss White, have gone to the same place with the intention to help on the glorious cause. Brother Luther Rice, who has formerly been in that country, and who has been preaching and traveling through the United States for some time past, intends, we understand, to return there again.

"And now, dear brethren, what remains but to impress your minds with the duty you owe to God and your fellow-creatures, that you may be induced to lend a helping hand and cast your mite into the treasury of the Lord to support such a glorious cause. Remember, that in time past ye walked according to the course of this world, fulfilling the desires of the flesh and of the mind, and were by nature the children of wrath, even as others. But God, who is rich in mercy, commanded the light to shine out of darkness, and hath shined in our hearts to give the light of the knowledge of the glory of God in the face of Jesus Christ. And how did our hearts burn with love and gratitude to Him who is able and mighty to save! And shall not the heathen world, when they are favored with the glorious gospel and the graces of the Holy Spirit, show forth the praises of Him who hath called them out of darkness into his marvelous light?

"While we are praying for the prosperity of Zion and the spread of the gospel of Christ, let our practice correspond therewith and prove our petitions to be sincere, by lending a benevolent hand to its support. If it be inquired what has God done, we reply he has done great things for us, whereof we are glad; and he will do greater things than these, that ye may marvel. Millions that are yet unborn shall, in their time, hear the gospel of Christ and believe in his name to life everlasting, for the prophecy is gone before, saying, 'he shall see his seed, the travail of his soul, and be satisfied, and the pleasure of the Lord shall prosper in his hands. And it shall come to pass, that in the place where it was said to them ye are not of my people, there shall they be called the children of the living God.'"

In regard to the personal character of our venerated brother, it may be stated that he was held in high estimation by all classes. In his familiar association with men he was cheerful, and sometimes, especially with the young, he would indulge in what might be considered an unjustifiable levity.

Elder Burgher lived to be very aged, and to the close of his life continued to adorn the doctrines of God his Saviour. For some time before his death he expressed a wish to be suddenly removed. In this wish he was gratified. The Lord's day before his death he preached in usual health. He expected to speak on the follow-Sunday, but on Saturday, after having been very cheerful through the day, just before night he walked into the garden, and returning, said to his wife, "I am dying." She proposed to send for some Christian brother, but he opposed it, intimating that before the breaking of day the conquest would be over. And so it was. That night he breathed his last; so softly, so sweetly, that those who were with him scarcely knew the precise moment.

He died November 12th, 1822, in the seventy-eighth year of his age. His funeral sermon was preached by Elder William Duncan, from the words of Simeon: "Lord! now lettest thou thy servant depart in peace according to thy word, for mine eyes have seen thy salvation."

RANE CHASTAIN.

THE parents of ELDER CHASTAIN were of French extraction, but settled in Powhatan County, where he was born, June 28th, 1741. When quite young he removed to Buckingham, in which county he remained the remnant of his days. Though his education was much neglected, his morals were of the most unimpeachable character. In his nineteenth year he was married to Miss Ann Ford, and soon after, under the preaching of Elder C. Clark, was awakened to the exercise of pungent conviction for sin. Such was the sense of his lost condition that he could not refrain from exhorting sinners to repent, although he was himself without evidence of Divine acceptance. "I knew," said he, "I should be lost, and they, too, if God did not have mercy on us, and therefore was compelled to tell my neighbors of their danger; for if I was lost, I did not wish them to be lost with me."

At length he rejoiced in Christ; and August, 1770, was baptized. Immediately, he conferred not with flesh and blood, but began to preach Christ to the people. In April, 1772, Buckingham Church was constituted, at which time he was ordained. He was at once chosen their pastor, and continued in this office as long as he lived, a period of fifty-three years.

From his first entrance into the ministry he manifested a zeal becoming this high vocation. At different times he supplied regularly Cumberland, Providence, and Mulberry Grove Churches, etc. The toils and responsibilities of the ministry were his chief glory. To be useful was his chief concern, and the Lord gave him the desire of his heart in becoming the means of conversion to hundreds of souls. In his history was evinced how much under the Divine blessing may be done by a man of comparatively feeble talents, who gives himself to the work. Many pious men, much his superiors in intellectual endowments, would have failed to fill as he did the pastoral office. An affectionate spirit, united with persevering patience, are absolutely essential to success, if a spiritual shepherd would feed and preserve from wandering the flock of Christ. These qualities were possessed in no small degree by the subject of this sketch. Not as lording it over the heritage of God did he serve, but with winning softness of manner he went in and out among the people of his charge. By his churches he was tenderly loved. They knew how to appreciate his labors, though it is much to be regretted they failed to supply such a support for his family as would enable him to devote more time and labor to their spiritual good. This was to some extent the result of ignorance, as they had not been taught their duty with regard to the support of him who labored for them in spiritual things. Their pastor in this particular was doubtless defective. It is an unscriptural delicacy a minister indulges, when he omits to present clearly and faithfully the obligation of a church to furnish him a competent support. Elder Chastain would sometimes say, if the Lord will keep me humble, the churches will keep me poor. And so it was, for he would often during the week be compelled to plough until the hour for public worship, and again returned to the field. He could truly say his own hands administered to his necessities.

Notwithstanding extreme old age and some decay of the mental powers, he retained his accustomed clearness of thought and honest zeal when engaged in preaching the gospel. At length, after an illness of five weeks, which he bore with Christian patience, he calmly resigned himself to death, in the eighty-third year of his age, having worn himself out in the service of his Lord and Master. When lingering on the confines of life he was asked, by one of the members of his church, if he wished to recover, he replied, "If my Master has anything more for me to do I am willing to stay, but if not I have no desire to recover; but," said he, "I do not think I have any will of my own; the will of the Lord is my will." He retained his senses to the close of life, and the last words he was heard to utter were, "I have made full proof of my ministry."

The following anecdote is related of him: during the imprisonment of several ministers in Chesterfield, he was requested to go down and baptize the converts, who from the prison had heard the word of life. He went, and on his arrival was ordered, on pain of imprisonment, to leave the county. Having refused, he gave notice he should preach at an arbor in that neighborhood. On the day appointed he attended, and having risen, a man with a bottle of rum appeared, and commanded him to come down and take a dram, or he would horsewhip him. Mr. C. replied, I do not wish to drink, and as I am not generally tedious you shall not be long detained. His gentleness of manner subdued the lion spirit before him, and he proceeded with great pungency to preach the truth. He afterwards said, I felt perfectly willing to receive stripes for His sake, who was so willingly stricken for me.

ELEAZER CLAY.

BORN May 2d, 1744. He was in early life the subject of serious impressions, having heard the word preached by Baptist ministers in Halifax County. For several years, however, he remained destitute of hope in Christ. In his own county he was entirely without the range of religious instruction, as the gospel in its purity was at that time but seldom heard. In the latter part of 1770 Elders William Webber and Joseph Anthony, having been successfully engaged in publishing salvation on the north side of James River, were invited to visit and preach in Chesterfield. At this time there was not a Baptist in the county. The Lord was with them, and many were brought to rejoice in his salvation. They met with the most violent opposition, and the magistrates themselves, becoming much enraged, issued warrants for their apprehension. They were thrown into prison and there remained for three months. "But the word of the Lord grew and multiplied." One of the subjects of this good work, an intimate friend of Elder Clay, became deeply concerned on his behalf, and having called to see him, was made the instrument of again awakening his mind to consider the value of eternal things. He soon saw and felt his need of Christ; and found peace in believing. Although persecution was raging, he at once acknowledged his new Master in the ordinance of baptism. This took place in August, 1771. His sincerity and firmness were indicated by the fact, that while he was at that time in prosperous worldly circumstances and possessing much influence in society, and while the Baptists were held in almost universal contempt, he nevertheless determined to identify himself with them.

He immediately commenced the ministry, and in 1775 was ordained and took charge of Chesterfield Church, which had been constituted a year or two previous. He entered with boldness upon the work of preaching Christ and him crucified. Although others were thrown into prison and in various ways most shamefully abused, he did not suffer by the hands of violence. He was a man of dauntless spirit, and the opposers feared to maltreat him. The following is a letter addressed to Elder John Williams, urging him to visit and assist them in preaching throughout the County of Chesterfield. At this time several were confined in the jail, and he being in comfortable circumstances, assisted much in supplying their wants.

CHESTERFIELD, July 21, 1773.

DEAR BROTHER WILLIAMS:

I have long looked for you to come down to see us and the prisoners. We would be glad to see you soon, for we wish you to baptize those that are now waiting for an opportunity. The Lord is carrying on a glorious work in our county, especially below the Court-house. Let Brother Watkin know that the Lord has not passed by Mrs. F., but, as some believe, has placed her name in the Lamb's book of life. The preaching at the prison is not attended in vain, for we hope that several are savingly converted, while others are under great distress, and are made to cry out, "what shall we do to be saved?" Time fails me this opportunity to tell all. The brethren daily look for you to come down; they talk much about you. Remember me to all the Christian brethren. The grace of our Lord Jesus Christ be with you all, Amen.

Yours, in Christ,

ELEAZER CLAY.

Elder Clay did not travel extensively beyond the limits of his own county. There, however, he labored faithfully. For several years before his death he became so infirm as to be unable to attend his regular appointments, or even to leave the house. During this long confinement he evinced strong trust in God and attachment to the doctrines of the gospel. Whenever he was visited by his friends, and especially by young ministers, he never failed to impart some wholesome counsel, the result of his own long experience. To a young ministering brother, who was introduced to him, before he was seated, and while holding his hand, he said, in substance, "I am glad to become acquainted with you, and especially to know you have entered the vineyard of the Lord, and design to labor for him in the great work of the ministry. Let me now advise you never to use ardent spirits. I have seen its baneful effects in the church, and among preachers of the gospel, and would warn every young minister against it."

Although at the age of sixty he could with difficulty see to read even with spectacles, yet for several years before his death his eyesight was entirely restored. He became more and more attached to the Word of God, and besides reading in the Old Testament, he made it a regular practice to read the New Testament through once every month. As he advanced to the termination of his course he manifested an increasing spirituality of mind. In prayer he enjoyed much. The writer will never forget an interview which he was privileged to have with this aged saint, a few months previous to his death. There was a remarkable vividness about his conceptions; and his memory in reference to the history of the church in the days of his youth seemed to be unimpaired. He entered with great spirit in conversation on the value of the great atoning sacrifice, and the necessity of Divine influence to bring the heart to rejoice in it. In alluding to his experience in spiritual matters he manifested deep feeling. He said, with tears rolling down his furrowed cheeks, that he had never known so much of the sweetness and richness of the Word of God as since his confinement to the house; that he had enjoyed secret prayer more than ever. During his conversation he remarked: "If Christians did but know how to prize communion with God, they would more habitually enjoy it; and that he had felt more real happiness during one hour spent in meditation and prayer, than the world knew in a lifetime spent in the pleasures of sin."

The author of this sketch again called to see him, hoping to enjoy the delightful opportunity of listening to his instructive conversation. But he had been the previous evening attacked by severe illness, and was unable to speak. Within a few days he breathed his last. He died May 2d, 1836, in his ninety-second year.

Elder Clay possessed naturally a strong mind. In his manners he was inclined to bluntness, but in all his intercourse with men, it is said, he made it his great business to recommend the subject of religion. He possessed considerable influence among the churches in Chesterfield County, and for many years occupied the Moderator's chair in the Middle District Association.

We will close this brief sketch by presenting a letter written by Mr. Clay to Rev. Isaac Backus, with whom he frequently corresponded. Mr. Backus, in referring to it, speaks of him as a wealthy and most agreeable Christian. The letter is dated March 29, 1799:—

"AGED AND REVEREND BROTHER:

* * * "In the church where I serve we have a great calm. Are not such times more to be desired than when the billows are breaking over our heads? Or, has not God set one over against the other, that we may learn to fear him who worketh all things after the counsel of his own will? In some portions of our district God has granted precious revivals, to wit, in the churches of Brother Sanders and Brother Flowers. Other ingatherings are small; iniquity abounds, deism prevails, and the spirit of the world comes in like a flood on every side.

"God has at last touched the hearts of our rulers, and they have listened to our memorial, doing away all we asked for; so that all the clouds which threatened religious liberty with us are blown over. The Lord grant that neither we nor our posterity may forget his favors, bestowed so freely on us. From your history, you were not then free from the hand of power. May God grant your request, after all your toils, and an abundant entrance into his heavenly kingdom, is the prayer of your unworthy friend and Christ's servant in the gospel!'

GEORGE S. SMITH.

AMONG Virginia Baptist ministers of the eighteenth century is found the name of ELDER GEORGE S. SMITH. He was a native of Powhatan County. He was accustomed from childhood to mingle with the best society, and inclined to be gay and thoughtless. His first serious impressions were produced by hearing a Baptist minister preach, being led to the meeting by mere curiosity; but the Lord overruled the circumstance, and made it the means of deep solicitude of mind. The minister passed on his way. Mr. Smith began to visit the social meetings of the few Baptists which were held in his vicinity. His sedate demeanor, and the spiritual interest shown by him in religious subjects, connected with the fact that he was an excellent reader, induced them to impose upon him the duty of reading for them. Thus, for some time, he was the leader of their worship: reading the Scriptures, while they sang the praises of the Lord and offered up, one by one, the fervent, effectual prayer for the Divine blessing. May we not believe that earnest supplications were offered for the young man, who had thus been providentially drawn into their assembly? God heard their prayer. Mr. Smith found his convictions deepened. He began to perceive the spirituality of God's law, and his own condemnation and ruin. Soon he was led to know Christ, in the exercise of a joyful faith. His countenance now bright, and his step buoyant, he comes with his new-born hope into the presence of the disciples as he had never before met them. Now he reads the Scriptures with new eyes, and in tones never before uttered by him. He is prepared, too, not only to perform the service of a mere reader, but to speak of the Divine reality and import of its precious truths. It was his to speak experimentally of their power, and to call upon all that feared God to come and hear what God had done for his soul. Joyful surprise was felt by all that little band. They welcomed him into their fellowship, and he was baptized as a member of Powhatan Church. This was in 1771.

It is probable that Powhatan Church was formed at this time, and that he was one of its original members, as Mr. Semple makes its constitution to occur in 1771. Mr. Smith now began to excite attention, and a time of refreshing from the presence of the Lord followed his baptism.

Having thus been brought into the kingdom, his consolations were strong and rational. He wished to tell every one he met the Saviour's love, and to recommend him as the chief among ten thousand and altogether lovely. He soon exhorted in public. Having a most excellent voice, he engaged the attention of the people, and by his faithful warnings many sinners were made to tremble. He became connected in the pastoral relation with the Powhatan Church, and for some time supplied Skinquarter and Tomahawk Churches, in Chesterfield County. In these positions, the Lord, through him, effected much good. But he was not long retained. Having made several visits to the State of Kentucky, he at length determined to remove thither, and in 1804 settled in Franklin County, about six miles from Frankfort. There also he was useful. He was, however, soon called forever to leave the field of ministerial labor. A short time after his settlement in the West he was subject to painful diseases, which gradually prostrated his strength, and in 1809 he resigned his spirit into the hands of Him who gave it.

John Taylor, who was associated with him in the same church, says of him: "George S. Smith was a man of great respectability as a man, and much of a doctrinal preacher. Simplicity attended his whole course. His preaching operated but sparingly on the passions of his hearers, for though his voice was strong and sonorous, yet, lacking soft melody of tone, like a Gibeonite in the house of God, he was better calculated to hew wood than to draw water. He continued preaching with zeal and usefulness about twenty years in Kentucky, and died in the pastoral care of a large church, in Jessamine County, called Mount Pleasant."

Elder Smith was, by nature, highly gifted. His appearance was prepossessing, being six feet in height, and of robust form. He weighed about two hundred and fifty pounds. He was an excellent singer, and his manner in the pulpit was peculiarly interesting.

ROBERT STOCKTON.

ROBERT STOCKTON was born December 12th, 1743, in Albemarle County, of parents who were connected with the Presbyterian church. Before he reached manhood he professed religion, and became himself a member of this body. Having been thrown into the society of Baptists, he was led to the examination of believers' baptism, and to the belief that it was his duty to be immersed according to the example of Christ. He was baptized by Mr. Harriss, in 1771, in Henry County. Immediately after his union with the Baptist church he began to testify to the truth that Christ Jesus came into the world to save sinners. Nor was he content to be called a minister of the gospel, without faithfully performing the duties of this office. His labors were abundant. He is said to have been one of the most distinguished ministers of his day for activity and faithfulness. Through his influence many were won to the service of Christ. He was among those who were most active in the formation of the Strawberry Association. Eleven of the churches which compose this body were constituted mainly by his instrumentality.

Elder Stockton possessed excellent colloquial talents. These were well employed in passing from place to place. Referring to this subject, Elder Semple states that he "had always an inclination to travel; and perhaps no man ever traveled to greater advantage. Possessing invincible boldness, it was altogether unimportant to him what kind of house he went to, whether saint or sinner, friend or opposer. He never failed, wherever he went, to enter largely into religious conversation; and having great command of his temper, and much presence of mind, he often made religious impressions upon those previously prejudiced. It was an invariable rule with him to propose, and if permitted, to perform family worship. In doing this, he would often exhort a half hour or more. It was very entertaining to hear Mr. Stockton relate the various adventures of his life respecting things of this sort."

For many years he was chosen Moderator of the Strawberry Association, and filled the office well. His influence was as merited as it was extensive. It is true that his sermons were not remarkable for originality. He did not astonish by the extent and variety of his knowledge, nor gain admiration by the elegance of his style. But he possessed a heart full of compassion for dying men, and an unquenchable zeal in seeking their salvation.

In 1800 he removed to Kentucky, and settled in Barren County. About this time the Green River Association was formed; Elder Stockton was called to the chair, and continued to preside over this body for many years. He was regarded by Kentucky churches no less than by the Baptists in his native State. About the beginning of the year 1825, he was called by his heavenly Master to give an account of his stewardship. In the early part of his sickness he suffered much from the fiery temptations of the adversary, but was enabled to gain the victory, and died in full assurance of hope. He had reached his eighty-first year, having been fifty-four years a preacher of righteousness.

JOSEPH REDDING.

THE parents of JOSEPH REDDING were Europeans by birth. He was born in Fauquier County in 1750. In very early life he was left an orphan, and, with six or seven other children, was placed under the care of an uncle. In consequence of this bereavement they received but little education, though some regard was paid to their morals, being brought up rigid churchmen. When grown, a circumstance occurred which resulted in Joseph's conversion. A Baptist having called to spend the night, the subject of religion was introduced, and a lengthy conversation ensued. The man of God was encountered in argument by Isaac Redding, a brother of Joseph, but was enabled not only to maintain his ground but to defeat his young antagonist. Isaac became deeply convicted. This so enraged his brother that he threatened to chastise him, but Isaac continued his inquiries until Christ was made the joy of his heart. A short time after, when they were together in a large company of young men, at the instigation of Joseph, his brother was caught, greatly abused, and every effort employed to compel him to renounce his religion. But he remained firm, while their cruel treatment was borne with lamb-like meekness. The mildness of his temper amid such provocations led Joseph to serious reflection, and he was soon recognized as a weeping penitent.

Shortly after, Joseph invited Elder William Marshall to preach at his house, and his convictions becoming deeper and deeper, he was almost overwhelmed with the consciousness of his guilt. He at length found pardon in Christ. At that time his views of the sovereignty of grace were so clear that a peculiar cast was given to all his future ministrations. He was baptized in 1771, and immediately began to preach. Possessing a strong voice and much zeal, he attracted notice wherever he went. In company with John Taylor he spread a Saviour's love over a great part of Northwestern Virginia. Having spent two years preaching in his native State, he removed to South Carolina, and there remained, laboring with much success, until 1779; he finally settled in Kentucky. There he became a prominent man, at first connected with the Elkhorn District, but afterwards a leader in the Licking Association. He died December, 1815.

JEREMIAH MOORE.*

Jeremiah Moore was born in Prince William, Virginia, June 7th, 1746. His parents, though not wealthy, were respectable. From an early period in life serious impressions filled his mind, which he supposed prevented him from running into many of the excesses of the times. This excepted, nothing of an extraordinary character marked his progress, until he reached his seventeenth year, when a considerable revolution took place in the neighborhood where he was brought up, under the preaching of the Rev. David Thomas, who was the first Baptist he ever knew. Until now, he never heard a doubt suggested with regard to the truth of the established religion. Curiosity induced him to go and hear this New Light, as Mr. Thomas was then called. He returned home greatly astonished at the gentleman's manner of preaching, the doctrines insisted on, together with his apt quotations from the Scriptures in support of the whole. This brought him to confess it was something entirely new, and looked so much like the New Testament, with which he had some acquaintance,

* By his son, Elder Francis Moore.

that it afforded him much matter for serious meditation; and, although it was several years before he was made to understand the principles of the gospel, he never could obliterate from his mind the effect of this sermon.

As his acquaintances were generally Episcopalians, he resolved, as much as possible, to hide his views from them; and this he found no difficulty in effecting, as his convictions went little further than to persuade him that Mr. Thomas and his Baptist friends were good people, and did not deserve the abuse generally bestowed on them.

On the 1st of November, 1765, being about nineteen years old, he was married to Lydia Renno, daughter of Mr. Francis Renno, whose ancestors were under the necessity of flying from France, their native land, on account of their religion, and taking refuge in the then British dominions. Settled in the world, he was tempted to fly to that false refuge, that it was no matter what religion a man might adopt, provided he be only sincere and moral. His having fallen into this snare himself, he has said, was the reason why, in his public preaching, he so earnestly warned others to escape it. Having come to this conclusion, he became more attentive to the established church, and carefully avoiding the Baptists, would never go to hear them preach, nor see any of them if he could help it. By this time they had much increased, and had advanced near his residence. Several of his acquaintances had joined them; while every mention of them brought up recollections that goaded him to the heart.

On Easter Monday, 1771, he went from home on business, and on his return his servants informed him that their mistress had gone with his mother to the Baptist meeting. As it was now some time in the afternoon he made no doubt they would soon return. But the evening came on without bringing any intelligence. As several of his father's family were at the place of worship, he was sure if anything out of the ordinary course had taken place they would have informed him. At about eleven o'clock at night he heard the company ride up, and Mrs. Moore call for a servant. He went out, and on inquiring if anything had happened, was informed they had waited to hear a man preach by candle-light. In conversation with Mrs. Moore relative to the preaching, he soon discovered her mind was much affected. She observed, "Until now I never knew anything about my situation as a poor miserable sinner, against the best of beings." The conversation was like a dagger to his heart; a heavy gloom oppressed his mind, to a degree he had never felt before. A few days after he went to meeting. The service was introduced by singing Watts's 30th hymn, 2d book:—

"Come, we that love the Lord,
And let our joys be known;
Join in a song with sweet accord,
And thus surround the throne."

But the following words, "Let those refuse to sing that never knew our God," came with power. He felt he knew not God; and deep distress filled his soul. For a considerable time he was left to mourn that he could not mourn. He was tempted to believe he had committed the unpardonable sin; that with him it was too late; God would not have mercy on him; and though he strove to pray, he was often led to conclude the mercies he sought were not for such as he. At length, through the goodness of God, he was enabled to feel the remission of his sins through the blood of the Lamb, to the unspeakable joy of his heart. No wonder, then, that the blood and righteousness of Jesus Christ should be the theme he dwelt on and delighted in for more than forty years. How could he, who knew his own salvation was all of grace, preach a conditional gospel to others?

Soon after he became a member of the Baptist Church at Chappawamsick, in Stafford County, Virginia. His baptism made no small stir among his friends, the most of whom were Episcopalians, and some of them enemies to the Baptists. Some pretended to pity his folly, while others treated him with contempt; and all agreed to give him up for lost as to any future usefulness to himself or family. By becoming a Baptist he gave up a small office in the establishment worth 2400 pounds of tobacco yearly, and with it the friendship of many influential characters. When Elder D. Thomas baptized him, he observed to a friend, "I think I have this day baptized a preacher;" and so the event proved.

Very soon after this a lady (it is believed to have been the mother of Judge French, of Kentucky,) proposed the opening a meeting in the neighborhood, for singing God's praise, reading his word, and prayer, to which he consented, not imagining the work in any way to devolve on him. Here, however, it may be said, commenced that ministerial work in which he was engaged nearly forty-five years, through difficulties and trials, with a zeal and ability that have fallen to the lot of few. Three times he was apprehended by the officers of the crown and conducted to the town of Alexandria, to be lodged in the public jail; and once committed by one of his Majesty's justices of the peace to jail, for preaching the gospel of Jesus Christ. This mittimus is yet in the hands of his family, and will, it is hoped, be preserved, as an evidence of his faithfulness in his Master's cause.

He was blessed with an uncommon degree of health, and with seeing many churches planted as the fruit of his labors. One in the town of Alexandria he mentions with peculiar pleasure, on account of its being located in the place where he was thrice called to answer at the bar of his country for preaching the gospel of a precious Christ, and where he received the sentence of the judge *to lie in jail during life*. From all these afflictions he was wonderfully, and in an unexpected way, delivered, not without hope of meeting in a happy eternity many of these his enemies and their posterity. No doubt is entertained but that the church of Alexandria, at this time, is in part composed of the families that have descended from his most bitter persecutors! The ways of God, oh how unsearchable!

About two years before his death his friends saw, with unspeakable regret, that his accustomed health was fast declining. He, nevertheless, continued to travel and preach, through a district of country from fifty to sixty miles in diameter. His last attempt to speak for his Divine Master was in the village of Centreville. In the winter of 1814, it is thought, by those who are qualified to judge, that his journeying to preach the gospel from place to place would, if directed to that end, have carried him twice round the globe. His preaching was principally confined to Maryland and Virginia; yet he visited North and South Carolina, Tennessee, Kentucky, Pennsylvania, Delaware, the Jerseys, and New York.

A few days before his death he observed to his son, "I have finished my course; the doctrines that I have tried to preach are the stay and comfort of my heart; I know in whom I have trusted. There is one thing, and only one, that gives me the least uneasiness, and that is, that I have not traveled more, preached more, and written more, and in all things been more industrious in the best of causes." His last moments appeared to be employed as was his life, in a desire to spread abroad the savor of His name whose blood and righteousness were all his hope. On February 24, 1815, he left this for a better world, leaving a widow, five sons and four daughters, to lament a loss to them irreparable.

In addition to what is said above by his son, it may be proper to mention that Mr. Moore published two or three treatises on religious subjects, in which more than ordinary talent is displayed.

The mittimus referred to above is in these words: "I send you herewith the body of Jeremiah Moore, who is a preacher of the gospel of Jesus Christ, and also a stroller." To escape imprisonment in this case, it was necessary to obtain from the authorities a license to preach at certain places. Thus, in common with many others of his brethren, he was subject to painful disabilities in attempting to recommend the Saviour he loved—and all under the cover of law.

On one occasion he was brutally assailed by a mob, headed by two magistrates. He and another minister were taken, with the intention of plunging them in the water. They succeeded in throwing his companion into the water, and then they were both released. At various times he was subjected to the scoffing and abuse of his enemies, they breathing out threatenings and slaughter against him.

Mr. Semple speaks of Mr. Moore as a man of commanding talents. He says: "Mr. Moore certainly stands in the front row of Virginia preachers. His person and voice are extremely advantageous; his style is strong and energetic, and indeed elegant, especially as he had not the advantages of early education. His ideas are brilliant, and flow upon him so abundantly, that by some of his friends it is thought to interfere with clearness of arrangement. He is well versed in the Scriptures, and often gives lucid explanations of difficult passages. His system is high Calvinism, which he presents with great ingenuity. * * * His talent for satire is probably equal to that of any other man in Virginia. This he is thought to indulge too lavishly in meeting his opponents. Solomon says, 'Though you bray a fool in a mortar, yet will not his foolishness depart from him.' If that be correct, then it is better, sometimes, not to answer a fool according to his folly. Admitting these infirmities, yet it is doubtful whether any preacher in Virginia has run a more honorable course than Mr. Moore; honorable to his God, honorable to himself, and honorable to his people."

AMBROSE DUDLEY.

A NATIVE of Spottsylvania, and was born in 1750. During the early part of the Revolution he was commissioned to the office of captain in the army, and while absent from home his heart was pierced by the arrows of truth. He saw that he had all his days been waging war against his Almighty Sovereign, and in deep humiliation he cast himself before the throne, pleading for mercy. He was heard; his iniquities were forgiven; he became a loyal subject, and avowed his subjection by being baptized, according to the direction of his King. This occurred while he was stationed at Williamsburg.

It is remarkable that, about this time, the church in his native county were, with great union and earnestness, imploring God to send them a preacher, they being at that time destitute. To their astonishment Mr. Dudley, with whom they had been acquainted from infancy, and who had left home an opposing transgressor, returned a changed man, sought communion with them, and expressed desire to devote himself to the ministry. They considered him as the gift of God in answer to prayer. He began to preach. His first efforts gave great promise of usefulness to the cause of Christ. His manner was zealous, yet dignified, and, under the persecutions which characterized those times, he exhibited the most fearless intrepidity; soon the church became satisfied of his call to the ministry. He was ordained, and continued in that region many years. In 1785 he removed to Kentucky, and, to the time of his death, was one of the most faithful and laborious ministers of the Western country.

Having settled in the vicinity of Lexington, he, with two or three other ministers, built up several churches of the Elkhorn Association. Although he did not travel extensively, yet within the limits of Elkhorn District he was indefatigable in his exertions, exercising a kind of watch-care over that large body. He is said to have been an excellent disciplinarian, and for many years in succession was elected to preside at the annual meetings of the Association. In 1792 his time was employed in visiting the churches, in the character of an evangelist, for the purpose of ascertaining their condition and promoting their spiritual improvement. In this capacity he was useful. Among other things which he urged upon the churches was the much neglected duty of making suitable provision for the support of their pastors. On this subject he avoided that false delicacy indulged by many ministers, and hesitated not to declare the whole counsel of God. In the explanation and defence of doctrinal truth he was intelligent, affectionate, and decided. His influence was extensive.

"His manners and general habits," says Mr. James E. Welsh, "seemed to indicate that 'he was born' for discipline. The very glance of his piercing eye was often sufficient to awe into silence. In his personal appearance he was unusually erect and neat, so that once, when a stranger asked, in Lexington, Kentucky, where he could be found, he was told to 'walk down the street, and the first man he met having on a superfine black coat, without a single mote upon it, would be Ambrose Dudley.' And but few men have ever lived and died in the ministry who 'kept their garments more unspotted from the world.' He was highly Calvinistic in his sentiments, and of unbending firmness where he thought truth and duty were involved. Whenever it was known that he had made an appointment to preach, the universal declaration was, 'whether it rain or shine, Brother Dudley will be there.' He never disappointed any engagement he made, unless sickness or some equally unavoidable providence prevented. In family discipline he was very decided; he never spoke but once. In political or worldly matters he took but little interest, except within the limits of his own plantation. He was a man of God, whose praise is in all the churches throughout the region where he labored. He 'died at the horns of the altar.'"

In 1818, an unhappy difficulty existed in the Elkhorn Association, which resulted in a division. How far he was to blame is not for the biographer to determine. The Licking Association was formed, and he became a prominent member. He continued to labor efficiently until his death, in 1823.

JOHN SHACKLEFORD.

THIS eminently useful servant of Christ was born in Caroline County in 1750. When about twenty-two years of age, he became a pious man and a preacher of the gospel. He was not ordained until 1774, when he undertook the pastoral care of Tuckahoe Church, Caroline County. In this position he remained until he removed to the Western country. His labors in the lower part of Virginia were arduous. Besides frequent journeys in the surrounding counties, he was compelled to toil with his own hands to minister to the necessities of those who were with him. In 1788 especial times of refreshing from the presence of the Lord were enjoyed in Tuckahoe Church, when he baptized more than three hundred persons.

The following is from the pen of Elder Andrew Broaddus: "It was said, and I think upon good authority, that at the time of his marriage his stock of learning amounted to little more than a knowledge of reading. Considering this fact, his proficiency in the science of preaching was really wonderful. About the commencement of my religious profession I heard him often. He discussed a subject with a considerable degree of method and ingenuity; was sometimes a little fanciful, being rather fond of allegorical preaching; but evangelical truth and practical godliness were enforced with warmth and effect, and he was a popular and a very successful preacher."

In consequence of pecuniary difficulties he was compelled, in 1792, to migrate to Kentucky. Alas, how many valuable men has Virginia lost by the neglect of her churches! Though it is the duty of a minister to preach, whether his brethren supply his necessities or not, yet his influence and usefulness will be very much circumscribed when they fail to discharge their obligations to him. It is unquestionably his duty to make provision for the support of his family. To do this, Elder Shackleford sought a home in another State.

After his removal, he received from several churches an invitation to settle among them as their pastor. At length he accepted the call of South Elkhorn Church, with which the venerable Lewis Craig had been connected. Here his ministrations were eminently successful: the church became so large that one hundred members were dismissed to form another body in the same vicinity. The new church was called Mount Pleasant, and soon was enlarged to three hundred and fifty members. As when he lived in Virginia, most remarkable revivals of religion were enjoyed under his ministry.

John Taylor thus bears testimony to his character: "Lewis Craig continued pastor of South Elkhorn for perhaps nine years, and then moved to Bracken County, near the Ohio River. Having been well acquainted with John Shackleford in Virginia, who had lately removed to Kentucky, he advised the church at South Elkhorn to call him to take the watch-care of them. I suppose Shackleford has been in the ministry at least fifty years, and was a prisoner of the Lord in early times in Virginia. He was a preacher of much respectablity from his youth, and his labors were attended with great success before he came to Kentucky. He has been the laborious pastor of Elkhorn Church for more than thirty years. Under his ministrations there have been great additions to the church, several revivals having been enjoyed there. About the beginning of the present century several hundreds were added in one year. A few years past, nearly two hundred were added in one winter."

This pleasing testimony, from one of Kentucky's reliable historians, serves to illustrate the sterling excellence of Shackleford's character, and the moral power he was permitted to exercise in the State of his adoption. Virginia lost much, but Kentucky gained more, because more she needed the zealous evangelist in her wide-spread destitution. Thus, what seemed at the time an evil, was overruled, by the great Head of the church, for good.

But this devoted man was not allowed to enjoy uninterrupted tranquillity in his work of love. The tenets taught by Mr. A. Campbell were introduced into his churches, and, to some extent, were successful in producing a division. Much disputation and unholy feeling were engendered among Christians, while the cause of Christ was exposed to the sneers of sinners. His pious soul was vexed, day by day, as he beheld some of the most fundamental truths of the Word of God assailed and ridiculed by these schismatics. Especially did it grieve him to see some of those whom he had begotten in the gospel so soon turning away to these heresies. He found, however, that his own heart was sustained amid these trials by the sacred doctrines which, from his earliest allegiance to Christ, had been his consolation. He died in 1829, having reached his seventy-ninth year.

JOHN TAYLOR.

Born in Fauquier County, 1752. When he reached his seventeenth year, having heard Elder William Marshall preach, he became impressed with the worth of eternal things, and began to ask, "what shall I do to be saved?" His distress was pungent and protracted. Considerable alarm was created among his friends in discovering his deep-settled gloom, lest he should be verging toward insanity. They were, however, little aware of the true cause of his grief, and consequently were unable to prescribe a remedy. His relief came from the Word of God. There he learned that God was, in Christ, reconciling the world unto himself, not imputing to them their iniquities. Upon this truth he built his hope, and here he found consolation.

In the quaint but nervous style of Mr. Taylor, we will allow him to relate his exercises substantially in his own words: "Through the intemperate use of spirits and what is generally connected with that vice, my poor father had so far consumed his living, that hard labor was my inevitable lot in my raising. He had moved to Frederick County, back of the Blue Ridge, on the Shenandoah River. Here Mr. William Marshall came, preaching the gospel of the kingdom. At one of his meetings I became alarmed. I was then about seventeen years old, and went to the meeting as I would have gone to a frolic. I had heard of the great effect among the people under his preaching. About midway of his discourse—for I had not noticed a word he said before—the truth pierced my soul as quickly and with as much sensibility as an electric shock. In a moment my mind was opened to see the truth of all he said. I felt as if then at the bar of God, and as if condemnation was pronounced against me. It may seem strange, but I instantly loved the very truth that condemned me and the instrument that brought it. I had never felt such an attachment to any human being before.

"From that time I felt a peculiarly tender attachment for all I could think truly religious, though it might be an old African; and, had the world been mine, I would have given all to have been like one of them, though with it I were a slave for life. Some things spoken of by Paul are as incredible as this. He often calls God to witness the truth of them.

"At first the attaining of true religion seemed so perfectly out of my reach and so great a thing, that it never could be mine. This heavy doubt sunk me into dark despondency. Perhaps I never attempted to put up a prayer to God of any kind for six months together. As I was to be lost at last, I concluded I had better try to enjoy myself, or, at least, to please my companions as best I could. Yet sin was a bitter cup, though I practiced it. So I continued for many days; I seldom heard preaching, and as seldom was in company with religious people, for all my connections held the New Lights, as they were called, in the utmost contempt. This early conviction gradually took deeper root, and sin grew more hateful, so that often when practicing it my guilt would become so heavy on my soul I would be ready to roar out aloud. To prevent my comrades from seeing the effect I would abruptly leave them, and, by myself, bemoan my miserable case. By this kind of compulsion I forsook my companions, and betook myself to reading the Scriptures. When I would think of prayer to God it seemed to me both awful and dangerous; awful for a sinner to approach an infinitely holy God, and dangerous, more, than to omit the duty.

"Thus I worried on, I think, a whole summer. At length I began to think that I had forsaken all my old comrades, and with them all my old vices, and read the Scriptures a good deal. I foolishly concluded that I was much better than before, and that I might now begin to pray; that I was now becoming good enough for the Lord to be pleased with my prayers. I became abundantly pleased that I should get to heaven as well as the Baptists, and make no fuss about it. Thus I had cured all my former sores, and was safe without Jesus Christ.

"Thanks to the good Lord, he did not suffer me to continue there. Joseph and Isaac Redding lived neighbors to my father. Immediately after their conversion they began to preach with great zeal throughout the neighborhood. The purport of their preaching was, 'ye must be born again, or never enter into the kingdom of God.' Under the preaching of the Reddings the poor rags of my own righteousness took fire and burned me to death. Till now, in reading the law, I only understood its external demands; but by the removal of the veil from my heart I discovered the sin of my nature. That law which required truth and holiness in the inward parts condemned me for the sin of my heart. Amendment was out of the question; for everything I could do was like the filthy fountain from which it came. Every spring of my soul seemed now an unclean thing, and my best efforts as filthy rags. My prayers, on which I had much relied, appeared abhorrent both to God and myself. My practical sins, that had been numerous, and many of them of a magnitude that, to this day, I can never forgive, were, in a manner, removed out of my sight by the late survey of this mighty port of ill-bred corruptions, that seemed to swarm through my whole soul.

"Should you ask what these corruptions were, I could only state their outlines: as spiritual ignorance, unlawful desires, hardness of heart, above all, unbelief, and all these generating their thousands, while my inability was such that I could not master any of these thousands. My first thoughts under this new discovery were, that my day was past; that time had been when I might have been saved, but now it was too late; and that I was given up of God to a hard heart and reprobate mind. Under these embarrassments I labored for many months. I ate no pleasant food, and enjoyed not one night's rest. My father's family took the alarm that I had gone beside myself, and, to tell the truth, I was driven to my wit's end, believing that I was sure to be lost as if I was then in hell. I was often on my knees crying for mercy, if, perhaps, it might be obtained.

"At length a new thought struck me, that was more distressing than all before, that I never had a day of grace; and though some quarrel with God about election, it had a very different effect upon me. I shall never forget where I was when this thought struck me. I was chopping fire-wood in the cap of a tree, and a deep snow on the ground, more than fifty years ago. Under this thought I was stricken with a tremor, as was Belshazzar when the hand-writing was on the wall. The axe dropped from my hands. I fell on my knees, not to ask mercy, but to acknowledge God's justice in my condemnation. For about one month I do not know that I willingly asked for mercy, though I was often on my knees, both day and night. The purport of my addresses was a confession of the justness of my doom. No spasm could more affect the body than these awful thoughts alternately affected my soul. My conclusion was that no one ever saw and felt what I did till just before God cut him off. A lonesome mountain, where nobody lived, was in full view of my father's home. There I intended to roam the balance of my wretched life. In what mode vengeance was to overtake me, whether by the violence of my own hands or by other means, I knew not. Such were my impressions; and perhaps no criminal ever went to execution with more agony of mind than I went to that fatal mountain. As it began to grow dark, in passing under an overhanging rock, it occurred to me to fall on my knees and acknowledge, what I had often done, the justice of God in this awful sentence. On my knees, I began to whisper something like this: 'Thy throne, O

God, shall remain unsullied and unimpeached when thy wrath is inflicted upon me.' While thus speaking, my thoughts took a new and pleasing turn on the subject of salvation: that the great grace of Jesus Christ has extended to cases desperate as mine; that Christ-despisers and Christ-killers had been saved by this glorious Saviour. I saw the fullness of the grace of Christ, but I could not call it mine. The effect of that view was a sweet peace and calm of mind, such as I had never felt before.

"The mere possibility of salvation was to me like life from the dead; for I had long thought, for reasons stated above, that salvation for me was not possible. What I met at the hanging rock, small as it may appear, was so great to me that I changed my resolution as to dying in the mountain or continuing there all night. I returned home a new man thus far. The style of my prayer was changed. I now began to cry for mercy, as the great grace in Christ had brought possible salvation to such a wretched sinner as myself. I believe I shall never forget the hanging rock while I live, nor even in heaven."

This narrative is thus quoted not to intimate that all these deep agitations of mind are essential to Christian experience. This was not his design. He knew and felt that they originated in defective views of the plan of salvation. The salvation he sought was nigh him, even at first; and he was compelled, after all his struggles, to come to Jesus, helpless, unworthy, and joyfully to confide in him as his only hope. Speaking of the blind man to whom Jesus restored sight, he said: "Though I neither saw nor heard anything, I began to feel as if the Saviour were talking to me, in company with the blind man; and when he answered, 'Lord, I believe,' and he worshiped him, the very language of my soul was expressed, and if I did not speak, my heart repeated it over and over: 'Lord, I believe;' 'Lord, I believe.' My soul so ran in the same way, and I understood more of Jesus Christ in one moment than I had learned in all my life before. I considered him as both Lord and Christ; that he was the proper object of worship; and that it was no robbery to think of him as on equality with the Father. The heavenly joy and peace exceeds my expression."

Hearing that the church of which James Ireland was pastor

would meet to receive members, he went with the determination of uniting himself with the people of God. He found the house crowded to overflowing, and was unable to obtain entrance, but stood at the window and listened to the relation which a number gave of the Divine goodness to them. While there, he was the subject of violent temptation. The suggestion came with great power, that all his religious impressions were a delusion, and that all with whom he was present were deceived. He was inclined to give way to universal skepticism. Returning from meeting in this state of mind, he knew not what to do or whither to flee. In the pleasures of sin he could find no enjoyment, and yet, concerning the truths of revelation, his mind was enveloped in darkness and doubt. He retired to a deep and lonely glen, far away from human habitation, and, as the shades of night came on, he found himself surrounded with so many testimonials of the Divine existence and glory in the spangled firmament above him, and in all the works of His hand, that the righteousness and justice of His law became more evident than ever. Again he felt the heaviness of that guilt which he had contracted, and his need of the gospel remedy. The adaptedness of this plan to his ruined condition rushed upon his mind The words of Christ to Thomas, "Reach hither thy finger," etc., were made the subject of profitable and consoling reflections. With Thomas he was enabled to say, "My Lord and my God." He returned from his hiding-place, willing to tell what the Lord had done for his soul, and shortly after was baptized by James Ireland. He joined the Happy Creek Church.

Mr. Taylor came forth from the doubt and perplexity in which he had so long remained, not only with a joyous elasticity of mind, but with a hearty purpose to live to God. The necessities of the times, as well as a sense of obligation to his Almighty Deliverer, prompted him to consider the question of entering the ministry. He says: "I was now in my twentieth year. I found the church no place of ease to me, for, among other distresses, I felt a new one occurred. I soon began to feel great anxieties to communicate what I felt and knew of Christ to my fellow-men. This was to me a great source of perplexity on account of my unpreparedness for so great a work. Joseph Redding soon moved to South Carolina. Isaac Redding holding meetings in the neighborhood, it came on as a thing of course, to give him some aid, so that, in a few months, I became a public speaker. My conclusion was, that I could live nowhere but with Joseph Redding. The next winter I traveled to South Carolina, to live there, or have him return with me. We returned in the spring, and the church called me to preach. Why the church did this is yet a wonder to me; for, though I was twenty years old, I was only a fit associate for mill or school-boys. My lack of information filled me with dismay. My boyhood was such, even in stature, that it seemed to forbid me to address grown people.

"About four years after I began to preach, I was ordained as an itinerant minister. The Presbytery that officiated were Lewis Craig, John Picket, John Koontz, Joseph Redding, and Theodorick Noel. In those days I had three gospel fathers: William Marshall, the instrument of my awakening and conversion; James Ireland, who baptized me, and under whose pastoral care I lived some time; and Joseph Redding, with whom I traveled nearly ten years."

With Joseph Redding Mr. Taylor was intimately associated. These two servants of Christ, with apostolic zeal and courage, carried the sound of salvation into regions it had never reached. They were two of the most daring spirits of that age. Very frequently their journeys were extended beyond the Blue Ridge more than two hundred miles. This was then a thinly settled country. In these western excursions they were received with open arms. They were not, like their eastern brethren, subject to the opposing rage of the established church; but they were not without trials. Most of their journeys were performed on foot, over a rugged and almost unbroken wilderness; and they were continually in danger of falling a prey to the savage barbarities of the Indians, as they passed on from fort to fort. The good hand of the Lord alone preserved them. In hunger and thirst, in watchfulness and weariness, did Mr. Taylor go forth to preach the gospel. He could say:—

"In these mountains let me labor;
In these forests let me tell
How he died, the blessed Saviour,
To redeem a world from hell."

As illustrative of the trials and exposures of this pioneer missionary, we extract a passage from his own account of these early labors: "After ranging through the large County of Hampshire a year or two, we contemplated passing the Alleghany Mountains to the back settlements on Monongahela River. Our destination was Tygarts Valley. This valley was estimated at fifty miles long, and newly settled by about one hundred families. I found but one Baptist, a woman; but I thought her a precious Christian. This tour was in the middle of winter, and the snow knee-deep. The distance from one settlement to the other was about fifty miles. The track was such that it took two days to get there; of course we camped out one night in the deep snow. For the first time we saw people living in a fort. We then set out for Greenbrier. The next June, I concluded to take a more extended tour. Monongahela River has five large branches; these were all peopled. Our first stop was at Ghent River, where a little settlement of Baptists was found. Here we worshiped awhile. All the settlements in the great glades, a space of sixty miles, had been broken up by the Indians. The next place was about thirty miles, bearing down toward Red Stone, where was a considerable settlement of people, and a small Baptist church, which had been constituted by John Corbley. After this, Mr Corbley's family was killed by the Indians. The house was filled with people who came to hear preaching.

"Thence we crossed over the Main River, and ranged up the main bank, where we had some happy meetings. From this settlement it was a day's ride to Buchanon River, where I think preaching had never been. The people were either forted or huddled together in block-houses. These poor creatures would risk all they had, and their lives also, that they might get together to hear preaching. There we had several meetings, and the people were much affected. From Buchanon, one day's ride, through gloomy forests, brought us to Tygarts River. The next winter, dreary indeed, I visited all these settlements again."

Another tour is thus referred to: "It was thirty miles from the upper house in the valley to the first house in the Greenbrier settlement, and over a tremendous mountain that divided the two rivers. The track was very dull; I was a stranger to the way, and without company. The river was from twenty to thirty yards wide where I set out, to the source of which I had to travel before I ascended the mountain. The river was so blocked up with ice that it seemed impossible for my borrowed, bare-footed horse to cross it. I thought of going back, but concluded to push on. I took my wrappers from my legs, and placed my horse's fore-feet in the middle of them, and tied them round his legs with my garters. But I could not get him to take a step on the ice. My only remedy was to lead him to some little steep bank two or three feet high, and suddenly push him on the ice, and then lead him across. This was often repeated, for we had to cross the river nearly twenty times. The cold was so intense that it was doubtful if my ears and hands would not freeze. I reached the house about sundown."

A volume might be filled with a reference to his exposures and sufferings in his numerous journeys over the Blue Mountains and Alleghany Glades. No difficulties hindered, no dangers affrighted, if he might but preach in these sparsely-settled regions the Word of Life. On one occasion he remained in a stupor for several days, after wading swollen streams and becoming nearly benumbed by the severity of the cold. At another time in crossing the Glades his horse escaped, and carrying on his back his saddle and bags, he wandered for nearly forty hours without food, spending one night in this exposed condition. His horse was never found.

"Taylor was not imprisoned as were many of his brethren in Eastern Virginia. But he was not free from persecution. He speaks of the 'rage of mobs' with which he was assaulted, and 'open contradiction while preaching.' On one occasion, 'armed with instruments of death, twenty young men approached him and his friends in the midst of their worship, beating some and driving the others from the place.'"

The labors of this indefatigable man were not confined to these frontier settlements. He says: "The apparent call for constant traveling bore with great weight upon my mind, though with much misgiving of heart arising from my own inadequacy. I not only kept up my range with Redding in the backwoods, but below the Blue Ridge on each side of the Rappahannock River, where

I became acquainted with several of the laborious servants of the Lord: as Theodorick Noel, Lewis Lunsford, Nathaniel Sanders, all the Craigs, George Eve, Thomas Ammons, John Leland, John Shackleford, John Picket, and many others, all of whom, from my soul, I preferred to myself."

In one of these visits to the Northern Neck, he speaks of a great revival of religion through that country, during which Lewis Lunsford and others had been baptized. He says: "In every direction there was such a call for preaching day and night, that it required the best of lungs in the speaker to bear the service. Though the nights were short, the houses would not hold the people. I have known the preacher stand in the yard, the bright moonlight such that without a candle hundreds would remain and listen to the gospel. Respectable young ladies would walk ten miles on those pleasant sandy roads, rather than miss the happy night-meetings. Perhaps our modern young ladies, who love carnal pleasure, novels, and theatres more than they love the worship of God, may blame them as imprudent; but God has decided already in their favor, and against these daughters of Diana and Venus. This revival spread over a great part of the Northern Neck, and many hundreds were baptized."

The ministry of this itinerant was greatly blessed; several churches were founded, mainly under his influence. In 1783, he found it, as he believed, his duty to seek a support in the fertile fields of the West, as, notwithstanding his toils in Virginia, the churches contributed but little to provide for his necessities. One year previous to this he was chosen pastor of the church he first joined. When he removed he settled in what is now called Woodford County, then comparatively a wilderness. He was well qualified to labor as a pioneer, having learned, by his previous hazards in Virginia, to endure hardness as a good soldier of Jesus Christ. "Often single-handed," says a brother who knew him well, "did he occupy this wide-spread region. He itinerated for ten years with much credit to himself and profit to the cause. He had a fine constitution and much bodily strength; was as bold as a lion, yet meek as a lamb. In preaching he attempted nothing but scriptural plainness. The weapons of his warfare were wielded with much power. No man knew better than he how to reprove, rebuke, and exhort, with all long-suffering and doctrine. When he used the rod of correction all were made to tremble. The Lord wrought glorious things by him. The Elkhorn Association soon increased to the number of thirty-four churches. This was the best organized body of Baptists in all the Western country. In 1800, more than three thousand souls were added to them."

The same hardships borne in Virginia were endured in his new Western home. He located in the wilderness in the midst of hostile Indians, preaching as often as possible to the scattered families around him. He says: "We had to pack corn forty miles, and then send a mile to grind, at a hand-mill, before we could get bread. As to meat, it must come from the woods. Soon after I settled in my little cabin, sixteen feet square, with no floor but the natural earth, without bedstead, table, or stools, I found that an old buck had his lodge a few hundred steps from my cabin, among the nettles, high as a man's shoulders, and interlocked with pea vines. Those nettles the next winter we found very useful in getting the lint, and, with the help of buffalo wool, made good clothing for our people. I went many mornings, hoping to get a shot at this buck, but had not the skill to get hold of him; at length I got a fire at him, and accidentally shot him through the heart. This was a greater treat to my family than the largest bullock I have ever killed since, for he was large and very fat."

Speaking of a single day's work, which seemed extraordinary, he says: "I name this day's work that it may be accounted for how I have cleared nearly four hundred acres of land in the heavy forest of Kentucky, besides making other improvements." Having married in Virginia an interesting lady, and now beginning to have quite a family, he thus found it necessary, in this early settlement in a new country, to toil laboriously with his own hands for their support.

"John Taylor was one of the most efficient preachers; his judicious zeal, strong faith, and remarkable industry, qualified him to be useful to many souls. He was always cheerful, yet solemn, and willing to preach when requested. His whole demeanor, at home and abroad, was uniformly Christian-like. The labors of his ministry extended from Kentucky River to the Ohio. It was his custom to visit six or eight Associations every year. His great skill in discipline and faithfulness in preaching endeared him to all the followers of Christ."

This testimony is borne by one of his surviving coadjutors in Kentucky. Nor is it to be considered as the extravagant eulogy of a particular friend. From other sources this statement is ascertained to be true. Says the same brother: "He was, however, only a man, for, in the latter part of his life, he opposed missionary operations." There is reason to believe that this opposition was the result of ignorance. He had failed to make himself acquainted with the design, plans, and success of the mission enterprise. His ignorance was indeed culpable, for it was his duty to examine well the claims of these measures. Had he, with unprejudiced mind, contemplated the condition of the heathen world, in connection with the mandate of the ascended Saviour; had he known what almost incredible success has attended the efforts of God's people in foreign lands, his pious heart would doubtless have rejoiced with unutterable joy, and his whole influence been given to the cause.

That this is true, will be evident from the allusion to this subject by another brother: "I mentioned to him," says he, "in 1830, that I wished some conversation concerning the pamphlet he had written against missions; when the aged saint replied: 'Oh never mind that thing; let it sleep in silence;'" so that there is reason for believing he regretted he had ever written so unadvisedly against the mission cause.

He removed several times, but at length settled near Frankfort, where he spent the remnant of his days. There he ended a long, useful, and happy life. At the time of his death he was in quite a joyful state of mind. It was his desire to depart and be with Christ. His removal took place in 1833, having reached his eighty-first year.

We close this sketch with an interesting quotation from a work he published, entitled History of Ten Churches. "The greatest encouragement I have found is from the Bible. There I saw the whole will of God, in point of both opinion and practice. What I saw in this heaven-born book I received as the voice of God, and it was the invaluable guide of my whole man. To this I appeal in all controversy, and by this I expect to be judged at the last day.

"Of all the outward religious duties in which I have ever been employed as to conscious satisfaction, baptism takes the lead, and in that blessed work three different days exceed. The first was the evening after I was baptized; the second was the same day, fifty years after my own baptism, when I baptized a number of people; lastly, on my birth-day, when I was seventy years old, I baptized eighteen persons. I suppose I have gone into the water hundreds of times to baptize others, and in every case a sweet peace of conscience attended me."

It is thought well to insert a few brief extracts, written by him on various subjects, as expressive of his views, and illustrative of his plain, strong, blunt style.

"*A barren ministry.*—Can anything be more plain, that the calls and invitations of the gospel are to be addressed to all mankind? To me, it is evident that nothing but a cold, cramped, disobedient heart could object to it; and the preacher who does not practice it, I know what o'clock it is with his soul; I consider him an apostate from the gospel spirit. I take the opportunity of confessing my own apostasy in this case. Of the fifty-four years of my ministry two-thirds at least I have been too destitute of that tenderness of spirit that becomes the gospel; and just in proportion to the coldness and barrenness of my soul have I neglected to invite sinners to repent of their sins and come to Christ. With shame before the Lord I confess my apostasy from a gospel spirit. In those days I would be as busy as ever, (for I was never considered a lazy man,) but it would be about trifles: as, whether Adam was a natural or a spiritual man; when he was first made; whether he died a moral or spiritual death; when he first sinned; whether God's election was so definite that it could not be added to or taken from; whether regeneration and the new birth were different or the same thing; and many other poor trifles of the same kind.

"*The tongue.*—The Saviour says, the good man, out of the good treasure of his heart, bringeth forth good things, and the evil man, out of the evil treasure of his heart, bringeth forth evil things. The way these good or evil things are brought forth is by the use or abuse of the tongue. A house of merchandise hangs out part of its wares that passengers may see what is in the shop. The tongue is an expression of what is in the man, and is the landing-port of all the cargo of the heart, whether the lading be good or bad, for out of the abundance of the heart the mouth speaketh. Please examine what kind of lading is discharged at tongue-port by you.

"*Tenderness toward the brethren.*—I have spoken of Christ's people as the apple of his eye. How tender a member is the eye, and especially the apple of it. Let us always touch each other with tenderness, being mindful that when we attempt to take a mote from a brother's eye we should first get the beam from our own While, with a silken cloth, my friend proposes to wipe the mote from my eye, let me take it kindly. As in that case the eye always gives its aid, by the flowing tear, to remove the mote from its painful location, so when my brother comes to me in the letter and spirit of the eighteenth of Matthew, let me feel his touch as with a soft hand, and with a melting heart and flowing tears let me aid him to remove the incumbrance.

"*Useless professors.*—The man that gives place to the devil so as to be nothing in the church, though nominally a member, is what the devil has made him, a mere cipher there. A hundred such would not make a church; a thousand ciphers will not make the number one. Every way they turn they seem to be nothing. There is more trouble to get them to fill their seats in the church than their services are worth.

"*The work of the Spirit.*—The word of faith, or the Scriptures, will ultimately overcome the world. The whole book of God is a birth of the spirit, for holy men of old spake as they were moved by the Holy Ghost. I consider every good sermon, exhortation, or prayer to God, a birth of the spirit; the bringing forth of those gifts the spirit has bestowed on His church for the benefit of mankind."

WILLIAM HICKMAN.

This venerable and truly useful servant of Christ was born February 4th, 1747, in King and Queen County, Virginia. He professed religion during those seasons of ecclesiastical violence when devoted and useful ministers of the gospel were seized and immured within the walls of prisons, and by various other methods most cruelly persecuted. The whole of Eastern Virginia at that period presented a spectacle of almost universal suffering among the despised Baptists. But the Word of God grew and multiplied. In the County of Chesterfield, while several ministers were preaching from the windows of the jail, scores were converted to God, among whom were many who afterwards stood up as public witnesses of the truth ; of this number was William Hickman, the subject of this memoir.

Referring to the period when his attention was first arrested by religious matters, he remarks: "Curiosity led me to go some distance to hear these babblers. The two precious men were John Waller and James Childs. When I got to the meeting I could not get sight of the preachers, there was such a multitude of people. God's power attended the Word, and numbers cried out for mercy. I went home heavy-hearted, knowing myself to be in a wretched state. I informed my wife what I had seen and heard. She was much disgusted for fear I would be dipped too. She begged I would not go again, but I told her I must go and see them dipped. I went the next day; and an awful day it was to me. One of the ministers preached before baptism, and then moved on to the water, nearly a quarter of a mile. The people moved in solemn procession, singing. Many tears were dropped, and not a few from my own eyes."

He afterwards removed to Cumberland County, where he first heard David Tinsley, one of the most distinguished men of his time. He refers in strong language to the first sermon he heard from Tinsley, from the passage, "Thou art weighed in the balance, and found wanting." He says: "He let us know how we are indebted to God's righteous law, and if we could live as holy as an angel in heaven to the end of our days, he asked, how are we to atone for all our past sins? God, by his Holy Spirit, I trust, sent it home to my heart."

After various conflicting emotions, he was led to proper views of the plan of salvation. When he could thus rely on Christ, he says: "That was one of the happiest nights I ever experienced in all my life. The next morning, when I rose and looked out, I thought everything praised God; even the trees, grass, and brutes praised God." He states that he "heard no voice," and "had no particular Scripture applied to his heart." The thought of "sins pardoned through the atoning blood of the blessed Saviour," was the all-cheering ground of his hope and joy. He adds: "I thanked God for all his favors. In the month of April I was baptized by that worthy old servant of God, Reuben Ford, who baptized my wife the fall before. We both joined the church after being baptized."

After making a public profession of religion he visited the State of Kentucky, and while there, in 1776, according to Elder John Taylor's history, he began to preach. Returning to Virginia, he was greeted by his brethren with joy as a herald of the gospel. Multitudes flocked to hear the words at his lips, and his message was attended with saving influence. In the southern part of Chesterfield County especially, was his ministry successful; for here, in 1778, he was instrumental in the formation of Skinquarter Church. He became their pastor, and sustained this relation until his removal to Kentucky. In 1781 the church called Tomahawk also secured his services, and enjoyed the benefit of his labors for three years.

His own quaint style is here quoted, as descriptive of his first visit to Kentucky: "On the 23d of February, 1776, I started from home with five others, to wit, George S. Smith, Edmund Wooldridge, William Davis, Thomas Wooldridge, and Jesse Low, and in the back parts of Virginia we were joined by Peter Harsten, Christopher Urvin, and James Parberry. We came to the resolution, three of us being professors, to have prayer every night. Our new companions in their hearts opposed it, but submitted, and behaved well. We had to travel over a small and miserable track, over mud, and logs, and high waters."

Exposed to the perils of such a journey, he passed on until what is now called Harrodsburg, Kentucky, was reached, on the first day of April. He speaks of the town as having "a row or two of smoky cabins," and the men found there "with their breech-clouts, hunting-skirts, leggins, and moccasins." He says: "I there ate some of the first corn meal raised in the country, though but little of it, as they had a very poor way of making it into meal. We learned to eat wild meat, without bread or salt. We went nearly every Sunday to hear Thomas Tinsley preach. Mr. Tinsley was a good old preacher; Mr. Morton was a good pious Presbyterian, and love and friendship abounded. I generally concluded Mr. Tinsley's meetings. One Sunday morning he laid his Bible on my thigh, and said, 'You must preach to-day.' I took the book, and turned to the 23d chapter of Numbers, and the 10th verse. I suppose I spoke fifteen or twenty minutes."

As already observed, he returned to Virginia and remained, toiling in the ministry with much success. Concerning his second visit to Kentucky, he says that he wound up his affairs, and started on the 16th of August, 1784. In preaching his last sermon he represents it as a failure, for he was entirely unmanned. He thus refers to the separation: "There were a number of preachers present, and a weeping time it was. When we began our journey Brother George Smith was with us, and assisted us in our packages. Several of our friends followed us a day or two, and Brother Smith went to help us along, for at least one hundred miles. My oldest son, about seventeen years old, was the best hand I had. The other boys did their part as well as they could. After our friend Smith left us we were more lonesome, and missed his advice and aid. We took plenty of provisions, and drove two milch cows, that gave milk for the children and my wife's coffee. The fatigues of the journey are too tedious to mention. We proceeded through the wilderness. It rained almost every day, which made it dreadful traveling. The waters were deep, and no ferry-boats. The children and myself were wet, both day and night. I had written to George S. Smith to meet us. The night before we got in he came loaded with bread and meat. The next day we arrived at his cabin, about an hour by sun, the ninth of November. Wet and dirty, poor spectacles we were, but, thank God, all in common health. The Lord was with us through the whole journey."

Thus this servant of Christ, literally a pilgrim, passed these weary days and nights in the wilderness. Nearly three months of exposure to savage Indians, and all the other dangers of the way, we need not wonder how joyfully he reached the few brethren who had gone before him. His arrival was on Saturday. We might suppose that the next day would be passed in repose; but no! he prepares for the public worship of God. He could well appreciate the words of an inspired writer, "How amiable are thy tabernacles, O Lord of Hosts!" "The next day," he says, "which was Sunday, there was meeting, and as unprepared as I was, I had to preach. Three other preachers were there. I spoke from the Fourth Psalm, 'The Lord hath set apart him that is godly for himself.' I was followed by a Methodist preacher."

He doubtless could understand and feel the purport of the text from which he discoursed, on that memorable day. The inspiring influence of the sentiment it was his to attest by happy experience.

Referring to a visit from John Taylor, he says: "Brother John Taylor came from the north side and preached at a Brother Robertson's. William Bledsoe was there. Brother Taylor took his text, 'Christ is all, and in all.' I fed on the food. It was like the good old Virginia doctrine."

Thus, in 1784, he became a permanent resident of the State of Kentucky. Here he encountered peculiar trials. The whole of that country was but sparsely populated, while tribes of wandering savages were continually making depredations on the property and lives of the settlers. But he did not allow himself to remain within the narrow compass of the neighborhood in which he lived. For a number of years, at the peril of his life, he visited the frontier settlements, carrying the tidings of redemption through the Son of God. The church known by the name of the "Forks of Elkhorn" selected him at that early period for their under-shepherd, and this position he occupied for many years. In this church alone be baptized more than five hundred persons. Besides the labor given to this church, he statedly served other churches in various directions. Elder John Taylor states, that perhaps no man in Kentucky has baptized more converts than William Hickman.

With reference to his labors in Kentucky, as illustrative of his attendant exposures and trials, a rather long but exceedingly interesting extract from his own narrative is herewith appended. After describing the circumstances of a providential call to visit a destitute and thinly settled portion of what is now Shelby County, and the many difficulties in his way, he proceeds :—

"We crossed the river one at a time, and swam our horses by the side of the canoe. When we all got over, and put our saddles on, the moon was shining. We then had twenty miles to go in the night. Sometimes it was snowing, and then the moon shining. We crossed Benson nineteen times. At some fords the ice would bear us over, at other fords some steps would bear us, the next step we would break in. We continued this disagreeable road until we fell on the waters of what was then called the Fish Creek. We passed a number of evacuated cabins, the owners of which had either been killed or driven off by the Indians. It was a very cold night. We had no watch along, but we judged it must have been two o'clock in the morning when we called at the fort gate for admittance. The old gentleman was not at home, and the old lady had all barred up. It was some time before we could convince her who we were, as she was afraid of a decoy. But at last she let us in. The weather being so cold, she had given us out; but she soon had a good fire raised, and a warm supper, or rather breakfast; put all to bed, and covered us up warm.

"Early in the morning she sent out runners to the different forts, and about noon collected one of the rooms nearly full of people. About two years before, a small church was constituted by two old ministers, Brother William Taylor, of Nelson, and John Whitaker, of Jefferson. I believe eight in number. The Indians were so very bad among them that they scattered, and kept up no government. They could not meet together, and nobody preached to them till I went as above named. I preached on Saturday night and Sunday to nearly the same people, and knew none of them but what went with me. On Sunday night I went about a mile to another fort, and I hope the Lord did not send me there in vain. On Monday morning I was to start home. This short visit attached our hearts to each other. They insisted very hard for me to leave them another appointment. At last I consented to come again.

"I repeated my visits to them, and baptized a number. The church grew. While going from meeting to meeting, sometimes twenty or thirty in a gang, we were guarded by the men. It looked more like going to war, than to a meeting to worship God. They urged me hard to move among them. I told them that request could not be granted; I had not long been moved to Elkhorn; I was attached to my people there; I could not leave them; besides all, they had given me a little home; I felt bound to them as long as I lived. Buying and selling never was my object. Then they told me if I could get some good minister to come and live with them, it would be what they wished. I told them I would do my best for them. Brother Joshua Morriss had just moved to the country, and I thought he would suit them. I saw Brother Morriss, told him the situation of that people, and their wish. He consulted himself and family. I told him if he would take a tour there, I would go with him. We both went. Himself and people were pleased with each other. Soon after he moved, and his labors were much blessed. The church grew and flourished; but many a tour I took with him, long circuits round, till at last, concluding they were well supplied, I gave out going so often. But now I know of no county in the State so well supplied as Shelby—flourishing churches and good ministers. Great changes have turned up in thirty odd years. I went in front there, through cold and heat, in the midst of danger, but my God protected me till now; blessed be his name!"

He lived to see a very old age. In 1822 it was remarked, by one of his most intimate fellow-laborers, "Though now about seventy-six years of age, he walks and stands erect as a palm-tree, being at least six feet high, and of rather slender form. His whole deportment is solemn and grave, and is much like Caleb the servant of the Lord, who at fourscore years of age was as capable to render service in the war as when young. This veteran can yet perform a good part in the gospel vineyard. His style of preaching is plain and solemn, and the sound of his voice like thunder in the distance; but when he becomes animated, it is like thunder at home, and operates with prodigious force on the consciences of his hearers. His mode of speaking is so slow that his hearers are sometimes in advance of him in the subject he is discussing."

The testimony of his intimate friend and Christian brother, John Taylor, is worth insertion here: "Mr. Hickman, in the spring of 1785, moved from the south side of Kentucky, and lived in South Elkhorn neighborhood. A number of his children joined the church. One of them, his son William, is now the pastor of a respectable church on South Benson. Under the labors of Lewis Craig, Hickman, Sen., and other visitors, South Elkhorn soon grew up to be a large and respectable church; they put up a framed meeting-house, not far from the brick one now standing, and it was the first house of worship of any kind on the north side of Kentucky. Though William Hickman and I were not members at the same time, yet we have been both connected with South Elkhorn Church, and are now near neighbors. This man has had a large range in Kentucky, for here he has been a faithful laborer nearly forty years. He is truly a seventy-six man, for in 1776 he paid his first visit to Kentucky, and here, the same year, he first began to preach. In early times, and in the face of danger, he settled where he now lives. For a number of years, at the risk of his life from Indian fury, he preached to the people of Shelby County and other frontier settlements."

He was twice married, and had the happiness of rearing a number of children, most of whom became the disciples of the Redeemer. One of his sons entered the ministry and has been eminently useful.

We approach the period of dismission from his labors. Well may he be accounted a laborer who had well performed the duty assigned him. Something like twenty churches had been constituted by him, and in a single year he had baptized more than five hundred persons. It was a sublime spectacle to behold this old man, scarcely relaxing his labors when he had reached his fourscore years. He says: "I have nearly come to the close of my poor

21 *

pilgrimage. I am now in my eighty-first year, and have a greater charge on me than ever. I am called upon to attend three other churches besides my own, which takes up all my time. But I want to spend my latter moments to God's glory. I am a poor sinner; but believing that the great God knew me from eternity, and included me in his great purchase, he called me by his spirit, and made me willing to be saved through faith, and that not of myself,—He deserves the glory." Such were the sentiments he breathed in his declining age, after a life-long proclamation of the blessed gospel. That gospel he loved as the foundation of all his hope, and he was willing to spend and be spent in making it known to others. He preached the Word to the very last. He had joined his son, and with him was employed in his cherished work. It is said that, being unwell, he turned his steps homeward, in company with his son; but he could proceed no farther than Frankfort, where, at the house of a friend, he sunk into the embraces of death as tranquilly as a slumbering infant in the arms of its mother. To the last he spoke of Jesus. That name was above every name to him. In the midst of his joyous contemplations and praises he passed away. This was in the latter part of 1830, he having reached his eighty-fourth year.

He was buried at the Forks of Elkhorn. Precious dust! It is a sacred deposit, over which his great Redeemer watches, and which will come forth again, at the resurrection morn.

GEORGE EVE.

George Eve was a native of Culpepper. He was born in 1748. During his earlier years he seldom, if ever, heard the gospel proclaimed in its purity, until Elder David Thomas and others visited the neighborhood in which he resided and made known the tidings of salvation. In 1772 he professed religion and joined the Baptist church. He soon began to exhort, and afterwards to preach. In 1778 he was ordained and became the pastor of F T Church, and, when Elder Craig removed to Kentucky, of Blue Run, in Orange County. For the space of twelve years he continued to preach with astonishing success in Virginia, and large numbers acknowledged him as the instrument of their conversion. But in 1790 he emigrated to the State of Kentucky, and settled near Georgetown. With his wonted zeal he engaged in ministerial duties, receiving the kindest attentions from those among whom he had determined to reside. No special influence seemed at first to follow his ministrations; but about the year 1800, a most extensive revival of religion was enjoyed, to some extent the result of his exertions. This was said, by one of his friends, to have been the most remarkable period of his life. His success in winning men to love the Saviour exceeded that of his whole previous ministerial career. Nearly all his time was devoted to the labor of preaching and exhortation.

As he had reached an eminence in popular favor, it might have been expected that some effect unfavorable to his Christian temper would have been produced. But it was far otherwise. He was the same humble, unassuming, spiritually-minded man he had always been, and indeed only seemed to shine the more in those respects the more he received the caresses of his brethren and friends.

In describing his person, a brother represents him as having been six feet high, of genteel figure, and handsome appearance; his eyes were blue, and his hair inclined to be light. In his general mien there was something peculiarly attractive, which, united with his naturally amiable disposition and his Christianly deportment, contributed so extensively to render him the subject of popular regard.

Thus Elder Eve continued to adorn the doctrine of God, his Saviour, until a very short period before his death, when, painful to relate, he allowed himself to be overcome by the intoxicating draught. Confession before his brethren in the most humiliating terms was made, and he was forgiven, but again he was overtaken. It being then the uniform custom to present the beverage of ardent spirits as a token of kind feeling, and moving as he did among the most refined circles, the temptation to indulge too freely was strong, and in his case prevalent. But this was no apology for his offence.

What a melancholy lesson does this teach his successors in the ministry! None are so lovely in character, so respected by the world, or so deeply rooted in the affections of the pious, as to be exempt from the temptations common to man. And the Christian minister will never reach a point, on this side of the grave, when he will not need to watch and pray that he enter not into temptation. This admonition of the Saviour ought every day to be heeded especially by him, for if *he* fall into sin, he sins not alone; others to a woeful extent are liable to be involved in unbelief, sin, and ruin.

JOHN KING.

JOHN KING was a native of Brunswick County. The circumstances of his parents were extremely dependent, and his opportunities of improvement were, in consequence, scanty. His attention to religious subjects was arrested in early youth. About 1773, Elder Samuel Harriss, with others, preached in the neighborhood where he lived, and many believed to the saving of the soul. A considerable excitement was the result. Crowds attended the ministrations of God's servants, some curious to see these New Lights, and others with sincere desire to hear and know the truth. The ordinance of immersion also, having been rarely witnessed, excited much interest. A baptismal scene was the means of arresting Mr. King's attention to spiritual things. He attended at Harper's Mill on one of these occasions, more for the purpose of amusing himself than to receive benefit; and, that he might enjoy his sport unobserved, he concealed himself beneath the mill-wheel. But the Lord's eye was upon him, and his laughter was turned into mourning. He came from his hiding-place with the arrows of the Almighty sticking fast in him, and with anguish unutterable he hastened homeward. The night was passed without rest, and he arose to behold the sun, but no hope beamed upon his benighted soul. In this state of mind he continued for many days. All society was cautiously avoided. He would wander for whole hours in the wilderness, brooding over his wretched condition, and for some time no person knew or suspected the cause of his gloom. It began to be supposed that he was suffering a temporary derangement of mind, and was called by many the distracted boy. After concealing his grief until he found himself more and more miserable, he determined to divulge his feelings to a Baptist minister, then in the vicinity of his father's residence. The man of God directed him to believe in the Lord Jesus Christ. He went away astonished and offended at the advice he had received. That his sin was great he was willing to acknowledge, but he could not perceive how a holy God might accept and save him until he should become a holy man. For this he was groaning and striving, and his heart cherished the hope that some method of making himself better would be recommended by his spiritual adviser. In all his inquiries, he was still informed that Christ died for sinners, and that he must be saved, if saved at all, by the mere mercy of God through Jesus Christ. At length his proud heart yielded. He saw that God could be just, and yet justify the ungodly through Christ. This humiliating truth became the joy of his heart. Now the plan of salvation was beheld in all its simplicity, freeness, and fullness. He returned to see the minister with a new song in his mouth, being willing not only to rejoice in, but to acknowledge the Saviour. He was shortly after baptized.

It has been hinted that he was at that time quite young. He soon cherished a desire to preach the gospel. For a long period, even after he began to exercise his talents in public addresses, he was oppressed with a fear that he was not called of God to this work. While anxious to do good to his fellow-men, he was ready to exclaim, "who is sufficient for these things?" In this early stage of his Christian career the Lord laid upon him his chastening hand. Some injury was sustained in one of his legs, which threatened the loss of life, and it became necessary to suffer amputation. During this confinement he was brought to the conviction that it was his duty to preach. He afterwards believed that the affliction was designed by his Heavenly Father to settle this question. The matter was indeed determined to his own satisfaction, and he was willing to count all things loss for the excellency of the knowledge of Christ Jesus his Lord. As soon as the maimed limb was sufficiently healed, he began in all the surrounding country to declare the unsearchable riches of the grace of God. Large numbers attended to hear the youth with a wooden leg preach, and many who went from mere curiosity returned to pray. Thus the trial through which he was brought redounded to the glory of God, and to the interests of immortal souls.

After Mr. King's devotion to the ministry he applied himself diligently to the cultivation of his mind. His progress in knowledge was rapid. It is said, that having married a woman of education, he received much valuable information under her tuition. She appropriated much of her time in affording such assistance as he needed. A great improvement in his manner of preaching was perceptible, and his influence was extended beyond his native county. He was for a short time pastor of Malone's Church, in Mecklenburg, and in that vicinity was quite useful.

A few years after his entrance into the ministry, he removed to Henry County, where he spent the remnant of his life. Within the limits of the Strawberry Association he exercised a commanding influence, and was much beloved by all his brethren. He officiated as pastor of Leatherwood and Beaver Creek Churches for many years. Until 1821 he continued to work for God, when he was released from the sorrows of earth and admitted to the joys of heaven. At the time of his death he was about sixty-four years of age. The Strawberry Association at its meeting in May, 1821, thus notices this event: "The Association is called with regret to announce that our aged brother, John King, has, since our last meeting, been removed to the world of spirits. He was long a zealous and successful advocate of evangelical truth in this district."

Elder King was a man of strong mind. As a preacher he was inclined to be doctrinal. He knew how to bring from the treasury of the Word things new and old. In Semple's History of the Baptists, published in 1809, a reference is made to his character as a minister in the following language: "Few men open their mouths in the pulpit more to the purpose than Mr. King; his language is strong and nervous; his ideas clear and perspicuous; his manner warm and animating, and his countenance grave and solemn. Though modest and unassuming out of the pulpit, when he ascends the sacred stand he speaks as one having authority; he lifts up his voice and commands all men to repent. His life has been an honor to his Master's cause, and when he has ceased to suffer here, doubtless his death will be glorious."

THEODORICK NOEL.

"WAS baptized (according to the notice of him in Semple's History) in August, 1773, being then a young man, it is thought some few years upwards of twenty. He shortly afterward began to exercise a gift in the way of exhortation and preaching, and soon became popular among the Baptists, and those who were attached to their meetings.

"Education among the common class in Virginia was far from being as diffusive at that period as it has since become; and ELDER NOEL's stock of improvement in that way was but scanty. With a considerable share of natural sagacity, however, and some degree of inventive power, his preaching talent was held in high estimation by the mass of his hearers; though it was in what is called *the gift of exhortation* that he was considered to excel. With a voice deep-toned and loud, but not harsh nor discordant, and a flow of words uttered in a sort of tuneful modulation, and attended with considerable unction, his exhortatory addresses were powerfully impressive, and stirred the feelings of many of his auditors to a high degree. I have often witnessed the effect of his declamations; and my own early religious impressions were, at such times, often excited and quickened. In the course of *the great revival,* (as it has been called,) in 1788–89, a season when the passions were more freely indulged in religious exercises than they have been of late years, it was nothing uncommon for numbers in the congregation to be visibly and audibly wrought on in a powerful manner; and this was more remarkably the case under Elder Noel's ministrations. The commotion generally appeared toward the close of the sermon.

Paroxysms of feeling were often excited, and crying out, and falling down, were not uncommon. Some were distressed with conviction. Some animated with rejoicing. In this state of things, of course there was often loud noise; but louder still, like the varied notes of a trumpet, was heard the thundering voice of the preacher. Then it was that his peculiar talent was in full operation; while standing among the people, or slowly moving here and there, he poured forth the full volume of his voice in declamation and exhortation to those around him, or in prayer for those who fell on their knees to express their desire.

"The life of Elder Noel does not appear to have been marked with interesting incidents. The 'young woman' mentioned in Semple's History as the first person baptized by Elder Noel, (on account of which her brother made an assault on him in the water,) was afterwards Sister *Goulden*, who lately died at an advanced age, a resident of Caroline. I have heard her relate the circumstance of the case."

The above tribute to the memory of a devoted, useful minister, was prepared by Elder Andrew Broaddus, who had been familiar with his whole history. This testimony was corroborated by Semple. "Few men," he says, "have been more successful in the ministry than Mr. Noel. It is probable he has baptized as many persons as any other preacher now living in Virginia; among them have been a number of preachers, some of whom rank high in the ministry as men of talents and usefulness. He is now, and has been for many years, pastor of the Upper King and Queen Church. The first that Mr. Noel baptized after he was ordained, was a young woman. Her brother promised to dip any person that should dip her. In fulfillment of his word he made the attempt, but could not succeed. Being pursued by some of the wicked, who resented this treatment of the preacher, he was obliged to make the best of his way off. He died a few weeks after, having first sent for Mr. Noel to ask pardon. Mr. Noel's talents seem singularly calculated for a revival."

The above statement respecting the success of Mr. Noel is sustained by the history of the churches he served, and by other churches in the Dover Association. He contributed not a little, if not mainly, to the origination of Salem Church, and was, at different periods, and for many years, pastor of Salem, Upper Essex, and Upper King and Queen Churches. These churches, through his instrumentality, received large accessions. He commenced his pastorate at Upper King and Queen Church in 1780, and for a succession of years, up to 1788, regular accessions were made. For two years from this period an extensive revival was enjoyed. "It was usual for Mr. Noel," says Semple, "to baptize at every monthly meeting; and for many months there were seldom, if ever, less than twenty baptized, but more frequently forty, fifty, and sixty; many of them respectable private persons, and three or four preachers."

The same was true of Upper Essex Church. At one time, in connection with his body, Elder Noel baptized seventy persons; and during the revival of 1812, under his ministry, the church letter reported an increase of three hundred and twenty.

Thus this honored servant of Christ lived and labored. He was ready, when called away to the rest of heaven. He died on Friday, the 27th of August, 1813. Few men were more beloved in life or lamented in death. Even to this day, the churches he served hold his lovely spirit and zealous labors in grateful remembrance.

IVERSON LEWIS.

Iverson Lewis was the son of John Lewis, whose father, Zachary Lewis, emigrated to this country from Breckwork, in Breckworkshire, Wales, in the year 1692, at which time he settled in the County of King and Queen, State of Virginia. Iverson was born the 4th of March, 1741, at the family residence in King and Queen, where he lived and died. He was educated in the established religion of his day. When he attained the age of manhood he considered himself so pious that he went to the communion-table on all sacramental occasions, and thought himself prepared for heaven. It had never entered his mind that anything more than a conformity to the regulations of the Episcopal church was necessary to obtain eternal life, the Word of God being scarcely ever read by him. Hearing of a preacher traveling through the country proclaiming to the people that they must be born again, he was astonished, and, Nicodemus-like, asked how can these things be? About this time John Waller passed through his neighborhood; he had heard of him, and entertained a contemptible opinion of his sentiments, considering him a wild enthusiast. But determined to hear what he had to say, he found a congregation assembled under a tree, while Mr. Waller was addressing the people from this text, "Ye must be born again." He paid marked attention to the sermon, and before the preacher had concluded he found his prejudices entirely removed, himself convinced that he had been shrouded in darkness, and, without repentance toward God and faith in our Lord Jesus Christ, he must be lost. He now felt the horrors of a guilty conscience; and, with a determination to seek salvation, he finally received pardon and peace to his troubled spirit through the blood of atonement. He soon considered it his duty to endeavor to convince all around him of the truth of that religion which he had before despised. His efforts were not in vain, for many, through him, believed and turned to the Lord Thus, before his union with any church he began to impart the knowledge of Christ to others.

Upon searching the Scriptures he became convinced that immersion was a scriptural practice, and believers the only proper subjects; he was accordingly immersed about the year 1770 or 1771.

Although his talents as a preacher were not above mediocrity, yet he accomplished much; his ardent zeal, his indefatigable industry, his unwavering faith, enabled him to overcome all opposition, and to make his way amidst persecutions of various kinds, so that he was instrumental in spreading the gospel all around him, and of enlisting numbers into the service of Jesus Christ. Few men possessed, in a more eminent degree, the gift of exhortation. He was always warm and pathetic in his public addresses. His manners were gentle and refined; and although it was his common custom, in public and private, to converse with and admonish all persons, yet it has been observed of him, that he was never known to give offence. He was so mild, so gentle, and yet so dignified, that all were struck with his superior excellence as a man and Christian, and were at once disarmed of their enmity to religion, and felt a reverence for his character. In 1775, he constituted the church called Mathews, in the county of that name, and continued to visit them once a month for many years, as pastor, a distance of about fifty miles. He also constituted two churches in the County of Gloucester, about the year 1790, and continued to visit them several years as their minister. The approach of advanced age, however, made it necessary for him to discontinue his regular ministrations to these distant churches, and to confine his labors to those in his more immediate neighborhood, in King and Queen, and Middlesex Counties, where he continued his regular pastoral duties until December, 1814. About the latter part of that year he became more feeble, and was confined to bed until the 5th day of January, 1815, when, in the full possession of all his mental faculties, with strong faith, relying on Him in whom he had believed, and without a pang, he gave up the ghost.

JOHN BOWERS.

This devoted servant of God was born in Nansemond County, in 1753; about 1774 he heard the gospel preached by Elder David Barrow. The Word was clothed with power from on high, and reached his heart; he was convinced of sin, and soon became a believer in the Lord Jesus, was received into membership by the church at South Quay, and baptized by Elder Barrow, in 1775. His warm and zealous heart was drawn out in desires for the salvation of sinners, and he soon commenced holding evening meetings, in which he would read the Scriptures and exhort the people to turn to the Lord. In a few years he settled in the neighborhood, and became a member of the church at Black Creek, Southampton County, where, in 1798, he was regularly set apart to the sacred work of the ministry.

After the removal of Elder Barrow to Kentucky, Elder Bowers was called to the pastoral care of Black Creek, South Quay, and Western Branch Churches, which he continued to serve during his life. Although his talents were not above mediocrity, yet such was his zeal that he became a useful and quite an acceptable preacher. He was seldom known to preach or to pray in public without shedding tears.

He was a great lover of Associations, and for many years, when present, presided as Moderator. He was an affectionate husband, a tender parent, an indulgent master, and a kind neighbor, and in every sphere of life in which he was called to act he proved himself to be a man of God. Having thus fought a good fight, finished his course, and kept the faith, he yielded his soul to God his Saviour, October 17th, 1815, aged sixty-two years.

BENJAMIN WATKINS.

Elder Benjamin Watkins was born in Powhatan County, July 5th, 1755. His father died when he was only three years of age. His mother, though a stranger to vital godliness, was not negligent of the externals of religion, but taught him short prayers, and endeavored to instil into his mind such principles as she supposed necessary to prepare him for usefulness in this world. She maintained a most rigid discipline in the management of her family, and required them regularly to attend the services of the Episcopal church. Benjamin from a child was remarkable for his strict moral habits. When but nine years old he was the subject of serious impressions, which were banished from his mind from time to time until he had reached his nineteenth year, when he became a happy believer in the Lord Jesus Christ. Until this period he had not been accustomed to hear the gospel in its purity; nor had he, amid all his convictions, been conscious of his entire guilt and helplessness. With reference to his conversion he says: "I was brought up strictly, and often went to church, said prayers, etc.; but after the Lord was pleased to send his glorious gospel in our land, I was convinced that I was a poor sinner, and could never obtain rest but in the Lord Jesus Christ."

Owing to strong apprehensions that he might be deceived, he

delayed connection with the church for more than two years. The great adversary knows well what is most likely to deter the child of God from walking in the path of duty. If he can disturb the mind by perplexing doubts concerning Divine favor, and thus prevent an active devotion to the Redeemer's will, his end is gained as well as when he can induce to entire thoughtlessness on eternal things. Having obtained clearer views of the plan of salvation, and exercised a more simple reliance on its provisions, Mr. Watkins was baptized, September 22d, 1776, and became a member of the church at Powhatan Meeting-house, then known by the name of Dupuy's.

When speaking afterwards of this event, he remarks: "I could not venture at first to give a relation of the work of God, lest I should impose on the church; not that I had any scruples relative to believers' baptism, for I was convinced of that by reading the Word of God. I have often wondered how Christians could neglect this plain command of Jesus Christ, but believe that the glorious time is rolling on when all the saints of God will see eye to eye, when infant sprinkling will be done away, with every other human tradition, and Jesus will be king of Zion and his name one. Then will all submit to believers' baptism, and embrace each other in heart and hand, and glorify together our Heavenly Father."

He began to preach in 1783, but was not ordained until March 19th, 1786. The Presbytery which attended his ordination were Elders George Smith, James Dupuy, and John Goode. For several years he was employed in teaching a school, and consequently was not then wholly given to the ministry. But from 1790, the greater part of his time was engaged in traveling, and in various respects he was made a blessing to the cause of Christ. Through him many were brought to God, and churches established and enlarged. In prosecuting his work he was laborious and persevering. He traveled extensively, proclaiming wherever he went the unsearchable riches of Christ. It was his ambition to occupy the most destitute portions of the Lord's vineyard. In the latter part of his life he annually performed tours throughout Chesterfield, Amelia, Nottaway, Brunswick, and Lunenburg, for the special purpose of doing good. His memory will long be revered by many in these counties. In him, when almost unsupplied with religious instruction, they found a friend willing to make sacrifices and endure hardships, that they might be benefited. His regular yearly visits were anticipated with unfeigned joy by them; and when he did come, he came in the fullness of the blessing of the gospel of Christ.

It is proper that something be said of his manner in the pulpit. He was to some extent eccentric, though without seeming to be aware of it. His illustrations and allusions were homely and sometimes wanting in dignity. No one, however, could accuse him of intention to amuse. While a smile was almost unavoidably produced by his anecdotes, he himself remained grave. There was a perfect simplicity in all he said and did. He was remarkable, too, for the earnestness with which he urged the doctrines and precepts of the gospel. His addresses were generally of the hortatory kind.

Mr. Watkins was peculiarly scrupulous in all his business transactions with his fellow-men. To "owe no man anything," was a maxim to which he rigidly adhered through life. Those who name the name of Christ cannot be too punctilious in the faithful execution of all their pledges; especially is this true with regard to him who calls himself a teacher in spiritual things. There have been those who acted as if it were a matter of comparatively little importance to discharge pecuniary obligations, and thus have seriously injured the cause of religion.

His piety was of the most uniform character. It was the result of principle. The great business of his life was to do good. Whether abroad or at home he was an Israelite indeed, in whom there was no guile. As the head of a family, he always manifested the deepest concern for their spiritual welfare. Of his ten children, nearly all became the subjects of conversion. He was also an ardent lover of good men, and exerted his influence to promote the harmony of the churches. "It is," said he, "a remark of the wise man, 'two are better than one, and a threefold cord is not quickly broken.' The brethren should be helpers of each other. The feeble state of infants, the unwary steps of youth, the decrepitude of old age, and indeed the inability of individuals to execute business of agriculture and mechanism, all evince the utility of society in civil life. Nor are the arguments in favor of union in religion less conclusive."

Elder Watkins was also a warm friend of those measures which are employed by the church to spread the knowledge of a Saviour through the earth. In reference to the prospect of accomplishing this object, he observes: "The days in which we live are pregnant with wonders. Are not these the days foretold by ancient prophets, when the stone cut out of the mountain without hands, shall fill the earth with the glory of God? Is it not the mighty angel flying in the midst of heaven, having the everlasting gospel to preach unto them that dwell on the earth, and to every nation, and kindred, and tongue, and people, saying, with a loud voice, 'fear God, and give glory to him; for the hour of his judgment is come'? In the distribution of the word of truth are not party names and prejudices to crumble, totter, and fall, and all the church in this grand work to become one? The beams of truth have begun to dawn on almost every land, and the Lord is adding to the church daily such as shall be saved." In giving encouragement to these efforts, he did not satisfy himself with appeals from the pulpit. He was a man of deeds as well as words. Regularly every year he called on a friend in Richmond, and deposited a sum of money to be appropriated to objects of benevolence. In his views of truth, he was sound and scriptural. When in the pulpit, he delighted to dwell on those doctrines which are most essential to be known. "Every parcel of truth," he used to say, "is as precious as the filings of gold. A man may sell his house, his lands, his jewels, but truth is a jewel that exceeds all price, and must not be sold. While error and ignorance are still abounding in the world, while Deists, Arians, and Socinians are active, let us, as the people of God, earnestly contend for the faith once delivered to the saints. Let us at all times and in all places watch and be sober."

It was the will of God that his servant should live to a good old age. He continued to labor in the ministry until a few days before his death. On the Sabbath before he died he preached twice with his accustomed warmth; his last sermon was founded on the prayer of the publican, "God be merciful to me a sinner." This was with him a darling theme. He had been frequently heard to say that this prayer was suitable to be offered by him: for he felt himself to be a sinner. About this time the work of the Lord began to revive among the churches of his charge. For this he had long been deeply solicitous, and was often known to say, if he could live to see another revival of religion he should rejoice to die.

The Wednesday before his death a church meeting was held to receive one of the first subjects of the work, which was then beginning to be manifest. He was too much indisposed to leave his bed. The church determined to meet at his house; and though he was quite ill, he proposed several questions to the candidate, and manifested a peculiar interest in the relation she gave. On Thursday and Friday he became much weaker, and was conscious that he was near his end. A perfect resignation to the Divine will was exhibited, and a comfortable assurance enjoyed that he should soon be with Christ. On Lord's day morning, July 17th, 1831, he breathed his last, in the seventy-sixth year of his age.

Thus died this venerable servant of Jesus Christ, who for the space of forty-eight years had been employed in his vineyard. During this period he had preached more than six thousand sermons, being rather more than an average of one hundred and thirty-two for every year he labored in the ministry.

The following extract of a letter written by him to Dr. Rippon, of London, will illustrate something of the spirit he evinced. It is dated Powhatan County, April 28th, 1800: "Although you are a stranger to me in person, yet I hope we are not strangers to each other in mind. I wish to have an acquaintance with you, as your name is familiar to us. I have, after my feeble manner, attempted to preach the gospel of Christ nearly seventeen years, and have lived to see several revivals of religion in Virginia, especially in different churches of the Middle District Association. Before the late work commenced wickedness had run to a very great height, infidelity and irreligion abounded on every hand, and professors had become very carnal; there were but few names in Sardis that had not defiled the garments. I had awful thoughts respecting our condition, and fearing that some judgment would befall our happy land. But, contrary to my fears, did the Lord visit us in a way of mercy, by first stirring up the people, causing them frequently to assemble together, and carry on his worship by fasting and prayer. The sacred flame has spread to and fro, in various parts of Virginia, so that we may truly say, 'the Lord hath done great things for us whereof we are glad.'

"Our church at Spring Creek has added by baptism, since the revival, upwards of one hundred and fifty members. Chesterfield Church also has received about the same number, or more. Powhatan Church about one hundred. Elder Webber's church, called Dover, belonging to the Dover District, yet hard by us, has added about one hundred members. The work has been chiefly among young people, while the old, who have lived to see several revivals, are still left out, exposed to God's wrath. The Lord have mercy upon them.

"Since the late revival in Virginia, the ministers have traveled more than formerly. Brother Jacob Gregg, one of the missionaries to Africa, paid us a visit last January. He appears to be a very intelligent man; his preaching was well received by the churches. He lived not far from Norfolk. My own home is about twenty miles from Richmond, the metropolis of Virginia.

"I shall conclude my letter with the words of Aaron and his sons, when blessing the people: 'The Lord bless thee and keep thee; the Lord make his face to shine upon thee, and be gracious unto thee; the Lord lift up his countenance upon thee, and give thee peace.'"

MARTIN DAWSON.

Martin Dawson was an efficient member of the Albemarle Association. He was born in the year 1744. When he had reached his thirtieth year his heart was brought under the influence of truth by the preaching of Elder David Paterson, by whom he was baptized. He at once began to preach, though with much fear and trembling, often being ready to yield to the impression that he was not called to the work of the ministry. However, he continued the practice of speaking in public, until it was judged by his brethren expedient to urge him forward as qualified to fill the pastoral office. On the day of his ordination Ballenger's Creek Church was constituted, and he invited to officiate as their spiritual shepherd.

As the pastor of this church he was eminently useful; several interesting seasons were enjoyed, when converts were baptized and added to the people of God. As might be expected under such circumstances, he was extensively known and beloved in the county where he labored. For many years he presided over the deliberations of the Albemarle Association with much dignity.

Besides the church called Ballenger's Creek, he served at different times several other churches. His talents, though not showy, were of the useful kind. He did much good. The confidence of all classes of men reposed in him as long as he lived. During his last sickness he conversed freely concerning his departure hence, and sometimes said, while he dreaded the pains of death, he had nothing to fear beyond the grave. He desired that no funeral sermon should be preached at his decease. To the rest of heaven he has doubtless gone.

He married in early life, and was the father of a numerous offspring, for whose support, by his industry, he made ample provision.

JAMES SHELBOURNE.

ALTHOUGH the highest attainments of human excellence are comparatively mean, it should be ours to "mark the perfect man and behold the upright," that we may follow him as he followed Christ. It is true, that excellence of temper and purity of life deserve our imitation, though they be seen in one who occupies an obscure station in the church; at the same time, there are men in whose lives circumstances appear of such marked interest as to force them upon our attention and demand our respect. In no case is this observation more forcibly illustrated than in the biography of ELDER JAMES SHELBOURNE.

This devoted servant of God was born in James City County, November 29th, 1738. He had the affliction to lose his parents in early life, so that he was destitute of many advantages which he might otherwise have possessed. At the early age of seventeen he removed to Halifax County, shortly after which, his mind was arrested to solemn inquiry on the subject of religion. This concern arose from a sermon delivered by Elder William Murphy, on Romans, xiv. 17. It appears, however, that these convictions were not of that lively character which produce repentance unto life, for it was not until 1769 that he became properly sensible of his character as a sinner, justly condemned by the righteous law of God. During this year he was so deeply distressed, that for the space of three months he was unable to attend to his domestic affairs, applying himself to a rigid course of fasting, prayer, and reading the Scriptures. In a trial of his own strength he was ultimately brought to realize his weakness, and to receive with consolation and hope the atonement of Christ. Having thus been delivered from the kingdom of darkness and translated into the kingdom of God's dear Son, he made a public profession of attachment to his cause by baptism, in 1770.

From this period his labors as a minister of the gospel commenced. He cherished a peculiar anxiety to be useful by publishing the way of salvation. So powerful was this sense of duty, that he has often been heard to say that it would be as difficult for him to desist from preaching as to hold coals of fire in his hand without shrinking; and that if he could not be allowed to preach without a pecuniary sacrifice on his part, he would labor with his hands six days to be allowed that privilege on the seventh. This restlessness of spirit did not arise from a wish to make a display of himself, nor from any visionary or unscriptural impression, but from a settled conviction of the wretchedness of a world lying in wickedness, and of the boundless sufficiency of Him who was made a sacrifice for sin.

In 1775 he was ordained, and took the pastoral charge of Reedy Creek Church, Lunenburg County, containing at this time thirty-six members. Having thus been made an under-shepherd over the fold of Jesus, he, for some time, without realizing his wishes, manifested a deep anxiety for the enlargement of Zion's borders. It, however, pleased the Lord, who hears the prayers of his people, to revive his work in the bounds of Reedy Creek Church, when about fifty were added to the Lord. Here we beg leave to introduce a quotation from Semple's History of the Virginia Baptists relative to this circumstance:—

"Mr. Shelbourne is one of the most religious men living. He seldom talks on any other subject. It is easily conceived, then, that whenever Zion languishes, he feels his portion of sacred sorrow expressed by the Prophet Jeremiah, ix. 1. It will also be admitted, that of this mourning, the church with which he stood connected in the solemn office of pastor would share her full portion. Such was the case for several years. The state of religion in Elder Shelbourne's church was truly lamentable; he felt it and mourned. God heard his groans and removed his complaints. He is often pleased, however, to take strange ways (strange to mortals) to effect his purposes. It was deeply impressed on Elder Shelbourne's mind, that if he would make a religious feast, or, in other words, if he would invite his neighbors generally to come to his house, and there, for two or three days, entertain them with such as he had, and at the same time employ every opportunity in exhorting them to repentance, etc., that the Lord would thereby begin a goodly work: he tried it and succeeded. He first made an appointment at the meeting-house, and thence invited them, one and all, to his own house. Many went, and the time was occupied in the most devout manner; singing, prayer, exhortation, were all in their proper seasons attended to; the heavenly shower descended; the souls of many were refreshed, and from that time the work went on to the conversion of great numbers."

Besides this, other times of refreshing were enjoyed under the ministry of Elder Shelbourne, so that at the time of his death, notwithstanding many removals and deaths, there were connected with the Reedy Creek Church one hundred and fifty members. Nor was his usefulness confined to the neighborhood in which he lived; the destitute churches belonging to the Meherrin District were frequently watered by his ministrations and established by his faithful advice.

As a preacher Elder Shelbourne was indeed much and deservedly loved. His pulpit efforts were characterized by an unostentatious simplicity, and, as he advanced in years, his head of silvery whiteness contributed much to increase the veneration in which his person was held. But his extensive popularity was not alone the result of agreeable manners. He possessed a benevolent heart, leading him to give frequent and substantial indications of good-will to his fellow-men. Such was the universal esteem with which he was regarded, that he often expressed a fear that he might deserve the woe of those concerning whom all men might speak well. But while he was thus beloved by all, he did not shrink from the defence of the humbling doctrines of the cross. These were his glory and his boast. Especially did he delight to dwell on the truths, that man is wholly depraved, that salvation is obtained alone by the righteousness of Christ received by faith, and that the depravity of human nature is overcome only by the special and direct influence of the Holy Spirit. For the long period of fifty years did he urge these and kindred doctrines upon the attention of his hearers.

As serving to shed light on the history and character of the subject of this sketch, an interesting extract will be subjoined from the writings of Dr. Alexander, of Princeton, one of the gifted and honored men of the Presbyterian denomination. This testimony is the more valuable because unsolicited. It is the tribute of an honest, humble, good man, to the virtuous and moral influence of a kindred spirit. The extract, though long, will repay perusal. The doctor having called to spend a night at the house of a friend, met with Mr. Shelbourne for the first time, and thus speaks of the interview and of the future friendship between them :—

"Mr. Yarborough took occasion to inform us that there was a Baptist preacher in his employment as a millwright, who would be at the house as soon as his work was finished. Accordingly, about the dusk of the evening, an old man, in coarse garb, with leathern apron, and laden with tools, entered the house and took his seat on the stairs. Neither Mr. Grigsby nor I had ever been acquainted with uneducated preachers, and we were struck with astonishment that this carpenter should pretend to preach. When we retired, Mr. Shelbourne, such was his name, was put into the same room with us. I felt an avidity to question him respecting his call to the ministry, taking it for granted that the old man was ignorant. I therefore began by asking him what he considered a call to the ministry. Mr. Shelbourne perceived the drift of my question, and, instead of giving a general answer, proceeded to a narrative of his own experience, and to state the circumstances which led him to suppose that God had called him to be a preacher. The substance of his story was as follows :—

"'I was born in one of the lower counties of Virginia, and, when young, was put to learn the carpenter's trade. Until I was a man grown and had a family, I never heard any preaching but from ministers of the established church, and did not even know that there were any others. About this time came into the neighborhood a Presbyterian minister by the name of Martin, whom I went to hear; and, before he was done, I was convinced that I was in a lost and undone condition. He made no stay, and I heard no more of him. But a wound had been left in my conscience which I knew not how to get healed, and no one about me could give any valuable advice as to a cure. I went from day to day under a heavy burden, bewailing my miserable state, till at length my distress became so great that I could neither eat nor sleep with any peace or comfort. My neighbors said I was falling into melancholy or going mad, but not one of them had any knowledge, from experience, of the nature of my distress. Thus I continued mourning over my miserable case for weeks and months. I was led, however, to read constantly in the Bible; but this rather increased than lessened my distress; until one Sunday evening I saw, as clearly as I ever saw anything, how I could be saved through the death of Christ. I was filled with comfort, and yet sorrow for my sins flowed more copiously than ever. I praised God aloud, and immediately told my wife that I had found salvation; and when any of my neighbors came to see me I told them of the goodness of God, and what he had done for my soul, and how he had pardoned all my sins. As I spoke freely of the wonderful change I had experienced, it was soon noised abroad, and many came to see me, and to hear an account of the matter from my own mouth.

"'On Sabbath evenings my house would be crowded, and when I had finished my narrative I was accustomed to give them a word of exhortation. And as I could be better heard when standing, I stood and addressed my neighbors, without any thought of preaching. After proceeding for some time in this way, I found that several others began to be awakened by what they heard from me, and appeared to be brought through the new birth much as I had been. This greatly encouraged me to proceed in my work, and God was pleased to bless my humble labors to the conversion of many. All this time I did no more than relate my own experience, and then exhort my neighbors to seek unto the Lord for mercy.

"'Thus was I led on from step to step, until at length I actually became a preacher, without intending it. Exercised persons would frequently come to me for counsel, as I had been the first among them to experience the grace of God; and that I might be able to answer their questions I was induced to study the Bible continually; and often while at work particular passages would be opened to my mind, which encouraged me to hope that the Lord had called me to instruct those that were more ignorant than myself; and when the people would collect at my house I explained to them those passages which had been opened to my mind. All this time I had no instruction in spiritual matters from any man, except the sermons which I heard from Mr. Martin. But after a few years there came a Baptist preacher into our neighborhood, and I found that his doctrine agreed substantially with my experience, and with what I had learned out of the Bible. I traveled about with him, and was encouraged by him to go on in the exercise of my gift of public speaking, but was told by him that there was one duty which I was required to perform, which was that I should be baptized according to the command of Christ. And as we rode along we came to a certain water, and I said, See, here is water, what doth hinder me to be baptized? Upon which we both went down into the water, and he baptized me by immersion, in the name of the Father, the Son, and the Holy Ghost. From that time I have continued until this day, testifying to small and great, to white and black, repentance toward God and faith in our Lord Jesus Christ; and not without the pleasure of seeing many sinners forsaking their sins and turning unto God.

"'Now,' said he, 'you have heard the reasons which induce me to believe that God has called me to preach the gospel to the poor and ignorant. I never consider myself qualified to instruct men of education and learning. I have always felt badly when such have come to hear me. But as for people of my own class, I believed that I could teach them many things which they needed to know; and, in regard to such as had become pious, I was able, by study of the Bible and meditation, to go before them, so that to them also I could be in some measure a guide. I lament my want of learning, and am deeply convinced that it is useful to the ministry of the gospel; but it seems to me that there are different gifts now as of old, and one man may be suited to one part of the Lord's work, and another to another part. And I do not know but that poor and ignorant people can understand my coarse and familiar language better than the discourses of the most learned and eloquent men. I know their method of thinking and reasoning, and how to make things plain by illustrations and comparisons adapted to their capacities and their habits.'

"When the old millwright had finished his narrative I felt much more inclined to doubt my own call to the ministry than that of James Shelbourne. Much of the night was spent in this conversation, while my companion was enjoying his usual repose. We talked freely about the doctrines of religion, and were mutually gratified at finding how exactly our views tallied. From this night James Shelbourne became an object of my high regard, and he gave abundant testimony of his esteem for me. Whenever I visited that part of the country he was wont to ride many miles to hear me preach, and was pleased to declare that he had never heard any of the ministers of his own denomination with whose opinions he could so fully agree as with mine. I had the opportunity of hearing him preach several times, and was pleased not only with the soundness of his doctrine but the unaffected simplicity of his manner. His discourses consisted of a series of judicious remarks, expressed in the plainest language and in a conversational tone, until he became by degrees warmed by his subject, when he fell into a singing tone, but nothing like what was common with almost all Baptist preachers of the country at that time. As he followed his trade from day to day, I once asked him how he found time to study his sermons; to which he replied, that he could study better at his work, with his hammer in his hand, than shut up and surrounded with books. When he had passed the seventieth year of his age he gave up work, and devoted himself entirely to preaching. Being a man of firm health, he traveled to a considerable distance and preached nearly every day. On one of these tours, after I was settled in Charlotte County, I saw him for the last time. The old man appeared to be full of zeal and love, and brought the spirit of the gospel into every family which he visited. He was evidently ripening for heaven, and accordingly, not long after, he finished his course with joy."

These things are not said to give false views of human nature, but to present as worthy of universal and habitual imitation the virtues that adorned his character. Neither is it wished to present him as living unconscious of imperfections. These doubtless he felt, and realized his daily need of the purifying blood of Jesus. But it may not be uninteresting to know how this man of God was supported in his last hours. He was confined to his bed but a short time, and throughout his illness maintained the most unwavering trust in the atonement of Christ. He met the terrific monster, not with the philosophy of a Stoic, but with the resignation and cheerfulness of a Christian. While on his death-bed he used every possible means to fortify his aged and amiable companion against the trying scene, by telling her not to grieve at his approaching dissolution, as they had been favored to live together so many years, and that it would not be long before they would meet again in the enjoyment of an eternal rest.

Although he was blessed with a competency of earthly good, no dissatisfaction was expressed at leaving it behind; his anxieties seemed to run out toward the church, whose interests he was about to leave in the care of others. A short time before his death he addressed himself to his son Silas (who previously had commenced the work of the ministry) in a most impressive and affectionate manner. "Oh, my son," said he, "the church lies heavy, very heavy on my mind. I fear that a cold and trying time is approaching, and that many will be seeking a more fashionable religion. Watch over their souls as one who must give an account to God, and keep yourself unspotted from the world. Do not aspire after men of great swelling words, but study the Scriptures, preaching the gospel in its simplicity; be meek, lowly, and unassuming in your manners, with all holy conversation, as becometh the gospel of Christ. Never aim at things too deep and incomprehensible for mortals to know, remembering that there is as much made plain as it is the will of our Heavenly Father we should know; for secret things belong to God, and things that are revealed belong to us. Throughout life, what difficulties soever you may have to encounter, never return railing for railing, but contrariwise, in doing which you will overcome ten where you will one by any other method."

It may be proper here to give an extract from the record of the Reedy Creek Church book, which was made shortly after his death, evincing the esteem in which he was held by his brethren in Christ:—

"On Monday, March 6th, 1820, departed this life, at his seat in Lunenburg County, in his eighty-third year, Elder James Shelbourne, who had been the diligent and affectionate pastor of this church about forty-five years. The last sermon he preached was on the first Lord's day in February last, from Luke, xxix. 30. In this discourse he had much freedom, and it was thought by many of his brethren to be the best sermon they had ever heard him deliver. On the monthly meeting in February we received his last visit, and being very unwell he did not preach, but delivered a short exhortation, stating to his congregation at the same time that he never expected to address them more in this world; then committing the church to the Lord, he returned home, from which time he was confined to his bed until his death. The day following, many of his friends having heard that his dissolution seemed to be fast approaching, visited him. He conversed with them as much as the depressed state of his respiration would admit. To some of his young brethren he spoke with peculiar energy, and seemed to enjoy the most peaceful resignation to the will of his Heavenly Father. Before his last illness he often said, that when he desired to realize death nature shrunk, but now it was quite otherwise; he was no more afraid of dying than living, yet he did not wish to die sooner nor live longer than it was the will of his adorable Creator.

"Shortly before his death he seemed to have some difficulty in breathing, and remarked, that the grace of God had always been sufficient for him, and always would be to his dying moments. One night he observed to one of his friends that he doubted whether he should live to see the morning-light; being asked whether he felt resigned, he replied, 'Perfectly, perfectly! I have no more doubt of Divine favor than I have of my existence; I could say, come, Lord Jesus, come quickly; but I feel resigned to wait his good pleasure; therefore, all my appointed time will I wait, until my change come.'

"During the whole of his illness he enjoyed the exercise of his reason, and was often heard to say, that he would not turn his hand to have his evidences brighter or his hope and confidence stronger. He seemed to have nothing to ask. A short space before his death he lost his speech, and about half-past five o'clock this shining light was extinguished. While dying he raised one hand toward heaven, and seemed, from his gestures, to be perfectly sensible and anxious to let all around him know that he was about to ascend to glory, for which event his life had been one constant preparation.

"By this dispensation of Providence this church is bereaved of an under-shepherd whom they dearly loved. Salvation by the cross of Christ, independent of human worthiness, was the darling theme of his ministry. Doctrinal truth he considered as the only foundation of evangelical obedience, and maintained that notions of religion, however correct, would prove of no avail, any further than their sanctifying influence was felt on the heart, and evidenced by a holy walk and conversation. His own exemplary conduct was a striking instance of the power of those doctrines he believed and taught. Integrity and uprightness were traits in his character acknowledged by all who knew him; he possessed a noble disinterestedness of spirit, seeking not ours but us: he was truly our servant for Jesus' sake. We are left without our teacher and guide; our father and friend is no more; we shall no more witness on earth the fervor of his zeal, nor the ardor of his piety, nor hear the sound of salvation from his impressive lips. The hand that so often broke to us the bread, and poured out to us the wine in commemoration of our Lord, is now cold in death. As a church we are sorrowing that we shall see his face no more, and yet thankful to God that he was so long spared to go in and out before us. He still lives in our memories and in our hearts, and we trust his precepts and examples will never be forgotten by us. We should feel ourselves wanting in justice to his memory did we not inscribe on the records of this church our testimony to departed worth, for of him it might be said, 'He walked with God.'"

In reviewing the life of such a man it becomes every lover of Zion to pray to God that our young ministers may be faithful unto death, and that many more may be raised up thus to labor in his vineyard.

JOHN WRIGHT.

JOHN WRIGHT became a convert to the service of the Redeemer under the preaching of Elder Elijah Baker, in York County, and was baptized by him in 1776. He began at once to preach the gospel himself, and having satisfied his brethren that he possessed the requisite qualifications, he was ordained, and in 1777 became the pastor of Grafton Church, York County. "Mr. Wright," says Mr. Semple, "was a blessed man of God. He was faithful to occupy his talents. No man could find him out of his place; he lived and died a pious Christian, and a faithful as well as useful minister of Christ. He was a poor man and had a family to support, which prevented him from being as extensively useful as he probably would have been under more favorable circumstances: but his vineyard, though small, was well kept; his duty was his delight. In discipline he was tender, yet vigilant and impartial. He died about 1795, much regretted by all classes."

WILLIAM CLOPTON.

Elder William Clopton, the only child of Walter Clopton, was born in New Kent County, in 1761. At an early age his parents were removed by death, and he was placed in the care of an uncle who became his guardian. By some means the property to which he was heir having been lost, his education was much neglected. He was simply taught the common branches of learning, and apprenticed to the wheelwright business. Before the age of twenty-one he intermarried with Elizabeth Clark, and, abandoning his mechanical employment, became a farmer.

About the time of his marriage he embraced religion and united with the Methodist church. On examination he became convinced that it was his duty to be immersed, and determined forthwith to deny himself and follow his Master into the liquid grave. He was baptized by Elder Elijah Baker, near the close of the revolutionary war. About this time Charles City Church was constituted, of which Elder Clopton became a member. He was appointed clerk of the church, and after the expiration of several years was called to the deaconry. This last office he filled with great propriety and usefulness. In 1804 they lost their pastor by death, and the duty of conducting all their social meetings devolved on the subject of this memoir. He took occasion to exhort his brethren and to urge on them the faithful execution of their various duties. The church were soon convinced that he ought to be encouraged in the exercise of his gifts. He continued to exhort, and occasionally to expound the Scriptures, until 1808, when, by request of the church, he consented to preside over them as their under-shepherd.

Though Elder Clopton was never distinguished by vigor of intellect or extent of information, and although his success in the conversion of souls was not extensive, he was, nevertheless, very useful. As a pastor he was zealous and faithful. The people of his charge esteemed him highly; for his works' sake he deserved their esteem. By all who knew him he was generally respected, both as a pious man and a preacher. Toward the close of life he devoted much of his time to missionary labor among the destitute churches in the surrounding counties.

A short time before his death efforts among the Baptists were commenced to send abroad the gospel of the Son of God. He was much interested in these plans, and to the extent of his influence encouraged them.

He was removed from the church on earth to the general assembly and church of the first-born in heaven, January 18th, 1816. Five days previous he saw the companion of his life breathe her last. On the day of her interment he was attacked with an epidemic fever, which, in a short time, brought him down to the grave. He died as he lived. Christ was his stay and his joy. With great earnestness he exhorted his friends to prepare for a happier meeting in a better world. His attendant physician was much struck with the scene of his death-bed, and frequently remarked he had never beheld so much composure in the trying hour. He left six children, one of whom, Elder James Clopton, succeeds him in the pastoral office, and labors much in the region between Richmond and Williamsburg.

JOHN GOODE.

Elder John Goode was born near Four Mile Creek, Henrico, March, 1738. At the age of twenty-one he removed to the County of Chesterfield, where he was united in marriage with Miss Sarah Brown. Some time in 1778 Elder William Hickman preached in the neighborhood, and Mr. Goode attended his ministry. The truth reached his heart, and such was his distress of mind that for some time he was unable to attend to his worldly business. In communicating his feelings to his companion, he expressed the belief that he should be forever lost; he saw no way of escape for such a sinner as he felt himself to be; but, to his great surprise, when hope was almost gone, the Lord appeared in mercy for his relief: his burdened soul was made to rejoice in the atoning blood of Christ. He called on all around to join him in praising God. His confidence was so great that he thought he could convince every one of the value of the gospel; and went from house to house, declaring what great things the Lord had done for him. He was baptized, and joined Skinquarter Church, in 1778; he soon began to hold meetings and to lead in exhortation and prayer. Before many months had elapsed he engaged in preaching the gospel, and having been approved by the church, was ordained June 18th, 1780; Elders Reuben Ford, John Dupuy, Eleazer Clay, and William Hickman constituted the ordaining presbytery. The church of which he was a member being destitute of a pastor, unitedly elected him to that office. He accepted the invitation, and labored with them until his death.

Elder Goode had not the advantage of an early education; at the time of his birth opportunities for obtaining useful information were enjoyed by few. He was, however, very zealous and faithful in his Master's cause. His labors were extensively blessed in the salvation of sinners, and in building up the church. He not only preached in his own immediate vicinity, but in various parts of the country. There are a few still living who remember the zeal and fidelity with which the cause of the Redeemer was advocated by him.

Of his sixteen children, eleven became hopefully pious, and united themselves with the Baptist Church. One of his sons entered the ministry. Like a shock of corn fully ripe, this aged servant of the Lord was gathered unto his fathers, the 12th of June, 1790. His death was peaceful. Precious in the sight of the Lord is the death of his saints.

JOHN ASPLUND.

John Asplund was a Swede by birth. Being devoted in early life to mercantile pursuits, for the purpose of obtaining business he visited England about 1775, and there, for a short time, obtained employment as a clerk. He then became connected with the British navy, and, while on the American coast, deserted and settled in North Carolina. There he became pious, and about 1782 was immersed by David Walsh, and united with Ballard's

Bridge Church, Chowan County. He afterwards removed to Southampton, Virginia, and commenced the ministry. In 1785 he returned to Europe, and visited England, Denmark, Finland, Lapland, and Germany. On his arrival in America, he traveled through the States, collecting statistical information concerning the Baptist denomination. In 1791 he published a small folio volume as the result of his efforts. It contains many valuable facts. Introducing this work to his readers, he remarks:—

"I have long been desirous, and have waited several years, to see a publication of the nature of the following. And though I was sensible I could publish nothing of the kind without the fatigue and expense of traveling over the greatest part of the continent, yet, at the request of many, I have been prevailed upon to make the tour of the Baptist churches, to obtain the necessary information. With a view to this, I have traveled about 7000 miles in about eighteen months, *chiefly on foot*, and have visited about two hundred and fifteen churches, and fifteen Associations. I am personally acquainted with two hundred and fifty ministers of our society, so that the Register may safely be depended upon in general, though after all, perhaps, a few churches and ministers may be omitted. It is probable, also, that the number of members in some churches may not be exact, as some do not associate; others who do, neglect to send forward their number; and some make conscience of numbering the people.

"Having been brought up with a view to the business of merchandise, I have been accustomed to keeping accounts; and I now prefer accounts of souls with their faces set Zionward, to those which only respect money or trade. I have a natural turn for traveling, and I am convinced I could not better spend my time than in itinerating to preach the gospel, and to collect materials which may assist the future historian; and though I have met with many discouragements from narrow-minded persons, whose illiberal souls are not concerned for the public welfare, I appeal to the Searcher of hearts, that my principal design is to make the Baptists better acquainted with each other, that union may more generally obtain among them.

JOHN ASPLUND, a Swede.

SOUTHAMPTON COUNTY, VIRGINIA, July 14, 1791."

He published another Register in 1794, when he traveled 10,000 miles, and became acquainted with 700 Baptist ministers. His talents as a speaker were quite plain, and, in this capacity, he was never distinguished. In the latter part of his life he was much injured by engaging in land speculations. Having removed to Maryland, he died suddenly, by drowning, in 1807.

EPHRAIM ABEL.

Although he whose character is now to receive attention was one of the most useful men of his day, his memory had well-nigh perished. While other men less humble and devoted have been admired, and have had their names handed down to the present age, no one seems, hitherto, to have taken pains to record the labors of Ephraim Abel. His most enduring record, however, is on high; and if in the Lamb's book of life his name be found, it is of comparatively little moment though the generation in which he moved on earth should ungratefully neglect him.

His native place was the County of Orange, where his heart was subdued to the obedience of the faith, and where he was baptized by John Leland, not far from the year 1788. Very soon after his connection with the Baptist Church he commenced his ministerial course. After his ordination he removed to Fauquier County. He was soon called to the pastorate of Hartwood, in Stafford, and it is believed he also undertook the charge of Brenttown, in Prince William. Besides this, he labored much in Fauquier County. The following testimony to the excellence of Elder Abel's character, and the success of his toils, is borne by one of the most judicious brethren of the upper country, who, for a series of years, was intimately acquainted with him:—

"He was a man possessing great worth of character, exerting an extensive and happy influence upon the communities in which he lived. Correcting with great judgment and tenderness the improprieties of the brotherhood, and giving by his amiable and pious life a mighty sanction to the truths which he diligently propagated for many years, he is most affectionately remembered by a few surviving brethren. He died, universally lamented, about 1809. When Fristoe's Ketockton History appeared, a few years after, it was a matter of profound astonishment that Elder Abel was not noticed according to his claims upon the historian. It will be explained, perhaps, by adverting to what will soon cease to be known except on the page of history. That historian, with all his native greatness and gracious goodness, was accustomed to rate men low who did not spend a large portion of their time in *degrading* (ideal) *Arminianism.* This, the subject of these remarks thought, was *best done* by preaching Christ and him crucified. The spririt of the age in which he lived led almost all men into bitter controversy in the pulpit. Such was the meekness of his spirit and the philanthropy of his heart that he preferred avoiding the theatre where he was likely, by circumstances, to have his soul brought under sectarian influence of a controversial character—hence he seldom visited Associations. His views of truth were of that kind which tend eminently to degrade human nature, and exalt the riches of Divine grace. There was a lovely proportion in his character, which commended itself to those who knew him best, as the result of a supernatural influence. Many were brought in under his ministry, and instances are still occurring which attest the fact that the Lord used him as the instrument of sowing seed to spring up long after he had entered upon the joys of a better state. He left several children; most of them are professors of religion.

"The field of his labor was extensive, he being for many years the only minister of our denomination for a large district of country. He was removed from earth by a lingering disease. His soul was calm, his faith unwavering, till he gently fell asleep in the arms of Jesus. It was said, by those who knew, that it was truly delightful to be with him during his illness. He expressed anxiety about the condition of his churches, and desired the brethren to meet together and keep up the worship of God. This was done as he desired until a successor was obtained."

From this extract the reader may justly infer that Elder Abel was, as a man and minister, well qualified to exercise a salutary influence among the circles in which he moved. May not the fervent prayer be offered up to the Lord of the harvest, that he would multiply many such laborers?

HENRY KEELING, SEN.*

WAS born in or about the year 1770, in Princess Anne County, Lynnhaven Bay, probably on the farm on which he was buried in the summer of 1820, making his life only fifty years. He was the youngest but one of a large family of children; the oldest of whom was Jacob Keeling, Sen., whose oldest son was the late Rev. Jacob Keeling, of the Episcopal church in Suffolk.

Contrary to the tastes and usages of this old Virginia family, who, from the earliest settlements on the James, had loved seclusion and planting, Henry was at an early age indentured, at Norfolk, to be a mechanic. His master was a man named Portlock, to whose savage treatment he ascribed the ruin of his constitution.

In his eighteenth year (1788) he professed religion, under the ministry of Major Thomas Armistead, of the revolutionary war, subsequently Rev. Thomas Armistead, first pastor of the Baptist Church in Portsmouth. This man combined in his person the military with the religious official life, as in cases of necessity has been done by persons of very high distinction. It is certain that young Keeling was a constituent member, at its constitution, of that venerable body the Portsmouth Church, for there was no church in Norfolk till many years afterwards, and within two years of his baptism was constituted the church, and the Association which borrows its name.

From his credentials, which are now on the desk of the writer of this notice, (in 1859,) on parchment, in the superior chirography of J. Flood, whose signature, with that of Davis Biggs, the

---

* By Henry Keeling, Jr.

then pastor of the church, is affixed, as Presbytery, he was ordained March 19, 1803, in Norfolk, the early home of his married life, by order of "The Baptist Church in Portsmouth and Norfolk." His license, on the same sheet, is of only eight days previous date, and signed by Deacon William M. Fauquier, of Keeling—through life the unchanging friend, and one of the fathers of everything good in the interest of the Baptists in Norfolk.

These data leave Elder Keeling only seventeen years of professional ministerial life, but the fifteen previous years had been scarcely less usefully employed. Of these, the three of the war of 1812–15 were employed in the pastorate of the Toppim Church, in Chowan County, North Carolina, where he was the companion and fellow-laborer of the Rosses, the Spiveys, and the Dorseys; the several previous years of the embargo, when all merchandise and every pursuit beyond mere necessity was suspended, he was pastor of the Pungo and Black-water Churches, where he was associated with the Caseys, Etheridges, Soreys, and Browns; and the last five years of his life, he sustained the same office with his old people, at London Bridge, among whom he had been born, and with whom he is buried.

The towns then, as now, and always, though small, had large influence on the surrounding country. The commanding interest, money, was in the hands of the merchants, who were generally either Englishmen or Scotchmen: the former Episcopalians, the latter Presbyterians; and with neither, much sympathy for Baptists. Hence, when our ministers settled in them, it was to follow some secular calling for support, while they labored as best they could in the towns and the adjacent regions: and hence almost every Baptist minister was, if in the country, a farmer; if the town, a merchant or mechanic, or perhaps a soldier. There were Havelocks then, as now; and every man was, though self-supported and at great sacrifice to himself and family, a missionary. Nor was it possible to be easily or soon loosened from such bonds. It must forever remain to us a wonder that, under such circumstances, they did, not so little, but so much. No telegraph, cars, or steam; Bibles, tracts, or papers, for circulation—nor the possibility of originating them. No Sunday-schools, nor colporteurs; no anything, but for each man to sieze his implements or utensils, and work where he could. If a forest presented itself, down with a tree; if a field, thrust in his spade or his sickle. Now we can easily and gratefully look back, and see how each opening providence and each enterprise, of social or individual origin, contributed to the great cause: but the beginnings of things are, of necessity, small and feeble, encounter difficulties, and are hard to originate. If Lott Carey had never seen a Latter Day Luminary, he might never have gone to Africa.

Elder Keeling was fond of learning, in common with many others who lacked opportunity. Had he lived in our day, he would have been whole-souled in the enterprises of this age. But neither his labors nor his person were known beyond a few surrounding counties: in these, and their churches, as the Minutes of the Portsmouth Association show, he was highly respected and much beloved.

Of him and many of his companions it may truly be said, briars and thistles are the monuments of their graves; but their memorial is with those who have followed them to the skies, and ought not to be less with us, who feel the moral influence of their lives, inducing much that is great and good in the present state of things, which some erringly think more in contrast than in unison with their labors and privations. They labored, and we have entered into their labors. Of these fields that surround us on all sides, some inviting, some promising, some luxurious and beautiful, calling us to labor and to reap, some hands must have felled the forests. Those hands were the hands of our fathers, whose memory we thus briefly record.

ABSALOM WALLER.

THIS servant of the Redeemer was born in Spottsylvania, Virginia, in 1772. His parents, several years prior to their marriage, were brought under religious influence by the instrumentality of Elder Samuel Harriss. Having heard from his lips the word of salvation, and embraced it in 1768, they became members of the

Baptist church. They had six children, of whom Absalom was the oldest. They were allowed not only to see them all happily married and settled in comfortable circumstances, but the followers of Christ and members of his visible church. The happy influence of parental counsel and example was strikingly exhibited in their history. With regard to this influence, their son Absalom thus speaks when he was nearly fifty years of age: "I have often remembered, with humble gratitude to God, my happy lot to be born of such parents. They used to converse with their children about the great things of eternity from the earliest dawn of reason, and as soon as we could read, the Bible was put into our hands; occasionally they would make us read, and then explain what was read to us, especially on the Sabbath day. Our father was, from my earliest remembrance, very punctual in the observance of family worship, which made a gradual and deep religious impression on my mind. About the commencement of my fourteenth year, I obtained an interest in the merits of our blessed Redeemer. Shortly after, the pastor of our church baptized a younger brother in our family, and, in the lapse of years, I had baptized two more of my brothers and our sister, together with my own wife, as also the husband of my sister, prior to their marriage. In our late revivals, the heavenly drops of Divine mercy came down again in rich profusion upon our highly-favored family, and the last of my brothers, four sisters-in-law, three nieces and a nephew, the youngest not thirteen years old, have bowed to the sceptre of King Jesus. Our parents, at the advanced age of over threescore and ten, are in good health, and full of piety and good works, waiting for a gentle dismission, in the earnest hope of a glorious immortality."

In 1786, as already referred to, he became a joyful believer in Christ, and some time during the next year was baptized by his uncle, John Waller, and united with the church at Waller's, Spottsylvania. When his brother John and himself became the subjects of conversion, a deep impression was made on the mind of their uncle and pastor, that John was designed of God to become a minister of the gospel. Connected with this impression, a remarkable incident is related. Elder John Leland, who then resided in Virginia, attended a meeting at which he met the youthful brothers, and had an opportunity of hearing them both lead in prayer. After rising from his knees he appeared thoughtful, and calling the attention of the pastor, said, "Brother Waller, you are deceived in your impressions: John will never preach; but that little white-headed boy," pointing to Absalom, "will be the preacher in your flock." For several years after his connection with the church, Absalom seems to have passed through sore conflicts with the great adversary. At the age of eighteen he imprudently cherished an attachment to an irreligious female, who proved unfaithful to the pledges she had given him, and thus the connection was prevented. In relation to this affair, he thus speaks: "When I became convinced that I was honorably delivered from this snare, I felt sweet thankfulness to God, whose great mercy had wrought deliverance for me. I had calculated on settling myself on a little farm detached from the noise of this busy world, where I might spend my days in the shades of obscurity. This was the scheme I had honestly formed; but God foresaw the evil that awaited me, dissolved the golden enchantment, and set me at liberty."

In his nineteenth year he became deeply concerned for the salvation of his fellow-men, and impressed with the conviction that it was his duty to devote his life to the work of preaching the gospel. In the consideration of this subject he suffered much mental anguish. Numerous objections to the work were suggested, and at times he was tempted altogether to abandon it. A sense of duty at length prevailed. "I was," says he, "a poor, trembling, doubting creature myself, and no way calculated to instruct others. I lacked education, and was timid to an extreme, and withal I was poor, and my future subsistence in life depended on my attention to business of some kind; but these objections were not sufficient to extinguish the flame which was burning in my bosom."

About two years after, he was publicly set apart by the church to the work of preaching and administering the ordinances of the gospel. This event was viewed in its true light, as one of the most solemn and important which could occur in the whole history of his life. It was preceded by deep searchings of heart and prayer to God for direction. That man gives but little evidence of a call to the ministry or fitness for the work who enters upon it in a trifling and prayerless spirit. The state of Elder Waller's mind will be indicated by the reference which he afterwards made to this period of his ministerial career:—

"In the month of July, 1793, a motion was made in church meeting to appoint a day for my ordination to the work of the ministry, and a resolution passed that the business should be attended to in August, and that assistant preachers be called in for the purpose of ordination. Although the church was unanimous in making this order, still I thought it premature, and expressed my sentiments to that effect; but the brethren appeared decided and immovable in their opinion that the Lord had most assuredly called me to preach his gospel, and that I ought to be ordained and fully authorized to go forward in the work. I spent much of the month of July in solemn prayer and meditation; I fasted and humbled myself greatly before a throne of grace. The language of my heart was, 'O Lord, thou knowest my motives and desires; if I am actuated by anything short of an humble desire for the salvation of sinners and the advancement of thy name's glory, I beseech thee to show it me and I will seal my lips in silence.' The presence of God was with me, and in my deepest hours of retirement I felt his love shining like a sunbeam in my soul. I became convinced it was my duty to preach the everlasting gospel. What could I say, or how dare I be disobedient to the heavenly vision? My soul was humbled into the very dust; and such were the views that I had of the excellency of my Master's service, that if crowns and sceptres had been presented to me I should have looked on them with contempt, and have said, 'God forbid that I should glory, save in the cross of our Lord Jesus Christ.' I was willing to forsake parents, brethren, houses, and land, yea, all for Christ and his cause. In this frame of mind I met the Presbytery that was called to attend my ordination, and I sat as a little child at their feet. I was examined, and publicly ordained as an assistant minister in the Baptist church at Waller's, when I had but just completed my twenty-first year. Directly after my ordination I went into the pulpit and preached to a large audience with much enjoyment. How marvelous are the works of God, and his ways past finding out!"

During the same year in which he was ordained his uncle, Elder John Waller, removed with his family to South Carolina. Three or four churches were, in consequence, left without an under-shepherd. But the Great Shepherd had designed to prepare a successor in the person of Absalom Waller. The eye of the destitute churches was at once directed to him as a suitable leader. He consented to take the oversight of Waller's, County Line, and Bethany, and for many years continued to labor for them.

In 1808, in taking a brief review of his pastoral life, he thus alludes to two of these churches: "The congregation which statedly attended my ministerial labors at County Line was large, and independent as to worldly circumstances; but the provision which they made for my support as a minister of the gospel was poor indeed. In fifteen years I received two hundred and fourteen dollars for the loss of my time, expense of clothing, riding horse, etc. If the laborer is worthy of his hire, this people were surely unfaithful to me. But the Lord will determine this matter at a future day. Notwithstanding the neglect of the brethren, I loved them tenderly, and served them in singleness and simplicity of heart. Through all my sufferings, the church at Waller's have been my helpers; they have freely administered to my necessities, and have assisted me more liberally in things pertaining to this life than all other churches among whom I have gone preaching the gospel of Christ; and, notwithstanding my own meanness, the King of saints has made me a blessing indeed to my mother church. I have seen the travail of my Master's soul, and have been satisfied therewith among my brethren at Waller's."

The ministrations of Elder Waller were much prospered of the Lord, particularly at the church at Waller's. Besides regular additions from year to year, several revivals of religion were enjoyed. The most extensive occurred in 1817–18, previous to which he had baptized more than 1500 persons. In 1817, after a season of much discouragement, in consequence of the depressed condition of the churches, he entertained serious thoughts of leaving Virginia; and, for the purpose of obtaining the most desirable situation, he spent several months in traveling through the Western States. During his absence he was the subject of the most painfully conflicting emotions, concerning the course he ought to take. He represents himself as entranced with the idea, that when comfortably settled in the "land of corn and wine," he should never more hear from child or servant the heart-rending question, what shall we do for bread? But a whisper, solemn as the voice of death, inquired, "and with whom wilt thou leave these few sheep in the wilderness?"

"I became convinced," he continues, "it was not the will of God that I should remove from my native State, *as yet*, and that perhaps my dear Master intended to make me the humble instrument, in his hand, of bringing sinners to bow to the golden sceptre of his grace. *Delightful thought, indeed*—'What, to be the means, in the hand of Heaven, of bringing home more of the lost sheep of the house of Israel;' and some of them perhaps from among my kinfolks, and the children of my old brethren and sisters, who have grown up under my infant ministry! Lord, it is enough. I'll tread this dirty world and all its mean appendages under my feet, and bear the cross of my Divine Master with holy zeal and fortitude. In exercises like these I reached home, and found my family and churches safe: I had, in many fervent prayers, committed them to the care of Heaven, and finding them under the protection of my great and good Father, and ready to receive me with open arms, my heart was overwhelmed with a sense of gratitude.

"In a few days after my arrival at home, Elder G. Hodgen and W. Warder, on their return from the Baptist Convention in the City of Philadelphia, visited the church at Waller's, and such was our dullness, that very few attended their appointment. They came, however, in the fullness of the blessings of the gospel of Christ; and from this period I began to entertain an humble hope that the set time to favor our Zion was at hand."

His relation of the various exercises of his own mind during the progress of this interesting work, will exhibit the concern he indulged for the salvation of sinners and the prosperity of the churches. The following is an extract:—

"In the middle of harvest the ministers before named came among us, in the spirit and power of the Lord Jesus; and afterwards preached in rotation four or five times, with all the simplicity of apostolic zeal, and great success, to vast crowds of people. The first sermon, especially by Hodgen, was a masterpiece, (at least to me;) it was on these words: 'He that goeth forth and weepeth, bearing precious seed, shall doubtless come again rejoicing, bringing his sheaves with him.' I never saw his face before; but he told me all my faults, and sweetly described all my sorrows and my joys.

"A great number of young people had grown up under my ministry in an unconverted state; still they seemed to show me very great respect; if they were to be married, I must perform the ceremony; if they were sick, I must visit them. One of my brothers in the flesh, and four amiable sisters-in-law, were unsaved; for these I had, almost times without number, prayed and wept before the Lord in secret. But, strange as it may seem, when the set time to visit our people came, I was unprepared to hail the rising beams of the Sun of righteousness. Having been formerly engaged in several precious revivals of religion, I was no stranger to the labors of an evangelist. Like Jonah, I was unwilling to run at the Divine command; and while the worth of souls, together with a full persuasion that the Lord had much work for me to do, was presented in all their force to my mind by day, and even in dreams at night, I strove, in a variety of ways, to excuse myself. Several pious ministers, who frequented the meetings of the Kentucky brethren, informed me that they could not feel any engagedness in the work; which seemed to be bursting forth under the ministry of those preachers. This tended very much to strengthen my excuses in secret, before a throne of grace; and I tried to believe that no sacrifices were required of me in the work, except the faithful discharge of my stated labors in the Lord's vineyard. But I tried in vain! My distress of mind continued to increase, from an inward conviction that I was disposed to roll in the lap of domestic indolence, while the great harvest of souls was ripening; until I became fearful it would settle down in a fixed melancholy. Sometimes I would endeavor to divert my mind by the conversation of a loving wife, and the innocent prattle of our children; but my efforts were ineffectual. I was in the frequent habit of retiring into a grove of pines, (where are deposited the remains of many of my relatives, together with two of my own children,) for the purpose of prayer; and having one cloudy morning felt more than common distress in mind concerning my own situation, as to my unwillingness to forsake all for Christ, I entered my usual retreat, for the solemn purpose of seeking communion with God. The lowering clouds, the thick cluster of pines, as also the graves of the sleeping dust, seemed greatly to increase the spirit of devotion; my very soul was lifted in strong cries to the throne of mercy, for Divine instruction concerning the way of duty. While I was thus engaged, the thought struck me, with great force indeed, that the souls of my dear departed children (near whose graves I was then kneeling) were at that moment in glory, singing the praises of the Lamb of God, who died for the redemption of lost sinners! and that I was surely a most ungrateful wretch, to feel unwilling to spend and be spent in the cause of Christ! I am unable to describe my feelings at that moment; I wept, under a sense of God's goodness and my own ingratitude—nay, more, I fell on my face and cried out, O Lord! send me, and I will go; I will forsake all for Christ, and try to spend my latest breath in exhorting sinners to repent and turn to God.

"Prior to the Association, which was holden on the first Saturday in September last, between thirty and forty persons (mostly young people) had professed to find pardon; and on my return from the Association I entered the great field of ministerial labor, and in the course of the five succeeding months I delivered over one hundred discourses (chiefly on experimental subjects) to crowds of weeping sinners, besides a great number of exhortations; and very few rest days passed without my being visited by some person under deep convictions for sin. The constant inquiry, 'What shall we do?' and my uniform answer, was, 'Believe on the Lord Jesus Christ, and you shall be saved.' The ordinance of baptism was regularly administered once, and sometimes as often as thrice a week; and generally from ten to fifteen were baptized at a time; several times as many as twenty, and, in one instance, twenty-five were baptized. The meetings for baptizing were generally attended with abundant displays of the Divine presence, as well as those appointed for hearing the exercises of the new converts."

He thus describes a baptismal scene: "The crowd to-day was immensely great; consequently I was compelled to preach in the open air; however, the Lord was with me, and while I had the immense concave of heaven for my sounding-board, I was enabled to raise my trembling voice, and preach that men should repent and believe the gospel; the effect was great indeed—many, very many, were on their knees, begging the prayers of God's people in their behalf. The church convened to hear experience, and six were received as candidates for baptism; among this number was one of my sisters-in-law, and a daughter of my eldest brother. Oh the goodness of God, in making me the humble instrument in his hand to the conversion of my nearest relatives!

"After church-meeting we repaired to the river; the place was vastly convenient for the proper arrangement of the spectators; and while I beheld the multitude standing in solemn order on the banks of the river, many of whom were in tears, I was reminded of the banks of Jordan, where thousands attended the ministry of the first Baptist that ever was in the world. The service was introduced by solemn prayer and praise, and then commenced a most heavenly scene. The candidates marched down into the water in pairs, singing as they went the high praises of God; so soon as they were baptized they returned in the same order; and to behold a pair of lovely children newly baptized meeting the welcome embrace of their weeping and pious parents on the bank, afforded a feast to the enraptured minds of God's people which I am unable to describe."

At another time he says: "In the early part of October the cloud of mercy began to extend itself over the congregation at Bethany, and on the third Lord's day, in the morning, I commenced the work of baptizing among those people; fifteen persons were on that day added to the church. The revival had now become general in three churches, and having none to help me I was almost exhausted in the labors of the vineyard, as well as in continual watchings by night and by day. But the Great Head in Zion was with me and supported my feeble frame, so that in the months of September and October I preached over forty discourses and baptized one hundred and forty-five persons."

Mr. Waller alludes to several special cases of conversion, some of which may properly find a place in this work: "A young gentleman of liberal principles, who had spent a morning in light and sarcastic conversation with a carnal neighbor on the subject of the revival of religion, on his return home, stated that he was suddenly seized with such an awful sense of his lost state and the omnipresence of God, that he was brought upon his knees to beg for mercy through a crucified Saviour; and from this period he became an attendant on public worship, a penitent and broken-hearted sinner; and finally, he obtained a full assurance of pardon for sin, and has since become a zealous member of the church which he once despised.

"Two Christian friends entered into covenant that they would unite in fervent supplications in behalf of a thoughtless acquaintance for whom they entertained great personal respect; and to their great joy and surprise in about three weeks afterwards the gentleman came to meeting—was struck to the heart with the power of conviction for sin; together with his lady. They have both since become members of the County Line Church. It was truly a melting sight, to behold him leading the partner of his earthly joys down into the watery tomb, while tears of contrition for sin, and humble gratitude to God for his pardoning love, through a Divine Redeemer, were rolling down his manly cheeks!"

"The family of an old member in the County Line Church was favored in a peculiar manner indeed. He had three daughters who were all converted within the space of twenty-four hours; his house was truly another bethel, and he observed to a friend shortly after, that he never witnessed so much of the goodness of God before. In the midst of this, a gentleman who had married an elder sister of the young ladies who had just obtained mercy, having heard the astonishing news, came in haste to hear the particulars of the case. The holy raptures of his sisters-in-law produced such a powerful effect on his mind that he rested no more until he found peace by the blood of the cross; and since, himself and his wife have become pious members of the church."

Elder W. did not confine his ministerial labors to the churches for which he statedly preached, but made extensive and frequent tours in almost every direction. There is reason to believe the seed thus sown was productive of fruit unto eternal life. The following interesting selection from his journal is inserted to illustrate the state of his mind in one of these excursions: "We went to the house of prayer and I preached from Heb. vi. 20, 21, to the multitude. About the middle of my discourse the fire of the Lord began to kindle and gently increased, until it burst into a flame, which appeared to fill the whole house; saints rejoiced and sinners trembled! Oh what a heaven of Divine love we felt! We remained at the meeting-house until a late hour, then adjourned to the dwelling of Mr. ———, directly on the sea-coast, dined, and preached again to a great crowd, heard experiences, and at ten o'clock P.M., went down to the water, which was about a stone's cast, carrying with us many lights; here I again exhorted a considerable while in the audience of a solemn, weeping multitude.

"Reader, you can hardly form an idea of this grand and awful scene. Fancy to yourself five hundred persons standing on the sand in silent awe; the proud waves of the sea lulled to sleep in the deep shades of night; and not a breeze stirring to disturb the smooth surface of the water. Numerous lights distributed among the crowd, the mild radiance of the moon, and ten thousand stars, all conspired to render the season grand and impressive. As I went down into the water, my heart filled with the delightful idea that the Saviour, who himself was baptized in Jordan to fulfill all righteousness, was present by his Spirit, beholding our order and obedience. Seven persons were buried with Christ, most of whom came up out of the water rejoicing like the jailor and his house who were baptized the same hour of the night."

Mr. Waller's numerous and pressing ministerial duties, connected with the care of a growing family, must have required unremitted toil. It would appear that while absorbed in the great work to which his Master had called him he did not neglect to provide for his own household. From his earliest devotion to the ministry he was accustomed often to preach from four to five times in the week, besides performing labor on his farm and spending some time in study. Speaking on this subject, he says: "It must not be supposed that I wholly neglected my family concerns; for the most part I rode home every evening, spent often most of the night in reading, meditation, and prayer, and would rise with the dawn of day attend to all my temporal affairs, making the best arrangements I could, and then ride perhaps eight or ten miles to meeting." This last quotation will lead to the mention of his views in reference to ministerial improvement. He labored under the continual consciousness of deficiency, and applied himself with becoming diligence that he might be a workman needing not to be ashamed; rightly dividing the word of truth. He was not possessed of extensive literary attainments, but he sought as far as possible, after his entrance into the ministry, to obtain them. Had the facilities which are now enjoyed by young ministers been at hand, he would doubtless have obtained an education. To some extent he prosecuted the study of the Latin language, but how far he succeeded in its acquisition is not distinctly known. The following paragraph shows his sentiments on the importance of an elevated standard of ministerial improvement:—

"The pastor who is faithful in the discharge of his duty must devote much of his time to study, reading, and prayer; otherwise, he cannot expect to profit his flock. He must strive to become mighty in the Scriptures, that he may be able rightly to divide the word of truth; and unless he devotes himself wholly to the work of an evangelist, he will prove a burden to himself as well as his hearers. It is a lamentable mistake which some Christians labor under in supposing, that because the aid of the Holy Spirit is promised unto the Lord's ministers there is no reason for them to read and study. A minister who falls into this delusion is very apt to became cold and formal in the discharge of his duty and an Antinomian in principle."

At another time he says: "The minister of Christ should be sound in the faith of God's elect and established in the truths of the gospel, that he may be able to feed and comfort his flock; he should spend much of his time upon his knees, in supplication to God for the people of his charge and for a Divine blessing upon his labors. He should not be satisfied with dry and formal services in the pulpit; but he ought to covet earnestly the best gifts, and labor night and day to become a scribe well instructed in the mysteries of gospel grace, that he might bring forth from his treasure things both new and old, for the establishment of the saints in their most holy faith, and for the conviction of lost sinners. The church is very soon reduced to cold and declining circumstances, when her pastor is satisfied with telling his own experience and traveling over his old ground once or twice a month. While it is all-important that a pastor should look to God for aid in preaching to his flock, it is also highly necessary that he should be unceasingly engaged in accumulating a fund of Divine knowledge."

His views of pastoral labor were sound and scriptural. It is much to be regretted, that many of those who undertake the work of an overseer over the house of God have no just conceptions of their responsibility. Elder W. remarks: "The pastoral duties are not confined merely to public preaching. It is the duty of a pastor to visit his people; to comfort those that are in affliction; to weep with those that weep; and to rejoice with those that rejoice. He should warn them that are unruly; strengthen the feeble-minded; and in all things endeavor to be to his flock an example of meekness, humility, and temperance. In the government of the church he should exercise no authority, save the counsel of a tender father; and as a member, he should be subject to the watchful care and discipline of the church. He should administer the ordinances and exhort the members to a faithful discharge of their duty, both in the house of God and in their families, as well as in all their transactions before the world."

Nor were the views he entertained of the obligation of the church to provide for the support of her pastor less judicious and consistent with the Word of God. He remarks: "The church should pay particular attention to the temporal support of her pastor. She should endeavor, as far as the means are in her power, to disengage his mind from the perplexing cares of his family, that he may give himself to the ministry of the Word. The Lord hath ordained that they who preach the gospel should live of the gospel. It is, undoubtedly, the duty of every member to contribute toward the support of his pastor as the Lord hath prospered him.

"There are many professors who say, that if a minister is poor, then it is our duty to assist him; but if he is otherwise, or in good circumstances, let him shift for himself. This excuse reminds me of a remark which I once heard fall from the lips of a poor old Baptist preacher. He said, 'That after having tried to preach the gospel *forty years*, he could safely say that he never received *forty shillings for preaching in his life!*' He is since dead, and a neighbor of his observed to me in a few months after, 'We never knew what a treasure we possessed until we lost him.' The time of retribution will surely come; and the congregation or church that lives in the habit of closing every door of temporal support against the man who watches over their spiritual interest have reason to fear the judgments of an angry God, who visits the sins of the fathers upon the children even unto the third and fourth generation of them that hate him; while he shows mercy unto the thousands that love him and keep his commandments."

It were well if these doctrines had been more faithfully promulged by our brethren in the ministry. When the popular sentiment had become fixed in its opposition to the duty of giving a full support to the ministry, it required no ordinary moral courage to meet this prejudice, especially as it so easily comported with the selfishness of human nature. Covetousness is a plant finding vigorous growth in the soil of the carnal heart, and if it can receive support from any apparent principle of Divine authority, it sends forth its branches but the more luxuriantly. To aim at the root of this evil, at whatever expense of popular favor, is the manifest duty of every Christian pastor. God's people should be guarded against the extreme of parsimony and the ruinous love of money, while a hireling priesthood is denounced as unworthy of support. The fidelity of Mr. Waller on this subject is worthy of imitation. He says:—

"The idea that if a minister is able, he is bound to support himself, is one of the most unreasonable things that ever entered the human mind. This wild notion embraces the following inconsistent doctrines: that our minister is to employ all his time and talents in serving the people; to procure his own books, clothes, food, and pay his taxes out of what he honestly raised by industry prior to his becoming our pastor, or on what his father bequeathed him by his last will and testament! I cannot believe that any who fear God can possibly believe a doctrine so pointedly contrary to Scripture, reason, or even common sense; for, in admitting this, we must believe that covetousness is an appendage in our religion. Abhorrent thought, indeed!

"*A covetous Christian* would be a monster in the world of grace. I am, therefore, disposed to think that the principal reason why the people are so prone to neglect the support of the gospel ministry arises from two sources. First, the ministers themselves, in declaiming against the despotism of the former establishment of religion, have taught the people to believe that religion was to be supported by miracles; and even where this absurd and mistaken notion began to vanish, the want of proper attention to the Scripture method of providing for the ministry has caused very considerable difficulty and even serious confusion to arise. Second, the people tremble at the idea of a pampered and lazy set of priests, who, like swarms of locusts, devour the good of the land in all countries where they have an existence. I wish, therefore, to make a few serious remarks upon each of these evils.

"First. The man who suffers his zeal to carry him to extremes when declaiming against error of any kind, is very often the means of forming prejudices in the minds of the people of the most unreasonable and unscriptural nature, which requires the lapse of generations to wipe off. Second. I observe that where the people possess the power of choosing the man who is to minister to them in holy things, and of discarding him at pleasure, they have nothing to fear from spiritual tyranny. The monsters of civil and religious despotism seldom show their heads in the tents of a virtuous people, but where the inhabitants of a country forsake the ordinances of heaven, throw down the altars of the most high God, and plunge into carnal mirth and pleasure; in process of time the whole body becomes a mass of disorder and wild confusion; every man wishes to do what appears to be right in his own eyes; the sword falls from the hand of the magistrate, and there is an end to all order, while even the right of private property becomes insecure. In this state of *chaos* the demons of spiritual and civil tyranny raise their heads. The one assumes the title of *Bishop*, or supreme head of the church, while the other marches through rivers of blood to the throne of cruel despotism. Then the sons of heaven-born liberty must fly their native country or be consigned to the horrid dungeons of the despot.

"The last thing which I shall notice is the proper method to be observed in the regular support of the gospel ministry. Every person should remember that whatever he gives is given unto Christ, or to aid in the support of his blessed cause."

Mr. Waller had been familiar with the sacrifices and sufferings of the older men of God, who, to proclaim Christ to the people, had gone on long journeys, and whose families had been allowed by the churches to suffer the want of food and raiment. He had witnessed their faith and patience, while, pressed in spirit, they beheld the multitude as sheep without a shepherd, and had gone forth to feed them. The following touching anecdote is related by him:—

"I am acquainted with a minister who once left home under great pressure, to fulfill a tour of six days' meetings. The wife of his bosom said to him, just as he started, 'My dear husband, what are we to do for bread?' The big tear of piety was swimming in her radiant eyes, for she feared Elijah's God. Her poor disconsolate husband replied, 'The Lord will provide' At that time the whole stock of grain, or last turn, was sent to the mill, and they had no money. The preacher went on to fulfill his appointments, trying to summon all the fortitude of a doubting Thomas, wishing, in the midst of his inexpressible tortures of mind, to lean on that promise, 'I will never leave thee nor forsake thee.' On the sixth day, after preaching to a large and solemn assembly, he felt more than common consolation, arising from an humble hope that he had been made the instrument of doing some good. Just as he was turning his face toward his house, a gentleman put a paper in his hand, and said, '*A few of us worldlings wish, sir, to make you a small present.*' The preacher received it with a silent bow; but what were his feelings, when, on opening the paper, he found it contained *forty* dollars! He alighted from his horse in a lonely wood, and, on his knees, returned thanks to Heaven, while, with flowing tears, he prayed for the salvation of the gentlemen who bestowed the present. The pious reader is left to judge as to the impression made upon the mind of her who participates in the joys and sorrows of the minister."

The duty of employing the avails of labor in part for the promotion of Christ's kingdom was often pressed upon the attention of his churches. He feared not, however unpopular it might be, to present this duty in its strongest light, believing that its neglect would be attended with the Divine disapprobation. He writes, in reference to it:—

"'The Lord loveth a cheerful giver.' A deacon once informed me, that 'a member in the church where he was also a member, observed to him, on paying his annual subscription, that he hated to part with his money for religion. That year the miser died; and his children have since spent hundreds at law concerning the division of his estate.' I have no sort of doubt concerning the Divine interference in all human affairs, and that God rewards or even chastises his own children in the present world according to their works. I often tremble at the thought of the dying bed of thorns which awaits worldly-minded professors, who are always too poor to give a small matter to the poor, or to cast their mite into the treasury of the Lord."

Mr. Waller's sentiments on the nature of Christian fellowship, in distinction from the kindness proper to be shown to men in general, as also the importance of fidelity in defending scriptural doctrines and ordinances, were sound, and fearlessly expressed. He was not a bigot. The good of every name he knew how to appreciate. And yet the will of the Lord, as ascertained from his words, was regarded as authoritative and binding on all his people. No false notions of charity would allow him to conceal or adulterate the truth. It was with reference to this subject that the following interesting statements were made:—

"Christian charity, or love, leads us to desire union and concord in both civil and religious society, and to follow peace with all men. James and John, two disciples of Christ, were very far from the exercise of this heavenly temper when they desired that fire might come down from heaven and burn up the Samaritans, because they neglected the doctrine of our Saviour; and our Lord sweetly rebuked them by saying, 'Ye know not what manner of spirit we are of.' Hence learn that the temper of our holy religion is not to kill and destroy sinners and refractory brethren, but to save them. The desirableness of union among all saints is sweetly represented by the Psalmist, when he says, 'Behold how good and how pleasant a thing it is for brethren to dwell together in unity.'

"But, it is necessary we should remark, that it is one thing to love and be charitable toward all men, and another to form a union upon improper principles. It is surely a lamentable circumstance, that many professors of religion seem more concerned about union among societies than they do about keeping the commandments of God. Although those declaimers about the necessity of union may appear in the eyes of thoughtless persons to possess the very essence of charity, yet the candid inquirer after truth will soon discover that this enchanting bait covers the deadly hook. If Luther had listened to the loud declamations of the Romish priest, respecting the necessity of union, the Reformation must doubtless have perished in embryo, since it is evident the Pope would have suffered him to retain his principles, provided he would have acquiesced in the voice and authority of the holy Catholic Church.

"The union of saints who profess our Lord's faith and baptism is radically different from a union of sects and parties. Notwithstanding there may be vital Christians among the various sects in the religious world, whose minds (for a season) may be beguiled by the subtlety of the serpent and the vain pomp of worldly wisdom and carnal philosophy, yet this by no means argues the propriety of giving countenance to the traditions of men. Supposing a man to be a Baptist, he is bound by the laws of Christ and the profession he makes to believe that infant baptism is a vain and useless thing, and one of the props and pillars of antichrist; and, consequently, that all Christians who believe in and practice it are in an unbaptized state. Now if a Baptist, under these impressions, should enter into communion with other societies—let all say, whether his conduct would not savor more of hypocrisy than Christian charity. The road to union among Christians is by the highways of obedience. We should say to professors of religion who seem to follow Christ only in part, We love you, and we pity your errors, but we dare not countenance you in our fellowship, until you are reconciled to follow the Lamb whithersoever he goeth. Then, and not till then, we can take sweet counsel together, go up to the Lord's house, and sit around his table in heavenly concord."

The subject of this memoir was not unmindful of his personal obligations, nor did he fail himself to grow in grace and in the knowledge of Jesus Christ. "How great," said he, "is the responsibility of those who preach the gospel! They watch for souls as those who must give account at the great tribunal." Thus, contemplating his solemn responsibilities, he continued to the close of life, steadfastly adhering to the service of his Lord. He made such full proof of his ministry, that among his brethren he was regarded with high esteem, and, toward the close of life, with veneration. For many years he was afflicted with partial deafness, and consequently found it difficult to engage in conversation; yet his opinion on difficult subjects was frequently consulted.

His death occurred not far from 1820. The summons did not surprise him. He had long been in readiness for his dismission. The following, written some years before his death, expresses the feelings which he seemed habitually to cherish, and which were peculiarly manifest in the closing hour. He remarks: "Oh how near is the period when these active limbs will slumber in the grave, the land of silence, forever to rest! Forever did I say? No; death, cruel death, thou mayest triumph for a season, and lock my bones in the prison of the grave, but Jesus will come, and will be thy plague and thy destruction; I shall hear his voice, and come forth from thine iron domains, and feeling in an instant the springs of an immortal body, I shall rise to meet him in the air."

The period of his dissolution was indeed an hour of peace and joy. He looked on the grave not only with composure, but triumph. He knew that his Redeemer lived, and felt happy in the prospect of beholding his face in righteousness. His attendant physician was much affected with the rational and elevated joy which he evinced as he walked through the valley of the shadow of death.

HENRY TOLER.

THE date of ELDER TOLER's birth is not known. He was a native of King and Queen County, Virginia, and remained in that county until he reached manhood. His parents, who were respectable, gave him such an education only as the common schools of the county afforded. Under the ministry of Elder John Courtney he received in very early life his first religious impressions, and these impressions continued to increase until they ultimated in a saving acquaintance with God's plan of salvation. He became a member of the Upper College Church, and soon began to speak in public. Such were the indications of genius, that he attracted the attention of Counsellor Robert Carter, a member of the Baptist church, and among the wealthiest men in Virginia. Mr. Carter was so much pleased with young Toler, that he prevailed on him to remove to Pennsylvania, for the purpose of improving his mind under the tuition of Dr. Samuel Jones, and generously contributed the necessary funds for his support.

While at school this young disciple applied himself to his studies with becoming diligence. He made rapid proficiency in those branches of learning which occupied his attention. Having remained at school about three years, he returned to his native county, greatly improved in all respects. Shortly after, he was ordained. His whole time was now consecrated to the delightful employ of preaching Christ and him crucified. Nor did he spend his strength for naught: in various directions the Lord accompanied his ministry with almighty energy, and made it his wisdom and power unto salvation. Having preached with much acceptance in the County of King George, in 1783, he was invited statedly to visit them. He ultimately settled in that county. After his removal, he consented, at the urgent solicitation of a pious lady, to preach in Westmoreland. At this period there were but two Baptists in the county, and they were females. The results of this visit, and of his future labors there, are thus narrated by Elder Semple, in his History of Nomini Church: "In 1783

Elder Toler was invited by an old lady, who had been baptized by Mr. Lunsford, to preach in the neighborhood of Nomini. He went, and but few people attended; these were distant and reserved; none, but a very poor man, invited him to his house; yet, how unsearchable are the ways of God! This meeting was the beginning of great events, as it respects this neighborhood. Light dawned; the prejudices of the people wore off; several persons of different classes were converted and baptized. This, says Mr. Toler, *was a gracious, glorious, pleasant time.* Those whom he had baptized, together with a few others who had been baptized previous to his coming, were formed into a church, April 29, 1786, having in all seventeen members. Elder Toler was chosen to attend them as pastor, and in a year or two moved here to live.

"On the same day, after the constitution of the church, five others were baptized; and, at the end of this year, the number was seventy-three. In 1787 it increased to one hundred and nineteen. In 1788 to two hundred and twenty-two. In 1789 to three hundred. In 1790 to three hundred and thirty-one. In 1791 to three hundred and forty-eight. In 1792 to three hundred and fifty-four. In 1793 to three hundred and fifty-seven. In 1794 to three hundred and sixty-seven. In 1795 to four hundred and eight. In 1806 the work of God again appeared. In a small time it spread to an extent beyond the former revival. In three months ninety were baptized, and at various times thirty, forty, fifty, and sixty were baptized at once, so that, from first to last in this revival, there were added between five and six hundred, bringing the number up to eight hundred and seventy-five. This was the most numerous church in Virginia."

By this extract the reader will learn something of the influence which attended the ministrations of Elder Toler in the County of Westmoreland. There are yet living several persons who were the subjects of God's grace in those revivals. By them the memory of their father in the gospel is greatly revered. They still love to speak of those solemn seasons when the majesty and glory of the Redeemer were displayed in subduing his proudest foes, and in making the cause of truth and righteousness triumphant where sin once fearfully abounded.

The labors of Mr. T. were not confined to the County of Westmoreland. He traveled extensively in the upper counties, and below in the Northern Neck, as well as between the York and Rappahannock Rivers. In these journeys he was excessively laborious. "Few preachers," says Elder Semple, "having families, have been more indefatigable in proclaiming the gospel than Mr. Toler." Between himself and Elder Lunsford there was for many years a most endearing intimacy. They labored much together. When Lunsford was taken to his reward in heaven, it became Elder Toler's mournful duty to preach a funeral discourse at two different places; one was delivered at Kilmarnock Meeting-house, Lancaster County, and the other in Essex, the county in which he died. These sermons were afterwards published.

At the annual meetings of the Dover Association, Elder T. was usually required to take a prominent part. "I do not think," says one who knew him well, "that he ever failed to attend the Association." For several years he was appointed their clerk, and frequently was chosen to preach on Lord's day. Some of the circular letters issued by this body were written by him.

Notwithstanding his successful labors in Westmoreland, and his high repute as a preacher, it is melancholy to state, that those for whose spiritual benefit he labored did not suitably contribute to his temporal support. On this account he was compelled to remove. He purchased a farm in Fairfax, but finding himself unable to pay for it, he relinquished his title and removed west of the Blue Ridge. Thence he emigrated to Kentucky. Thus the claims of a dependent family obliged him to seek a home among strangers. In adopting this course he followed the example of many of the most talented and pious Virginia ministers, who remained in their much-loved native State, preaching for churches without a just renumeration, until they were driven to find a livelihood in the rich lands of the West.

On this subject he thus speaks: "Much is required at the hands of ministers without regard to their inconveniences or sufferings; and for all their services they may sometimes receive the extraordinary reward of a little lifeless praise, and, if they choose it, a rich Sunday-dinner. If they should not appear well-dressed, they are blamed as lazy slovens, although they have little or no time to work for themselves; and, if they struggle hard and furnish themselves by their own industry, it is either said their accommodations are too good for them, or that they can very well shift for themselves, and serve others day and night too."

This neglect of ministerial support has been the reproach of Virginia Baptists. To this is to be attributed the fact, that the labors of many of those who remain are necessarily divided among three or four churches. Even when this division has been allowed, the minister gives most of his time and attention to secular concerns to save his family from want, and preaches mostly on Lord's day to the churches he serves. The pastoral office has been reduced to a mere name. Even in preaching the gospel, the mind becomes so much secularized that it is disqualified for entering upon the work with becoming energy. It is strange that the duty of providing for the necessities of their pastors should have been so long neglected by our brethren, especially as this obligation is obviously authorized by the Word of God. May it be the determination of all the churches no longer to allow such guilt to be indulged. They should at once place their pastor in circumstances of comfort, and require of them their entire services. Then would sufficient time be allowed to "give attention to reading," to visit from house to house, to "reprove, rebuke, and exhort with all long-suffering and doctrine."

To this remissness, of which mention is here made, there have been some honorable exceptions. A few individuals, who highly prized the labors of Elder T., contributed what they could for his support. A pious female connected with the Nomini Church, at her death, left the sum of ten pounds to be annually applied to his benefit as long as he retained his pastoral relation.

Concerning his talents as a preacher, it may be said that they were above mediocrity. He was not as remarkable for vigor as sprightliness of mind. His style, though not distinguished for clearness, was flowing, and his manner usually animated His voice was clear and musical. He delighted much to dwell on those sentiments of the Word of God which tended to abase man and exalt the character of Christ.

As illustrative of his views of the plan of salvation, the following is taken from one of his discourses: "The absolution of sin flows through the blood of the Son of God, the crucified Lord of glory, who, by the mysterious union of his Divine and human nature, became God and man, in one person, that he might be one, real, proper Mediator, and in him the infinite law might be honored in the complete salvation of sinful men. Without the shedding of his blood, the smallest sin could not be forgiven, but by it all manner of sin shall be remitted. In wonderful kindness, he humbled himself and became obedient unto death, even the death of the cross; thus fully meeting the preceptive and ending the penal part of the law, that God may be faithful and just to forgive us our sins and to cleanse us from all unrighteousness."

Proceeding with this train of thought, he says: "The sinner, being truly humbled and by the power of faith drawn to Christ, as a guilty offender, he receives a generous and entire pardon from God, whose prerogative alone it is to forgive sin. He does not receive it because he becomes worthy of it by sincere obedience, repentance, faith, or any other thing in himself; for then he might demand it, and it would not be a pardon at all; but, by the atonement of Christ. All his sins of every shape and size, his sins of nature and sins of practice, his more than ten thousand times ten thousand complicated acts of rebellion, are fully and freely forgiven, so that, in this ocean of merit, every trace of them is drowned and sunk out of memory."

In these passages, culled from his sermon, the reader is put in possession of his style and sentiments. In a certain sense, Toler himself is presented, and we listen to him. Treating of the reluctance with which the sinner lays hold of the plan of salvation, he observes: "By nature man is dead in sin, and not only in darkness, but darkness itself. He is entirely ignorant of his own guilt and utter depravity, as well as the spotless purity and extent of the Divine law. He thinks his crimes small failings, his duties great performances, and either trusts in some confused notions of general mercy, or expects to appease an offended God by some sincere future obedience. When first awakened from this sleep of carnal security, instead of flying, like a dove, over his obstructions to Christ, he struggles, worse than a mole, to clear them all out of the way. He must stop for greater alarms, for sharper convictions, to suffer more for his sins, to experience sufficient humility, self-mortification, sanctified tempers, that he may render himself an acceptable object of pity, before he can venture to come to the Saviour. But let the sinner twist and shift as he will, until he does come to Christ, he must be under the curse, just as naturally as the fire emitted from a burning mountain would certainly consume him if within its range, however much he might exert himself to quench the flames."

Extracts like these might be multiplied, exhibiting his views of truth and manner of presenting them, but the present limits will not permit. It may be sufficient to say, but few Baptist ministers in the State entertained clearer apprehensions of all those great doctrines which, as a people, we have delighted to cherish, and but few have more earnestly and successfully defended them.

It has already been stated that Mr. Toler, after a long, laborious, and efficient career of usefulness in his native State, migrated to the West. He became pastor of the church in Versailles, Kentucky, where he remained until his death, which occurred in March, 1824. How far his efficiency was kept up after the change in his position, the author has no means of determining. We doubt not that, with Noel, Semple, and Lunsford, the associates of his earlier years, he now swells the song of redemption in the bright world above.

ROBERT B. SEMPLE.

Robert Baylor Semple was of Scotch descent. His father, John Semple, who emigrated to this country in early life, was one of thirteen children, and the son of very wealthy parents. According to the custom of the Old Country, his eldest son inherited the whole estate, while the others received as their only patrimony a liberal education. Two of the younger sons, John and James, came to America, and settled in Virginia. James became a clergyman of the Episcopal church, and was the father of the late lamented Judge Semple, of Williamsburg. John Semple engaged in the practice of law, and, after the acquisition of a large property from his profession, married Elizabeth Walker, in 1761.

R. B. Semple, their youngest son, was born at Rose Mount, King and Queen County, January 20th, 1769. His father died when Robert was only twelve months old. By this event, Mrs. Semple was left, with four children, nearly penniless. Having become security on behalf of several friends for a large amount, the ample estate which had been accumulated was nearly all required to meet the claims of creditors. The wreck which was left after the payment of debts was bequeathed to the eldest son, while Robert inherited nothing but the affectionate regard and guidance of his surviving parent, "with," as he used afterwards to say, "the wide world to seek his fortune in." This depression in the external circumstances of his family may have been one of the necessary links in that chain of events by which God intended to magnify the riches of his providence and grace in calling him from darkness to light, and in making him the instrument of spiritual good to hundreds of his race.

Mrs. Semple was a rigid adherent of the established church, and left no means untried in endeavoring to instill into the minds of her children the principles she had imbibed. They were regularly taken to public worship, and accustomed to all the forms of the church. Such was Robert's attention to the externals of religion, when still a youth, that both his friends and he had formed a high estimate of his attainments in piety. After he became a converted man, and a minister, he was heard frequently to allude to the influence which these early instructions produced on his mind. Though pharisaical pride was indulged, and his heart remained for a time unchanged, yet he always considered that the religious habits he formed in the beginning of life resulted in keeping his conscience tender, and prevented him from running into the vortex of skepticism.

When quite young he was placed at school with a Mr. Taylor, as his mother cherished a peculiar anxiety to give him a good education. The late Rev. Peter Nelson, known throughout Lower Virginia as one of the most distinguished teachers of the State, was afterwards his preceptor When Mr. Nelson removed to the Forks of Hanover and established an academy, Robert's mother, unable to sustain the expense of boarding and tuition, began to apprehend that she must decline the purpose of educating her son, excepting so far as an opportunity might be allowed by the common schools of the neighborhood. But Mr. Nelson, discovering in his young pupil much sprightliness and a considerable aptitude for the acquisition of knowledge, magnanimously tendered to him his board and tuition free of expense. With Mr. Nelson he studied the Latin and Greek languages, and at the age of sixteen he had made such proficiency as to become a most valuable assistant teacher in the academy.

Having finished the course of studies prescribed at the academy, he was recommended by his tutor and friend as well qualified to conduct the education of youth, and obtained a situation in a private family. Here he commenced the study of law. No one, acquainted with his natural vigor of mind and his powers of discrimination, could doubt that in this profession he might have risen to distinguished eminence. But He who has the hearts of all men in His hands had determined to elevate him to a distinction still higher, by calling him to the work of preaching the everlasting gospel. His was to be the noble work of vindicating the ways of God to man, and to plead with guilty rebels to be reconciled to their sovereign. While prosecuting his studies, preparatory to the practice of law, notwithstanding the influence of maternal instruction, he became strongly tinctured with the sentiments of infidelity. In these he sought refuge from the occasional convictions of guilt which he experienced. Frequently was he lured from the path of morality, in which, in his earlier years, he had been accustomed to walk. Being necessarily thrown into the society of the gay and wicked, he was tempted to indulge in their practices. To paralyze the strokes of conscience, an endeavor was made to disbelieve the truths of the Bible; but still he was restless and unhappy. According to his own confession he was often compelled, amid the frivolities of the ball-room, to seek relief by retiring to pray.

During this period of painful contest between conscience and inclination he sought opportunities to converse on religious subjects. So far as he was inclined to believe in the reality of inspired truth, he urgently defended the forms of the established church. About this time the Baptists were much prospered in their attempts to save men from the delusions of sin. Although, for the most part, their ministers were men of limited attainments, yet they possessed strong native sense, and ardent, humble piety, while the Lord was with them, bringing many, through their means, to a knowledge of the truth. Mr. Semple seems to have indulged quite a contemptible opinion of them and their system. Among others whom he encountered in argument was a pious and aged member of the Baptist church, by the name of William Skelton, who resided near him. This man, being an industrious and respectable citizen, though unskilled in science, became the subject of Mr. Semple's sympathy. He was regarded as a deluded enthusiast, and was visited by his youthful friend with the avowed purpose of convincing him of the error of his way and restoring him to the bosom of the church from which he had departed. In the execution of this purpose, Mr. Semple plied his arguments with warmth and skill; but he failed to change the mind of the aged disciple. His arrows were pointless. To his utter astonishment, he found this man's mind well stored with scriptural knowledge. He could not gainsay or resist the truth, which, in simplicity and godly sincerity, was brought to bear on his understanding and his heart. He determined to make himself more familiar with the Bible, and doubted not that he should be able still to triumph over his opponent. The controversy was renewed, but with the same result. Mr. Skelton extorted from him a promise, at the close of the second interview, that he would carefully read the New Testament, and note all the passages which related to the points in dispute. This examination was productive of lasting good. "The law of the Lord is perfect—converting the soul." The whole character of the young disputant was now changed. He was no longer the petulant cavalier or the self-approving Pharisee, but the humble, broken-hearted inquirer. His proud heart was subdued; for he saw, what to him was before unknown, that he was a ruined sinner and deserved to perish. Now, the sentiments which had been advanced and vindicated by his aged neighbor were seen to be truths of lasting importance. The further his investigations were pursued the more wretched he became, until the plan of salvation, in all its simplicity and fullness, was beheld and trusted in by him. A new world was opened to his vision; Christ was made unto him wisdom, righteousness, sanctification, and redemption, and became, in his estimation, the chief among ten thousand, and altogether lovely.

In adverting to the means by which the spirit of God effected a change in the heart of this young formalist, a number of important suggestions occur to the mind. The first is, the sovereignty of Divine grace. Here is an individual presenting himself in the attitude of an opposer; he wages war against God and his Christ, and God subdues, not by confining him in chains of darkness, but by taking away his stony heart and giving him a heart of flesh. God's purpose is accomplished, too, not by human wisdom or human eloquence, but in the manifestation of truth by a plain, uneducated farmer. Another thought deserves to be remembered: the Christian knows not what grand results may grow out of his endeavors to do good, however feeble. An old man, with no capacity to encounter the learning and wit by which he was assailed, might have satisfied his conscience with the utter hopelessness of making an impression. He might have apprehended only an exposure of the cause he wished to defend, or the fear of exposing his own ignorance might have prompted him to keep silence. But no; he determined to open his mouth boldly, and speak on behalf of Him in whom he trusted and whom he loved. And what was the result? A soul is converted. An individual is brought over from the enemy who is to become a leader in the army of the Lord, and through whom many are to be won to the standard of the Prince of peace. The most obscure follower of Christ may, by a well-timed conversation, or a single word uttered in a right spirit, be the occasion of events intimately or remotely connected with the eternal well-being of thousands of his race.

But to return to the narrative. The subject of this biography was not simply delivered from the wrath to come and adopted into the heavenly family; his grateful spirit submitted with joy to the Redeemer's sway, and his prayer was, "Lord, what wilt thou have me to do?" He sought his duty from the pages of inspiration, and, contrary to early prepossessions, determined to attach himself to that sect which pre-eminently, in his day, was everywhere spoken against. In taking this step he had nothing to gain but the answer of a good conscience and the approbation of God; while, in respect to temporal things, there was every prospect of sustaining loss. But for the excellency of the knowledge of Christ Jesus his Lord, he was willing to count all things loss. He was baptized in December, 1789, by Elder Theodorick Noel, and joined the Upper King and Queen Church.

The same month he began publicly to testify to the faithfulness of the saying, "That Christ Jesus came into the world to save sinners." It has been before stated, that at the time of his conversion he was qualifying himself for the practice of law. When the excellence and love of Christ were revealed to his soul, he immediately conferred not with flesh and blood, but relinquished the hope of worldly elevation, that he might preach among his fellow-men the unsearchable riches of Christ. His first attempt was made at the house of Mr. Loury, Caroline County, December 24th; and it is said this effort was far from giving promise of eminence as a preacher. A late distinguished statesman and lawyer being present at this time, expressed himself very freely concerning the sermon, and predicted that young Semple would never, in the character of a minister, gain the attention of the community. On the same occasion a ministering brother, still living, whose praise is in all the churches, preached his first discourse. Although Elder Semple commenced the solemn work in much weakness and with trembling, he was not discouraged. He was willing to sacrifice his pride while he could entertain the hope of doing something to promote the cause and glory of his Master. The characteristic decision which he exhibited through life was evinced in his earliest efforts. His second discourse was delivered at a private house, from Hebrews, ii. 1. One who had an opportunity of ascertaining something of his juvenile attempts, remarks that "his manner was extremely awkward, and his ideas, though obvious to his audience to be clear and well conceived, were expressed with a labored and unpleasant gesticulation." Encouragement may be furnished, in his example, to young licentiates to persevere in determined endeavors to improve in style and manner. For several months this young disciple labored in the neighborhoods adjacent to his own home with great zeal. In 1790, Bruington Church was constituted in King and Queen, under the instrumentality of that excellent man, Elder James Greenwood. After their constitution they unanimously called the subject of this memoir to take the oversight of them. On the 26th of September, 1790, a Presbytery, consisting of Elders Robert Ware, Theodorick Noel, and Iverson Lewis, proceeded to examine and ordain him to the work of the gospel ministry. He continued to sustain the pastoral relation to Bruington Church as long as he lived, a period of forty years.

On the 1st of March, 1793, he was united in marriage to Miss Ann Loury, daughter of Col. Thomas Loury, of Caroline County. A few months previous this estimable young lady had attached herself to the Baptist Church, and had given the most indubitable evidence of devotion to the cause of Christ. Her husband was often heard to express gratitude for the direction of his Heavenly Father in this event. She was a help-meet indeed. They commenced the married life without property, but being vigorous in health, and independent in their feelings, they determined, by industry and rigid economy, to avoid embarrassment, that he might more fully prosecute the duties of the ministry. This was rendered the more difficult as they had both been accustomed to move in affluent society. After two or three temporary removals, they ultimately settled in King and Queen County, on a farm called Mordington. Here they spent the greater part of their lives. At this place, for a number of years, he conducted a school. As an instructor of youth he was much approved, and highly useful. In this employment, in connection with the cultivation of a farm, he was soon placed in very comfortable circumstances, and before the close of life had acquired considerable property.

In a few years after the entrance of Elder Semple into the work of the ministry, it was the will of God that he should attain a very high reputation among all classes of men. Notwithstanding his necessary confinement in school, he made extensive and frequent tours throughout all parts of Lower Virginia, preaching the gospel and confirming the disciples. His visits to the churches were eminently blessed. Itinerant labors like these he continued until the close of life. His regular ministrations, however, were confined to King and Queen, and King William Counties. Within this region a number of infant churches had been originated when he began his ministerial career. These churches, chiefly under his instrumentality, were greatly enlarged, embracing many of the most intelligent classes of society. It is to be regretted that the minutes of the Dover Association do not, for a number of years, give the statistics of the churches, by which might be ascertained something of the increase in those regions occupied by Elder Semple.

The following extract of a letter addressed to a Christian friend, alludes to the state of things in his congregations in 1822: "To-morrow I am to attend at Upper King and Queen, (one of the churches of my pastoral care,) for the purpose of baptizing fifteen or twenty persons recently converted, and at the same place, in July, I baptized twenty-three in one day. This, I am sure you will say, is good news; I can also say of them that few revivals in my acquaintance furnish characters of whom stronger hopes may be entertained of their wearing well. Although many of them are the poor of this world, I feel persuaded they are rich in grace. In another church of my care a revival has gone on for some months, chiefly among the people of color. About one hundred and seventeen have been baptized, of whom more than one hundred are colored; I wish my hopes of these were as sanguine as they are in respect to the subjects of the other revival. So closely are ignorance and superstition united, that I find it hard to keep these poor creatures from building upon visions and dreams. In many of them, however, the clearest evidences are furnished of a work of grace. In Bruington Church, the other church of my care, we have had rather a warm season for about twelve months past, and during that time have baptized about thirty; of whom many were persons of high standing in civil society. When in York, last May, I baptized two ladies, from whom I entertain great hopes of usefulness. They are Mrs. B——, and Eliza P——, my niece. I correspond with them, and Eliza writes to my daughter: from their letters, as well as their conversation, I entertain these hopes They seem to be very pious."

An interesting fact may be inferred from the above letter, which deserves the attention of the biographer Not only were the intelligent, refined, and wealthy brought under the influence of his ministry, but the ignorant and the indigent. They shared largely in his sympathies and ministrations. It is said some of his happiest moments were spent in the cabins of the poor, while recommending to them the Divine Saviour, who humbled himself that they might be rich. Hundreds of those who occupied the humbler walks of life were accustomed to hail him as their spiritual father, their counsellor and friend.

Until 1783 there was but one Association in Virginia, called the General Association. This body was then divided into four districts, and the General Committee organized. While the four District Associations met regularly, to consult the welfare of the individual churches, they each appointed four delegates to the General Committee, to deliberate on the interests of the denomination at large. This was dissolved in 1794, but in 1800 representatives were appointed by several Associations, and the General Meeting of Correspondence was formed. Elder Semple was usually a delegate from the Dover Association, and in 1808 he was appointed their Moderator. In this office he continued until its dissolution. From his entrance into the ministry he was one of the most regular attendants at the Dover Association. It is doubtful whether he was absent from any one meeting for the space of forty years. This Association, the largest in America, and perhaps in the world, owes much of its efficiency to his exertions. At an early period he was chosen Moderator, and continued to receive this appointment from year to year, until his death.

In the early efforts of the Baptist denomination to send abroad the gospel among the heathen, Elder Semple became deeply interested. His benevolence was enlarged, like that of Christ, embracing the whole world. He thus refers to the subject of missions:—

"The whole glory of the salvation of sinners is due to God; but the means must be used by his people. Go ye and preach, said Christ, and I will be with you. Do you use the outward means, and I will make them effectual. To preach is the duty of the preacher; but are there not duties incumbent upon others as well as preachers? Doubtless there are: nothing is plainer in the Scriptures than that ministers must not go on this warfare at their own charges. But missionaries differ from stated pastors.

They have to go out into the world to preach. Pastors preach to churches who will feel themselves bound in justice to support them. The question then is, are any bound to aid in the support of missionaries whom they are never to hear? We answer, not by the principles of justice; yet, they are bound by the principles of charity; that charity which seeketh not his own and loveth his neighbor as himself. Who that feels (as a Christian ought to feel) for the wretched state of mankind, starving for the bread of life, but will be willing to throw into common stock his money, or his services, or both, for the purpose of supplying their wants, by sending them the gospel? This is Divine generosity. It is alms of the highest grade, on which a rich reward awaits.

"In order to concentrate the energies of the friends of the gospel, missionary societies have been formed in various parts of the earth. The individuals of these societies combine their efforts to send the gospel into destitute places, whether heathen or nominally Christian. Preachers are sent out under their direction, and are supported or compensated from their funds. These funds are raised by the contributions of the members of these societies, by private donations, and by public collections, etc. These measures, like all others requiring money, have met with opposition. Where is the Scripture proof? say some. We answer, abundant proof is to be found in the New Testament.

"The Lord Jesus himself, while preaching the gospel, received support by the contributions of his followers. See Luke, viii. 23. After his ascension, his disciples, impelled by a holy desire for the spread of the gospel, and by Divine charity, cast all they had into one common stock. This might very properly be called a missionary fund, by the aid of which the gospel was propagated in Jewish and heathen countries. And hence the Apostle says to the Gentile churches, their debtors they are. See Romans, viii. 27. The Gentile converts, on their part, repaid the debt, by sending aid to the Jewish, impoverished by their extraordinary liberality. The church at Philippi is applauded by Paul as having been the first among the Macedonian churches who contributed to his necessities; and still more commends them because they had done this once and again. Right reason speaks the same sentiment. Can anything be more reasonable than to contribute, for godly purposes, a part of the abundance which God gives us? Can we receive from him so much as to be able to fare sumptuously every day at home; show finely abroad; expend hundreds in the education and dress of our sons and daughters; build fine houses, etc.; and, even after such expenditures, have wherewithal to make purchases of lands, etc.,—shall we be thus kindly treated by him, and refuse or neglect to make any return, by contributing out of this abundance for the advancement of his cause? Nothing would be more unreasonable. Objections have been raised upon the ground of practicability. Is it not a hopeless undertaking? say they. No! by no means. Great success has already attended the efforts of missionary societies."

Elder Semple was among the first in Virginia to engage in the delightful work of promoting the mission cause. To his influence, in a great measure, is to be ascribed the regard which was manifested by many individuals and churches toward this object. He was a member of the first meeting of the Baptist General Convention, and afterwards uniformly attended, to the period of his death. Whoever else might be absent from the anniversaries of Virginia missionary societies, Elder Semple was always in his place. From the origin of the Richmond Foreign and Domestic Society (afterwards the Virginia Baptist Missionary Society) he was its most active and devoted friend. For a series of years he presided at their annual meetings. The General Association of Virginia, for supplying the destitute parts of the State, had also a large share of his affections. He was usually Moderator of this body and President of its Board of Managers. Nor was he less interested in the cause of education. Indeed, every object which promised to be advantageous to his fellow-men met his most cordial approbation. He acted upon the general principle that it was right to do good unto all men, as far as he had opportunity.

To do good was his delight. It may not be inappropriate here to insert a few sentences written by him, expressive of the interest he took in the subject of colonization:—

"If the colonization plan should fully succeed, a radical change for the better will be effected in three distinct nations: our own nation will be rid of a most deadly evil; the African race among us will take their stand as an independent, civilized people, cultivating the soil, and breathing the air which Heaven seems to have destined for them; the savage tribes on the African continent will, through them, rise to refinement and civilization; and, what is infinitely better, will acquire a knowledge of that gospel which brings life and immortality to light. Why should not our free colored population go back to the land of their forefathers? It is believed that the Jews are again to possess the country given them of God. If the sons of Abraham are to return to the sepulchres of their fathers, why not the sons of Ham? Both these people have for centuries suffered the chastisement of offended Providence; both have been preserved a separate people in the bosom of other nations. Will the Father of mercies, whose loving-kindness is to be seen even in his chastisements—will he be angry forever with the one people, and ultimately show forgiveness to the other? But I am reminded that it is a delicate subject, and must be treated cautiously. Very true! No people can be more aware of that than Virginians; and, I think, no Virginian more than myself. When I say or do anything on this delicate subject, I strive to call up my soundest discretion, to think again and again; and lest, after all, I may be misled by some vain imagination, I endeavor to ask wisdom of the Father of lights. Such should be the course of all. It is, however, one thing to act with caution, *great caution*, and another, and a very different thing, not to act at all. We must not abstain from doing good lest our good should be evil spoken of. The way is, indeed, narrow and perilous; and fiery spirits may pull down evils upon themselves and others; yet the wise and prudent may walk the same way and effect much good without any evil. The late disaster in Liberia is indeed discouraging; but a kind Providence can easily remedy the evil. The Israelites had to go through many purgations before they could settle in peace in the promised land. So had the American Colonies."

Among other objects that engaged the attention of Elder Semple was the Columbian College, in the District of Columbia. This institution became deeply involved in debt, and its existence as a Baptist College seriously periled. To save it from ruin, and restore public confidence and patronage, it was found necessary that some individual of known integrity, judgment, and industry should be selected to take charge of its financial concerns. The eyes of the board were directed to Semple, and he was pressingly invited to assume this responsibility. In considering the propriety of accepting the appointment, he saw that ties most powerful must be sundered, and many painful sacrifices made. But he yielded to the convictions of duty, and determined, at least for a time, to remove to the City of Washington. This removal took place in July, 1827. In this station, as President of the Board, he remained until the period of his death. With his characteristic diligence and energy he prosecuted the important work committed to his hands, and the whole denomination were inspired with hope that the College would soon be relieved from its embarrassments. In a letter from Elder Abner W. Clopton, dated College Hill, October 29th, 1828, reference to this subject is made in the following language: "Dr. Semple, the main-spring, the very soul of the institution, is still here; and with the vigilant concern and unwearied activity of an honest, faithful, and tender parent, is endeavoring to arrange, and pay off as rapidly as the means can be obtained, the enormous and chaotic mass of debts. Scarcely any other man in our denomination, though many others possess excellency of character, could have entered upon this herculean task with any hope of success. Perhaps no other, while scarcely sun or moon or star shed a beam of light through the threatening clouds, would have remained firm at his post." The cheering anticipations expressed in this extract, and indulged by all the friends of the institution, were not realized. He who overrules all events saw it best to remove his servant from the sphere he occupied on earth to the rest of heaven.

It becomes proper to refer to the labors of Brother Semple as an author. Some time in 1809 he published a catechism for the use of children, which was highly approved. In 1810 his principal work, the History of Virginia Baptists, with several biographical notices appended, was issued from the press.

This history must have cost its author much expense of time and labor in the collection of materials, as well as in its preparation for the public eye. There might be found by the critic some defects in the style of this work, and it is questionable whether the references which were made to men then living were not calculated to have an unhappy tendency. In presenting it to the public, he employs the following language: "Unless the compiler is wholly deceived in himself, his attempt to write a history of the Virginia Baptists did not spring either from the love of money or the love of fame. To say that these things never entered his thoughts, would be saying what no one would believe. His motive was an ardent wish for the prosperity of truth, which he really thought could be greatly promoted by a plain and simple exhibition of God's dealings toward his people. The rise and rapid spread of the Baptists in Virginia were so remarkable, that there are but few who do not believe that some historical relation of them will be productive of real advantage to true religion. So much were our revolutionary reformers persuaded of this, that they made arrangements as early as 1778 to collect materials and publish a history; as may be seen by turning to our history of the Proceedings of the General Committee. If his book does not recommend itself by its deep erudition, polished style, or rhetorical flights, he thinks that it possesses qualities that are more valuable in such a work. Candor and simplicity in church history appear to the author properties of primary importance. He has faithfully recorded the foibles and failures, as well as the virtues and praises of his own people."

No doubt an important benefit was conferred on the denomination by the publication of this history. It enabled the churches to become more familiar with each other's rise and progress, and tended to bind them together in a closer and more endearing fellowship. It was important, too, that the peculiarly interesting circumstances which accompanied the origin and early history of the Baptists in Virginia should be made known to the world. In addition to these works, it devolved on Elder Semple to become the biographer of the lovely and lamented Straughan. This memoir was well executed, and reflected much credit on its author. He was also frequently appointed to write the circular letters of the Dover Association. All these are good, containing much valuable matter, and two or three of them may be called superior.

Elder Semple was never distinguished as a controversial writer.

Had he turned his attention particularly to polemics, he doubtless might have excelled. But he was always more disposed to engage in some work of faith and labor of love, than to spend his time in vexatious controversy. It has been thought by some, that his letters in reply to Mr. Campbell had rather an injurious influence. These letters were too hastily written, and, moreover, in his early correspondence with that wily errorist, there was too much of disposition to recognize him as a Christian brother; defective, indeed, in some of his views, but not in essential matters. This discussion inclined many in Lower Virginia to become readers of Mr. Campbell's periodical, some of whom were led away by his enticing words. It must not be understood that Elder Semple thought lightly of these errors. In one of his communications he speaks of Mr. Campbell's views as constituting "one of the most poisonous schemes that the present generation has witnessed."

The following extract of a letter from him, addressed to the editor of the Herald, deserves a place here. Referring to a conference of churches which had previously met, and adopted resolutions against this system, he says: "Let it be distinctly remembered that there are certain great leading truths which constitute the essence of Christianity. Put off these, and adopt anything else in the place of them, (no matter what,) and you lose everything in the character of a Christian worth having. You may retain the name and the forms of godliness, but you deny the power thereof. A word with regard to the season; was it the proper time? had suitable forbearance been exercised? I would answer, years have elapsed since this religious leprosy made its appearance, and became dangerous to our religious body. Having watched its progress and perceived its malignant effects, the most experienced disciplinarians became satisfied that the time had fully arrived when measures should be adopted to put out from among us those who clearly and obstinately adhered to a system so unlike the real gospel. It is believed by the most dispassionate, that if there be any error, it has been in being too tardy in resorting to the proper measures. In Kentucky, where the erroneous system spread more alarmingly than in Virginia, strong measures have been adopted; and it is said to have produced very desirable effects. Another question will be asked. Is this the proper course? I answer, under existing circumstances, it does appear to me to be the wisest course that could be pursued. The evil having become general, something like a general remedy was plainly called for. Associations are looked at with a jealous eye by many excellent men. These being periodical bodies, it was apprehended that if once such matters should be taken up by them, they would grow into something alarming. For single churches to act separately would be likely to produce discordance, and thereby weaken the remedy. A conference, therefore, made up of committees from aggrieved churches, seems to me to commend itself to every prudent man's judgment. Those churches having the disease prevalent among them would be most likely to fall upon the remedies best adapted to the case. The committees, too, selected from these aggrieved churches, would be for the most part tried and experienced men, fathers in Israel; such would march directly to their object with a firm step, not biased by false delicacy on the one hand, nor by party heat on the other. All things fairly considered, I do most cordially recommend the course advised by the conference, and do hope, earnestly hope, that a course substantially like it may be adopted by all our churches; and that we may in this most distressing state of things all move together."

Some allusion has already been made to the exertions of this devoted man as a minister of Jesus Christ. Few men have possessed a wider or more commanding influence, or have been more useful in the vineyard of the Lord. There have been those who have risen rapidly in the world, and for awhile have excited attention, but whose relaxed zeal or improper conduct has thrown them back into the shade, from which they have never again emerged. Others have attracted, and continued to attract the admiration of those around them, while their real usefulness has been confined within a very limited compass. Semple's progress was gradual, but it was onward. His influence was practically felt. And what was the secret of his success? Did it consist in eccentricity of manner, extraordinary powers of mind, or overpowering pulpit eloquence? In neither. It was the result of other qualities which he possessed in an eminent degree, and to which the attention of the reader should be directed, or this sketch would not be complete.

I. Among the most marked features of his ministerial character was prudence, united with great decision. These important attributes were exhibited in conferring with inquirers on the subject of salvation and Christian duty. He was always prepared to give discreet advice. Nor was he unfrequently called upon to afford instruction both within the sphere of his pastoral labor and to distant correspondents.

The following letters were written in reply to inquiries made by one who was settled in a neighborhood where the Baptist ministry seldom visited:—

"Your last came to hand in a very short time after date: it brought me the first intelligence of your baptism, and of the Gloucester meetings. It was, indeed, in every respect a pleasing communication. You have witnessed a good profession in a part of our country where Baptist principles have been very little understood, or rather have been greatly misunderstood. Your situation in life will cause you to be much observed by all. The friends of truth will fix the eye of hope upon you, and look for a Divine blessing on your good conversation in Christ Jesus. The opposite party, made up of various descriptions, under more various motives, will watch for your halting. The personal enemies of the Baptists, from religious and other motives, will say, 'their principles are too rigid for any good person to be happy among them.' You know of whom it was said, in old times, 'as for this sect, it is everywhere spoken against.' It does indeed require a large stock of prudence, or rather of Divine grace, to make a consistent and useful Baptist. But looking to God with constant and humble reliance, there will be nothing too hard. Surely he can make rough ways smooth, and crooked paths straight; and, moreover, he says, 'these things will I do, and not forsake you.' As it respects society, you will doubtless sometimes be at a loss: you cannot go all lengths with your old friends who are not changed, and of course must, to a certain extent, withdraw from them; and a refined mind cannot fully enjoy the company of the unrefined, even though pious. But this you will take as a part of your cross. In the mean time be at work, and you will find your labor not in vain in the Lord. Talk, advise, write, pray, etc., and you will find your society improved upon your own terms. Some of your friends who pitied your weakness, perhaps persecuted you, will be among the number to seek your religious association. I have seen these things more than once."

Again he writes: "Your letter, by taking a wrong direction, did not reach me until a few days past. Its contents were most satisfactory and consoling. Your experience of grace was surely from God, for no person can feel thus unless God be with him. You speak of being 'assailed with doubts and fears.' It is questionable whether a faithful experience is ever without them. They are not from God, but he overrules them for the Christian's confirmation. Satan will worry whom he cannot devour. In this, like all his other attacks upon the children of God, he causes only momentary pain, which is succeeded by lasting peace. The barking of the wolf drives the sheep nearer to the fold and the shepherd. I am more than commonly pleased with the calculations you seem to make, that the Christian is not to be carried to the skies on flowery beds of ease. Young Christians often overrate the duration of their comforts and underrate their trials, so that, when their conflicts come, they are not prepared for them, and 'count it strange' that they should be visited by such fiery trials. It is to their advantage to keep in mind that through much tribulation we must enter into the kingdom of heaven. I am also highly pleased at discovering, from your letter, that you have right views of prudence and waiting upon God. The enemy of souls has often done much mischief among zealous professors, by persuading them to neglect one set of duties to attend to others; that the immediate and direct duties to God are not paramount to domestic and social duties. It is not so: all duties should be done to God. Hence, Colossians, iii. 3, we are told, 'Whatsoever ye do in word or deed, do all in the name of the Lord Jesus,' etc., and immediately the duties of domestic life are enumerated and enjoined as to be done for God. See the same subject, Ephesians, v. and vi. This must be done by waiting upon God and seeking his direction as to the proper mode of attending to each duty, so as to be found rendering unto

God the things which are God's, and unto man the things that are his. This is the sure way of letting our light shine.

"Baptism is so very distinctly revealed in the New Testament, that for more than thirty years I have been astonished how there could be more than one opinion upon it among the readers of the Testament, especially the pious; that repentance and faith should precede baptism, is as plainly laid down in the above book as words can speak. Philip, when asked to baptize a certain man, said, 'if thou believest with all thy heart, thou mayest.' You speak of obstacles: you cannot do wrong to wait on the Lord to remove them, and make your conversion and baptism a blessing to many others; and by a judicious use of your privileges, you will have much solid happiness here, and will meet your Saviour with more pleasure when you find yourself among those to whom he will say, 'These are they who have followed the Lamb whithersoever he went.'"

In the social circle, he always demeaned himself in a manner becoming his exalted station. Many ministers who act well their part in the pulpit, are lamentably deficient in their daily intercourse with men. Their undignified demeanor and indiscreet remarks tend to neutralize the most instructive and eloquent discourses. But it was not thus with the subject of this memoir. He always seemed to carry about with him the recollection that he should watch for souls as one who must give account, and all his words and actions were judiciously adapted to leave, both among saints and sinners, a good impression.

His government of the churches over which he presided, and the course he took in the Dover Association and other large deliberative bodies, furnished also a test of his character for sound judgment and firmness of purpose.

II. Another invaluable trait in his character was unwearied diligence in the discharge of ministerial duties. For punctuality in attending his own appointments, and all the more important denominational meetings of the State, he was proverbial. And, while at these meetings, as well as in the fulfillment of pastoral duty, whatever his hands found to do, he did it with all his might. It will be appropriate, in this place, to furnish an extract from a communication, written by one who was doubtless prepared to give the most accurate information. In this extract the writer alludes to the course Elder Semple pursued at an early stage of his ministry. Having referred to his industrious habits in teaching and farming, immediately after his marriage, the writer proceeds:—

"During this time he ministered to three congregations, two of them twenty miles distant from his residence. He labored incessantly, making it his religious duty to undertake nothing which he did not complete, and to have no appointment that he did not fulfill. So strictly did he observe this rule, that I have heard him say that he has rode through the most inclement weather to a distant church, and when getting there found the nearest neighbor absent, and preached on such occasions to a congregation of not more than four or five persons. His labors at this time were peculiarly arduous. The Baptist church in that region was in its infancy. There were few persons who belonged to it, and those the most illiterate and unpolished. The prejudices of the public were against it, and the young man of learning and talent was deemed irreclaimably infatuated who could devote his time to the service of a church which brought neither honor nor emolument. Panoplied, however, in the armor of conscious rectitude, he went forth to battle these prejudices and to disseminate truth. In a short time the fruits of his labor were awarded him. A church, equal in number and respectability to any in the State, grew up under his ministry, and old Bruington still stands a monument to the zeal and piety of its never-to-be-forgotten founder."

In a sermon delivered on the occasion of his death, by Elder Robert Ryland, the following allusion is made: "He was eminent for his PERSEVERANCE. I have known many men of equal, perhaps superior abilities, who fell far short of his usefulness, because they wanted his decision. He was deliberate in forming his conclusions, but when formed he acted on them. He felt that the ground on which he stood was solid, and he therefore stood erect and fearless. His course through life was, consequently, not an irregular one, vacillating from one extreme of doctrine to another, now manifesting an excessive zeal, and now settled down into a frigid insensibilty; but it was uniform, steady, dignified. You always found in him the same man. Human energy is often wasted because it is applied to some point for a short time with great vehemence, and then diverted from that to another before the first is accomplished. Such was not the custom of Mr. S. He never abandoned a project because it proved to be difficult or unpopular, but went right on until a fair experiment had convinced him what was expedient. Hence it was that he acquired so much weight of character in the community. Every person confided in the soundness of his judgment, and in the energy with which he executed his purposes. If he had appointments to fulfill, he suffered no impediment which mortal enterprise could subdue to interrupt them. His congregations would go out to hear him in cold and rainy weather, because they were sure of his attendance. This trait in a public man is doubtless more valuable than it is usually regarded. In the course of a long life, its influence is capable of effecting a large amount of good, while the patriarchal sentiment is found to be true, 'Unstable as water, thou shalt not excel.'

"He was one of your *practical* men, that set themselves to work in good earnest, and 'from the same fixed and faithful point' never decline until their aim is accomplished. It ought to be set down also to his credit that he was *constitutionally* indolent. His physical nature seems to have been changed by the force of principle. Whatever of activity he displayed was the result not of natural temperament, but of grace Divine, urging him forward against the current of his feelings,—the effect of holy, ardent love, prompting him to spend and be spent for the salvation of souls. Many men are endued with a restless temper that makes them energetic by starts. Their motions are rapid, but uncertain and eccentric. Their zeal is blazing, but misguided and injudicious. They rarely effect much good. But this man's energy was steady and efficient. His zeal was uniform and salutary because guided by a sound judgment and directed to a hallowed end.

"The only additional remark which I shall make on this part of the subject is this: That no man probably felt a deeper interest in the general welfare of Zion. While the disciples are classed into so many little families, there is danger lest they feel an undue solicitude each for his own family, and disregard the common cause. Mr. S. felt a lively anxiety for his whole denomination, and for the progress of the gospel in every part of the world. He could have said, with Paul, 'Besides those things that are without, that which cometh upon me daily, the care of all the churches.' Indeed, when his reputation had increased, he was so much importuned to preach in distant neighborhoods, that his own people felt his loss. Wherever he sojourned, there he went to work as if it had been his particular charge. And, on this account, he was looked up to by all the churches as a kind of apostle; was called upon to decide controversies, and to adjust more serious difficulties. One of his darling themes in the pulpit was the enforcement of brotherly love. His soul was oppressed by the schisms which have in some instances perplexed our churches. To the variant parties his private and public counsels were excellent. If, however, he ever displayed an authoritative spirit, it was while preaching on this subject. He had little patience for the senseless quarrels of those who profess to be disciples of the Prince of peace, and children of the God of love."

III. It may be observed, in addition to the qualities to which the attention of the reader has been called, that he was distinguished for the *practical* character of his preaching. By manifestation of the truth he commended himself to every man's conscience in the sight of God. His discourses were remarkable for their appropriateness, and were always delivered in simplicity and godly sincerity. To amuse men was never his design when he stood up to recommend the weighty truths of the Word of God. No one could sit under his ministry without being convinced that the great object at which he aimed was to do good. It was said by a pious lady that she never heard him preach when she did not retire resolving to be more holy and devoted to God. Possessing an intimate acquaintance with the heart, and feeling the superlative value of eternal realities, he was habitually prepared to speak with pungency and faithfulness. It must not be understood that he was deficient as a doctrinal preacher. It was the delight of his heart to dwell on the love of God to his people, the Divine nature and glory of the Redeemer, the necessity and happy influence of the Spirit's work in regeneration, and all the other truths of the Bible; but he never theorized on any one of these doctrines without making some practical inference, and pressing them upon the consciences of his hearers. This was evidently the apostolic plan. Paul, in his writings, manifests a peculiar concern that purity of sentiment should prevail in the churches; but, in recommending the precepts of the gospel, he descends to particulars, and with emphasis urges all the duties of social life, as well as those of a devotional character. Thus did Semple. His style was sometimes negligent, but his manner always impressive. An extract from the funeral discourse, delivered by Elder A. Broaddus, will be here introduced. It furnishes an accurate description of the ministerial talent and spirit of him with whom, from early youth, the speaker had been intimately associated in the work of the gospel ministry:—

"Among the gifts and endowments of my valued friend, we do not reckon an eloquent tongue and a fluent speech. The early part of his career was marked by frequent embarrassments, from the want of a ready and happy appropriation of words to the ideas which labored in his mind. But then, you still saw the idea of sterling worth, big with important meaning, and weighing powerfully in the scales of the sanctuary. You saw the object toward which, with resolute pace, he was marching up; and though he might sometimes be impeded on the way, still he marched on, (for perseverance was one of his distinguishing features,) still he marched on till the point was gained. And if, even in the maturity of his ministry, he never attained to excellence in ready utterance, the worth of his matter more than made amends for the want of this faculty—a faculty which, though it has its worth, is often found to exist in connection with a slender stock of mind and meaning, a pompous parade of words, a body without a soul.

"Divine truth, from the lips now sealed in silence, came to knock at the door of our hearts, not with the tap of the gloved-hand, but with the stroke of the brazen knocker. It entered not with the bows and compliments of a stranger, but unceremoniously, like the owner of the castle come to claim his mansion. Nor did he lack a holy warmth, a heavenly unction, in his ministrations; for God was with him. To have the best feelings of the heart engaged and kindled up in the cause of Christ, and under the influence of his redeeming love, was the delight of his soul. Often has he said: 'I would give nothing for that religion which excludes these heavenly feelings.' And if he was not eminent for those appeals which produce a more powerful excitement, you are witnesses, my friends and brethren, how often a sacred pathos mingled itself with his addresses; how often, ere we were aware, a transition took place from the current of argument and instruction, to a feeling and even a melting sense of the excellence of Christ's holy religion, its blessed enjoyments and immortal prospects.

"Various are the gifts with which God has favored the Christian. The distinguishing excellence of our brother, in his ministerial capacity, appeared to me to consist in a fund of knowledge of human nature, applied, as occasion called for it, to the various workings of the heart; and in what the Apostle calls 'instruction in righteousness;' or an exhibition of the duty and advantage of practical godliness. Having been instrumental, under the influence of God's gracious spirit, in turning many 'from darkness to light, and from the power of Satan to God,' he was earnestly engaged in his ministrations, in building them up in the faith of the gospel, and training them to active diligence in all good works."

Says Mr. Ryland: "As a public teacher of religion, our lamented brother was deservedly eminent. He was always appropriate. The variety of his sentiments, the originality of his manner, the solid, earnest, and devout constitution of his mind, made him profitable to all classes of hearers. I think those familiar but beautiful lines of Cowper suit him as well as any man I have ever seen:—

'Would I describe a preacher such as Paul,
Were he on earth, would hear, approve, and own,
Paul should himself direct me. I would trace
His master-strokes, and draw from his design.
I would express him simple, grave, sincere;
In doctrine uncorrupt; in language plain,
And plain in manner; decent, solemn, chaste,
And natural in gesture; much impressed
Himself, as conscious of his awful charge,
And anxious mainly that the flock he feeds
May feel it too; affectionate in look,
And tender in address, as well becomes
A messenger of grace to guilty men.'

"One quality, which distinguished our venerable brother, was his intimate acquaintance with the human heart. This was one of the chief sources of his greatness and usefulness. Pope says:—

'The proper study of mankind is man.'

This study is important to all professions; but to the preacher it is indispensable. He has to deal emphatically with the heart of man. He should know how to touch alternately the chords of hope and fear, of love, joy, sympathy, gratitude, and devotion. Mr. S. applied his mind more to this subject than to books. If he addressed the unconverted, they were often astonished at his perfect insight into their feelings. Like the woman of Samaria, they were constrained to say: 'He told me all the things that ever I did.' He described them so faithfully that they found no way of escape, and had to confess they were the very sinners whom he had designated. If he spoke to Christians he seemed to know their trials, their secret exercises, their besetting infirmities. He expatiated on them more correctly than they could have done themselves. And he was well skilled to apply a remedy suited to their spiritual diseases; to administer comfort to the depressed, caution to the unguarded, and reproof to the disobedient. Perhaps this is of all others the most delicate task assigned to the messengers of truth; to adapt their instructions to the character and circumstances of men. It is not sufficient that they understand what is truth; but they should know what particular ideas to advance for the various stages of experience; when to apply the promises, when the admonitions, and when the threatenings of the gospel. In a word, they should rightly divide the Word of truth, giving to each one his portion in due season. This can be done only by knowing, in some measure, what is in man. Possessing a large share of this quality, Mr. S. succeeded remarkably well in performing the duty above alluded to. He aimed his darts not over the heads of men, but at their consciences, and they felt their point. He abhorred the disposition which prompts some to attempt great things merely to attract the stare of the ignorant. The useful was preferred by him to the ornamental, and the homely phrase that conveyed his thoughts was

28 *

selected rather than the classic one, which would be understood only by the learned."

It will not be unsuitable or uninteresting to the reader, here to introduce a few extracts from the pen of Elder Semple. They will give a just idea of the sterling excellence of those sentiments which were at all times advanced by him, both in the pulpit and by the pen. It ought to be remarked that he very seldom wrote sentimental letters, although his correspondence was extensive. As he was frequently consulted in reference to the interests of individual churches, or the cause at large, he was accustomed in each case to confine himself to the subject, and to give plain, practical advice.

The first extract furnished will exhibit his views of the gospel ministry. It is from a letter addressed to a young brother, who was agitating the question, whether it was his duty to enter upon this solemn work: "Yours of the ninth instant is now before me, and I sit down to answer it. It contains one general proposition by way of asking my advice, viz., Shall I preach the gospel? To which I might answer shortly, Yes! But you would have it more in detail. You seem to be satisfied that God has impressed it upon your mind, or at least you ought to be satisfied, if your exercises are as you describe them. Such exercises prove *the call of God.* If God has committed a dispensation of the gospel to you, a woe betides you if you do not preach. On the contrary, if you preach willingly and faithfully, you will have a reward. Such are the terms of God's house. But the part in which I hope to be of some use to you, is respecting the difficulties of this holy occupation. Of these you should be forewarned. When God called Saul of Tarsus, he said to Annanias, 'I have showed him what great things he must suffer for my name's sake.' A faithful and true minister must make up his account, that he is to endure hardness as a soldier of the cross. He is appointed thereunto. It would seem that God will accept no services unless they can stand the fiery ordeal. His way is full of fire; and wood, hay, or stubble will soon burn up, while gold shines so much the brighter for having passed through the fire. The Apostle found it as God had told him; hence he gives us a long catalogue of sufferings which he had endured. And when he compares himself with others, he asks, Are they ministers of Christ? and his answer is worthy of note, '*I am more:* in labors more abundant, in stripes above measure;' and he goes on to enumerate his sufferings, as if they made him more than a minister of Christ. This you will say is a dark picture. True, but you will find it a true one, if you are a laborious and faithful minister of the gospel. But there is also a bright side to this picture. Ay, one that if rightly viewed, will dazzle not only the above prospects, but all the bright hopes and schemes of worldly aggrandizement. The man who has right feelings toward God's work, and faith as to its reward here and hereafter, would not hesitate in making choice of a holy minister's office, in preference to the office of prime minister of the most potent kingdom upon earth; nay, of the crown itself of such kingdom. But it requires peculiar feelings, such as God only can give. Your course is plain: wait upon God, wait upon him without weariness. Follow his leadings. Be still until God says, Move; and then move with zeal, judgment, and humility. Do not forget Jeremiah's question and advice to Baruch, 'Seekest thou great things for thyself? Seek them not.' I am desperately mortified at seeing some of our young preachers. They seem to have accepted the call of God only upon condition that they may be great preachers, and may get great salaries. It requires a stretch of charity beyond my measure to even hope, that pride and selfishness have not a large share in their ministerial exercises. These seldom succeed in doing good. All things considered, I hope you will engage in the holy work, and that you will do it from the purest motives, and with extensive success. Yours in gospel fellowship."

The brief selections which follow, will, without doubt, be read with pleasure by many who have heard from his lips the words of eternal life; and to those who have no personal acquaintance it will be gratifying to see specimens of the style in which he was accustomed to illustrate and enforce truth.

"*Holiness, a rare principle.*—So refined a principle is true holiness, and so contrary to the natural propensities, that few, either in the Old or New Testament, are represented as having attained to high degrees in it. But few spotless characters are exhibited among the sons of God, that presented themselves in worship in the days of Job; it is said of none that he was a perfect and an upright man, except Job himself. Of the thousands in Israel, Moses seems, at some seasons, almost to stand alone faithful to his God. Many thousands assembled in the Plain of Dura, and doubtless many Jews, yet three only continued immovable, and would not bow to the king's golden image. When the Lord Jesus was betrayed, a few women, and perhaps one male disciple, adhered to him.

"*The true church.*—The fairest and only proper mode of ascertaining the visible church in the present day, is to search for the visible church in the days of inspiration, and then inquire among what people her characteristics, as laid down in the Bible, may be discovered.

"*Charity.*—A charitable spirit is not a mere disposition to give alms to the poor. This is only one of its many excellent effects. It is rather that mind that was in Christ Jesus, which prompted him to love mankind in their sins, and to determine him to save them at the expense of his own life. By one writer it is defined to be 'a principle of love to God, and good-will to men, wishing well to all.' A charitable spirit, in a Christian, is the fountain whence most of the other graces spring; and, we may add, it is the source whence all the real good practiced among men takes its origin. Forbearance, forgiveness, long-suffering under injuries, gentleness, mildness, etc. are some of its many fruits. Feeding the hungry, clothing the naked, visiting the sick, acting the part of a father to the fatherless, of a friend to the friendless; to make another's suffering its own; to rejoice with those that rejoice, and weep with those that weep, are a part of its holy works. A charitable spirit views the faults of its possessor with abhorrence, those of its neighbor with grief, and those of its enemies with forbearance and forgiveness. This spirit never aggravates, never propagates the follies of others. It spreads its mantle over a multitude of faults, and would fain blot them out of existence. Envy, evil-speaking, whispering, backbiting, pride, selfishness, flee from her train. Faithfulness, candor, prudence, philanthropy, happiness, are its constant attendants. It sometimes wounds, yet never but with a view to healing. If it frowns, it is the frown of reform, and its chastisements are the chastisements of peace. In prosperity it warns not to be too much elated, and in adversity it strengthens the feeble knees and lifts up the hands that hang down. It is heaven-born, and nurtured near the eternal throne. It is a visitant on earth, going about pointing out the road to glory and happiness, and leading all to the abodes of peace who will follow its advice or example. It is a plant of paradise, which never thrives in human soil, unless moistened with the dew of heaven, and cultivated according to the rules of Holy Writ. It seeks no rank on earth; but with equal readiness becomes a guest to the prince or the peasant, the sovereign or his subjects. Faith and hope are its principal ministers in this world, but in heaven, its native clime, it needs them not. There it forever lives and sings, when inferior spirits shall cease.

"*Pride.*—Few things can be imagined more unreasonable in a follower of Jesus than pride. His first admittance into the kingdom of Christ being wholly through sovereign mercy; his preservation therein, by given strength; all his virtues, and all his gifts the offspring of grace; a beggar and a bankrupt as to himself, he may be well asked, What hast thou to glory in? Unreasonable, however, as it may be, there are few, very few, if any of the church militant, who are exempt from its baneful influence. It is a noxious plant, that springs up spontaneously in the breast of man, and will destroy everything good, unless by close, diligent, and holy watchfulness it be dug up and kept under. It is a spirit marked with deep ingratitude. It often rises highest in those who are most favored of God. Beneficiaries of his distinguishing goodness, they are prompted by this spirit (like Satan) to put the crown upon their own heads. Hence we may account why the best men are often most afflicted. Lifted by their Master to the third heavens, a thorn in the flesh is given them, lest they should be exalted above measure. Well then may we account them happy who endure.

"*False teachers.*—Satan transforms himself into an angel of light, and it is not uncharitable to believe that a large proportion of the religion that is in the world is the offspring of satanic inspiration. In this way we are to account for the various unscriptural doctrines of most of the sects of Christianity. Professing to be guided by the Word of God, they suffer themselves to be misled by the devices of Satan. They call meteors stars, and gewgaws jewels. But in the church, this side of heaven, however sound in doctrine and however regular and strict in discipline, individuals will be found who privily creep in and seem destined to disgrace the cause in which they embark; such was the case in the Apostolic Church, as sacred history records; and the best authenticated profane history leaves us without a doubt that no subsequent age of the church has been exempt from these calamities.

"*Discipline.*—God seldom works but Satan imitates. God makes Christians, and Satan makes hypocrites. Time, however, will make manifest who are on the Lord's side, and true scriptural discipline will separate the precious from the vile. Discipline is like the refiner's fire; it makes the faithful shine like pure gold, while the false and faithless are consumed like chaff.

"*Source of true greatness.*—Many excellent lessons may be learned by turning our reflections to our own day. Various characters have passed before our view. Some have risen to great usefulness and weight of character; and some, like the glow-worm, have glutted for a moment and sunk into oblivion. What are the causes? It will be found, upon impartial examination, that whatever might have been the effect of talents, connections, or popular sentiments, the far greater part of their high standing ought to be ascribed to the successful cultivation of a meek and Christian spirit, and that the insignificance or downfall of the opposite party oftener arose from that pride which precedes a fall than for the want of mental or personal endowments.

"*Bigotry.*—Bigotry often claims the exclusive credit of being a defender of the faith, of candor, of faithfulness, of holy courage, and casts contempt on everything that opposes. With it, meekness is meanness, prudence is the fear of man, moderation is apathy, and the love of enemies is hypocrisy. A contentious spirit is always forming and fomenting parties. Its own party is flattered and caressed; the opposite is slighted and brow-beaten. When much heated, it is not uncommon to resort to still baser measures; to seize trifling foibles in its opposers, and magnify them into great faults, and occasionally to spread, if not fabricate, base falsehoods. It is against this spirit the Apostle labors in his First Epistle to the Corinthians: 'For,' says he, 'it has been declared to me that there are contentions among you. Whereas, there is among you envying, and strife, and divisions, are ye not carnal? For while one saith, I am of Paul, and another, I am of Apollos, are ye not carnal?' In another part of the same epistle he says, 'If any man seem to be contentious, we have no such custom.' To Timothy he complains of some who doat about questions and strife of words.

"*Indolence.*—Indolence does much harm negatively, by not doing the good that it ought and might. The slothful man sees innumerable and insurmountable obstacles in the enterprises presented to his view. Tell him to arise and work for his God, he immediately saith, There is a lion in the way, I shall be slain in the streets. He will sometimes rouse up and commence a work, but seldom or never brings it to perfection. He may hunt and may take the prey, but his sloth lulls him to sleep, and he roasts not that which he took in hunting. He may undertake to cultivate a field or vineyard, but if you go by it, you will find it all grown over with thorns. A professor of religion who gives way to a slothful spirit, is a cipher on the left hand that counts for nothing; a barren fig-tree that cumbers the ground. In the useful, active labors of God's house, he does nothing to perfection. Appoint him to any active service, and you hear no more from him, or hearing, it is only an apology for not doing. Sluggards in religion are not always so in worldly matters. Some of them are eager enough in pursuit of their own things, but have no time, no temper, no talents for Christ's work. Some of them can stir themselves on a Sabbath day, and travel some miles to pay a social visit, but seven or eight miles to worship is too unreasonable for man or beast.

"*Idle curiosity.*—Idle curiosity often leads its possessors into barrenness of soul, and others into miscalculations. The curious are always in pursuit of novelty. Those who are infected by the spirit of curiosity, and do not check it, are disgusted with everything of long standing. They find out new preachers, new books, new people, etc., and these, while new, are always the best; but as soon as the novelty wears off they quickly look out and find others more to their taste. A curious spirit sometimes manifests itself in searching into deep and mysterious subjects, or dark and difficult texts of Scripture. The common maxims or plain doctrines of God's word are overlooked as insipid and useless; those full of dark metaphors and inscrutable mysteries are the food of this spirit. Doctrines involving inexplicable points are sought as pearls from the bottom of the ocean; more valuable, because more rare. Some of these discover their error and reform. They then tell us that their former course afforded no permanent pleasure or profit, and that plain and common things are found, on fair trial, to be most valuable.

"*Worldly religion.*—The religion of the world, like Nebuchadnezzar's golden image, is for the most part pompous, and crowded with ceremonies and sensual gratifications. God is always best pleased with his people when in simplicity and godly sincerity they have their conversation in the world. Paul was jealous of the Corinthians, lest their minds should be corrupted from the simplicity that is in Christ.

"*Christian intercourse.*—Frequent and familiar associations of Christians, accompanied by prudence and watchfulness, often check a wrong, and enkindle a right spirit. The association of the pious upon right principles is of great efficacy towards producing and preserving a holy frame. In our best estate, we are often blind to our own faults.

"*Depravity the source of error.*—Depraved as man is, it would be vain to hope that he would not abuse any treasure (however precious) to which he could have access. Sinful, fallen man can never touch and not pollute; can never wear and leave the garment unpolluted. Pure religion is handed to us directly from heaven. But, alas! how much is there that bears the name of religion, that is nothing more than the production of man, and, indeed, of a power worse than man.

"*Prayer.*—Humble prayer has a most happy tendency toward softening the ferocious passions of nature. The very approaching of God as our Father tends to produce in us a meek, mild, and childlike temper. A soul with a praying spirit loses (for a season at least) all malice, all arrogance. He either trembles at his Master's frowns, or melts at his smiles. But besides this, humble prayer receives an answer. He, therefore, who feels his proud and resentful temper too stubborn to be subdued by himself, has but to wait upon that God who giveth more grace to the humble.

"*Patience.*—Patience in this world of woe is not only right, but indispensable to vital piety. In the character of Christ it was notable indeed. Being a man of sorrows and acquainted with grief, his whole life exhibited proof of the prevalence of this spirit; and to induce us to imitate him, he promises that if we suffer, we shall reign with him. A calm and serene temper in the midst of trials and sufferings displays the genius of Christianity more favorably than any other attitude in which the follower of the Lamb can be placed. This seems to be the true secret why the pious but prosperous Job must pass through fiery trials. God, who searcheth hearts, knows that he is a perfect and upright man; but those who look on things after the outward appearance, think they see in his wealth and prosperity sufficient inducement to serve God; and, therefore, dispute the purity of his motives. The Lord would cut off all occasion for doubt or reproach, and accordingly brings Job down to the lowest state of adversity and affliction. His patient spirit under his sufferings is named and applauded in the New Testament. Most of the favorite servants of God have been *like* sufferers. It was while Daniel's soul was in bitterness and grief he is so often called a man greatly beloved. David's forbearing and forgiving spirit in the midst of unrelenting persecutors seems to have had no small share in procuring for him the honorable appellation of 'a man after God's own heart.' Moses, though raised in a royal court, must also drink of the bitter cup; and the patient spirit displayed by him in Egypt and in the wilderness, under the severest conflicts, seems to be the brightest trait in his character.

"*Hospitality.*—So valuable is a virtuous hospitality in the sight of God that he has sometimes crowned it with distinguished blessings. The widow of Zarephath, or Sarepta, by entertaining Elijah, was miraculously fed for many days, and the great woman of Shunem, by her hospitable kindness to Elisha, obtained a son, the first desire of her heart. And Isaac also, the promised seed, seems to have been promised by the angels when filled and cheered by Abraham and Sarah's cordial kindness at their house, though probably not known to them as angels at the time. Abigail, by feeding David and his men, averted a heavy curse from her family and procured for herself a royal husband. It was in a house of hospitality that Jesus said, 'This day is salvation come to this house.' But, probably, the most important advantage which arises from hospitality is the advancement of the Redeemer's kingdom. It causes the gospel to be preached under private roofs at times and seasons when circumstances prevent it at public meeting-houses; sometimes also in neighborhoods where there are no houses of public worship, and where, but for such accommodation, the people would be left destitute of the Word of Life. It promotes intercourse among the pious, by which their faith is strengthened, their hearts are warmed, their principles confirmed, and all their powers animated in the heavenly warfare. It invites inquirers into the society of the godly, with whom they can have free conversation, and who can 'expound unto them the way of God more perfectly.' Hence, ministers of the gospel are specially required 'to be given to hospitality,' that their houses may supply the lack of service of the pulpit; that their conversation might do what was left undone by their ministry, and what, in many instances, the public ministry could not so well effect.

"*Conversation.*—Frothy and vain conversation should be avoided as the bane of Christian society; worldly things, if introduced, should be talked of moderately and in the fear of God; but, above all, religious subjects should not be named with levity. Foolish talking and jesting on any subject is said not to be convenient, but religious conversation, conducted with levity, is shameful. Cheerful gravity and grave cheerfulness fit best the followers of Him who was never seen to laugh, but who, nevertheless, bade his disciples be of good cheer.

"*A generous spirit.*—A generous spirit never enjoys his possessions more happily than when he shares it at the hospitable board with his friends or with the needy and distressed. The very reflection that his house is filled with God's people has often melted the pious man's heart into the sweetest delights. When he deals to them the food or drink, water or napkin, or lights them to bed, or takes care of their horses, etc., his heart is in all he does, and he actually realizes our Saviour's words: 'He that would be the greatest let him be the servant of all.' Such a host, while he renders himself happy, is sure to impart pleasure and delight to his guests. If, from poverty, his fare should be coarse, it nevertheless becomes delicious by his mode of administering it. He turns water into wine and wild gourds into palatable food by the delicious seasoning of affection. He proves, by actual experience, that a dinner of herbs, with love, is better than a stalled ox without it. He serves up one dish, without which the finest dainties are deceitful meat, viz., a hearty welcome. If his guests must lodge on beds of straw, they will, if good men, repose more softly than on beds of down struck over with the thorns of malevolence. What view of human nature can be more celestial than to see a circle of religious friends sitting around the hospitable room, elucidating mysterious passages of Holy Writ, or mingling their voices in the songs of Zion, or reciting past experience, narrating the holy tidings of each neighborhood, giving and receiving sacred instruction and consolation? When they approach the family altar, with what earnest solicitude will they invoke blessings on their affectionate host and his family. How cordially do they desire that his bread, thus cast upon the waters, may be seen after many days! And will not God hear such prayers? We answer, that he will hear, and grant the blessings too.

"*Connection of commands and promises.*—It is worthy of a believer's notice, that God's exhortations are so frequently accompanied by his promises. If he exhorts us to work out our own salvation with fear and trembling, he also promises to work in us to will and to do of his own good pleasure. Now the grace of God works in us through faith, and the support of faith is the promises of God. Hence we are said to live by faith.

"*Perseverance.*—The true believer perseveres in proportion as he is sanctified; the pretended one as he is gratified. The one holds on his way, though surrounded with temptations and trials; the other faints when persecutions and distresses arise on account of the Word. The one, like the ship, heads up to the anchor when tempests blow and billows rise; the other is carried about with every wind of temptation. The one will finally arrive safely in the port of everlasting rest; while the other will be wrecked upon the rocks of sinful pursuits, never to rise again. It will always appear that apostates greatly disgrace the cause in which they engage, and great, no doubt, is their punishment. In this world they experience severe terrors of conscience, called in

Scripture a fearful looking for of judgment; in the world to come, like the servant that knew to do his Master's will and did it not, they will be beaten with many stripes.

"*Christian friendship.*—The food which is eaten among friends at the hospitable board, seems sweeter 'than to eat our morsel alone.' This, probably, is one reason why the primitive Christians 'did eat their meat with gladness and singleness of heart.' Having all things common, they were mutually hosts and guests to each other.

"*Self-examination.*—He that does not keep his heart with all diligence will often find the issues of death instead of life. A Christian should not be too easily satisfied with himself. By close examination he will often find things not as well within as he had supposed. He will discover secret faults which would otherwise lie hid. Hence the prayer of the Psalmist, 'cleanse thou me from secret faults.'

"*Disinterestedness.*—Primitive Christians seem to have forgotten their own interest and to have been wholly absorbed in that of their Master. No man called aught of the things which he possessed his own. So much were they divested of self and self-interest that they accounted it an honor to be whipped and to endure ignominious persecutions for Christ's sake. Nothing recommends more forcibly the Redeemer's cause to unbelievers than an unselfish, disinterested spirit among professors. When a sinner's mind is staggered by the arguments of the gospel he looks around at the conduct and temper of the friends of the gospel. If he sees them acting a noble and disinterested part, and ready to make any sacrifice to promote its prosperity, he quickly makes up a favorable opinion. But if he sees a selfish, contracted, scheming spirit, pretty generally among them, he either gives up the pursuit or turns his attention to some other denomination. Much damage has been done to the cause of truth by a selfish spirit.

"*Covetousness.*—Covetousness is a demon that haunts the church. This spirit is the more deceptious, because it assumes to itself the names of virtue and duty. Some of the best maxims of social life are plausibly quoted to justify its course. He that provideth not for his own has denied the faith and is worse than an infidel; industry and frugality are the handmaids of Providence; exercise and temperance are the best means of health; competence and independence are necessary to happiness; something for my family and something for my friend enables me to be hospitable; a little to spare furnishes a fund for the poor and for religious expenses; such like maxims as these, though misapplied, afford ease to the conscience of the covetous; they often stint their family under the pretext of providing for them. He talks of preparing something for the poor, but when the opportunity offers he finds some excuse in the unworthiness of the object, in the hardness of the times or the inconvenience of the present season. He talks of being sociable with a friend, but seldom or never finds time or inclination to attend to friends. He longs for wealth, that he may be liberal to religion, but his sacrifices are rarely to be found upon the altar, or when found, consist of the blind or broken, the maimed, scurvy or scabbed. The love of money is the root of all evil, and in professors of piety it is the fountain of many sorrows, the source of many errors, and the wretched clog of every noble enterprise. This spirit has a most voracious appetite, always crying, Give, give! but, unlike any other being, its appetite increases with its gratification, and the more it receives the more it wants. It often infects the minds of both preachers and people, and sets them at variance. The one is often too eager to receive, the other too willing to withhold. Crimination and recrimination are frequently the result, while the sacred cause of the Redeemer bleeds from every pore. How strong are the words of our Lord against this propensity! Ye cannot serve God and mammon. It is easier for a camel to go through the eye of a needle, than for those who trust in riches to enter the kingdom of heaven.

"*Public worship.*—A steady attendance upon a faithful gospel is a fountain from which we may often draw and drink the spirit of holiness; and this more especially, if we combine with it a diligent reading of the word of Christ, until it dwells in us richly in all wisdom.

"*Mortification of sinful appetites.*—Mortification of the flesh is indispensably necessary. Hence, the Lord Jesus speaks emphatically about self-denial and taking up the cross, and hence Paul declares that he was in 'fastings oft.' It seems pretty obvious, also, that it is with this view that God afflicts his people. He turns his hand upon us, that he may thoroughly purge away our dross. He sees that the flesh must be mortified, and what the saint does not do by voluntary self-denial, he effects by his chastening.

"*The church subject to changes.*—The true church is sometimes compared to the moon, and like her she waxes and wanes. Revivals and declensions are symptoms of God's peculiar people. Hence it is said, 'when the Lord turned again the captivity of Zion, we were as men that dream. Then were our mouths filled with laughter, and our tongues with singing.' On the other hand, we read of the complaints of God's people in times of declension. 'How can we sing the songs of Zion in a strange land. Our harps are hung upon the willows!' How much do these things look like the revivals and declensions among God's people of the present generation!

"*Willingness to labor for God.*—A laborious spirit, or a willingness to labor for God, is of more value than many are aware of. Most men are inquiring for talents, and ascribe success or the want of it to the presence or absence of talents. Talents certainly have their weight; but what are talents unless they are occupied? It is labor which renders talents successful; and small talents well occupied are often seen accomplishing more for the cause of Christ than very conspicuous ones, used only when convenient. Our country affords strong proof of this position. We have seen a religious establishment entrenched around by human laws, supported by power and wealth, defended by preachers of learning and talents, pulled down to the base by illiterate and unpatronized ministers of Christ. To an experienced man it is easily explained. These illiterate men were steady, unwearied laborers. The others were idlers. The one set was as the ox in the yoke, pulling at his burden; the other was as the ox in the stall, too well fed and too fat to labor much. Every day's observation shows us the exceeding benefit of a laborious spirit. What great things have even private members effected by keeping their eyes steady to their Master's honor, and doing such work as may fall to their share! A laborious spirit should be never laid aside. It is applicable to all states of the church. The labor may, and ought to be varied; but the spirit must remain. Like the industrious husbandman, who finds one sort of work for the spring, another for the fall, one sort for dry, and another for wet weather, the diligent servant of God adapts his work to the season. In revivals, in declensions, in lively or languid times, in discipline, in prayer or preaching meetings, the devoted Christian finds something still to do; and this is his support and consolation, that his labor is not in vain in the Lord. He knows that in whatever lawful way he labors his reward is certain. He is assured that both he that soweth and he that reapeth shall rojoice together. Let not these remarks be exclusively applied to ministers. They are applicable to private individuals as well as to preachers. All have their work to do, and all should be at it."

The biographer will proceed to state that not only were the piety and talents of Mr. Semple highly appreciated within his own State, but throughout the whole denomination he wielded a powerful influence. He was everywhere known as a man of unfeigned devotion to Zion's interests, and one on whom reliance could be placed in every great practical effort. In the year 1820 he was elected president of the Triennial Convention, which station he filled to the time of his death. "This election," he remarks in his journal, "although flattering in some respects, was mortifying in others." The idea of taking the place which might have been filled by other aged and venerable servants of God seemed to distress him. "I felt, however," he adds, "much of the spirit of prayer, and hoped that God would overrule it for good." In 1815 Brown University, Rhode Island, conferred on him the honorary degree of A.M. In 1814, from the same university, he received the degree of D.D., and in 1826 the College of William and Mary also conferred the degree of D.D. But the latter honor he declined, from an impression that he did not deserve it; as also on the ground that it was altogether inconsistent with the interests of religion, and in contravention to the express command of Christ. Unquestionably he deserved such a distinction far more than many upon whom it is bestowed; yet, aside from the mandate of his Lord, his unambitious spirit would not allow him to be called Rabbi, and thus in title and by name to be elevated above his brethren in the ministry. As early as the year 1805 he was invited to the presidency of Transylvania University, which invitation he did not conceive it his duty to accept.

While our venerated brother was thus permitted to reach an honorable eminence in usefulness and influence, he was not without the experience of most painful trials. These were mostly of a domestic character. His place of residence in King and Queen County was exceedingly unhealthy, and his family were consequently often visited with sickness. Of twelve children, only four were living at the time of his death. Says one of his surviving sons, in alluding to his father's trials: "Besides these several afflictions caused by the death of his children, his family's health was in a most precarious state for several years, which was a source of constant unhappiness to him. From 1825 to 1827 his home was a perfect hospital, from which disease was scarcely ever absent. His wife, who was always his comforter in affliction, became herself deeply afflicted. Of a family of sixty, black and white, I have known forty to be ill at one time. There were not enough well, at some times, to attend to the sick, the dying, and the dead. Himself at the time in good health, his mind was deeply exercised at the scene around him; two of his six children just conveyed to the tomb, two more expected every moment to follow them, and his wife, the strongest tie that united him to earth, prostrate and senseless from insatiate disease. It was truly a situation that was calculated to call forth all the philosophy and religion he could command. He bore it as a Christian. No murmur escaped his lips. But relying upon the declaration which he often repeated, that 'whom the Lord loveth, he chasteneth,' he awaited the issue with calm and Christian composure."

Perhaps some of the most shining excellencies of this good man's character were the result of that severe discipline through which his Heavenly Father saw it necessary to lead him. Those who are deservedly esteemed as ministers of Christ are liable to be exalted above measure, amid the many kind attentions they receive from their Christian brethren. Pride is easily engendered in the exercise of gifts which God bestows, and which ought to be wholly employed in his glory. Under these circumstances, a thorn in the flesh may be needful; and He who is all-wise to ascertain the necessity, will in paternal love cause it to be experienced. And not unfrequently does he carry through the furnace of affliction, for the purpose of calling into livelier exercise the graces of his Holy Spirit, and to prepare for more eminent usefulness in his kingdom. Some of the most distinguished of God's people for humility and active devotion to the honor of Christ, have known what it is often to drink the bitter cup of affliction. Thus it was with the venerated Semple, as stated in the letter of his son. The following communication, addressed to a beloved friend immediately after the death of one of his grown sons, will afford some idea of the state of his mind at that painful hour:—

"*May* 24, 1822.

"Dear Sir:—

"Yours of the twenty-first instant, directed to my dear John, reached me just as Mr. Broaddus was about to commence his funeral sermon. He left us on Wednesday, about twenty minutes after nine o'clock. His evidences of Divine acceptance seemed to brighten as he approached his dissolution. He said to several of his friends, that death had no terror to him; that he had no desire to live for his own sake; that except for the sake of his connections, especially his parents, he would rather die than live. He said to one of his young friends, who had paid him great attention, I have witnessed that

'Jesus can make a dying bed
Feel soft as downy pillows are.'

He was manifestly dying all day on Tuesday, but on Tuesday night he began to sink rapidly, and I was sent for, having been called from home on ministerial duties. He said to his friend, Dr. Fleet, has my father been sent for? He told him yes. Well, said he, I hope my pulse will hold out until he comes. This was just the case; I found him, on my arrival a little after sunrise, in his senses, and dying fast. He gave me his hand affectionately, but said not much. His debility was so great that he could not speak but with great exertion. He died apparently very easy. My reflections on his death are mixed with pleasure and pain. When I think of my loss and the loss of my remaining family, it is painful beyond description; but when I consider him as called by his gracious Redeemer to his precious embraces, I am filled with holy delight. The attention paid him by his and my friends, while here and on his travels, exceeded my most sanguine hopes. I owe them a debt of gratitude which I must forever owe. Your kindness was never named by him but with the most tender emotions. He seemed to think there never was anything like it before. Oh, how shall I do justice to such disinterested friendship! As I cannot make you suitable returns, I hope my Heavenly Father will abundantly bless you. His weakness toward the last was such as to render it necessary for him to see but few of his friends. This was very painful to him, when any came and could not see him. Indeed, we were obliged not to let him know when they came, lest it might excite him too much. How deep, how unfathomable are the ways of God! If we had the direction of the shafts of death, how differently should we have sent them! But He does all things well.

'Peace, all our angry passions then;
Let each rebellious sigh
Be silent at his sovereign will,
And every murmur die.'"

There is some reason to believe that his own health, and perhaps his life, became a sacrifice to the variety and pressure of those toils in which he felt it his duty to engage. When he left King and Queen County, in 1827, he remained awhile in Washington, but at length settled in Fredericksburg. The management of college concerns on the one hand devolving on him, and the care of the Bruington Church on the other, it was necessary to travel much, both to King and Queen, a distance of sixty miles, and then to the City of Washington. In addition, he engaged to preach twice in each month in Fredericksburg, and once in Washington. In reference to his declining strength, in writing to a brother, dated May, 1831, he remarks: "I have nearly determined against attempting the ride to Lynchburg. I think it too much for me. This is the first General Association I have missed, if I miss this, and I assure you I do it with great reluctance. But the wheels of nature will run on in spite of us, and we must feel the wearings of time. I am now upon the list of the silver grays, and can only fight when there is not a great deal of marching."

Though his health had become impaired during the year 1831, it was little expected that he was soon to be removed from the sphere of labor in which he was so usefully engaged. But He, whose judgments are unsearchable, was preparing him for a dismissal from the toils of earth, and an introduction to the repose of another and a better world. It is a deeply interesting fact, that the last year of his life was crowned with the special indications of Divine favor. The church at Bruington, which had previously suffered in consequence of erroneous sentiments imbibed by some of its members, experienced a season of refreshing from the presence of the Lord. The venerable pastor, in the month of September, baptized, at one time, thirty-two, and before his death had the unspeakable gratification of seeing more than one hundred obey their Lord in baptism, and unite with the Bruington Church. Like Simeon, with the blessed Saviour in his arms, he was ready to say, "Lord, now lettest thou thy servant depart in peace, for mine eyes have seen thy salvation." His last visit to Bruington was made about three weeks before his death. It is thought, although he was then enjoying his usual health, that he had some presentiment of his approaching end. His text on Saturday was selected from 2 Corinthians, xiii. 11: "Finally, brethren," etc. It was the sentiment of many who heard him that he would soon be taken from them. The last sermon he was allowed to preach was founded on Exodus, xv. 11. Returning home, he found himself affected by the extremely inclement weather through which he was compelled to ride.

When it was suggested by some of his family that it was probably necessary he should go to Washington to attend to some business connected with the college, he replied that he felt like a dead man, and could not venture from home again. Shortly after he was seized by a chill, and continued to grow more unwell, until his disease began to assume a dangerous form. During the early stage of his sickness he requested his daughter, whom a few weeks previous he had baptized, to read for him the first chapter of Philippians, and frequently referred to it afterwards in his conversation with those around him. Until within a day of his death, nothing serious was apprehended by the family. But death had marked him as his victim. The following letter, written by his son to the editor of the Herald, will state more explicitly the circumstances of his sickness and death:—

"WOODLAWN, *December* 25, 1831.

"DEAR SIR:—

"The melancholy duty devolves on me to announce to you the death of my venerable father. He left us this morning at ten minutes before ten o'clock. He was seized, this day week, with a fever, which we all thought was nothing more than the influenza, which is now raging in our neighborhood. Monday morning a physician was called in, who pronounced it a pleurisy, but so mild in its features as not to create any alarm in his or our feelings. It gradually grew more serious in its character till Friday, when he dispatched a messenger for my brother, the only one of his children absent, and whom, to his last moments, he expressed a *great desire* to see. He declined rapidly from Friday until this morning, (Sunday,) when he expired without a struggle or a groan. From the first moment of his attack, he affirmed that it would be his last illness; and so impressed was he with that thought, that the remedies prescribed failed to effect the desired results, as his physician believes, from the great influence which his mind exercised over his body.

"He died as he lived, a bright and shining Christian. His frequent ejaculation was, 'I am anxious to depart and be with Christ.' Tuesday afternoon he sunk into a comatose state, from which it was difficult to awaken him. On one occasion he awoke with a placid smile on his countenance, and said to me, 'Oh ask Brother Ball to come here again.' What Brother Ball? said I. 'Mr. Eli Ball,' he replied; 'is he not here?' No, said I. 'Well,' he observed, 'I thought he was conversing with me just now.' He again sunk into this state, and made no other remark till some time during the night he awoke up in the same way, and said, 'This night, forty-two years ago, I preached my first sermon;' and then inarticulately said, 'I have fought a good fight, I have kept the faith.' I have never seen such perfect composure. He requested me, early yesterday afternoon, to look into a certain drawer in his secretary, and bring his will. I did so, and at his request I read it aloud to him. 'Well,' said he, 'I am satisfied; my spiritual condition is such as I wish it; I can depart in peace. The great divisions in the churches sometimes make me unhappy, but I hope they will be healed.' Such were some of his dying observations. I give them in great haste, and under feelings you can more readily conceive than I describe."

Thus fell one whom God and men delighted to honor. The intelligence of his death, as it passed from one circle to another, caused many a bosom to heave with emotion, and many a tear to fall from eyes unused to weep. By hundreds he was most tenderly loved as a father in the gospel, and by most of the churches in Virginia he was regarded as a judicious counselor and devoted friend. All felt that a chasm was created which could not be easily filled. In his removal the whole denomination sustained a loss. Throughout the United States the name of Semple was associated with all that is lovely and of good report; and his active, untiring co-operation in plans of benevolence, had placed him among the principal standard-bearers in the army of the Lord. A discourse, occasioned by this mournful event, was delivered by Elder Robert Ryland, then pastor of the Second Baptist Church, Lynchburg. A discourse was also delivered by the author, then pastor of the Second Baptist Church, in the City of Richmond, from 1 Samuel, ix. 1, 19. In this address the speaker took occasion to refer to the lively interest which the lamented Semple had taken in the welfare of the Second Church, particularly in its early history. Another funeral sermon was preached at Bruington, before the church of which he had been pastor for so many years. An individual who was present, thus refers to the solemnities of that day:—

"The funeral of this eminent servant of God took place at Bruington, on the fifth instant. The occasion was the most solemn and imposing we ever witnessed. Though the day was inclement, the large meeting-house was crowded with a weeping congregation. Every eye, as it entered the house, was fixed upon the vacant pulpit, which was hung around with crape, until the suffusing tear obscured the sight. A thousand sighs that burst from as many feeling hearts, and the tear that bedewed every dejected countenance, spoke in a language that all could understand, how much that venerable old man of God was esteemed. The funeral sermon was delivered by the Rev. Andrew Broaddus. The religious services were opened with the following hymn, from Dr. Rippon's Selection:—

'Lord, when we see a saint of thine
Lie gasping out his breath,
With longing eyes and looks divine,
Smiling and pleased with death.'

"The throne of grace was then addressed by the Rev. Philip Montague in an impressive manner. The text selected for the occasion was taken from 2 Tim. iv. 6, 7, 8: 'I am now ready to be offered,' etc."

The following are the closing remarks of this discourse:— "May I not say, brethren, that what he preached to others, he lived himself? It is not my intention, in what I am saying, to delineate a strictly perfect and faultless character. No! were I to attempt this, I should seem to myself to see the spirit of my departed friend looking down on me with a frown of disapprobation. No! as one of the fallen family of Adam restored by grace to a spiritual life, he still felt and mourned the lingerings of the mortal disease, and 'a sinner saved by grace,' was the motto which he wore.

"Still, however, I may justly say, that he lived himself what he preached to others. No self-denial was inculcated on others which he was not willing to undergo; no religious and moral duties enjoined which he did not practice. Nor did he appear to suffer himself to be engrossed by one class of duties, so as to disregard and neglect another. Standing in different relations in life, it appeared to be his aim (as it ought to be the aim of all) to estimate each of these relations according to its importance, and give his attendance to each accordingly. He knew, indeed, that there are no duties which really clash with each other; they only appear so when we do not pay a just regard to the various relations which we occupy.

"Thus, with a zeal that never grew cold, with a perseverance that never tired, did our much esteemed brother hold on his course, exposing himself, I suspect, even beyond the bounds of prudence, till the last fatal disease laid him on the bed of affliction and death, to call him from his labors, to that eternal 'rest which remains for the people of God.'

"Indulge me a little further. I shall presently be done with this sketch, and bid you adieu. Some have remarked, from the traces of my friend's countenance, that he seemed to possess, by nature, a temper and disposition bordering on the austere. Allowing this to have been the case, we ought the more to admire the influence of that heavenly grace, which, from its throne within, shone so obviously through his features, softening the whole into a kindly expression, and giving a moral lustre to his countenance. Yes; we ought to admire that heavenly grace, which wrought in his soul Christian condescension and affability toward the lowly, and Christian benevolence toward all classes.

"My friends! have I said too much? Have I said enough? At least I have aimed to be faithful, in this imperfect sketch of our departed brother. And now I am done with the character: and here we are about to bid our lamented and beloved Brother Semple a solemn adieu! He is gone! No more shall we see him here among us! No more shall the eyes, now darkened with the shadow of death, rest on the sacred page of this pulpit Bible! No more shall the lips, now sealed up in silence, speak forth to you the message of life! But long and deep in the heart shall his memory be embalmed. And hark!—there is a voice that tells me we shall see him again! Though death presses heavily on him, and waves over him his iron sceptre, it is but a short-lived reign which he holds; and the immortal Judge comes to release his servant—all his servants from the dominion of the tyrant. Yes; brother of my soul, I shall see thee again. Semple will arise. All the saints shall arise, dressed in immortal robes, for 'the marriage of the Lamb.' The chain of death shall be broken; the prison-doors of the grave shall burst asunder; and the redeemed shall come forth to sing the song of triumph, and gather around the throne in deathless felicity. O my friends, are we ready for that great meeting? Christians, are you watching? Are your lamps trimmed, your lights burning, your spirits waiting for the coming of the bridegroom? My unconverted friends, are you lamenting that you have not hearkened to the voice you can hear no more? Will you now turn to God? will you now come to Christ, who ever lives? Oh turn! that you may meet the Judge in peace—and your old preacher, and all the redeemed in glory. Farewell!"

WILLIAM LEIGH.

WILLIAM LEIGH was born in the year 1761. In his seventeenth year he became a subject of conversion, and a short time after joined the Baptist church. The profession thus made was adorned by a consistent life. It is not known at what precise period he entered the ministry, but having been called to preside over Petsworth Church, Gloucester County, he retained this position for twenty-five years, and is said to have been happily instrumental in causing many to seek the remission of their sins. When brought to a bed of sickness, his mind was composed, being stayed upon Him in whom he had believed, and to whom he had committed the interests of his soul. He died at his own dwelling, in Gloucester County, March 22, 1832.

JAMES RUCKS.

ELDER JAMES RUCKS was born in Chesterfield County, January 22d, 1751. In his twenty-eighth year he became a professor of religion, and united with Skinquarter Church, in his native county. Shortly after his mind became concerned respecting his duty to publish the gospel, and after much prayerful reflection, he resolved to preach Christ and him crucified to his fellow-men.

For thirteen years he continued to labor in various directions in his Master's work. At length he was called by Tomahawk Church to go in and out before them as their spiritual shepherd. He was ordained August 11th, 1792, Elders Clay, Smith, and Watkins officiating as the Presbytery. His connection with the church as pastor was retained six years, when, in consequence of delicate health, he was compelled to resign. For twelve years he suffered so much with infirmity of body that he was unable to walk. He still preached, frequently at his own dwelling, and at Skinquarter Meeting-house. When unable to stand alone he was borne to his horse by brethren, and then into the house of God, where, seated in a chair, he addressed his fellow-men on eternal things.

He was always considered a plain, experimental preacher, being often exceedingly zealous in his appeals to the congregation. He died May 12th, 1818.

EDWARD KELLY.

ELDER EDWARD KELLY was one of the most esteemed and useful Baptist ministers of Southwestern Virginia. Though a man of plain understanding and limited opportunities, by a course of unblemished piety and patient labor in the cause of his Divine Master, he accomplished more than many learned but less devoted men. When he commenced the ministry he resided in a comparatively new country, and therefore was the less disqualified by an uncultivated mind for the duties of his station.

He was a prominent member of the Washington Association, and his ministry was mostly confined to the Counties of Scott and Russel. His labors were blessed to a remarkable extent in the conversion of sinners. In 1801 especially, a season of refreshing from the presence of the Lord was enjoyed, when two or three hundred souls were brought into the fold of Christ, and two or three new churches constituted. He continued from time to time to be blessed in his ministrations. As he advanced in years he increased in the affections of the people, and finally came down to his grave like a shock of corn fully ripe. He has been but a few years dismissed from his stewardship.

ROBERT LATHAM.*

ROBERT LATHAM was born in the County of Culpepper on the 2d of November, 1769. His parents were members of the Baptist church, and of respectable standing in civil society. He was baptized when about twenty years of age, and joined some church in Culpepper County. He was married shortly after to Miss Cundiff, of respectable family, in the County of Prince William, where he settled, and pursued the business of a carpenter for some time; then became a farmer. He moved his membership from Culpepper to the Little River Church in Loudon County, near to the Prince William line, and commenced speaking in public about 1806 or 1807, and was ordained about 1809. In this year he became the pastor of Little River Church. In June, 1810, he took the charge of Long Branch Church, in Fauquier. He also preached for awhile to a congregation in Prince William, where, in 1812, a church was constituted, called Bethlehem, of which he became the pastor.

In consequence of a misunderstanding between him and the church at Little River, in 1824, the pastoral connection was dissolved, and he joined the church at Bethlehem. In 1827 the connection between him and the church at Long Branch was dissolved.

His system was high Calvinism, and to some he seemed to border on fatalism; but this he himself denied as a consequence growing out of his views. He could not, however, see the consistency of holding to salvation by grace, and exhorting sinners to the exercise of evangelical repentance, faith, etc. Notwithstanding these views, it is believed that he had occasionally considerable conflicts of mind upon these subjects. At one period

---

* By Elder George Love.

he spoke to the writer of this article in very high terms of Fuller's Essays, and seemed as if his difficulties were removed; but this did not abide. He appeared to fraternize freely with his brethren who differed from him, and when warm in his feelings, and out of sight of his system, would preach very acceptably upon practical and experimental subjects. He was unassuming in his ministerial character, humble as a Christian, and exemplary in his moral deportment. He departed this life on the 15th of April, 1833. The Columbia Association, at their session in August, 1833, instructed a committee to draw up some article relative to his decease. Upon the report of the committee, the following article was adopted by the Association :—

"The Association sympathize with the church at Bethlehem, and with his bereaved family, in the death of our aged and venerable brother, ELDER ROBERT LATHAM. He was called by the grace of God in early life to the knowledge and profession of the truth as it is in Jesus, and through a long life was enabled to keep the faith, and to contend for it. His life was a living comment on the blessed gospel he preached to others, his guide through life and his support in the hour of death. While we sorrow 'that we shall see his face no more,' we are consoled, with his numerous friends, by the consideration that his death was as happy as his life had been holy and useful. He came to his grave in peace."

His first wife made no profession of religion. By her he had four children; two of them are still living. His second wife was Miss Sarah Rust, a Baptist lady, who yet survives him.

WILLIAM RICHARDS.

ELDER WILLIAM RICHARDS was born in Essex County, in 1763, of highly respectable parents. At the early age of eighteen, it pleased God to translate him from darkness into his marvelous light, through the instrumentality of the Baptists. He had enjoyed the opportunity of hearing some of their most zealous preachers, and was won by the truths which they proclaimed. At that time in his native county the Episcopal church was the popular sect, while the Baptists were everywhere spoken against. It need not therefore excite surprise, that his relations and friends should be violently opposed to his immersion. Every expedient was resorted to that it might be prevented. But, having examined the Scriptures and learned the path of duty, he was immovable in his determination to pursue it. He became a member of the Baptist church in 1781. It was his portion to suffer many painful trials as a follower of the Redeemer. All these, however, were borne with Christian meekness; and such was the manifest influence of the gospel in purifying his heart and life, that the mouths of gainsayers were at length stopped, and he was no longer the subject of contempt and persecution. Those who had most ridiculed were compelled to respect him as a good man.

Very soon after this change he conceived it his duty to preach the gospel. His earliest attempts at public speaking were unpromising; and by many it was judged that he would never stand high as a preacher. But in this their judgment was erroneous. It should be stated that most of his first efforts were made in North Carolina; but in 1794 he was induced to remove to the County of Mecklenburg, Virginia. Here he spent the remnant of his life, and with justice it may be said, that few men, within a similar sphere of labor, have risen to greater eminence than he, especially as it regards the purity of his life

The same year he removed from North Carolina he was chosen pastor of Blue Stone, now called Bethel Church. In 1799 a revival was experienced, which resulted in the accession of more than one hundred members. The year previous he consented to serve as their pastor, Sandy Creek Church, Charlotte County, and in 1802 a most refreshing season commenced, which continued for eighteen months, and during which a large number were added. His labors were extended to different parts of Mecklenburg, Lunenburg, and Charlotte, for many years, to the joy and edification of the people of God.

His principal attention, however, was given to Blue Stone, or Bethel, this church being in the vicinity of his own residence. Very few country churches in Virginia have exceeded Bethel in its influence and usefulness. In their pastor they found an example of Christian loveliness, and in most respects they followed him as he followed Christ. They, with their pastor, were not only prompt in their labors for the salvation of sinners at home, but made vigorous efforts on behalf of the wretched heathen in distant lands. For many years they were in the habit of raising a large sum for foreign missions, while the Bible cause and other good objects received their hearty approval and liberal contributions.

Elder Richards was highly distinguished for the unaffected simplicity of his character. Whether in the family, or mingling in society, or in the pulpit, there was the same unassuming artlessness of manner. This softness and meekness were not merely the result of natural temperament. In this respect he was willing to say, "by the grace of God I am what I am."

While he was thus exhibiting the harmlessness of the dove he was not deficient in firmness. When truth was to be defended or discipline in the church enforced, he was resolute in purpose to discharge his duty. He was an excellent disciplinarian. No abuses were allowed to remain uncorrected, nor did transgression among his brethren pass unrebuked. A mighty sanction was given to his influence in supporting a wholesome discipline in the church by his own bright Christian example. None could look at his life without being compelled to approve and admire. Nor was his influence in ruling well among his brethren confined to the churches he served. It was felt in the Meherrin Association, over which, as Moderator, he presided for a number of years. This body owed much of its strength and efficiency to his labors. In its early history he was in the habit of passing almost every year among its churches, supplying the destitute with the preached word, and giving encouragement and support to those which were feeble. At their annual meetings he occupied the chair with peculiar dignity, aweing into silence the turbulent, while all the members of the body were compelled to respect and love him.

As a preacher he was esteemed—among the more judicious and pious, highly so—not for profundity of thought, or elegance of diction, but the peculiar simplicity and energy with which scriptural truth was exhibited. He always gave evidence that the subject of his discourse had been well studied. It is true, he had not access to a well-furnished library. This, had it been practicable, would have yielded peculiar satisfaction. His principal works of research were the Bible and concordance; from these he collected and arranged such arguments and illustrations as his subjects required. He was pre-eminently *a preacher of the cross.* To dwell on the person and work of Emanuel was his chief delight. Many now living can well remember the impassioned and yet artless simplicity of manner with which the plan of salvation was explained and recommended.

For several years before his death feebleness of body compelled him to relinquish all his pastoral connections. Still the house of God was not forsaken. Nothing furnished a richer satisfaction than the society of his Christian brethren and the services of public worship. But at length the hour of his dismissal came, and it found him ready. He knew in whom he had believed, and joyfully did he commit the mighty interests of eternity into the hands of his Divine Redeemer. He died on the 13th of July, 1837, in the seventy-fourth year of his age, having been about fifty years in the ministry.

WILLIAM CREATH.

Elder William Creath was a native of Nova Scotia. He was born December 23d, 1768. His father emigrated to Granville County, North Carolina, in 1786, and became a permanent resident of that State. Previous to this removal his son William was brought under the influence of Divine truth, and was enabled to cherish the gospel hope. No public profession of religion was made until 1787, when he was baptized by Elder Henry Lester, and joined a church in North Carolina, of which Elder Thomas Vass was pastor.

The same year, being then about twenty-years of age, he began to preach Christ and him crucified, as the way to God. Possessing promising talents, he was invited by Elder John Williams, of Lunenburg County, Virginia, to reside with him, for the purpose of improving his mind by a course of general reading. With Mr. Williams he remained for two or three years, during which time he made considerable progress in knowledge. In his instructor he found not only a warm friend, but a pious and talented man.

In 1791 the subject of this memoir was married to Miss Lucretia Brame, with whom he lived for more than thirty-one years in the County of Mecklenburg, Virginia. They had sixteen children, some of whom died in infancy. His wife proved an efficient helper in his labors as a minister of Jesus Christ.

He was, according to Semple, the means of originating the churches called Allen's Creek and Wilson's, and for some time supplied Malone's, all in Mecklenburg County. These churches, even though in his immediate vicinity, did not, to any great extent, prosper, arising from the fact that he was but comparatively little at home. He was in the habit of making lengthy tours through different parts of Maryland, Virginia, and North Carolina. For many years he was scarcely employed in any other way than as an itinerating preacher. It could have been wished that he had occupied a more circumscribed sphere and been more regular in his circuit, as in this way he might have shed a more effective influence on the cause of Christ.

He was in many respects qualified, as a public speaker, to command the attention of his auditors, and generally called out, wherever he preached, large congregations. That some idea of his talents and manners may be obtained, the following testimony from the pen of Elder Semple will be introduced. Mr. Semple, being well acquainted with Elder Creath, was qualified to give a correct judgment. Referring to Wilson's Church, he says: "This church was planted by the labors of Elder William Creath while he was pastor of Allen's Creek. At first they were small; but in 1802 God sent them a time of refreshing, when about forty were baptized. Since then, there have been deaths, removals, and expulsions, sufficient to counterbalance their additions; so that their number at present is only fifty-four. Although they have not for some years been blessed with a revival, yet, under the care of their active and laborious pastor, they enjoy peace, love, and good order.

"Elder Creath is a man of strong mind and deep research, in matters of divinity; and were his manner equal to his matter, he would be among the greatest of preachers. He is thought by some to be too fond of polemic points, so as to lessen his usefulness by exciting unnecessary prejudices. One thing is certain, that in subjects of dispute, there is a time to speak and a time to be silent; and when we speak unreasonably, and especially if it should be intemperately, we damage the very cause we profess to espouse. But with this (if this be so) Elder Creath is a very useful man. He seems willing to spend and be spent for the honor of his Master."

It is painful to be compelled to state that, in the latter part of Elder Creath's life, he was charged with the use of spirituous liquors, even to intoxication. The hearts of his brethren were grieved, while the cause of religion sustained an injury which, perhaps, he was never able fully to repair. The charges alleged against him were acknowledged, and there is abundant reason to believe that he was truly penitent. Before a large congregation he expressed deep sorrow for the wound which he had inflicted on the interests of Christ's kingdom, and became pledged, in the strength of the Lord, no more to indulge in this habit.

The clerk of Meherrin Association refers to this circumstance in the following language: "Let this stand as a beacon to all unwary mariners on the boisterous ocean of life, that they run not on those rocks upon which many have dashed, to the reproach of that good name by which they were called."

About two years after this circumstance he was called to give an account of his stewardship. He left home on the 4th of July, 1823, on a tour of preaching in the lower part of North Carolina. From this journey he was not permitted to return. On his way home he was arrested by an inflammatory disease, and was confined to the house of Mr. John Blunt, in Edenton. On the ninth of August he died, in the fifty-sixth year of his age.

"It is said by those who had heard him for a number of years, that they had never known him preach with such power as he did on his last tour. He spoke as though he knew it was the last battle, and in full confidence of victory. The last time he preached he seemed to be in full view of heaven, and observed, as he arose, that he could scarcely stand; but, as he firmly believed it was the last time, he was more anxious to gain a triumph than he ever had been before. That was on Thursday, and on the Saturday following he fell asleep in the arms of Jesus.

"In the whole of his illness he manifested a noble indifference to himself, with the most tender and sympathetic concern for his dear family and for the church of Christ; and with great fervor he poured out his affectionate petitions for them. The day he died he tried to preach to all that came to see him from these words, 'Thy kingdom come;' and when he could not preach he prayed.

"The following are a few of the many passages of Scripture which he repeated: 'Whom have I in heaven but thee, and there is none upon the earth that I desire beside thee; I have fought a good fight; I know on whom I have believed; I know that my Redeemer liveth; O death, where is thy sting! Come, Lord Jesus, come quickly' His fortitude was unshaken, and his faith strong. Without a struggle he inclined his head on his Saviour's breast, and breathed his life out sweetly there. And just as his joyful soul was about to take its flight he repeated this verse:—

'Farewell, vain world, I am going home;
My Saviour smiles, and bids me come;
Bright angels beckon me away
To realms of everlasting day.'

"He left an affectionate spouse, who assisted him in his ministerial labors, and thirteen children, all of whom have since become members of the Baptist church; five of this number were ministers."

It will not be out of place, in closing this sketch, to notice the character of this excellent lady, since she contributed in no small degree to the efficiency of her husband. She was the daughter of Thomas and Elizabeth Brame, of Granville County, North Carolina. It was her extreme affliction to be left for thirty years with a large family dependent upon her instruction and guidance.

The writer remembers to have seen her a short time after this painful event, and was impressed with the simple confidence she seemed to repose in the widow's God. Cheerfully and trustfully did she cast herself upon the Almighty arm. Nor was this faith a mere idle speculation. She entered upon the duties of her position with patient energy, resolved that all her responsibilities should be fully discharged. The affairs of her household were guided with discretion.

Especially as a Christian mother did she excel. Her whole life was a refutation of the argument, that the practice of believers' baptism militates against the proper religious education of the young. She was a zealous advocate of this, as a practice warranted by the Evangelical Lawgiver. She was able to defend, and often did defend this practice. But never was a Christian more intent or more intelligent in fulfilling the duty of bringing up her children in the nurture and admonition of the Lord. She instructed them in the knowledge of the Scriptures, and in all the duties they owed to God and their fellow-men.

Such was her intimate acquaintance with the Bible, that she was able to converse intelligently on the higher doctrines of the gospel, having selected and arranged ready for use those passages which might be needed to sustain them. In the absence of her husband, who was often away on tours of preaching, she was in the habit of leading in family worship, and requiring her children to memorize and repeat portions of the Bible. It was her earnest desire that her children might all be Christians, and frequently said that, like Hannah, she was willing to give them all to the Lord, to be used by him for the promotion of his glory. The fact is worthy to be recorded that, long before her death, she was able to entertain the hope of meeting all her sixteen sons and daughters in the heavenly world. She rejoiced also to know that five of her sons had entered the ministry. In a good old age, like a shock of corn fully ripe, she descended to the grave. Being in Western Virginia, she desired to return to her friends in Brunswick, that she might die there and be buried with her family. Her wish was gratified; a few days after her arrival in Brunswick County she calmly yielded her departing spirit to her Father and God, maintaining to the last a joyful trust in the Redeemer, to whom she had committed herself, and in whose service, for more than sixty years, she had so humbly and faithfully engaged. May her large posterity, nearly one hundred in number, all be followers of her, as she followed Christ.

NATHANIEL CHAMBLES.*

ELDER NATHANIEL CHAMBLES was the son of William and Elizabeth Chambles, both respectable members of the Baptist church. He was born in Sussex, February 4, 1762. He had religious impressions from an early age; but it was not until his twenty-sixth year that he was enabled to throw himself as a helpless sinner upon the mercy of God in Christ Jesus. In July, 1787, he was baptized and cordially received into the fellowship of the High Hills Church. In 1803 he commenced preaching, and in 1806 was, by the unanimous wish of his church, solemnly ordained to the work of the ministry. For many years he was the faithful and affectionate pastor of the High Hills and Sappony Churches.

Nothing remarkable occurred in his history as a minister from the period of his ordination until 1822. At this time he was deeply affected by the coldness and darkness which pervaded the churches. With unusual warmth he exhorted the members of his churches to be diligent in searching the Scriptures, faithful in self-examination, and fervent in prayer. A day of fasting and humiliation and prayer was appointed by the church at High Hills. God was preparing them to receive a blessing. About this time several laborers were providentially sent into this part of the vineyard. A blessed revival now commenced. In about a year sixty or seventy persons were converted, baptized, and added to the churches. During this season of "refreshing from the presence of the Lord," the heart of our aged brother was filled with gratitude and delight; he seemed to have become young again; with

---

* From Minutes of Portsmouth Association.

all the warmth and tenderness of a young convert he would exhort, and pray, and weep.

In 1825 his constitution evidently began to fail from old age and a disease of the lungs; he was, however, permitted to continue his public labors until within a few weeks of his death. His last sermon was preached from 1 Peter, v. 6, 7. He was blessed with uncommon freedom in speaking from the latter part of the text. God, perhaps, was preparing his children to "cast their care on him" in the heavy affliction they were soon to undergo. A few days afterwards he was attacked with a bilious fever, which terminated in a palsy. Every effort was made by his kind friends to prolong his life, but the hour appointed for his release from sin and woe was at hand. His mind during the period of his severe and protracted illness was serene and heavenly. To a brother minister, who asked him if he was willing to die, he replied: "I have nothing to fear." For about two weeks before his death he was rendered speechless by a paralytic affection, so that his family and friends were not permitted to receive the dying advice which he would otherwise have imparted. A niece, perceiving that he was in his right mind, said to him, "Uncle, you will use your tongue yet." He could only move his hand significantly toward heaven and smile. His countenance indicated the tranquillity of his soul. On the 4th of December, 1827, he fell asleep in Christ. His funeral sermon was preached from Rev. xiv. 13. His body was followed to the grave by a numerous train of relatives, friends, and brethren, and committed to the house appointed for all the living, to repose till the resurrection morn.

It is not easy to delineate the character of a good man; his excellencies, like the colors of the rainbow, are so mingled that it is difficult to distinguish them. He was not a cold, heartless professor of Christianity—a Christian only in name and appearance. He believed the doctrine, imbibed the spirit, followed the example, and heartily espoused the cause of Christ. His religion was sincere, warm, and constant. The whole family of Christian graces dwelt and flourished in his heart. We can exhibit only a few which attained the greatest perfection in his life.

He was eminent for humility. No man possessed a deeper sense of his sinfulness and insufficiency than he did. He could heartily subscribe to the saying of the pious Newton, "I am nothing, I have nothing, and I can do nothing." He literally "esteemed others better than himself." A discerning man could not long be in his presence without admiring his modesty and gentleness; these were the robes in which he was adorned.

Our venerable brother distinguished himself by acts of beneficence. His heart was warmed with love to God and men, and his hand opened to supply the wants of the needy. He considered himself only a steward of God's bounties. He was one of the ready and liberal supporters of the benevolent institutions of the day: believing them calculated to promote the good of men, he listened not to the objections which ignorance and avarice frequently urge against them. For several years he maintained a minister in his own house, and gave him twenty dollars a year, besides the salary raised by the churches, for his services. He fully imbibed the spirit of that saying of our Lord, "It is more blessed to give than to receive." His benevolence was free, full, and constant.

He possessed a remarkable control over his tongue. His intimate acquaintances well know that on all subjects he spoke with the utmost caution. Foolish jesting, trivial conversation, and censorious expressions, never fell from his lips. "Swift to hear, slow to speak," was never more descriptive of any man than himself. With his friends he would sometimes converse freely, and his conversation was both interesting and instructive. Alas, how few employ their tongues as if they expected to give account to God for every word!

As an economist, he has rarely been equaled. His affairs were conducted in the most perfect order; by industry, perseverance, and God's blessing, he made ample provision for the support and comfort of his family.

As a minister, our respected brother never gained great applause. His education was slender: he embarked in the ministry at a late period in life, and was always surrounded with the cares of a large family: it is not, therefore, to be expected that he became eminent in his profession. He closely studied the Bible, and was a plain, solid, faithful, and affectionate preacher. Though not a *great*, he was a *good* minister. He was always solemn and dignified in the pulpit. One trait in his character, as a minister, ought to be particularly noticed: he was not *envious*. The more popular and useful his brethren in the ministry were among his churches, the more he was delighted. Indeed, it seemed to be no part of his object to be admired and lauded by men. Though he would not needlessly offend men, he sought only to please God. His conduct ought to put to shame those preachers who are pained at the prosperity of their fellow-laborers in God's vineyard.

SAMUEL SHREWSBURY.*

SAMUEL SHREWSBURY was born in Hanover County, Virginia, in the year 1736. Some time in the year 1766, he removed and settled in the County of Bedford, Virginia, where he became a convert to the Christian faith, and was baptized about the year 1770, by a traveling Baptist minister who tarried for a short time in the vicinity of his residence. In 1772 he commenced proclaiming the gospel of the grace of God, in which he steadily persisted until the year 1784, when he fell a victim to the intermittent fever, which he was thought to have contracted at the Big Lick, in Botetourt County, when returning from a tour to warn his fellow-creatures to flee from the wrath to come. He died at the early age of forty-eight years, and appears to have been cut off in the midst of his usefulness, and thus furnished additional evidence that the ways of God are inscrutable to man. After a lapse of more than half a century, it is difficult to collect specific information in relation to Mr. S.—so difficult, indeed, that no attempt would now be made to rescue his memory from oblivion, were it not for the fact that he lived and labored in portentous times. We are at but little loss to determine of what manner of spirit a man is, when he espouses an unpopular cause, and earnestly contends for the faith once delivered to the saints, against an overwhelming current of opposition created by the lordlings of the

---

* By Elder William C. Ligon.

country. It is no meager compliment to record the name of an individual as a *Baptist minister*, zealously laboring in Virginia between the years 1772 and 1784. We claim for such a one more than presumptive evidence that we record the name of a Christian and a patriot. Well might a highly reputable and influential citizen of Kanawha County say, in a letter now before me, "I am proud that I am a descendant of Samuel and nephew of Nathaniel Shrewsbury."

It is doubtful whether Mr. S. was ever ordained: facilities for ordination were rare in the then frontier country of his residence; but be that as it may, there is positive evidence that he was an exemplary and successful preacher of the gospel. Elder William Leftwich says, in relation to him: "I have no acquaintance with him, but I have no doubt, from what I have heard from others, (now fallen asleep,) that he was a worthy man of God, and an acceptable preacher." Of particular exercises of mind about the time of his dissolution, I have no information, (my principal informant being, at that period, a child of only six years of age, and orphaned by his death,) but if we are permitted to deduce a particular conclusion from current facts, we feel justified in saying the end of Samuel Shrewsbury was *peace*.

NATHANIEL SHREWSBURY.*

THE subject of this sketch was born in the County of Hanover, Virginia, in the year 1739, and removed, in company with his brother Samuel, to Bedford County, in the year 1766.

The two brothers appear to have made a profession of religion about the same time, were baptized by the same man, and commenced the ministry together. Indeed, the history of the one seems to be the history of the other, so united were they in their lives and labors, until they were separated by the death of Samuel, the elder. From Semple's "History of the Baptists in Virginia,"

---

* By Elder William C. Ligon.

it will be seen that Nathaniel Shrewsbury constituted Goose Creek, Little Otter, and Buffalo Churches, in the bounds of the Strawberry Association. Of the first and last named churches he was the early pastor.

The brief and indefinite history which the excellent Semple has written of Buffalo Church is to be lamented; because, when joined to his table of the Strawberry Association, it is calculated to mislead the reader and leave the impression that Elder Nathaniel Shrewsbury was the individual to whom he alluded in the following remarks: "A good preacher is one of the best gifts of heaven to a pious people; but if he unfortunately forgets his sacred office, and neglects to keep his body under, and thereby becomes a castaway, the affliction is more than commensurate with the former blessing. Buffalo found it necessary to exclude her once useful minister." Who that "useful minister" was, I have no means of determining, but facts are conclusive in favor of the idea that it was *not Nathaniel Shrewsbury.* In the year 1798 he removed to the State of Kentucky, and settled in Adair County, where, in the language of one to be relied on, and well acquainted with the fact, "he continued his ministry till his death, in 1825." My informant also adds that Mr. Shrewsbury frequently remarked, "that the necessary separation from his several churches gave him more pain than he had power to express." He died at the advanced age of eighty-five years.

Elder William Leftwich, of Bedford County, in a letter now before me, says: "I was acquainted with him; have heard him preach often. When I first became acquainted with him, he had the care of Goose Creek Church. I think he must have been the pastor of that church as far back as 1780. He was likewise the pastor of Little Otter Church from the time of its constitution, which took place in or about the year 1785. These two churches he served, aided generally by Brother William Johnson,*

* I have endeavored, but in vain, to collect sufficient information to compile a biographical sketch of Mr. Johnson. Where or when he was born, or the time and circumstances of his demise, does not appear to be known by any to whom I have applied for information. That such a man settled in the County of Bedford, in the character of a Baptist preacher, about

(than whom a much worthier man never lived,) until the year 1798, when, like many other Baptist preachers, he removed to Kentucky. While connected with these churches, he sometimes made excursions abroad. Among others, the Cow Pasture had his occasional visits. As a preacher he was popular, with many he was very much so. He was truly an affectionate and exemplary minister of the gospel; his labors were owned and blessed of the Lord. Under his fostering care, his churches in the main were prosperous. His talents as a preacher, there is no doubt, were above mediocrity in his day and sphere of labors."

Elder Leftwich's opinion of the talents and usefulness of Mr. Shrewsbury is amply corroborated by the testimony of others; and no doubt can be entertained that he was a highly gifted and useful preacher. He too lived and labored in the days that tried men's souls; when Baptist minister was a term of reproach in Virginia, and when such a one wrought in the Lord's vineyard with full knowledge of the fact that he was thereby exposing himself to bonds, stripes, and imprisonments. God was pleased to protract his days to see the ball of the Revolution wound up; to taste the sweets from the cup of religious liberty; to sit under his own vine and fig tree, and worship agreeably to the convictions of his own mind, nor fear nor hear the voice of the oppressor.

JEREMIAH HATCHER.

As respects the early part of the life of Elder Jeremiah Hatcher, we have no information whatever, although some pains have been taken among his surviving friends and relatives to obtain it; all those from whom *such* facts might have been

---

the year 1778, and that he was the immediate contemporary and active and successful fellow-helper of Elder Nathaniel Shrewsbury, appears to be incontestibly true.

While we have cause to lament the loss of his record on earth, no little consolation arises from the confident belief that Heaven has been less remiss; that the record is, doubtless, *on high.*

derived are *now* no more. Yet there are a few well-ascertained circumstances worthy the attention of the biographer, which, as a testimonial of esteem for his memory, should be handed down to posterity.

Elder Hatcher was a native of Chesterfield County, and it is said his ancestry were highly respectable. His ministerial career commenced at least as far back as 1778. He is stated to have been the first pastor of the church called Tomahawk, in the County of Chesterfield, which was constituted in 1777. This church he served about two years, and then removed to Bedford County, where he labored with much acceptance and usefulness, and in a very short time became the pastor of the church called Northfork of Otter. Whether this church was constituted before, or subsequently to his removal to Bedford, is somewhat uncertain; but we incline to think it was about this time. This church was built up principally under his ministry, and enjoyed his indefatigable labors without fee or reward until the time of his death.

His labors were not confined exclusively to this church; he made frequent excursions in the surrounding country, and exerted an influence in the cause of his Divine Master that will tell when time shall cease to be measured by days, months, and years. Elder Hatcher was one of the most uniform and exemplary men; his general deportment was a comment on his profession—humble, grave, solemn, and unassuming—thereby commending himself to every man's conscience in the sight of God. He was greatly beloved by the people of his charge; and by all that knew him, whether saint or sinner, he was recognized as a devout man of God. He was an uncompromising Calvinist. In sentiment, as a preacher, he was plain, pointed, and consistent. His talents, though not highly cultivated, were of the useful sort, and were not employed in vain, for the work of the Lord prospered in his hands.

Some time in the year 1804 he bid adieu to the toils and labors of a life not spent for naught, and entered, it is believed, into that rest that remains for the people of God.

JOHN POINDEXTER.

THE ancestry of JOHN POINDEXTER were highly respectable. His grandfather was a French Protestant, whose adherence to religious principles compelled him to leave his native land and seek shelter from papal oppression in the Island of Great Britain. At this time he was the head of a large family. Shortly after his arrival in England, one of his sons, Thomas Poindexter, became attached to a young lady, whom he addressed, and who reciprocated his affection. As there was considerable disparity in their circumstances, the father of Thomas was much displeased, and expressly forbade the connection. More effectually to prevent it, he gave his son a handsome estate, and sent him to Virginia. This being made known to the young lady, she determined to follow in search of her intended husband, and for this purpose indented herself as a servant for four years. She succeeded in reaching the shores of Virginia. The young Frenchman having heard that a vessel with servants had arrived, and desiring to obtain one, made application, when, on examining, he discovered his once intended spouse. The meeting was joyful. They rushed to each other's embraces. He paid the stipulated price, and she became his wife. From these sprang all the Poindexters known in America. One of their sons was the subject of this memoir. When quite young, he indicated considerable sprightliness of mind, and the best advantages for education which the country at that time afforded, were enjoyed by him.

It was not until he became a married man, that he manifested interest in the subject of religion; on the contrary, he was understood to be an opposer. At that period when the gospel was first proclaimed by the Baptists in the County of Louisa, where he resided, he employed all his influence to resist the truth. But the Lord was mightier than he, and the truth became effectual in his own family. His wife was turned to the Lord, and rejoiced in him as her Saviour. This circumstance created in the bosom of Mr. Poindexter mingled emotions of surprise and rage. His opposition was exhibited in a more marked and decided manner. When his companion desired to be immersed, and to unite herself with the Baptists, he entered his express prohibition against it. In secret places she often wept, and sought God on behalf of his cause and her unbelieving husband; nor were her entreaties vain. The Lord heard her prayer, and brought her companion to feel his own guilt and ruin, and to sue for mercy. The circumstances of his conversion are thus modestly referred to by himself:—

"Two women, Mrs. H. and Mrs. P., who lived near each other, about the year 1788, professed conversion, but were not baptized, because of opposition. The husband of Mrs. P. was most pointedly against her being baptized, and equally so against her attending Baptist meetings. These women often met in secret, to converse about religion, and to enjoy each other's company as travelers to Zion. In the course of their conversations, they expressed their desire to introduce the Baptist ministry into the neighborhood, and concluded that an application should be made by them to the husband of Mrs. P. This attempt, the most unlikely to succeed to human view, was made, and treated at first very indifferently; but ultimately, it was observed by him that he had no objection to the Baptist preaching on his land—perhaps it might benefit some of his neighbors or their children—that if he did not go to heaven himself, he was willing they should; but he must choose the preacher. He stated his objections strongly against noisy preachers, and observed that some years before, he had heard a clever old gentleman preach, by the name of Goodloe; if he could be had, he might preach on his land, and that preparations should be made for the accommodation of a congregation. The two ladies were well pleased. Elder Goodloe was notified, a day appointed for the first meeting, an arbor built, and seats prepared for the congregation.

"Though Mr. Poindexter had been much opposed to religion, and would not attend on the preaching of the gospel, he was apprehended by the spirit of God, and under serious conviction before the meeting came on. Elder Goodloe attended, and to a large congregation preached with considerable liberty, from the words, 'Ye must be born again.' His audience appeared serious, and the sermon had good effect. Particularly the poor criminal,

John Poindexter, was much affected. The next meeting was appointed August 29th. Previous to this the prisoner was brought forth, the sentence pronounced against him, which he acknowledged was just, and saw no way by which he could be pardoned; although he beheld a fullness in Christ for sinners, he could not realize a hope that it would be extended to a sinner so vile as himself. But God, who is a God of grace, showed unto him how he could save him. He manifested the richness of his grace by opening the prison doors and proclaiming his pardon.

"By this man the Baptists had been despised; all other professions of religion were preferred to that of the Baptists; but, after having experienced the pardoning love of God, he esteemed them above all people. He had uniformly opposed baptism, upon profession of faith, by immersion; but now he was thoroughly convinced of its propriety. His wife, who had been for nearly two years desirous of being a Baptist, and whom he had heretofore prevented, was, August 29th, 1790, led into the water by her husband, together with Mrs. Henly, and they were all baptized by Elder Henry Goodloe. The news had spread far and wide, that the baptism above alluded to would take place on that day, and people attended the meeting from every adjacent county, and very generally from the county of Louisa. There was an anxiety in the minds of the people to know the truth of this affair; numbers doubted, and others attended to gratify their curiosity. Many were the conjectures of the people about the baptism of that hardy rebel, John Poindexter. Some supposed he joined the Baptists from pecuniary motives; some that it was to gratify his lusts; and others supposed in six months he would be as he was before. But grace knows how to support its own. Thanks to our redeeming Lord, they were false prophets. From the time of this baptism, not only Elder Goodloe, but Elders Waller and Webber, attended the meetings; and at times foreign ministers. The Word of the Lord grew and multiplied. On the approach of winter, meetings were held in the house of John Poindexter. The congregations were large; and such numbers of people dined at his table, that the devil changed his voice and began to pity him and his family. Now, instead of charging him with pecuniary motives, he declared that the Baptists would eat him out of house and home. But the devil was a liar then, as he is now; for God prospered him. A certain lawyer passed through his plantation, and looking on the crops, declared that he would be a Baptist too: for he never saw such crops of corn as Poindexter made since he became a Baptist."

About a year after his baptism he began to speak in public, testifying both to small and great repentance toward God and faith in our Lord Jesus Christ. In February, 1792, he was publicly ordained to the work of the ministry. A church called Roundabout (after a creek of that name) having been constituted near his house when he was converted to God, he was unanimously invited to take the oversight of them. This relation he sustained for many years; and it was well sustained. As a preacher, he was eminently successful, especially in the early part of his ministry. Within twelve months after his ordination he baptized upwards of one hundred, and the church continued to increase until more than three hundred were added. His labors were extended into the neighboring counties, and with great power did he exhibit the truth as it is in Jesus. He was instrumental in forming a church in Albemarle, called Bethel, which soon numbered more than one hundred members.

For some time also he labored in connection with William's Church, and his ministrations here were eminently successful. "Under his ministry," says Mr. Semple, "they enjoyed a pleasant revival of religion, conducted with harmony, solemnity, and order, in which about ninety or one hundred were baptized; of these only about fourteen were excommunicated in ten or eleven years, and yet their discipline has been regular." Such was the success of Mr. Poindexter's endeavors in proclaiming the gospel, that in 1798 another congregation was constituted as a branch of Roundabout Church, and called Siloam. This was itself, when organized, a strong body.

Elder Poindexter was a man of no ordinary talents. His discourses were highly doctrinal, and usually displayed much thought and discrimination. He seldom preached without preparation, giving evidence that in no common degree he was a scribe well instructed in the things of the kingdom.

From a few notes in possession of the writer, it is manifest that he was not satisfied with a cursory view of things. To dig deep in the mines of truth was his delight. Nor did he labor in vain. The precious ones were brought forth, and subjected to the crucible of investigation. Many a precious gem, thus brought to light, enriched its possessor, and imparted good to others. No one could listen to him without deriving instruction. Indeed, it is doubtful, from the specimens of his style of writing which yet remain, and the testimony of those who have listened to him, whether among the ministry of his generation we have had a more able man.

The influence of Elder Poindexter was extensive and merited. For many years he was the clerk of Louisa County; and, as a member of the community, was highly useful. He always exhibited a prompt and Christian-like benevolence in the use of those means which were intrusted to his care by a kind Providence. He seemed to feel the sentiment, that it was more blessed to give than to receive. His pecuniary sacrifices in promoting the cause of God at different times were numerous.

Whatever related to the spread of evangelic truth was regarded with peculiar interest. He was ready for every good word and work. Though diligent and faithful in attention to secular duties, it was evident to all that the highest place in his affections was occupied by the interests of Zion and of souls. When the missionary enterprise was introduced to the notice of Virginia Baptists, his whole heart entered into it, and he was ready with his tongue, pen, and purse, to promote its interests. Said he to Luther Rice: "Command me and my services, as far as my feeble powers will allow, in supporting that good work, and I will obey. I hope that the good Lord, who rules in the heavens and on the earth, will prosper the endeavors of all who are found sustaining the glorious cause of Foreign Missions."

The doctrinal sentiments of Elder Poindexter were what are usually denominated Calvinistic. He, however, avowed his confidence in the simple teachings of the Bible, calling no man master. He loved to contemplate the Divine Sovereignty in the plan of redemption, and the work of Providence. Especially was Christ in all his character, offices, and work, the object of thought and love. One of his manuscript volumes is made up of an examination of the various names appropriated to the Son of God, and exhibits strikingly the leading tendencies of his mind in respect to doctrinal truth. He desired to know nothing but Christ Jesus and him crucified, hanging not only his own hope of salvation upon this doctrine, but urging it upon others as worthy of all acceptation.

His views of the structure of a gospel church are eminently sound. They deserve to be recorded and preserved In them is indicated the general sentiment of Baptists, a sentiment which distinguishes the denomination from all others. They have been rigid in their adherence to the great principle, that a church of Christ cannot scripturally exist excepting as it is made up of baptized believers; and that all its internal affairs are to be conducted by itself, without the exercise of power on the part of any higher tribunal. This is regarded as fundamental. No warrant is found in the Word of God for any other constitution of God's people as a Christian church. These views are introduced by Mr. Poindexter. He says:—

"The term 'a gospel church,' has been, and is now, thought by many to be somewhat equivocal, and consequently has had different meanings attached to it, suited to the opinions, prejudices, inclinations, and pecuniary interests of men placing themselves at the head of different sectaries or societies, called by them gospel churches. But it is evident to all who disinterestedly attend to the Scripture account of the nature of a gospel church, that, more or less, men who have assumed to themselves the prerogative of new modeling the church of Christ have not so much attended to the directions given by Christ and his apostles as they have to their own opinions; and we are sorry to say that such conduct has had a tendency to divide professors of our holy religion, and subject them to the opinions, prejudices and views of their different leaders. * * * * * *

"The sense we give to the term church, when applied to the people of God, is a company of men and women called out of the world: 'Unto the church of God, which is at Corinth, to them which are sanctified in Christ Jesus, called to be saints.' 1 Corinthians, i. 2. Clearly, then, a gospel church must be holy, independent, and regular—a visible society of men and women. * * * The terms of union or the door into the church is *not* baptism; all members who enter into a gospel church must previously hear, believe, and be baptized. Such persons may be received into a church state. To form a gospel church there must be *fellowship*—a mutual compact or agreement voluntarily entered into by baptized believers. It is clearly to be seen the first churches were made up of baptized believers; when additions were made none but baptized believers were admitted. * * * Every voluntary agreement between baptized believers ought to be upon the principles of *truth, peace, holiness,* and *order.* An assembly who have thus given themselves to the Lord and to one another by the will of God, may properly be called a Christian church, and while they walk together in the order of the primitive churches will be, in the eyes of beholders, 'comely as Tirzah, and terrible as an army with banners.'"

Speaking of discipline, he thus writes: "A government in all societies is necessary, but more especially in the church of Christ. Notwithstanding the church is composed of persons professing faith, yet none are exempt from the imperfections of human nature, and have to lament that the pollution of their nature often indisposes them to submission to the will of God. Discipline then becomes necessary to correct the disorders occasioned thereby, that the honor of Christ and his gospel, together with the peace and happiness of his church, may be maintained. The government of the churches was instituted by Jesus Christ.

"We shall not stop to consider those who endeavor to establish Presbyterial government over the churches. Christ Jesus deposited his authority to administer discipline *in the churches.* It was not deposited with the ministry *as such,* because the Apostle Paul acknowledges Church authority. Christ's words are, 'If he shall refuse to hear them, tell it unto the church,' etc. * * * The plain meaning of all the Scriptures is that the authority for carrying on and administering discipline is delegated by Jesus Christ to his church as such, inclusively, and that authority is not given to one member above another, and distinct from the church, but to the whole body, as every member thereof may stand related to each other in each respective church."

Some remarks on schism are worthy to be recorded in letters of gold: "What is called schism," he says, "in a religious sense, is division and dissension, whereby the hearts of men are split into opposite factions and interests, so as to make a separation in the church. This is one of the most detestable monsters that ever appeared in the church of Christ; and yet the schismatic is often received with the greatest applause. The causes of this evil are pride, self-love, jealousy, hatred, evil-speaking, covetousness, lust for pre-eminence, immoderate thirst after the honors and pleasures of this world. We shall not stop to show by long argument that these are causes of division, because they are self-evident. Pride is at the bottom; self is the idol to be honored; jealousy is in company lest others should be more honored; then hatred, malice, envy, and evil-speaking take place, each endeavoring to disgrace the object in view, that everything may contribute to the honor, emolument, and pre-eminence of the schismatic himself. The description is given by Paul to Timothy: 'Lovers of their own selves, boasters, proud, truce-breakers, false accusers, fierce, despisers of those that are good, heady, high-minded, lovers of pleasure more than lovers of God.' The Apostle marks with severity this character. 'Now, I beseech you brethren, mark them which cause divisions among you and offences, contrary to the doctrine which you have learned, and avoid them.'"

Notwithstanding he filled the clerkship of the county up to the time of his death, and in this capacity was prompt and vigilant, he did not neglect his Master's service. To the close of life he was, in season and out of season, endeavoring to do good to all men. The Goshen Association, of which he was a member, enjoyed the advantage of his counsel and influence. For a series of years he was elected to preside over their deliberations. Although inquiries have been made, no definite information has been received concerning the precise time and circumstances of his departure from this world. His death took place the latter part of the year 1819.

ELISHA PURRINGTON.

MANY of those who have labored in Virginia as the heralds of the Cross were natives of other States. The subject of this sketch, it is believed, was born in New England, and came to this State about 1772. In removing hither, his principal object was to teach the science of sacred music. He succeeded in obtaining patronage in Louisa, Goochland, and Fluvanna Counties, and having formed a matrimonial engagement with a Miss Todd, finally settled in the first-named county. Although he was a member of the Baptist church when he removed to Virginia, he was far from being zealous in spiritual things. But a happy change took place in his religious feelings, which resulted in the conviction that God required him to work in his vineyard. He began to exhort, and ultimately to preach At first his efforts were very unpromising; many believed that he would never overcome the obstacles which impeded his progress, and he was often, on this account, the subject of despondency. But, with the most indefatigable industry, he applied himself to study, and by degrees acquired an extensive fund of knowledge. He became one of the most intelligent preachers of his day. His acquaintance with the Scriptures was deep and thorough.

As he advanced in life his influence increased, not only among the private members of the church, but his brethren in the ministry. At Associations and other meetings he was frequently consulted by the most intelligent in reference to difficult passages in the Word of God, while his opinions were received with the most respectful attention. As a theologian he deserved respect. His views were generally judicious, being the result of patient and laborious investigation. In the pulpit he was inclined to be doctrinal; but he did not, therefore, neglect practical religion. His style was clear and forcible, while his manner, though not impressive, was interesting; he failed not to commend himself to every man's conscience in the sight of God. Mr. Semple refers to him as having possessed "valuable gifts which were exercised in a useful way."

Such was the favor with which his ministry was received, that the old and intelligent church in Goochland, called Williams, gave him a unanimous call to become their pastor. They had previously enjoyed the labors of some of the most eminent men of that day; and it was a flattering indication to request him to engage in this labor. Their invitation was accepted. He entered upon his work with the most praiseworthy zeal. As a pastor, he was much beloved. The influence gained over the hearts of his flock was not altogether the result of intelligence in the pulpit, but of frequent and affectionate intercourse. There was a softness and ease in his manners which were the spontaneous product of a benevolent heart. If a spiritual guide would obtain the confidence of those placed under his care, he must give frequent and indubitable proofs of his affection. It must be seen that he seeks not his own, but their interest, and thus, like the apostle, very gladly spend and be spent for them; though the more he loves, the less he might be loved. He must be gentle among them, even as a nurse cherisheth her children. Mr. Purrington was such a man. He loved the people of his charge, and exhibited that attachment in his whole deportment. This constituted one of the elements of his great influence among the churches. Another reason to be assigned for the esteem in which he was held was the uniformity of his Christian character. His piety was fervent and habitual; eternal realities engaged his supreme attention. He acted in accordance with the great object of his creation, and sought to glorify God in his body and spirit which were his.

Such a man could not but be loved. It need not be a subject of surprise that he was useful. Many accessions to the churches were made during his pastorate, but especially in the edification of the pious was his usefulness manifest. Mr. Purrington excelled in his knowledge of the science of music; it has been already stated that he originally came to Virginia as an instructor in the art of singing. He continued to employ his talent in this way for many years. It ought, perhaps, to be said that he was not thought to be a good financier, having been frequently embarrassed in his worldly concerns.

The death of this good man occurred about the year 1820. As the circumstances of his last hours are not known to the biographer, this memoir must necessarily be brought to a close.

SAMUEL WOODFIN.

Elder Woodfin was a native of Virginia, and born September 21st, 1722. He was among those whose lot it was to stem the tide of prejudice and opposition which resisted the Baptists in their early history in Virginia. He was a zealous laborer in his Master's vineyard, and not until within a short time previous to his death, when age and infirmity compelled him, did he abandon the work. He was a man of industrious habits, diligent in business, fervent in spirit, serving the Lord. Not only in the gospel of His Son did he endeavor to please God, but by rigid faithfulness in fulfilling his worldly engagements; evincing to all around a tenacious adherence to the principles of justice and integrity. In his declining years he took great pleasure in retrospecting scenes of former days, and recounting the labors of his yet unwearied feet when he first entered the ministry. He would refer to those times when, after working with his own hands at the anvil during the week, at the close his journey was commenced, often on foot, to meet a congregation ten or fifteen miles distant from his home; while his customers would find him at his shop early on Monday morning. As long as he continued to preach, he was remarkably punctual in attending his appointments, allowing no weather, however inclement, nor any trivial circumstance, to prevent his presence where it was expected.

As a preacher, Elder Woodfin was plain, experimental, and practical. Like most of his contemporaries, he indicated the want of early literary advantages. His system of divinity was in accordance with the generally received views of the Baptist denomination. As a pastor, he was affectionate and attentive, and by the people of his charge was much beloved. He accepted the pastoral vocation in Muddy Creek Church, Powhatan, in 1784, and retained this connection up to the period of his death. He died in peace, January 13th, 1832.

If Father Woodfin had foibles, they were perhaps more conspicuous to himself than others, yet he had enemies disposed to magnify them. We would, however, entomb them with his mortal remains, in the silent grave, whence, we confidently hope, he will in the morning of the resurrection arise, clothed in the righteousness of Jesus, and appear in the presence of God without spot or wrinkle, to dwell with him forever.

JOSEPH PEDIGO.

Elder Joseph Pedigo closed his earthly labors some time in the year 1837, being more than threescore years of age, and having been long employed in the ministry of the gospel. He was a resident of Henry County, and was for many years an active member of the Strawberry Association, generally occupying the chair at their annual meetings. When the Pig River Association was formed, in 1824 or 1825, the church of which he was a member became connected with that body. In the new Association he exercised considerable influence, and to the time of his death was their Moderator.

At different times during his ministerial career he served several churches, and was instrumental in promoting their increase and edification. As a preacher he was highly regarded by his brethren, being distinguished by a plain, affectionate manner in his addresses from the pulpit. His information was very limited, having enjoyed no opportunity in youth for the improvement of his mind. During most of his ministerial life he was able to employ but little time in reading, being quite poor, and compelled to labor for the support of his family. His preaching was not strictly of the expository character, while at the same time, to the utmost of his ability, he delighted to recommend the offices and work of the Saviour of sinners. With a character highly exemplary, by all classes he was much esteemed.

Elder Pedigo was opposed to all the efforts which are now employed to send the gospel among the heathen, as well as Sunday-schools, tract operations, etc. etc. But the writer of this sketch is confident that this prejudice was the result of circumstances. If he had lived in other sections of the State, where he might have mingled with brethren engaged in these exertions, and where he would not have received inaccurate statements concerning their designs and consequences, his opinions would have been of a different stamp. During the year 1836 the writer had an opportunity of spending a night under his humble but hospitable roof. In riding to his door, the inquiry, with some coolness, was made, whether or not he was addressing a "Missionary Baptist." The answer was, that it afforded peculiar delight to see the gospel published to sinners everywhere, and that no appropriate means ought to be neglected to send it to every creature. An invitation was extended to tarry for the night. After some general remarks, a most interesting conversation occurred on doctrinal and experimental religion, while the aged brother seemed astonished that a "Missionary Baptist" should be so far from the indulgence of Arminian sentiments. After some time, the conversation was directed to the benevolent movements of the day, and it was quite astonishing to the writer that so little correct information respecting these things had been obtained by him whom he addressed. He had entirely misapprehended their whole character and tendency. In the morning, on separating, with the kindest and most affectionate manner Elder Pedigo extended an invitation to visit him again. It was a delightful interview, and on leaving the spot, the impression was forcibly made upon the mind that acquaintance and free interchange of sentiment, with mutual forbearance, would do more toward the production of unity of sentiment and action among brethren, than all the acrimonious debates or even well written and dispassionate essays could accomplish.

BENJAMIN HARDWICK.*

God often moves in a mysterious way to accomplish his wise designs. He changes the purposes of men by the interposition of his providence. This assertion is proved by the life of Mr. Hardwick. He was born during the memorable revolutionary war. His parents were poor and illiterate. He was brought up in the field to hard manual labor, and experienced many of the hardships to which motherless boys are subjected when under the control of stepmothers whose only ambition is to rule father and children with an iron rod. No pen can describe what such children have felt and endured. Benjamin was industrious. His father taught him to regard labor as the essence of human excellence. He ignored the claims of his children to mental culture; and while others enjoyed the rude advantages afforded by a sparsely settled country, his sons were toiling to increase his wealth.

Benjamin was anxious to be wealthy. He spent many hours of night in working for a few pence, which he was careful to retain. In early life he married a young and beautiful lady, Elizabeth Flowers, of Buckingham County. Not content with the slow, but sure and truest, process of accumulating by labor, Mr. Hardwick commenced speculating, and then sporting. The fame of his race-horses went out into distant parts of the State, and his companions envied his success. God apparently smiled upon him. Money flowed into his hands: he was soon surrounded by the comforts of life; a splendid farm, on Slate Run, with hands and stock, were the fruits of his accumulations. His family was large and growing.

God called him to reflect, repent, and believe the truth. The call was not disregarded. The truth, mighty to conquer, grappled with the strong powers of his soul, and they were conquered.

---

* Prepared by Rev. J. B. Hardwick.

The Spirit, ever potent to renew, changed his vile nature, and so felt—oh indescribable emotions!—that Christ was formed in his soul the hope of glory! God had a work for him. He had been faithful to the wicked one, and felt the importance of more than ordinary faithfulness to God. He was called in mid-life to preach. What was he to do? The groans of a lost world, the sighs of degraded and wounded humanity, were continually sounding in his ears. His early education had been totally neglected. Unable to read the Bible, inspired with a high sense of duty, he essayed to exhort his fellow-men, and then, assisted by the Spirit, to teach them what he had learned and felt.

He felt that he was not his own. Christ had redeemed him, and he belonged to him. Some would have plead a want of fitness for the work, and dragged out a dissatisfied life in some secular calling. The claims of his Master were imperative. To preach, he must consecrate himself to the work. His children were at school; blessed with vigorous minds, they progressed with great rapidity. Judge what their surprise was when their father accompanied them daily to school, and commenced learning the nature and power of letters. We have no means now of ascertaining how long he was at school, but he learned enough of the English language to read the blessed Bible, and teach the people its blessed precepts. Blessed with extensive means, he preached often, and invariably at his own charges. Think of it, young man, as you repose beneath the towers of Zion, and enjoy the advantages that the best schools afford for mental improvement, that for much of our present denominational felicity we are indebted to men whose manners and sermons would now be considered by some intolerable. The father at school with his own sons! What but the love of Christ constrained him? We leave this picture, that has encouraged one mind, if no more, to seek that information essential to success in teaching men what Christ has commanded.

God never fails to reward men for their deeds. He that is swift to gather up may expect to have it scattered, either by himself or others. Much of Mr. H.'s property was obtained by sporting, and God no doubt placed a curse upon such gains. The war of 1812 found him independent. It was followed by an unparalleled demand for tobacco: he speculated largely, with his sons. The article suddenly fell to a low price, and he was pecuniarily ruined. Now an old man, with a large number of children, he is thrown again upon his own resources for a support. He emigrated to Tennessee, and settled in Smith County. He did not complain. God had ordered all things right.

He was a preacher of good natural abilities. His manner was earnest, pathetic, and solemn. Some of the living fathers of the State still remember him. Many precious souls claimed him as the chosen instrument of their conversion. He would never take the care of a church. He thought God never called him to be a pastor, but a preacher. How great his awe must have been for that office! While others would have rushed into it, he hesitated and declined; preferring others, and esteeming them better than himself. If an old preacher, half a century ago, shrunk from so responsible a station, with what feelings ought men now to revere it! Mr. Hardwick lived to see Baptist churches increase and multiply with great rapidity. His children all grew up, and the most of them became members of the church he loved so well. Several of them were distinguished as political and professional men. His youngest son is now a minister of the gospel, and two of his grandsons—the children of his son Samuel—are ministers of the Baptist church in Virginia.

Full of years, rich in faith, far from the scenes of his early and eventful life, he went down to the grave. If he was poor in this world's goods, he was rich in that love that is worth more than the universe! His Saviour had taken away his gold, that cankered, and rendered the heart morbid and avaricious, and given him gold tried in the fire. He found a sepulchre among strangers, and now rests near Charlotte, the county-seat of Dickson, Tennessee. His grave has passed into other hands, but his freed spirit has entered the heavenly rest, 1835; whither his wife and many of his children have gone.

> "Part of the host have crossed the flood,
> And part are crossing now!"

SAMUEL HILTON.

ELDER HILTON lived and died in Scott County, Virginia. He possessed a vigorous intellect, and although the stores of learning were not placed within his reach, this deficiency was in some measure supplied by the habit of close thinking and the thorough investigation of those subjects upon which he brought his mind to bear. In the early history of Virginia Baptists he entered the ministry of reconciliation, having himself felt the power of the gospel in his own salvation. He continued, until within a few years back, a faithful, laborious laborer in the kingdom of Christ. He was highly respected and esteemed by all classes, and was eminently useful in the work of preaching the gospel.

JOHN JENKINS.

JOHN JENKINS was one of the most distinguished ministers of the Roanoke Association. He was born December 25th, 1758, in the County of Loudon, of indigent and irreligious parents. From statements furnished by himself, it is ascertained that little or no attention was paid to his morals in early life, being allowed to indulge himself in a course of folly from childhood until he was grown. He is reported to have said that the most laborious days he ever spent were Sundays occupied in a species of gambling. During the revolutionary war, having removed with his parents to Pittsylvania, he was employed as commissary by the United States, and in this capacity passed through some of the upper counties of the State. Shortly after he left this occupation he returned to his native county, and engaged himself in conducting a common school. There, through the instrumentality of Jeremiah Moore, he became a follower of Christ. He was baptized by Elder Moore in 1792. Though his whole life had been peculiar for neglect of eternal things, and, indeed, for its viciousness, it was the Divine pleasure to pluck him as a brand from the burning. The grace of God can triumph over depravity of heart and licentiousness of life; that where sin abounds grace may much more abound.

On his removal to Pittsylvania he became a member of Allen's Creek Church. Here he commenced the ministry. His ordination took place in the year 1796. It was then thought by his brethren that he possessed but little talent for the work of the ministry. But in this they were mistaken. The beauty of the marble may be concealed, as it is taken rude and unpolished from the quarry; so intellectual power may remain undiscovered until, by peculiar circumstances, it is called into exercise. Thus an impulse, produced by a solemn sense of the importance of his new vocation, was given to his habits of study and reflection, and a perceptible change was wrought in his whole intellectual character. Having engaged in the solemn work of teaching others the truths of the Bible, he began to apply himself diligently to study. He obtained a very considerable acquaintance with the Latin, Greek, and Hebrew languages. His knowledge of history became enlarged and accurate. Few were more thoroughly acquainted with the geography of the earth. It is said that, being unable to purchase globes, he prepared a pair for his own use, which were well executed. Nor did he satisfy himself with a knowledge of the languages, or of men and things generally. He was a close student of the Word of God. At all times he seemed unwilling to appear as the spiritual instructor of others without aiming to become thoroughly acquainted with the truth. His attainments in learning would have been creditable under the most favorable circumstances; but, when it is known that throughout life he was compelled to struggle with poverty, his proficiency may well excite astonishment. His example, in this respect, deserves universal imitation. No man should begin to preach the gospel who is not willing to become studious, that he may be a workman, needing not to be ashamed, rightly dividing the word of truth.

His preaching talents, after a few years' exercise, were of a high order. He possessed agreeable, animated, and impressive manners, with a strong and well-toned voice. Notwithstanding a deformity under which he labored,—a stiffness in his eyelids, which prevented him from raising them, and rendered it necessary, when he would look before him, to throw his head very much back and apply his hand to the forehead to draw up the lids,—his appearance, after he commenced preaching, was prepossessing.

His discourses were highly argumentative, interspersed with frequent and apposite illustrations from history and from the Word of God, and enforced by appeals of the most powerful eloquence. His style was chaste and perspicuous, sometimes highly ornamented by the most lively and beautiful figures. An anecdote is related, which may serve to show the power of his eloquence. A lawyer of some eminence, on his way to an adjoining county, passed on Sabbath one of his meetings, and concluded to stay during preaching. He knew nothing of Jenkins, but went in and listened to the sermon. Upon returning to his residence, in relating the circumstance to his friends, he stated that he had heard one of the most powerful bursts of eloquence to which he had ever listened; that the preacher, as it were, suspended him over the burning pit, and that, so horrific was the representation, that his very hair stood on end.

In the year 1806 he published a discourse of sixty pages, on the Final Perseverance of the Saints. In this work considerable talent is discovered. He writes like a man who feels conscious of being panoplied in the armor of truth. Referring to the objection that many professors of religion who appeared well do fall away, he says: "It cannot be proven that such shining professors were ever real saints; many will run well for a time, but in the season of trial will fall away, not *from* saving grace, but *for want* of it. The foolish virgins had lamps, but no oil; had a profession, but no grace. The stony ground hearers received the word with joy, but afterwards withered, for want of the moisture of grace. Many in our world make a great parade in religion, pretend to great attainments; but all is not gold that glitters. The only proof of sincerity in religion is a steady perseverance in it. Not he that endures for a time, but he that endures to the end, shall be saved. Many take law terrors for gospel grace. They are alarmed by the threatenings of the law, and affrighted by the horrors of a guilty conscience; are shaken as it were over hell, and made to cry out, 'Lord, save, or I perish.' In the bitterness and anguish of their souls they will promise to obey God, yea, they will agree to any terms, agree to any conditions, rather than go to hell. A soul in this situation, not dead to the law, will hold on to anything from which they may hope for relief. Satan may persuade them that Christ has heard their prayer, that he will certainly save them, if they will only serve him. Their fancy may suggest that Christ has saved them on these conditions. Unskillful physicians, or legal preachers, will not fail to heal the wound slightly, crying peace, peace, when there is no peace. Such souls may be wretchedly deceived. They may go on with great zeal for a time, and finally fall away." In 1821 he commenced a monthly periodical, styled the Roanoke Religious Correspondent. This was continued for two years, and was conducted with much judgment. So far as it was circulated it was productive of good, but the patronage was not sufficient to warrant its publication after the second year.

Another work of considerable merit, on the subject of baptism, was published in the year 1827. This treatise exhibits an enlarged knowledge of ecclesiastical history, and a spirit becoming the candid controversialist. He was also frequently called upon by the Roanoke Association to prepare their circular letters, several of which are valuable and reflect credit on their author.

The piety of Elder Jenkins was of an ardent and elevated character. Although, by a boarding-school, which at different times he conducted, and which he was urged to continue, he might have realized a handsome sum, he chose rather to devote himself chiefly to the ministry. Wherever he went his good works were seen adorning the doctrine of God his Saviour. In his journeys he rarely tarried a night with a family without engaging in something more than the ordinary exercises of family worship. Whenever it was known that he had reached a neighborhood, the people, without invitation, would collect, and the evening be spent by him in religious services. In his more private intercourse with his fellow-men there was a dignity, united with tenderness, becoming his ministerial character. One of the most intelligent ministers of Virginia, now living, states that his mother, in very early life, was induced seriously to consider her latter end, by a simple question, which he proposed to her on entering the dwelling of her father. With an inexpressively benign and solemn countenance he asked, "Does Christ dwell here?" It resulted in her conversion to God.

He was a man of much prayer. This was one of the secret causes of his influence as a minister. He communed much with God, and imbibing His spirit, went forth prepared to do good to all with whom he mingled. He continually indicated a quenchless desire to promote the prosperity of the churches, and the good of his fellow-men. The following extract from his pen will show something of the state of his mind on these subjects: "While we are often hearing of the triumphs of the cross in foreign countries; while our ears are cheered with the animating news that the gracious work is spreading in every direction in our highly-favored country; while thousands of heaven-born souls are daily emerging from darkness into the marvelous light of the gospel, mingling their prayers with the elder saints, and uniting their voices in lofty songs to God and the Lamb,—we remain still and inactive; our harps are hung upon the willows, and we pass it off by faintly saying, 'we wish we could see a revival among ourselves.' But why is it thus with us? Is the Lord's ear heavy, that he cannot hear? or is his arm shortened, that he cannot save? Not so; we must look for the cause at home. Let every preacher, every deacon, and every private member of the church examine himself strictly, as in the presence of the living God, and if he finds that he has been remiss, or negligent in any Christian duty, let him repent, return, and do his first works; let every church be stirred up to use all diligence in all the duties of her charge. In short, a reformation must first begin among professors, before we can expect to see it among the unconverted."

The labors of this man of God were extensively blest. Several churches, through his instrumentality, were commenced and built up. To one of his churches, during the years 1801 and 1802, two hundred and fifty persons were added under his ministry. Other extensive revivals were realized at different times through his labors.

He reached an advanced age. Toward the close of life his

influence and usefulness were somewhat diminished. Those, however, who knew him best, and who were with him in his last days, still witnessed the evidences of devotion to the Master whom it was his delight, for a succession of years, to honor and obey. He was for some time confined by sickness before his departure. In the expectation of death he was almost constantly in a rapturous state of mind, and, on the 24th of January, 1824, he fell asleep in Jesus.

EDMUND JOHNS.

Elder Edmund Johns was born in 1766, but in what portion of Virginia is not known. His junior years were spent in devotion to the god of this world; nor was he led to the contemplation of his guilt and ruin, as a transgressor of the Divine law, until he had reached his thirtieth year. About 1796, his mind became seriously impressed with the worth of eternal things; and, guided by the spirit of truth, he was induced to rejoice in the atoning righteousness of Christ.

Soon after his conversion, such was his conviction of duty in reference to the ministry, that he began to warn his fellow-men, and to beseech them to flee the wrath to come. As he continued to exercise his talents, his brethren encouraged him to persevere, and after sufficient trial he was regularly ordained.

His ministrations were mostly confined to the County of Campbell, where he spent most of his days. From his own vicinity he scarcely ever traveled, and was, therefore, not very extensively known throughout the State. But his own vineyard he cultivated industriously, and was not without evidences of usefulness. By reference to Semple's History, the churches he served are known by the names of Ebenezer and New Chapel.

It was hoped by the author that some more particular information would have been received respecting Elder Johns; but in this he has been disappointed. Nothing is known respecting the circumstances of his death excepting that it occurred on the 29th of December, 1836.

One who was well acquainted with him thus refers to his character: "This venerable man needs no eulogy from the pen of friendship. His praise is in the churches. His record is on high. His goodness has erected a monument in the hearts of all who were acquainted with him. The writer of this has often heard him deplore the time and talents which he so long prostituted to the service of the world, the flesh, and Satan; and adore the riches of that grace which opened his eyes, and turned him from darkness to light, and from the power of Satan to God.

Being a man of ardent temperament, what his hand found to do he did with his might. While he was not slothful in business, he was fervent in spirit, serving the Lord. Having felt the bitterness of sin, and tasted that the Lord was gracious, his heart was filled with compassion for his blinded and dying fellow-men, and he could not refrain from calling upon them to taste and see that the Lord is good. Forty years of his life was devoted to the ministry; during which time he studied to show himself approved unto God, a workman that needed not to be ashamed. He was a man of sound speech that could not be condemned. His life was a beautiful commentary upon the religion he professed. He was greatly beloved by the household of faith, and had a good report of them that were without. As a husband, a father, a master, and a citizen, he was not only free from reproach, but truly exemplary. In short, he lived the life and died the death of the righteous. His path was indeed the path of the just, widening and brightening to the perfect day. As his outward man perished, his inward man was renewed day by day. He spoke of his departure with composure and delight, conversed freely and affectionately with his family and friends, and requested the venerable partner of his joys and sorrows to resign him cheerfully, as he was ready to depart and be with Christ.

JAMES ELLISON.

THE father of JAMES ELLISON was originally from the State of New Jersey. Having removed to Virginia, and married, he settled in the western part of the State. James was the eldest son, and was born in Farley's Fort, New River, April 29th, 1778. Not long after his birth, his parents became the subjects of religious concern, and united with the Baptist church. They were poor, and unable to educate their children. In his eighteenth year, the subject of this sketch married Miss Mary Calloway, a person who was near his own age and circumstances in life. About a year after this connection was formed, he was the subject of great alarm on account of his sins. He saw himself exposed to ruin, and determined to reform his life. For several months he was a most rigid formalist, maintaining family worship, and regularly attending the house of God. But he again relapsed and became more wicked than before. To all human appearance he was likely not only to neglect his soul's interest, but to become a reckless opposer of the truth. But the omnipotence of Divine grace was displayed in plucking this brand from the burning: a conversation between his father and a minister of the gospel was made the means of again arresting his attention. Many efforts were made to banish serious impressions from the mind, but all in vain. Wherever he went he felt himself to be a miserable man, and what seemed most to increase the anguish of his heart was the recollection of previous failures. The wrath to come was felt to be justly deserved, and being ignorant of the righteousness of God, the most fearfully conflicting emotions were experienced. In such a state of mind, how cheering are the invitations of the gospel! These furnish hope to the most wretched and guilty. In these he found relief. He joined the Indian Creek Baptist Church in 1800.

He was soon discovered to possess talents which might be useful, and was frequently invited to conduct social meetings. For three years he embraced every opportunity of exhorting those around him to prepare for death. At length, he was licenced to preach. Considerable portions of time were now employed in study, and a prevailing thirst for improvement was evinced; every leisure moment being husbanded with the utmost care. Several valuable books were presented by friends, and perused with great interest; but the Bible was the volume he was chiefly accustomed to study, and from this uncorrupted fountain he drank largely of the truth as it is in Jesus.

Elder Ellison was not ordained until 1808, being then about thirty years of age. At this time he took charge of the church with which he first united, but afterwards moved to the Coal Marshes in Fayette. When he settled in this county, he was less abundant in labors, and less efficient in his Master's cause than formerly; but having met with a variety of trials, he renewedly consecrated himself to God, and to the work of the ministry. For many years he was one of the most active ministers of the Greenbrier Association. The urgent necessities of the churches, and the repeated solicitation of his brethren, kept him almost constantly employed. In the Counties of Giles, Monroe, Greenbrier, Bath, and Nicholas, he traveled much, dispensing the Word of Life; and while he preached Christ publicly, he neglected not to warn from house to house. Great pleasure was manifested by him in conversing on the subject of religion, and in this way he was quite useful.

His views of truth were similar to those entertained by the great body of the Baptists. Those doctrines which lay the sinner in the dust, and leave him dependent on the mere mercy of his Sovereign, were often introduced and defended in his public discourses. No less faithful were his exhibitions of human responsibility. While he taught that it was a crime of unspeakable heinousness not to love God with all the heart, so also he considered the refusal of sinners to believe the gospel equally sinful.

"With regard to his manner of preaching," says one who had opportunity of forming a judgment, "when he commenced the ministry, he was generally uninteresting, and at a great loss for words. He seldom ever confined himself to any particular method until he had been preaching several years, when he became more systematic. He was justly called a doctrinal preacher, but failed not to apply the truth to the hearts of his hearers, and often in such a way as to excite deep interest. He was a considerable reasoner: some of his appeals to the unconverted, in the latter part of his life, were very powerful. If he may be regarded as delighting to dwell on any one theme more than another, it was the adaptedness of the gospel to the necessities of sinners."

Elder Ellison was an uncompromising friend to the cause of missions. To know that the glad tidings were finding their way to the idolatrous nations of the earth, created the most unaffected joy. He delighted to refer to those prophecies which speak of the glory of the latter day. Any means which might, under the Divine blessing, contribute to the accomplishment of these prophecies, he most willingly employed. His addresses on the subject of missions were productive of good, by leading the churches to feel their obligation to send abroad the gospel. There was scarcely a benevolent institution but found in him not only an advocate, but a patron. He delighted to do as well as say, and thus his example stimulated others to act. It is said, in the latter part of his life he gave away to various good objects more than he received from the churches.

During one portion of his ministerial career, Elder E. was much embarrassed in his pecuniary concerns. It is possible, in this particular, he did not exercise sufficient caution. There may be cases when a good man may unavoidably become involved in debt, but in most instances such difficulties are the result of imprudence. It is an apostolic injunction to "owe no man anything," and this precept is no less binding than salutary. Every man, then, and especially every Christian minister, should cautiously circumscribe his expenditures within his resources. Nothing tends more to lessen the influence of a preacher, than the disregard of this rule. It is believed that the ministrations of our brother were less efficient on this account. Notwithstanding this, he was a useful man. Considering his large family, having reared twelve children, and the fact that he was dependent on his own exertions for a livelihood, it is rather surprising that he should have improved so much, and preached so frequently. The neglect of the churches in failing to provide more bountifully for his support is painfully apparent.

We now approach the close of his life. In the spring of 1834 he determined to attend the General Association, which was to meet in Richmond. Accordingly, with his son, he left home in May, and on his way visited several congregations where he had previously preached. He also attended the Strawberry Association, and a protracted meeting at Deep Run, near Richmond. Owing to indisposition, he did not go into the city until the second day of the anniversaries; from that time, though quite unwell, he never failed to attend either night or day, until compelled to leave to meet appointments previously made. The morning after leaving the city he was extremely hoarse, and unable to preach until Sabbath evening; he then addressed a very attentive assembly, from the words, "As Moses lifted up the serpent," etc. Two days after this he became too unwell to travel, having reached the house of a friend between Liberty and Fincastle.

Two days after his confinement, he observed to some one present that he had traveled much in preaching the gospel, but this was his last journey; he also remarked that the condition of the churches had occupied much of his thoughts, and that he felt a strong desire to see them more prosperous. The same subject was renewed the next day. "I have," said he, "been thinking all night of the happy influence which Christians might have over one another; I am distressed that the Church of Christ is so divided; the disciples should rally their forces and be united; they might wield an almighty power." After worship, he said: "I have reason to be ashamed of myself,—so few prayers offered in faith." The same day, he adverted also to the condition of the colored people, lamented that their religious privileges were so much abridged, and especially that they were unable to read the word of God.

On the twenty-first of the month, he conversed much on the great salvation of the gospel, and the duty of sending it to every creature; spoke also of the temperance reform. At night, commented on the love of David to Jonathan; his mind uncommonly clear. The twenty-second being the Sabbath, he requested his son to read the seventeenth chapter of John, and some of the succeeding chapters, and manifested peculiar delight in contemplating this portion of the word of God. For several days he continued to decline, during which time he was frequently heard to speak of Christ and his salvation. In expressing his conviction of what the Christians in these United States should be willing to do, he said: "They ought to consecrate themselves, their time, talents, and money, to the Lord: not inquiring when or how they could make the most or live the easiest, but where or how they could do the most good." In reference to his own future condition he was satisfied. He would say, "I am the chief of sinners, but the blood of Jesus cleanseth us from all sin;" and "his atonement is my only hope." On the evening of the twenty-seventh, after lying for some time as though he was asleep, he opened his eyes; with a smile, he raised his feeble emaciated hands toward heaven, and exclaimed, Glory, glory! Soon after repeated,

"All my capacious powers can wish,
In Thee doth richly meet;
Nor to my eyes is life so dear,
Nor friendship half so sweet."

A friend came in and asked him how he was; he replied, "If I die I shall be well." About sunset he became unable to speak, but still manifested great pleasure in what was sung. Between two and three o'clock he bid farewell to earth's cares, and mounted upward to dwell with God.

JEREMIAH CHANDLER.*

Jeremiah Chandler, according to the best information that can be obtained, was a native of Caroline County. He was born in the year 1749. From Caroline he removed into the County of Orange. But little is known of his early life, or as to the

* Prepared by John Pierce.

circumstances or time of his embracing religion. More than forty years ago he moved into the County of Spottsylvania, where he continued to reside until his death. He was, at the time of his removal, a Baptist minister; but how long he had been preaching before is unknown. He had the care of two churches: North Pamunky, in the County of Orange, and Piney Branch, in Spottsylvania; both of which he continued to serve, so long as he was able, with unwearied zeal and more than ordinary punctuality.

Elder Chandler's opportunities for ministerial improvement were very limited; having a large family of children dependent upon his own exertions for support, he had but little time to devote to any other object. Nevertheless, his was a successful ministry, and affords another to examples already innumerable of the scriptural truth, that "it is God who giveth the increase." Among the seals to his ministry may be reckoned two Baptist preachers, both of whom occupied a distinguished place in the affection of Virginia Baptists.

The chief excellency of Elder Chandler's preaching consisted in a plain and simple delivery of the truths of the Christian religion as taught in the Scriptures. He lived to the advanced age of eighty-five years; having enjoyed, at least in his latter years, an unusual portion of health. As to the manner of his departure the writer of this knows nothing personally, but has been informed that he died in the triumph of faith.

MILES TURPIN.

MILES TURPIN was born in Henrico County, October 21st, 1775. He grew up with few advantages for the cultivation of his mind, and, at the time of his conversion, was quite illiterate. This event occurred in 1803, about two years after he had entered the marriage relation. Although uneducated, he cherished a desire publicly to exhort his fellow-men, and, with the sanction of the church, for many years employed his talent in this way. He at length began to preach the gospel. The support of a numerous family devolving on him, this privilege was not very frequently enjoyed. In consequence of his numerous domestic cares but little proficiency in knowledge was made, nor did he rapidly improve as a public speaker.

The responsibilities of the Christian ministry were not fully assumed by him until 1821. In the spring of this year he was ordained by Elders John Courtney and Andrew Broaddus. He then began to devote more time to the work of preaching the gospel. The church at Four Mile Creek gave him an invitation to settle among them as their pastor, and, after much prayer, he consented to enter upon this relation. His usefulness now became more apparent, although his efforts were not much extended beyond the county in which he resided.

The talents of Elder Turpin as a speaker were not of a superior order; still he was usually heard with attention. Artless and plain in his manner, when he stood up to recommend the character and service of Him he most loved, it was evident to all that he was influenced by the best of motives. Though the graces of elocution and the beauties of style were not to be discovered in the delivery of his discourses, nor even depth of thought, he nevertheless enjoyed the respect and confidence of those who sat under his ministry. Nor was he without manifest tokens of his Master's approbation; many, through his means, were brought to a knowledge of the truth. The unaffected goodness of his heart and the blamelessness of his life contributed more to his usefulness as a preacher than his talents. The unadorned presentation of the truth, sustained as it was by the winning influence of a holy example, could not be without salutary effects.

As a pastor Elder Turpin was, to a considerable extent, successful. A large and flourishing church was built up under his labors. When he entered the pastoral relation there were only four male members, and the number of females was comparatively small; at the time of his death there had been an increase of more than three hundred. He had the happiness of seeing most of his numerous family the subjects of Christ's kingdom before he was called to his reward in heaven. What was to him an unspeakable satisfaction, one of his sons entered the work of the gospel ministry with the promise of usefulness in the kingdom of the Redeemer.

Elder Turpin's death was unexpected. Being suddenly arrested by disease, after a few days of suffering he was received by his heavenly Master to the rest of the upper world. In referring to this painful event, one of the members of his church thus speaks: "The Lord's day previous to the last that he lived to see, he preached, and had administered the ordinance of baptism a very short time before. And, in his dying hours, nothing seemed so much to concern him as the future prospects of the people of his charge. His chief anxiety was that sinners might be converted and the piety of the saints cherished.

"That his family would continue to enjoy the kind guidance, almighty protection, and necessary provisions of Providence, he seems to have felt not a doubt. In life he had been devoted to the service of God in laboring for the salvation of souls—concerned only to acquire a competency for his family: in death he had nothing to do but to 'depart and be with Christ, which is far better.' He was fully aware of his approaching dissolution. Indeed his family think that he had felt, for many months, a presentiment of his death. In the entire exercise of his reason until the last, he confidently resigned his spirit without alarm to the hands of the great Redeemer."

The editor of the Religious Herald alludes to his character in the following language: "Endued by nature with a kindly disposition, Elder Turpin exhibited in his spirit and deportment a degree of good-will and benevolence we have rarely seen excelled. The pervading element of his mind was love. It gave a cast to his whole character. He was kindly affectioned toward all men. His language ever appeared to be, 'Grace be unto all who love our Lord Jesus Christ in sincerity.' He was also ardently attached to all the benevolent institutions, which have shed such a lustre on the present age. Though not blessed with a liberal education himself, he was sensible of the value of knowledge to a minister of the gospel, and he ardently rejoiced at the formation of the Virginia Education Society, and ever manifested a deep interest in its welfare He also encouraged a missionary spirit among his people, not only by exhortation, but example. He felt anxious that the gospel, which to him was the power of God unto salvation, should be preached to every creature. He was also a decided friend to the temperance cause."

As expressive of the estimate in which he was held by the church of which he was pastor, we close this tribute to the memory of our brother by an extract from their Minutes:—

"There is a peculiar pleasure, as well as propriety, in paying honor, at death, to those excellent men who have staked their *all* in defence of the religion of Jesus Christ. And if religion is the highest glory of our nature, and if to have much of the spirit of Christ is to be eminent in religion, it must be confessed there have been few men who have appeared more worthy of honor and everlasting remembrance than he whom we now lament. The very foundation of his character seems to have been a habitual sense and reverence of God. He exhibited much of the fear of God; a fear which, far from being abject and servile, seemed constantly cherished by a filial, ardent, active love. He enjoyed God in all things, and all things in God. In an eminent sense he walked with his Maker, and appeared habitually to converse less with his fellow-creatures than with Him who is invisible. The man who converses much with God will be humble. This was a conspicuous trait in our deceased friend. Indeed, humility, that cardinal virtue of a Christian, made up a great part of his character. He had deep and extensive views of human depravity and of his own indwelling corruption, and went mourning under a sense of them. Hence he experimentally felt and highly appreciated the importance of a Saviour, his atonement, his intercession, and the influence of the Holy Spirit. Hence he prized the peculiar doctrines of Christianity. He felt that they only laid a foundation sufficiently broad and deep for the salvation of a sinner. On *these* he ventured his soul and his eternal hopes. They not only supported him in death, but sweetened and adorned his life."

SAMUEL LAMKIN STRAUGHAN.*

SAMUEL LAMKIN STRAUGHAN was born in Northumberland County, Virginia, July 30, 1783. He was the son of Samuel L. and Phebe Straughan, who was Phebe Lewis. His family, on the side of both father and mother, though not opulent, was respectable. His father, who followed the business of a farmer, required his sons to work on the farm; and this was Samuel's employment as soon as he was of sufficient size to be engaged in labor. He went two or three years to ordinary schools, at which he made the best use of his time, and had acquired, at eleven or twelve years of age, sufficient skill in the various branches of an English education to become an assistant storekeeper for his uncle.

During his childhood he was remarkable for his serious and manly deportment; often asking interesting questions, and manifesting but little inclination for childish play. He took great pleasure in reading, writing, and all such employments as tended to improve his mind in useful knowledge. At a very early age he became fond of reading the Scriptures and other religious books, and making inquiries of his parents respecting religious subjects, insomuch that his father used often to call him his preacher. He was never known but once to use a profane expression, and, being chastised for this by his mother, he was never afterwards guilty of a similar offence. After he became a preacher he frequently mentioned this circumstance, as a proof of the advantage of religious and moral education, and how easily bad habits may be prevented if the evil be corrected in time.

His deportment, while living with his uncle, was so amiable as to gain his confidence and cordial affection; and having no children of his own, he declared that it was his intention to make his nephew his heir.† He continued in this situation until his uncle declined the mercantile business, and then, by his recommendation,

---

* Abridged by R. B. Semple.

† His uncle, however, died without will, and Samuel received only his portion among the other relations.

went to live in the store of Mr. James Smith, a merchant of high standing, at Northumberland Court-house. Samuel was then eighteen or nineteen years of age. While acting as storekeeper for his uncle, such was his eager thirst for knowledge, that with scarcely any other assistant than books and the occasional instruction of a sea-captain, he acquired an accurate knowledge of arithmetic, surveying, and navigation. He pursued, afterwards, the practice of surveying, in which he was accounted a great proficient.

It was while at Northumberland Court-house that Mr. Straughan obtained an interest in the merits of the Redeemer, and experienced the power of vital religion. From early childhood he had frequent convictions, often made resolutions of amendment of life, and as often relapsed into former habits; but the time now approached for him to be effectually arrested. In April, 1802, he first saw his fallen condition as a sinner before God. He could no longer build up his fallacious hopes, founded on works of morality and social goodness; but he found that his most righteous endeavors, so far from meriting a reward, were stained with sin and required the blood of atonement to wash away their guilt. He became an earnest, humble seeker of salvation, and so continued for several months before he was visited by the intimations of Divine acceptance.

Being at some distance from the regular administration of the word and ordinances, Mr. Straughan did not find an opportunity to be baptized until the seventh of the next April. Mr. Jacob Creath had, at this time, the care of the Moratico Church. He baptized Mr. Straughan without, probably, once suspecting that this young man was to be his successor, and one among the most brilliant lights in his day and generation.

Within a few months after he was baptized, he began to labor in his Master's harvest. His first essays were in the way of exhortation, in which he occasionally succeeded so well as to enkindle hopes in the minds of the discerning that he might become an acceptable and useful preacher. Mr. Straughan was singularly modest, and would not push himself forward. He seemed, through all the stages of his life, to have set less value on his own abilities than any one else did who knew him well.

This disposition, together with his narrow circumstances, his limited education, the charge of a family by an early marriage,* probably tended to keep him, for a season, out of public view. It was two or three years before he came into much notice, though a few friends had at an early period of his labors spoken of him as a promising young preacher.

Toward the close, however, of 1805, he began to shine forth with too much splendor to be kept any longer in obscurity. On the 20th of March, 1806, he was ordained to the ministry, and about that time began to be everywhere spoken of in high terms. He attended the Dover Association, held in York County this year, and being chosen as one of the preachers for the Lord's day, he preached to the comfort of many, and to the astonishment of all such as had not previously heard him. From year to year his reputation increased, not only in his own neighborhood, but throughout the adjoining churches; and although still but a young man, he was often, indeed almost constantly, preferred by the hearers to the more experienced.

On the day of his ordination he took the care of Wicomico Church, being called to this charge by unanimous vote. This church had been constituted a year or two previously, with but twenty-four members, but it soon began to increase under his labors. The mere approbation of mortals was not the only fruit of his ministry; his God also spoke approbation, and great success attended his endeavors. A refreshing revival ensued. His preaching reached the hearts of his hearers, and there were many humble and contrite inquirers. Mr. Straughan's soul revived with the revival. He went forth day and night, to rich and poor, where there were openings. In the pulpit he lifted the gospel hammer with mighty strength, and many a rocky heart was broken. When there were meltings in the congregation, he would move among the people, from one to another, offering the most appropriate exhortations and the most fervent prayers. He had, indeed, a singular gift at exhortation on such occasions, and he used it with much diligence and success. In the course of a few

* He was married at about twenty-one years of age, to Mrs. Alexander, a young widow with one child.

years, Wicomico Church, from being a mere handful, became two hundred and eighty in number. Of these, there were many who had not previously any fondness for the Baptists, but, on the contrary, were highly prejudiced against them.

In 1807 he was unanimously chosen to the care of Moratico Church. He accepted the call, and held the charge until his death. In this church, also, he had some blessed seasons. Gradual additions of useful and pious members were made from time to time, but in 1816 they had a considerable revival, in which forty or fifty professed to be converted and were baptized. In this work Mr. Straughan was deeply engaged. In several other revivals, there were many useful as well as pious members added to both the churches of which he had the care, and these churches continued in a flourishing and happy state until his death.

In the Association of 1812, Mr. Straughan's first essay as a writer came forth. He composed the Circular Letter for this year, on the subject of *itinerant preaching.* It was admired for its simplicity and excellent sense. In the year 1814 he was chosen by the Missionary Society of Richmond to travel into certain parts of Maryland, where it was supposed there was a great call for evangelical preaching.

Mr. Straughan had once visited that destitute section of country, by special invitation, and had been found to be highly acceptable. This consideration, added to his known talents, his persevering firmness, his unabating zeal, and, above all, his spotless purity of character, marked him out as the proper laborer in this new and difficult field. He was unanimously chosen, and his conduct on receiving this notice is worthy of a place in these memoirs.

The intelligence produced on his mind a weighty solemnity, attended with fear and trembling. He was perplexed to decide how duty called him to act. He had the care of two large churches, which required all his attention; and he feared to neglect them, lest he should not be found a faithful watchman. On the other hand, the Maryland call seemed to be more than human, and could not be slighted. In this dilemma, he pursued the godly man's course. He laid the matter before his church, and they agreed to appoint a day of fasting and prayer, for the purpose of seeking the Lord's direction. The result was a determination to accept the appointment, and notice was accordingly given to the society. In a short time he sent on his appointments, and commenced his labors of love in this benighted region. Many were the difficulties encountered by this man of God in discharging the duties of this mission; difficulties more than sufficient to appall the spirit of any man less resolute than Samuel L. Straughan.

His amiable deportment, his simplicity of manners, his unaffected piety, his unabating zeal, his indefatigable labors, his excellent talents; and withal his spiritual, scriptural, and evangelical doctrine, commending itself to every man's conscience in the sight of God, soon began to make him useful. From enemies many became friends, and from despisers they became admirers.

Mr. S. kept a journal of all his travels in Maryland. In this journal he frequently relates interesting anecdotes of occurrences and conversations which took place in his travels; some of which show the state of public opinion among those people, and exhibit the dealings of God in support of the truth.

Mr. Straughan's visits to Maryland continued to be made steadily and faithfully several times in each year, until he was arrested by the disease of which he died. He often met with great discouragements, but was as often supported under them, either by the internal operations of God's grace, or by external occurrences in his Providence, in which he thought he frequently saw the hand of his Master stretched forth for his encouragement and aid. On one occasion, he tells us in his journal, he had serious fears that his going on this mission was displeasing to God. It was at a time when he had taken much pains to make appointments in different places, and in most of which they had failed, through the inattention of those to whom they were intrusted. In one case, where an appointment was made, he could obtain no house to preach in, though he offered a woman who kept a tavern a dollar an hour for the use of her house. She alleged that she had no objections, but that her preacher had disapproved of it. To counteract these discouragements God gave him many tokens of his special regard.

The great ignorance as to the Scriptures among the people,

most of whom were Catholics, was very discouraging; but it seemed to call the more loudly for a faithful ministry. Some, in speaking of the Bible, would say: "I don't like it, sir;" and some would say it was a Baptist Bible, and ought not to be allowed in their houses. Mr. S., however, drew some encouragement from the judgments of God against opposers. In one instance, some young men went to a place of water, and there, in a profane way, dipped one another in the name of the Holy Trinity! One of them (a ringleader) some time after, in a fit of despair, went to the same water and drowned himself. Mr. Straughan's remark is: "God will not be mocked!"

On some occasions he seems to have had his soul wound up to a high degree of confidence and consolation, while his preaching had visible and hopeful effects upon the people: some weeping and mourning for sin; some inquiring with anxious minds; a few young and a few old professors rejoicing with warm hearts; and all exceedingly affectionate toward him.

One or two of these instances may be referred to. He says: "Many prejudices have been removed. I will mention a case or two: The last summer I was in company with a well-disposed Methodist, and, after having conversation on religious subjects, he observed to a friend, 'How I have been deceived!' He had heard many tales about the Baptists that had given rise to his prejudices, which he now found to be groundless. He is now a pretty constant hearer.

"Another instance: A class-leader had written to one of the members of the society, at whose house I had preached, forbidding the like liberty to be granted again. After some time this person came to one of my appointments and was so prejudiced that he would not sing; but when I went again he sent for me to call and see him. We conversed freely together. He acknowledged that he had been opposed to me, but hoped I would forgive him, and said his home would always be open to me.

"What shall we say to these things: if God be for us, who can be against us? I firmly believe the missionary cause is the cause of God, and that he will own and bless it. My only grief is, that the society has made such a poor choice, and that I can do no more in so great and good a cause. Did I but possess such gracious qualifications and mental improvements as a missionary ought to possess, it would be my glory to be laid out for the furtherance of Immanuel's kingdom, in any way and in any direction whither Providence should lead and a sense of duty impel."

At another time he writes, under date of May 9th, 1820: "In the month of March I passed through the missionary ground in Maryland. I found that the anxieties of the people to hear the Word of the Lord were increasing, while a conviction of the necessity of heart-religion is gaining ground. The people in Maryland are generally remarkable for hospitality, and are much more tolerant in respect to religious privileges and intercourse than formerly. The very neighborhood in which old Brethren Moore and Hagen were persecuted, and the latter plunged in the water, until he said he believed they meant to drown him, now affords one of the largest and most respectable congregations that attend upon the ministrations of your missionary."

In his visit in April, 1817, he relates a very solemn parting with his young Christian brethren. "Brother Perry came by to accompany me to the ferry. We joined in prayer on the shore before we parted." On this occurrence he makes the following reflections: "Oh how religion unites souls to each other in the strong bonds of Christian affection! Oh what a place heaven must be! where all the saints of God shall dwell secure from all the insults and distresses which they now have to bear; where all the angels of God are; and where the eternal triune God displays his glories and sheds abroad his love, through the glorious medium of the once-suffering but now exalted Immanuel! Oh, may it be my happiness to be there, to bear a part in the never-ceasing song of Moses and the Lamb!"

At one time he had an appointment at some public place in St. Mary's, where there were few or none who felt any interest in the occasion, but where there were a number of persons round about the house. He began with only seven or eight present; but to excite the attention of others he raised his voice loudly in singing: in a little time the people began to come in, and before he had finished his sermon he had a respectable audience.

He was very remarkable for his punctuality in fulfilling his appointments. Sometimes he had to leave home under the most discouraging circumstances. His family sick, himself in low health, (lower indeed than he was aware of,) his affairs in confusion, his churches destitute and complaining, and his spirits deeply depressed. And though, from these considerations, he often hesitated, doubtful whether it was his duty to go on, yet in almost every instance he pressed through these difficulties, and often returned solemnly impressed with the belief that God had guided his course. Once he left home when several of his family were sick, and with many fears that he should not find them all alive on his return. He ventured, however, to go on, and had a prosperous journey; and on his return found his family almost well, while several of his neighbors had sickened and died in his absence. This melted him into humble and grateful acknowledgments to God.

His frequent indispositions hindered him from being as regular in attending to the mission as his pious and active spirit would have prompted. In 1819 he was compelled to withdraw for a considerable time, but in November of that year he ventured to go again; and on his way he makes the following remark in his journal: "During this day I had some pleasant exercises of mind in reflecting upon the privileges of returning to the missionary ground in Maryland, having been laid aside for about six months. Oh for a heart to trust and praise God! and may the angel of his covenant go with me, and give testimony to the word of his grace." In consequence of his long absence he made his journal much longer than usual; and at the close he inserts the following pious reflections: "Oh how much love and praise do I owe to God for all his goodness toward me! for health and good weather during this long trip.

'Oh to grace, how great a debtor,
Daily I'm constrained to be!'

I have been enabled to have fifteen meetings for the last fourteen days, and have filled them up with much comfort to myself, and, I hope, with advantage to many others."

In the beginning of 1820 his health was apparently much better, and great hopes were entertained, by himself and his friends, that his pulmonary symptoms would entirely subside; in consequence of which he ventured to extend his labors, especially in his missionary field. He made one tour to Maryland in March, and left appointments for another in May; while the intermediate space was almost entirely filled up with appointments in Virginia. Having about this time much of the spirit of preaching, he was peculiarly animated, and extended his sermons to an unusual length, often preaching, with laborious exertion, for more than two hours.

These unremitted labors, added to his exposure in many instances to unwholesome weather, appear to have brought on his pulmonary affections with double violence. A distressing hoarseness seized him early in April; but he thought it no more than a common cold, and continued his labors though often quite feverish. His towering soul was reluctant to be put back. His spirit was willing, though he felt his flesh weak and still weakening. He was willing to be spent in his Master's cause; and so indeed it turned out. While on his missionary tour in May, he was enabled for awhile to go through his labors without much inconvenience to himself, and with great satisfaction to his congregations; but, after a few days, he began to fail, and every day found his disorder increasing upon him. He still, however, pursued his appointments, though sometimes obliged to cut short in the midst of his discourse.

At last, on the thirtieth of May, about a fortnight from the time he left home, he was finally arrested at Nanjemoy Meeting-house, Charles County, Maryland. He began to preach, but after a few minutes he was constrained to close, and to close indeed forever as to his public ministry. From the force of his disorder, added to unseasonable weather, he could not attempt to travel homeward for some days. He reached home, however, on the sixth of June, and was from that time almost wholly confined to his house until his death.

Shortly after reaching home he sent for medical aid. Physicians of the highest reputation in the adjacent counties generously attended him, and continued to do so while there remained any hope of his recovery. But, alas! what avails the most exquisite skill of the most eminent physicians when God has determined to cut the thread of life! He had a fixed consumption, and no medical art could reach his case. With some temporary revivals in his feelings, his disorder, as usual in that disease, grew worse and worse until his death.

It is desirable to be made acquainted with the spiritual and religious exercises of a man so eminent for piety and usefulness, at the awful crisis when earthly hope was flying fast away. At this trying season he seems to have shone with more than usual lustre. Shortly after reaching home he concluded that he should never recover, but seemed to feel very little concern on that account. He would say there were two considerations which made him willing to live longer—his churches and his family. On the other hand, there were considerations of some weight which prevented him from any anxiety to live. He said that it had been his unvarying wish, indeed his earnest prayer, that God would rather take him out of the world than suffer him to disgrace his cause, or become a stumbling-block in the way of religion; that many, who were apparently worthy characters in the early stage of their progress, had in the decline of life fallen into sins and follies, by which their own names and their Master's cause had been much injured; that God had thus far preserved him from any material downfall; and as he was about to finish his course, he viewed it as a great mercy that he should die without bringing any serious reproach upon so good a cause.

During the last week of his illness he had some very heavenly seasons. Finding himself fast approaching his dissolution, he said at one time, with much feeling, "Farewell, sin and sorrow!" at another, "O death! where is thy sting? O grave! where is thy victory?" And again—

> "I cannot, I cannot forbear
> These passionate longings for home."

When told by a friend that he was going, he said: "Blessed be God! Glory to his holy name!" and then took another farewell of his family and all present.

On the day of his death Mr. Dunnaway, one of his particular friends, came to see him, and began to apologize for not having come, according to promise, some days sooner. He replied, that the Lord had ordered the matter; that he had come at the right time; he would now see him die. He then requested his friend to shave him, and put on his shrouding clothes, which he had prepared some time before. Mr. D. replied, he would do that in the morning. "Ah!" said he, "I shall be in glory before morning."

He continued to converse until a little after sunset, and was composed during family worship. Shortly afterwards he became speechless; and about two o'clock on Saturday morning, the 9th of June, 1821, he expired!

"The feeble taper, glimmering round the room,
Display'd the corpse amid the solemn gloom;
But o'er the scene a holy calm reposed;
The door of heaven had open'd there, and closed."

Thus died this man of God, in the very zenith of his age, being not quite thirty-eight years old. While pausing at this solemn event, a question presented itself to our minds, "Why should such a man be allowed so short a course?" Ah! but this is not for mortals to know. The solution of such a question lies among the unsearchable counsels of the all-wise God; the abyss of whose providence is

"Too deep to sound with mortal line,
Too dark to view with feeble sense."

It is singular that the section of country in which Mr. Straughan lived and labored has twice experienced nearly the same afflicting scenes. The Baptist churches there were almost all planned and built up under the labors of the excellent Lunsford, who was in his day one of the most burning and shining lights ever known in that part of the country, or perhaps anywhere else. He, after running a short though glorious race, died at about forty years of age. After a lapse of about ten years, Samuel L. Straughan was raised up, and became a shepherd to Lunsford's scattered flock; and was instrumental in filling their thinned ranks with many new converts. He became as eminent and as useful as his predecessor; and, as if the Lord would teach us, by painful lessons, that all our help is in him, Straughan also died, and at an earlier period than did Lunsford.

The writer has ventured to say, that "Straughan became as eminent and as useful as Lunsford;" and he feels justified in the assertion, although some, perhaps, may think otherwise. He was intimately acquainted with both, and conceives them both to have been of the first grade of good and great men of God; very *different* indeed in their tempers and talents, yet both pre-eminently pious, and signally useful in their Master's cause. In temper, Lunsford was bold, energetic, and fearless of man; so persevering that nothing could appall him; so determined and courageous that nothing could deter him. He kept his eye fixed with steadiness on his object, and marched directly to it. He had a lion's heart.

Straughan was a lamb—a lamb, indeed, of the mildest kind. He was calm, meek, mild, forbearing, and forgiving. He loved his fallen fellow-men, and was willing to weep over them, to persuade them; indeed, to spend and be spent, to live and die for them. He was by no means deficient in spiritual courage; but his disposition led him to win by gentleness rather than to conquer by power. Nor was Lunsford by any means destitute of meekness; but his majestic spirit rose so conspicuously as to draw off the observer's attention from his other excellent qualities. Lunsford's feelings prompted him to command all men, everywhere, to repent; Straughan's, to pray them, in Christ's stead, to be reconciled to God. Each had much of the Divine image; each had beheld, as in a glass, the glory of the Lord, and was changed into the same image; but the features of their Master seem to have been differently impressed on each. Lunsford imbibed much of his Saviour's sublimity; Straughan, much of his simplicity. Lunsford was cheerful without levity; Straughan was grave without sternness. Lunsford excited most admiration; Straughan, most affection. Lunsford, more free and open, ate and drank with sinners, though without subjecting himself to reproach; Straughan, more backward and reserved, was civil to all, but familiar only with the friends of Zion. They were, to all that knew them both, standing monuments of the diversity of gifts arising from the same spirit, "dividing to every man severally as he will."

In some great points they were much alike. Nature had done much for both. In regard to genius, it is hard to say which had shared most largely. They were both eminent. Neither had much advantage from education. Lunsford was almost wholly self-taught; Straughan, with a small opportunity, had become a tolerable English scholar. Neither of them was inattentive to the means for improvement in useful knowledge. Lunsford read more extensively and took a wider survey of the field of divinity; Straughan confined himself more to the Bible, and was, in deed and truth, "mighty in the Scriptures." They were both diligent, laborious, persevering, warm, heart-searching, and successful preachers.

To be more particular in characterizing Mr. Straughan, we may venture to say that we have never known, in any instance, his superior, either as a pious man or an evangelical minister. One of his own members says of him: "In every relation of life he was the greatest pattern of piety I have ever seen." We may add, he was, in our estimation, one of the most faithful and exemplary ministers of the gospel we have ever known.

As to talents, it is hard to say in what grade we should place him. Certainly, in the pulpit he was, *in matter*, inferior to none. In the *arrangement* of his subjects, or in his *manner*, he was not to all the most acceptable; but with those who heard him most frequently none stood higher, even in this particular. His voice was remarkably sonorous, and rather pleasant than otherwise. His style was often elegant, always nervous and strong, never low nor disgusting. His address was simple, sincere, and exceedingly animated. His countenance was prepossessing to a very high degree; perhaps none more so. In a word, it may be said that he spoke as one having authority; and, by his forcible manifestation of the truth, commended himself to every man's conscience in the sight of God.

In his manner and style there were, nevertheless, some deficiencies. His articulation was too rapid, especially in the early part of his ministry; and in the *arrangement* of his matter he was not, perhaps, sufficiently methodical to be entirely perspicuous. He said nothing but what was good, generally most excellent; yet his truths were sometimes so intermixed as to lose, in some degree, their bearing and connection.

His countenance, while in the pulpit, was in the highest degree expressive of unaffected devotion to God and holy affection for man. His countenance indeed, everywhere, spoke much for him. His action, though not exactly conformable to rhetorical rules, was rather agreeable and becoming than otherwise; never strained, never affected. His discourses were more remarkable for argument and Scripture illustrations than for oratory or eloquence; yet, doubtless, he was sometimes truly eloquent; and what gave it more weight was that it was obvious eloquence was not his aim. He seemed to rise imperceptibly to himself; and, animated with celestial fire, he mounted, as on the wings of an eagle, or rather of an angel, and never failed to carry his audience with him. On such occasions he often excited the astonishment of his hearers by the sublimity of his style—a style which the most learned might gladly imitate. In his doctrine he was clearly and plainly *evangelical*. He might be termed a moderate Calvinist.

His manners in private life were pleasant and engaging in a high degree, especially in small circles. He was at times rather inclined to taciturnity; but when he fell into such company as seemed to furnish him an opportunity of doing good or of affording pleasure to others, few men excelled him in edifying and agreeable conversation. He was particularly pleasant as a traveling companion. A leading member of his church, who frequently traveled with him on long journeys, has often said: "The better you know him the better you will like him." That character seems to have a fair claim for goodness which grows in our estimation as our acquaintance increases.

With these admirable traits of character, Mr. Straughan was one of the most modest, unassuming men that ever lived. He literally esteemed others better than himself; was always ready to take the lowest seat; and when invited to go up higher ever seemed reluctant to do so.

In the several relations of social life he acted the most exemplary and spotless part. As husband and father, master, friend, and neighbor, he pursued his various duties with undeviating attention. His labors, as a minister of Christ, were considered paramount to every other duty; but when these did not demand his attention, he was as assiduous to the calls of domestic life as could be required by reason or prompted by the most tender affection.

In every place and in every relation he still carried with him a holy unction, so that, whatever he did, either in word or deed, at home or abroad, he did all in the name of the Lord Jesus, giving thanks to God in all things.

It is hard to say whether his singular piety shone most in his modesty and meekness when lifted by prosperity and popular applause, or in his patience and resignation when brought down by adversity and affliction. He had certainly learned, and learned well, too, both how to abound and how to be abased. Too much can hardly be said of his piety and godliness. He should be placed among the foremost in the foremost rank. He was, in the Scripture sense of the phrase, "a perfect and upright man." His zeal, meekness, and patience, his temperance, charity, and faith, and indeed every Christian grace shone so brightly, that his intimate friends could not agree which of them was most conspicuous.

After all, we do not wish it to be understood that we consider our departed brother as one who had no spiritual infirmities to lament. This was not the case. He whom grace had made acquainted with himself and with the purity of God's law, knew his own defects and mourned over them. He lamented his infirmities, and looked for deliverance to that state which he has now attained—the state of "the spirits of just men made perfect." May all who read these memoirs be excited to zeal and perseverance, in running with patience the race that is set before them.

In addition to what is said above by Mr. Semple, we may add that the lamented Straughan took lofty views of the responsibility of a Christian minister. He considered him as deriving his authority to preach from Jesus Christ; not, indeed, miraculously, but still really from Christ. Mere impressions were not, with him, a sufficient guarantee that a man was called to preach. He indulges in the following reflections on the subject:—

"There can be no Christian who feels not more or less concerned for the salvation of sinners. But this is not all that ministers of the gospel ought to feel. We are inclined to think that some good-meaning men, who have felt these exercises, may have mistaken them for a call to preach the gospel; and without properly considering the nature and importance of the work, have begun to preach, and then, ascertaining their mistake, have desisted; while others have continued, rather to the disadvantage of the cause of Christ.

"Preachers of the gospel must not only have a sense of the fallen, guilty state of man, and the way of recovery through Christ, but must have a dispensation of the gospel committed to them. Those who have this treasure committed unto them, have a deep sense of their own inadequacy to perform so great a work, and notwithstanding their ardent desire to glorify God and benefit mankind, have, at first, raised objections to excuse themselves, as Moses and Jeremiah did, and to say, with Paul, 'who is sufficient for these things?' But the authoritative command of God lying upon their minds, makes them say again, notwithstanding these difficulties, 'Woe is me, if I preach not the gospel!'"

PEYTON NEWMAN.*

The subject of this sketch was born of Irish parents, December 24th, 1760. He enjoyed none of those advantages of education which have advanced men of inferior minds to places of distinction in the literary world. In early life he was addicted to occasional gambling, and participated, though to a limited extent, in the train of vices which are almost invariably the attendants of that highly pernicious habit.

From Henry, he removed to Stokes County, North Carolina, where he was awakened, under the preaching of Emanuel Hill, and subsequently became a member of Clearspring Church. But little appears now to be known of his ministry, until after his removal, in 1806, to Big Sandy River, Kanawha, now Cabell County. In the vicinity of his new residence he continued his ministerial labors, not only with acceptance but with profit. The time of his ordination does not appear to be known, but it was some time previous to the year 1814, and was conducted by

---

* By Elder William C. Ligon.

Elders John Alderson, George Guthery, and John Young. He was the stated pastor of Big Sandy Church, which was probably brought into existence through his instrumentality. When the convention met to form the Teay's Valley Association, Elder Newman was reported as one of the delegation from Big Sandy Church. His labors appear to have been confined within the limits of that Association until August, 1822, at which time, it is confidently believed by those who knew him best, he died the death of the righteous. Although the materials which can now be collected to form a history of the life and labors of Elder Newman furnish but little in detail, much may be collected to justify our saying of him, as Luke said of Barnabas, "He was a good man."

RICHARD DABBS.

THE name of RICHARD DABBS has been very extensively and favorably known, throughout Virginia and North Carolina, as a minister of the gospel. He became pious in early life, but did not enter the ministry until several years after his conversion. He was among the number who formed Ash Camp Church, Charlotte County, at its constitution in 1803. When their pastor, Elder Henry Lester, removed to the West, in 1808, they procured his services, and were by him regularly supplied for some time. The churches also of Mossingford and Staunton River enjoyed, for many years, his ministerial labors. In these various stations he was, to considerable extent, useful.

It was not in the performance of pastoral duties that he was thought to excel. It is true his views of church dicipline were scriptural; for, in a circular letter prepared by him for the Appamattox Association, he makes many judicious observations on that subject. But his sentiments were not wholly carried into practice under his administration. When he resigned the care of his churches, for the purpose of removing to the West, he left them in a rather enfeebled state. They had been trained to little or no systematic exertion to extend the influence of truth and righteousness, and consequently they were an inefficient people. But this is not all: under the influence of a lax discipline, disorders were allowed to exist, which materially injured the cause of Christ. Their pastor was not in the habit of watching over them with the determination to correct abuses and impartially to preserve purity of Christian character. No pastor can, to any extent, be successful who does not determine that a rigid, wholesome discipline be maintained in the church. So varied are the dispositions of those who name the name of Christ, and so numerous the temptations to which they are exposed, that the utmost vigilance, firmness, and discretion will be required in one who presides over them as their spiritual shepherd.

While Elder Dabbs did not possess, in eminent measure, the requisites of a skillful pastor, it ought in justice to be stated, that it was in all probability the result of peculiar devotion to itinerant labor. He was not an indolent man, nor was he absorbed in secular pursuits. He consecrated his undivided time and energies to the ministry. Had he remained at home among his own people, and given himself wholly to the duties of the pastoral vocation, and had his mind been relieved from the care of maintaining his family, it is probable he would have excelled in this department of usefulness.

As already hinted, Mr. Dabbs was much devoted to the work of an itinerant. He delighted to visit associational and other large meetings of his brethren in Christ, and, when among them, contributed not a little to their edification and comfort. His excursions were very numerous and extensive; and, while abroad, his time was well occupied. He scarcely ever traveled without preaching at least once every day. He was in the habit, too, of visiting those parts of the country where Baptist churches had not been constituted, or where they were feeble and declining. Thus portions of the truth which seldom fell upon the ear of the people were faithfully dispensed, and frequently with good effect. Among the happy results of these efforts may be mentioned the origin of the Baptist Church in Petersburg. It was mostly through his influence that the few Baptists in that place were induced to unite under a regular constitution, and to make exertions for the erection of a house of worship. He consented regularly to supply them as their pastor, though he did not long continue to serve them. He was for some time engaged in collecting funds for the meeting-house, and was to a considerable extent successful. About this time, also, he accepted the invitation of the Portsmouth Missionary Society to labor as their missionary within the limits of the Portsmouth Association.

During the year 1820 he was employed one-fourth of his time in assisting to supply with preaching the church in Lynchburg. His ministry there was very popular, although it is not known that many, through his instrumentality, were added to the church. He did not remain sufficiently long to accomplish any permanent good. It has already been remarked that he was fond of itinerating; and there is reason to believe, while he accomplished much good in this way, he was less useful in those places where he engaged regularly to labor.

Elder Dabbs's views of truth were consonant with those of the great body of the denomination. In his pulpit exhibitions, he manifested a partiality for what has been called the spiritualizing system; frequently selecting, as the basis of his discourses, some passage from the Songs of Solomon. Although he often displayed much tact and ingenuity, there is reason to apprehend that, in those allegorical disquisitions, there was more of the showy and curious than solid and useful. While the wonder and admiration of an auditory may be excited at these specimens of skill in finding a spiritual meaning to every fact and incident in the sacred history, much serious injury may be the ultimate result. It tends to produce the impression that the Bible is a book of riddles, and in surveying its pages the simple obvious meaning is liable to be overlooked, while something mysterious is made the object of anxious search.

It must not be understood, from these observations, that the subject of this memoir preached no other than metaphorical sermons, or that he condescended to all the ridiculous absurdities which have characterized some preachers of this stamp. On the contrary, it may be said in truth, that many of his public addresses were clear and faithful exhibitions of gospel truth. It ought also to be stated that his manner in the pulpit was exceedingly fascinating. With a musical voice and happy faculty of illustration, he rarely, if ever, addressed a listless congregation.

One of the most interesting traits of Elder Dabbs's character was his concern to be useful to those around him. He did not often neglect an opportunity of conversing with the unconverted in the social circle. He would sometimes relate an appropriate anecdote, or repeat a solemn passage of Scripture, and close his remarks by an affectionate exhortation. In these personal appeals he was remarkably felicitous in the selection of suitable seasons and topics of remark. Often having addressed a word of warning or invitation to a careless friend, he would sing some suitable hymn, which, in connection with the conversation, would produce the most solemn effect. Many now living can bear testimony to the happy influence of these appeals. This is one method by which a minister may be exceedingly useful. In his daily intercourse with men, numerous opportunities are furnished for the recommendation of the truth of God. While in public, Christ and him crucified are to be preached, and all the doctrines and precepts of the Bible enforced, and while in these, the appropriate duties of the ministry, success may be expected. There is also an inviting field of action opened in the social circle. Here an acquaintance with individual character may be obtained. An ascertainment of peculiar disposition and habit may be made. Honest objections may be satisfactorily answered, while the caviling of the presumptuous sinner may be met and resisted.

Perhaps in no other department of his vocation should the Christian minister more constantly study to show himself approved. The colloquial powers should be cultivated. In all attempts at the special enforcement of religious truth, an affectionate spirit and manner should be maintained. It will require also much practical wisdom in the selection of suitable times and circumstances for engaging in this work.

It has been thought by some that Elder Dabbs manifested too much disposition to make proselytes to the denomination with which he was connected. But it is questionable whether this opinion had any foundation in fact. If a Baptist minister is more solicitous to convert a Pedobaptist to his own practice than to bring a sinner to Christ, he unquestionably acts below the dignity of his character and office. But while his great business consists in leading men to God, it is his imperative duty to teach converts to observe all things whatsoever Christ has commanded. He ought to be desirous that the ordinance of baptism, as taught and practiced in primitive times, should be observed by every believer. While it would be unwise to refer to this subject in every discourse, he should be careful to allow it a due proportion in his public ministration. This he should do regardless of the frowns or derisions of those around him. The same may be said in regard to any neglected duty. As Elder Dabbs extended his labors over a wide surface of country, and frequently addressed his brethren of other denominations, he did not hesitate faithfully and affectionately to warn them against the sin of neglecting a positive and significant institution of their Lord and Master. Nor were his efforts in this respect vain. He had the pleasure of seeing many yield obedience to a long-neglected command. It is to be regretted that there was so much looseness in admitting persons to baptism. Wherever he could find a person ready to be baptized, even though in the vicinity of a Baptist church, he would perform the ordinance, and leave the individual either to remain in a Pedobaptist church or in the world. This practice was undoubtedly wrong.

It would not be improper here to introduce a brief reference to this servant of Christ, from Mr. Semple's History: "Since he commenced the ministry," says the historian, "few persons have risen into notice as rapidly as he. And, at present, in point of popularity, as a preacher, certainly none in those parts surpass him, if any can be said to equal him. He is surely the most indefatigable of preachers. He travels almost incessantly; and is thought by some of his intimate friends, for some years past, to have preached more sermons than there are days in the year. He does not preach in vain. There are seals to his ministry wherever he goes. His talents do not consist in deep investigation or close reasoning; not in full and fair explanations of mysterious texts of Scripture, or of abstruse points of divinity. He says clever things, and he says them in a winning manner. Besides, his voice is harmonious, his person agreeable; and his manners, both in and out of the pulpit, affectionate and pleasing. He sings well, and is fond of it. His exhortations are warm and pathetic. With all these advantages, it would not indeed be strange if Mr. Dabbs's talents were somewhat overrated by many. Be that as it may. Unquestionably, such gifts as he really possesses he improves to the greatest possible advantage; and if he should not become biased by excessive popularity, nor be weary in well-doing, he will reap a plenteous harvest in that day."

This harvest there is reason to believe he is now reaping. Having removed to Tennessee in the year 1821 or 1822, he became the pastor of the Baptist church in Nashville. He was ill for many months before his death, and during his confinement gave evidence that he was ready to bear as well as to do his Father's will. He died on the 21st of May, 1825, in full assurance of a blessed immortality.

FRANCIS MOORE.

It is a pleasing task to refer to the life of him whose name stands at the head of this sketch. He could not be said to belong to that class of men who labored as pioneers in extending the triumphs of truth and righteousness in Virginia, nor was he, strictly speaking, identified with the present race of Virginia Baptist ministers. He was one of those endeared names who might be considered as connecting links between the early fathers of our State and the present generation. Francis Moore was the son of Elder Jeremiah Moore, one of the most laborious and useful preachers of the eighteenth century. He was born in Fairfax County, September 18th, 1766. At an early age the grace of God was manifest in his conversion; he was baptized by Elder David Thomas. Immediately he began to preach a crucified Saviour, and after a sufficient trial of his qualifications, was ordained at Zoar, in the County of Jefferson.

On the 8th of November, 1792, he was united in marriage to a lady of high respectability, in Montgomery County, Maryland.

After this event he removed and settled permanently near Harper's Ferry, in the County of Jefferson, Virginia.

In referring to the labors of Elder Moore, it may be stated that during most of his ministerial career he regularly served three or four churches. He was the pastor of Pleasant Valley, in Maryland, and of another church in Montgomery County of the same State. He was also pastor of Zoar Church, in Jefferson, Virginia, and of Ebenezer, in Loudon County. For limited periods, and at different times, he also supplied other portions of the Lord's vineyard. Being a man of industrious habits, he applied himself diligently to the work of his Master both as a pastor and an evangelist. Few men of his day were better qualified to exercise an extended influence, and perhaps no Baptist minister of Northern Virginia was more universally admired and beloved. Nature had done much for him in mental endowment, and his powers of mind had been improved by a good English education.

Of a social disposition and agreeable manners, he endeared himself to all those with whom he became acquainted. In the pulpit the attention of his hearers was engaged by simplicity and clearness of style, as well as an easy and persuasive elocution. His discourses were usually doctrinal, and in the treatment of controverted points he contended earnestly, while he avoided that reckless vituperation by which too many polemics are distinguished. He was a great admirer of Dr. Gill, and considered the sentiments usually denominated Calvinistic as clearly taught in the Sacred Scriptures. But his character had been shaped in the gospel mould, and he could therefore most cordially love all who love the image of the Saviour, although in some particulars they might differ from him in opinion.

Although he was removed from his earthly labors before a separation had taken place between those who style themselves "Reformers" and the Baptists, he frequently expressed the confident belief that it would become necessary. At a very early period of Mr. A. Campbell's career he saw that there was reason to apprehend a fearful turning away from the truth. On one occasion, in 1824, a friend, now living, heard him say: "Many of the Baptist denomination are preparing to receive the most baneful heresies, as Mr. C. has commenced a crusade against benevolent operations, and by the ridicule he is casting upon these efforts, he will induce many to follow him upon that ground; and having thus gained their confidence, a favorable opportunity will be furnished to lead them into the most dangerous errors. He has commenced a voyage on the ocean of speculation without helm or compass, and many will follow him to their sorrow. I think," added he, "there is a desire on his part to be the inventor of new things; but mark it, he will revive some old exploded errors." He frequently warned his brethren against this system, and urged them to betake themselves to the more diligent and prayerful perusal of the sacred volume.

The cause of education found in Mr. Moore a liberal patron; his contributions were frequently bestowed to aid in building up the Columbian College. He was also a warm friend of missions. A sermon preached by him in 1826, at Zoar, on the importance of zealous efforts to spread the gospel throughout the world, will long be remembered by many. He not only recommended this good cause to others, but was himself a frequent contributor. He solemnly believed it to be the purpose of God, that the light of the gospel should shine upon the whole earth, and therefore felt it his duty to labor as an instrument in promoting this glorious design. The following remarks on this subject, from his pen, will illustrate his views. He says: "If the wicked one designs some special mischief to the church of Christ, he adopts means most likely to accomplish his ends. When ecclesiastical establishments will enable him to torment the saints, kings and emperors must march in front, inquisitions, with fire and sword, fill up the train. But now, the powers of darkness may pause. Superstition and bigotry have to recede; the Bible is disseminated abroad; the excellent Carey and Judson, with their brethren in the East, are holding forth the Word of Life, yea, many are engaged in this noble work; the Bible is spreading far and wide, and ere long will be translated into every tongue, so that, from the prince in his palace to the Indian in his wigwam, all may read, as on the Day of Pentecost, in their own language, of the great salvation. What, oh what, says Satan, must be done to preserve our kingdom now in danger? The answer is at hand. If possible, establish a union between the church of Christ and the world; this produced wonders when effected by force of arms; how much more will it advance the views of his satanic majesty if it can only be effected by common consent!"

In 1827 he was one of the instruments of originating a Domestic Mission Society in the Ketocton Association, for the purpose of supplying destitute portions of that region with the preached Word. Its constitution was prepared by himself, and is very similar to that of the General Association Auxiliary Society, being entitled to representation in proportion to the amount contributed, and individuals to a seat by the payment of two dollars.

We now approach the hour of his dismissal from this world. On February 15, 1831, the slender thread of existence was suddenly broken by an attack of apoplexy, which some months before had threatened him. In October, 1830, he returned home from the ordination of P. Klipstene, at Mill Creek Church; while sitting in his chair at supper he was suddenly seized with an unusual sensation, under which he labored a few days, accompanied with great debility; but was eventually restored to strength and usefulness, and permitted a little longer to stand as on the margin of the tomb, and privileged a few more times to sound the gospel trumpet. On Saturday previous to his death he went to Mr. Robert Classet's, under whose hospitable roof he had frequently tarried the nights prior to his fulfilling his monthly appointment in Pleasant Valley. He was during the evening in usual health and spirits, and very fervent in his devotion at the family altar, after which he retired to his room with two of the young Mr. Classets. In the night he arose, lifted the window and lowered it again; he then laid down, and in a few minutes began to moan as if under great oppression, but as he said nothing, nothing was spoken to him. Not rising at his usual early hour in the morning, Mr. Classet went to inform him that breakfast was ready, but received no answer, and upon approaching his bed found vitality was fast retiring from its citadel and the organ of speech forever untuned. His amiable wife, who was immediately sent for, just arrived in time to see him expire. She approached him scarcely noticed; he was unable even to whisper a last adieu. He remained nearly in the same situation until Tuesday morning about six o'clock, when his disembodied spirit took its flight to the shores of a blissful immortality, where the inhabitants shall no more say I am sick. On Wednesday morning, the 15th, his remains, accompanied by his wife and children and sorrowing friends, were conveyed to Virginia and deposited in the silent tomb.

JACOB GREGG.

HIS name is familiar to many Baptists in North America, and especially to the churches of Virginia. He was an Englishman by birth, and continued in his native land until he had risen to manhood. When very young he professed religion by uniting with a Baptist church, and soon commenced the ministry. After he began to preach he was induced to enter the Bristol Baptist Academy, and there prosecuted a limited course of study. Very soon after he left the institution he received an appointment from some society as a missionary to Sierra Leone, on the coast of Africa. This station he did not long retain; for having some misunderstanding with the governor of the colony, he determined to settle in America.

Having arrived at Norfolk, he served at different times the church in that borough, and the churches at Portsmouth and Upper Bridge. While in that region he married a Miss Goodwin. In a few years he removed to Kentucky, and became the pastor of a flourishing Baptist church. But this State he soon left and visited Ohio, there remaining but for a short period. In 1808 or 1809 he returned to Virginia, on a visit to his wife's parents, who were residing in Richmond. At their earnest solicitude he consented to remain in Richmond and open a school, which he conducted for several years. During this period he was generally employed in preaching, either in the vicinity of the city or for the First Church, then under the pastoral care of Elder John Courtney. In the capacity of a teacher he was highly approved, having a large number of youth under his direction. His acquaintance with the Latin and Greek was not very thorough, but he was considered an excellent scholar in all the branches of English literature. His readiness in communicating instruction, and the aptness of his illustrations, rendered him exceedingly popular with the young.

During his residence in Richmond it became apparent to his intimate friends and brethren, much to their grief, that he was in the habit of using too freely the intoxicating draught. How mournful the fact, that, with his capacity for usefulness in the kingdom of Christ, the best of his life should have been yielded to the gratification of this vile appetite! When by some of his brethren his fault was faithfully exposed to his view, he confessed his guilt, seemed deeply penitent, and promised amendment. As, however, he did not utterly abandon the use of spirituous liquors, he was afterwards, in several instances, overtaken by the same vice. In the year 1816 or 1817, he left Richmond, and remained some time in Philadelphia and its vicinity. During this period he was chosen to the pastoral oversight of Market Street Baptist Church, in Philadelphia. Subsequently he settled in Virginia, and was employed sometimes in the instruction of youth, but, toward the close of life, mostly in preaching as an itinerant. There are not many men whose lives have been more subject to vicissitude than his, especially in regard to location. As will appear from the rapid survey already taken, he remained but a short period in any one place, and therefore did not exercise the ministerial function in particular churches sufficiently long to create a permanent influence.

In referring to the talents of Elder Gregg it will not be a departure from the truth to represent him as possessing extraordinary powers of mind. Perhaps the most remarkable trait in his intellectual character was a tenacious memory. This formed the foundation of all his greatness. While he remembered almost everything he ever read, he possessed a peculiar aptness in selecting and arranging, from his ample stores of knowledge, as circumstances might render necessary. As an evidence of the retentiveness of his memory, it is said that while on the ocean, after he left his native land, he memorized the Old and New Testaments, with the whole of Watts's Psalms. During his whole future life, he was able to repeat at pleasure entire chapters and hymns.

Very frequently, in conducting family worship, instead of calling for the books or using them when brought, he would commence and go through lengthy portions from the Bible, and line out the words of a hymn, with perfect accuracy. In his sermons he sometimes introduced lengthy quotations from the sacred writings without referring to the volume before him.

His illustrations in the pulpit were usually apposite and forcible, and his style, while it was simple and chaste, was remarkable for its copiousness. He was an excellent sermonizer. The natural fertility of his mind and his extensive information pre-eminently qualified him for the pulpit. There was sometimes too much division in his discourses, and perhaps a disposition to make portions of the Bible teach what they never intended to inculcate. He was peculiarly fond of seizing some historical incident recorded in the sacred volume and making it the basis of a discourse. At other times he would indulge in the spiritualizing vein, and, with peculiar ingenuity, often to the amusement of his auditors, endeavor to elucidate some dark and mysterious passage, or deduce doctrinal truth from the fragment of a verse. The writer has in possession a curious skeleton of a sermon founded on the clause, "O wheel!" His sermons, however, were generally judicious and highly instructive. While thus much may be said respecting his talents as a preacher, he indicated but little judgment in the common affairs of life. There was possessed a small measure of what is usually denominated common sense; in the management of his own pecuniary and domestic matters he was a mere child, and in mingling in the social circle there was seen but little regard to the courtesies of life. He was rather awkward in his address, excepting with a few intimate friends, and then as a companion he was peculiarly interesting. His colloquial powers in such a circle were excellent.

In sentiment he was strongly Calvinistic. A superior sermon on predestination, delivered before the Dover Association, was, at their request, printed. About the same period a circular letter on the subject of close communion was published, and excited considerable regard.

For the last few years of his life he was a warm friend of the temperance cause, having himself abstained entirely from the use of ardent spirits. His standing, too, among his brethren, was entirely regained, although as a preacher, with men generally, he was far from being regarded as in former days. How dangerous for ministers to parley with temptation! How disastrous the effects of their sin when they fall! Elder Gregg died in Sussex County, after a few days' illness, in 1836.

We subjoin two or three passages from his sermon on Predestination, as illustrative of his views and of his style:—

"The Apostle expresses his comfortable assurance, 'that all things work together for good to them that love God, to them who are the called according to his purpose.' By the term purpose, counsel, pleasure, or decree, we are frequently to understand the whole plan of operation adopted by the Almighty—comprehending the great design he has in view in creation, providence, and redemption. Would it render the subject more plain or intelligible, we may substitute the word *plan* for either of the preceding terms. Thus, when we read, 'according to the eternal *purpose* which he purposed in Christ Jesus our "Lord,"' it may be rendered according to his eternal *plan*. Again, when we read, 'there are many devices in a man's heart, but the counsel of the Lord, that shall stand,' the passage would sustain no injury were we to render it, the *plan* of the Lord. Also, where it is said of the Redeemer, 'the *pleasure* of the Lord shall prosper in his hand,' it may be read, without any injury to the cause of God and truth, the *plan* of the Lord shall prosper in his hand. This plan is also the decree which the eternal Son hath to declare. See Psalms, ii. 7.

"By this time a question arises in the minds of some, What is this *plan* of the Almighty, of which you speak? To this, my brethren, I would reply, it is a plan of *holiness;* it is a plan of *grace.*

"It is a plan of *holiness.* 'According as he hath chosen us in him before the foundation of the world, that we should be holy and without blame before him in love; having predestinated us,' etc.

"It is a plan of *grace.* For 'he hath saved us, and called us with a holy calling, not according to our works, but according to his own purpose and grace, which was given us in Christ Jesus before the world began.' According to this plan, we are the called; according to this plan, we are predestinated, as will appear by consulting our text and the passage immediately preceding: 'Who are the called according to his *purpose*,' or divine *plan;* 'For whom he did know, he also did predestinate.'

"Some persons have styled our text the great golden chain of a believer's salvation. They have said, 'foreknowledge makes one link; predestination, two; calling, three; justification, four; and glorification, five.' But the passage will not, at this time, be so considered. We shall contemplate it as comprehending and illustrating one great subject. We shall view the doctrine of *predestination* as the centre, in which all the lines or subjects meet. And oh! may we all, beholding the Divine character, as displayed in this glorious principle of our Saviour's religion, be changed into the same image from glory to glory as by the Spirit of the Lord! * * * *

"The sentiment that God predestinates, or hath predestinated, persons to a future state of bliss, on foreseen virtue in them, as an inducement, is contrary to plain matter of fact. 'For,' said the primitive Christians, 'we ourselves were sometimes foolish, disobedient, deceived, serving divers lusts and pleasures, living in malice and envy, hateful and hating one another. But after that the kindness and love of God our Saviour toward man appeared, not by *works of righteousness which we have done, but according to his mercy he saved us.*' If works have no influence in procuring Divine favor, when they are wrought, how can we suppose they could have any influence on the Divine decree? If they are destitute of merit when performed, and if after we have done all, we are taught to confess that we are *unprofitable servants*, without any merit or desert, can we possibly think that these works could be foreknown as any meritorious consideration in the Divine plan? On this supposition the foreknowledge of God must be chargeable with error or mistake; and, of consequence, it could be no foreknowledge at all. But, after all, did God foreknow these things as performances of ours, without his immediate and special influence on our hearts? or did he foreknow them as things he would operate in us by his Holy Spirit? Certainly, as things that he would operate, as we have before proved. Then it will consequently follow, that whatever good he foresaw in us, he beheld it, not as native excellency, or acquired by us independent of him, but as the fruit of his own Spirit in our hearts; and, of course, not meritorious on our own account.

"Do you ask, what I understand by foreknowledge? I reply, by the foreknowledge of God I conceive that we are to understand that he, from everlasting, foreknew all those persons who would, through his own Divine operations on their hearts, seek an interest in his favor through Christ, and perfect holiness in his fear. I believe he had the most exact and critical view of their whole characters; that he knew the depraved state in which they would be born, the opposition of heart they would feel against renewing grace and the plan of salvation through a Mediator. 'I knew,' said he, 'that thou art obstinate, and thy neck is an iron sinew, and thy brow brass; I knew that thou wouldst deal very treacherously, and was called a transgressor from the womb.' But he also knew that, in a day of grace and Divine power, they would receive conviction of sin, repentance toward God, and faith in our Lord Jesus Christ, and be disposed to glorify God in their bodies and spirits, which are God's. Is it inquired, what avails this foreknowledge? I reply, that God's exact and perfect view of the unfavorable part of our character, while we were enemies to him by wicked works, proves that his plan of salvation is a plan of grace; for nothing but free, unmerited grace could design the felicity of such unworthy creatures as he foresaw we should be; but his perfect acquaintance with the favorable part of our character, when we are the subjects of his special operations on our hearts, proves that his plan is a plan of holiness; that holiness is its grand object or intention; that in this plan felicity is connected with, and springs from, holiness.

"From these remarks, it must appear that the accomplishment of the design of predestination commences in the obedience of every renewed soul to the call of God. As soon as a sinner is born again, and becomes a partaker in this Divine calling, he immediately exemplifies the dignified, pure, and heavenly exercises of a member of Christ, a child of God, and an expectant of the kingdom of heaven. 'To him, now, to live is Christ, and to die is gain.' The experience of the Apostle is now his: 'I am crucified with Christ, nevertheless I live, yet not I, but Christ liveth in me.' The grand design of predestination being to produce and establish the image of God in all its objects, as in our calling that image becomes measurably reinstated, it follows, of course, that the design of predestination is, in part, accomplished; at least it is so far accomplished, as we become a holy people. But, in our calling, its design is not fully completed; therefore it is added, 'and whom he called, them he also justified.'"

In his admirable tract on close communion, he employs the following language:—

"Hitherto we have only endeavored to show the impropriety of open communion, as it respects Christian societies in general. We shall now exhibit that impropriety with regard to the Baptists in particular.... This will appear—

"1. By reflecting on the nature and design of the mission of John the Baptist, viz.: to make ready a people prepared for the Lord, (Luke, i. 17,) to make ready a people for the kingdom of Christ, or for the gospel church. How was this design accomplished? See Matt. iii. 1, 5, 7. 'In those days came John the Baptist, preaching in the wilderness of Judea, and saying, Repent ye, for the kingdom of heaven is at hand. Then went out to him Jerusalem and all Judea, and all the region round about Jordan, and were baptized of him in Jordan, confessing their sins.' This is called the beginning of the gospel, (Mark, i. 1, 2, 3, 4.) This was the original pattern given for preparing persons for a gospel church state; and the ordinance of the Lord's Supper being confessedly a church ordinance, the Baptists, of course, entertaining these views of things, must act extremely improper were they to practice open communion. For, in such a communion, persons are received who were never made ready for the Lord, or for a gospel church, according to the original plan; hence, in their reception there must be a violation of the well-known rule: 'See that thou do all things according to the pattern shown thee in the Mount;' which precept will apply to the law from Mount Zion equally as to that of Mount Sinai.

"2. The impropriety of Baptists uniting in an open or general communion will appear, by considering how Christ received his disciples. In John, iv. 1, it is said, he made them disciples and then baptized them. See this confirmed by John, iii. 22, 23, 25,

26. Hence, we infer, if our Saviour received persons to communion with himself by the administration of this ordinance, it cannot be improper for the Baptists to adopt the same mode, and follow the same unerring example, in receiving persons to communion in the church of Christ now in the present day. 'For even hereunto are ye called, because Christ also suffered for us, leaving us an example that we should follow his steps,' (1 Peter, ii. 21.)

"3. It is improper for the Baptists to practice open communion, because 'in the beginning it was not so.' These were the words of the Lord, when the Jews inquired if it were lawful for a man to put away his wife for every cause. Our Saviour replied: Moses, for the hardness of your hearts, suffered you to put them away, but 'in the beginning it was not so,' bringing them back to the first institution of marriage. The question is now asked, is it lawful for persons baptized or unbaptized to break bread together at the table of the Lord? We reply, that a number of pious persons have submitted to it, 'but in the beginning it was not so.'"

JACOB DARDEN.*

Jacob Darden, the eldest son of Elisha Darden, was born in Southampton County, Virginia, August 24th, 1770. In early life he was volatile; but when arrived at manhood he evinced more steadiness of conduct, and moved in select circles of society with considerable dignity, but unfortunately imbibed deistical sentiments, which he continued to foster until 1809. From that time he renounced his former sentiments, and made religion the subject of close investigation. His convictions were pungent, the power of which he could not conceal from his friends. He resorted to the throne of grace in secret and there confessed his sins to the infinite Majesty, and implored forgiveness in the name of Jesus, whom he had persecuted. It was not long before the Lord

* From the Minutes of the Portsmouth Association.

answered his supplications and freed his soul from the guilt that tortured his mind. He soon requested admission into the church at South Quay, and was baptized by Elder John Bowers.

Soon after, his mind was deeply impressed with the worth of souls. His views of the lost state of man and the fullness of the gospel moved him to enter the field of labor, to recommend salvation to all around him. In this work he engaged with all that fervor which became a minister of Jesus. Such was the discipline of his mind, and the regulation of his judgment in the selection and management of plain passages of Scripture, that the church of which he was a member granted him license to preach. The time he occupied as a licentiate is not definitely recollected; he was, however, examined by a Presbytery, and ordained to the ministry October 2d, 1813.

The life of Brother Darden was, what the life of every Christian should be, a commentary upon his principles; his faith was exemplified by good works. His life was devoted to the cause of Christ; he not only possessed the ability to be useful, but "whatever his hand found to do he did it with his might." By his humble boldness in the cause of Christ he did much in promoting its interest. His example is worthy of imitation; his zeal, his prayers and exhortations will long be remembered by the pious. He "ruled well his own household," and displayed a talent in the management of his family and domestic concerns seldom evinced. He manifested the most ardent solicitude for their welfare, and sought to train them up in the nurture and admonition of the Lord. As a minister of the gospel, member of the church, clerk of the Association, and justice of the peace, he maintained a dignity seldom equaled. He was nice in his calculations, deliberate in all his decisions, and sincere in all his pretensions in church and State. Of his judgment in courts of justice it is said, by shrewd attorneys, few were his equals. He was reverenced and caressed by all the respectable part of society who knew him. To him the language of Solomon was justly applicable, "When a man's ways please the Lord, he maketh even his enemies to be at peace with him."

Not long after he commenced his ministerial labors he was admonished, by a great weakness of the lungs and spitting of blood, to desist from his former exertions. He traveled but little, except to the neighboring Associations and churches. He preached but seldom during his tedious indisposition; consequently was not much known as a public minister at a distance from home. During the progress of a glorious revival, such was the solicitude of his heart, he could not forbear public exercises again, under the pressure of which his feeble tenement was soon prostrated, so that he was confined to his room almost continually until his dissolution. Under his affliction he manifested unusual resignation, and entire dependence on Christ Jesus. About one week before his departure he was visited by an old minister. He requested him to shut the door and take a seat by his bedside, and addressed him in the following language: "Dear brother, I feel a great anxiety that young converts of the late revival should be instructed much in the leading doctrines of the gospel. There are so many sentiments existing in the Christian community incompatible with the true spirit of the gospel, I fear much that many young Christians may be led into error. I request that you will take much pains, in the spirit of meekness, to guard them against the heresies of the day, especially the Unitarian and Socinian doctrine, which has already overthrown the faith of many; I expect this is the last interview we shall have in time; I therefore make it as a dying request."

Two days before his death, he said to a young brother who visited him: "Brother, I am glad to see you; I thought this morning I should have gone before now; but I was resigned; I seemed to be passing along pleasantly; I have had the presence of Jesus." After a moment's pause, he gave some instructions concerning the records of the church, and then added: *"I have fought a good fight,* and my trust is in the Redeemer for the crown of righteousness."

He continued thus tranquil and resigned until the fourth Sabbath in October, 1827, when he fell asleep in Jesus, and his happy soul, as we doubt not, was conducted by angels into the presence of God. His funeral was attended on the ensuing day by Elder S. Murfee.

JAMES HEALY.*

THE subject of this memoir was born in Middlesex County, July, 1756, of poor but reputable parents. On account of the death of his father, which took place when he was quite young, his education was limited. His mother sent him to school about thirteen months to a very ordinary teacher; being a boy of good mind, he obtained a knowledge of the elementary branches of education. Most of his early life was spent in working upon the farm. In his youth, the revolutionary struggle began, and, at sixteen years old, he enlisted in the continental army for the space of three years, served his tour at the North, and was in one or two actual engagements, where he narrowly escaped death by a musket ball. This, however, made no serious impression on his mind. His time having expired he was discharged, and returned to the place of his nativity, but not to enjoy this happiness long. Within a few weeks a press-master passed, and he was draughted to serve two years in Georgia and North Carolina. During this period, Cornwallis besieged Little York, and he received orders to march thither; when Cornwallis was forced to surrender, and he again returned home to his friends. Although he was prudent in saving his wages while in the army, yet it profited him nothing. He was paid in continental money, which immediately failed after the war, and he lost it all. Shortly after, he was married to Miss Ruth Bristow, and, by their united industry and economy, they were placed in easy circumstances. He was enabled to purchase a farm, to which he attended with great success, and soon became independent in his circumstances.

It is not remembered at what time, or in what way, he was brought under Divine influence. Suffice it to say, that in the Lord's good and appointed time and way, the *rebel* was changed to a *friend*, and the *hater of God* was brought to love him. According to a memorandum, in his own hand-writing, he began to publish the news of salvation through a crucified Redeemer, in

---

* By Nathan Healy.

the winter of 1804, in the forty-eighth year of his age. From the humble view he always had of his own qualifications, he no doubt was induced to embark in this noble work from the great desire he felt for the conversion of sinners. He was invited to take the pastoral care of Pocorone, King and Queen County, at the time of its constitution, August 29th, 1807; which he seemed unwilling at first to do, saying that he was too unworthy and incompetent for so high and responsible a station. The *love* which he bore to his *Divine Lord* soon hushed all objections, and he proceeded to hold a stated monthly meeting with that church, and to administer the ordinances of the gospel, to their great satisfaction and the gradual increase of their number, to the day of his death. For several years his labor was confined principally to this church and its vicinity, going from house to house, holding evening-meetings, and preaching on the Lord's day in private houses. Some time about the year 1809, he, with the few Baptists near the central part of Middlesex, built a new house of worship on a corner of his land, called Clark's Neck Meeting-house, where a monthly meeting was held. This meeting he regularly attended; and whenever the pastor of Hermitage was prevented by any cause to attend, he never failed to fill the vacancy.

In a few years after this house was built, it pleased God to call away by death, the pastor of Hermitage. Being now left destitute, ELDER J. HEALY was called to the pastorate, which call he accepted, and labored one Lord's day in a month with that body, one at Clark's Neck, one Lord's day at Pocorone, and the other he preached, sometimes at the old church, King and Queen, sometimes at Ware's, and at other places. In 1815, his eldest son, John Healy, died, and Zoar Church was left without the bread of life. After a year or two, their great destitution and repeated applications induced Elder Healy to take charge of this church. Thus he was constantly engaged in supplying four congregations until he was removed by the Master of the vineyard.

He was very plain in dress, and remarkable for simplicity of manners; he was reserved before strangers, but open and accessible to his friends and brethren; economical in his habits, yet humane and hospitable to all, and especially charitable to the *poor*. In him the orphan might find a father and the widow a friend.

It is worthy of observation that, immediately after the late war, corn became so extravagantly high that with great difficulty did the poor obtain bread. Although he was in the yearly practice of shipping the larger portion of the corn he sold, yet, seeing the distress of many that year, he declined sending off any of his corn, and retailed it out on credit to his poor neighbors, and the poor widows around him, for less than many asked in cash for theirs; and to the poor widows who bought of him he gave employment, that he might better enable them to liquidate their accounts.

As a preacher his address was not prepossessing, his voice being sonorous and boisterous; he was sound in the doctrines of grace, and seemed to speak with a holy unction, which always commanded attention. Though not eloquent, he might be said to be a good doctrinal preacher. It is stated by one of his cotemporaries, that after Elder Healy had commenced preaching, he was thrown into a state of darkness, that led him to think he had committed a sin in attempting it; he therefore prayed to God that he would forgive him, promising that he would do so no more. But, from his subsequent life, we find him more bold, energetic, and indefatigable, after the temptation was removed, than before. As he approximated the end of his earthly career, he seemed to possess an increasing intellectual power and ardor of address, while his preaching was truly in the power and demonstration of the Spirit.

In the last years of his life he enjoyed good health, with short interruptions. The day week on which he was attacked with his last illness, he was called upon to preach a funeral sermon in a neighborhood where he had not for some time visited, and the brethren and he were much delighted on meeting each other. When asked how he was, he replied, "As well as when I was a boy, only I am not as active." After preaching, he returned home, and in a few days after was seized with a violent bilious fever. In his illness, his intellect was greatly impaired. When in his right mind, he bore his pain with calmness and resignation. He avoided speaking much upon the subject of his death, it is believed, to prevent giving pain to his family. When all his family were out of the room, except his oldest son, he communicated to him his persuasion that his final dissolution was at hand. The day before his death, he conversed pleasantly with the doctor and his friends, showing no anxiety nor fear, but by his composure and cheerfulness seemed to say, I am ready whenever my change shall come. The morning of his death his speech began to fail him, and early in the evening of October 4th, 1820, his spirit took its flight. He died in the sixty-fifth year of his age, and sixteenth or seventeenth of his ministry, leaving a widow with five children, and numerous friends to mourn *that loss* which was *his unspeakable gain.* The Rev. Robert B. Semple preached his funeral sermon at Clark's Neck Meeting-house, from Matthew, xxv. 21: "His Lord said unto him, well done, thou good and faithful servant; thou hast been faithful over a few things, I will make thee ruler over many things; enter thou into the joy of thy Lord."

WILLIAM BELL.*

William Bell was a native of Scotland, whence he emigrated to this country in 1817, and for the last seventeen years had been a resident ot Pattonsburg. He was for some years a minister of an independent Pedobaptist church in Scotland, having separated from the Presbyterian, the established church, on account of errors in doctrine and in church government. Having taken the word of God as the only rule of his faith and practice, he found he had been in error both as regarded the subject and mode of baptism. Deeply affected, he publicly confessed his error, and directed the attention of his brethren to their duty as believers; the result was, that he, together with the members of his church, were solemnly immersed in the name of the Father, Son, and Holy Ghost. But in consequence of the want of an evangelical Baptist minister to administer the ordinance, the series of baptisms was commenced by one of the elders of the church who had been set apart for that purpose, but who was not himself immersed until after he had first immersed the subject of this notice. Under

---

* From the Religious Herald.

his ministry others received the truth, and he had the pleasure of seeing, previous to his leaving Scotland, some hundreds obeying the Lord, by following him into the watery grave, and by continuing steadfastly in the Apostles' doctrine, and in fellowship, and in breaking of bread. After his migration to this country, the wants of a large family and the peculiar nature of his employments confined him constantly to the place of his residence, consequently his acquaintance was limited, and his usefulness circumscribed to a small sphere. Nevertheless, from his settlement in this country to the Sabbath before his death, (upon which day he walked a mile into the country and preached for the last time from Acts, xv. 9,) he ceased not to preach that gospel which had been the power of God in his own salvation, as opportunity offered, both in the town in which he resided and in the adjacent country. He also sought the acquaintance of ministers of the gospel, professors of religion, and serious persons, and endeavored affectionately and forcibly to point out their errors, and to expound unto them the way of God more perfectly. Although not blessed with more than an ordinary English education, he had by close study, particularly of the Scriptures, acquired a more thorough knowledge of the word of God, and clearer views of the plan of salvation by grace, through faith in the Lord Jesus Christ, and a more perspicuous and forcible method of carrying knowledge to others, than that of any public minister with whom the writer of this is acquainted in this country.

JOHN HEALY.

The subject of the following memoir was a man of sincere piety; and, although not eminent for erudition, the Lord made him the instrument of much good in his generation. He was the son of Captain James and Mrs. Ruth Healy, residents of Middlesex County, who were remarkable for piety. He was a preacher above the ordinary standard, and filled that station with efficiency, being successful in his labors, and, as a pastor, was sincerely beloved by his church and congregation.

He was born about the year 1785, and, removing from his father's family when young, resided in Matthews County, where he lived at the time of his conversion. In the year 1806, he was taught of God to understand and feel his need of Christ, and immediately on his baptism became a minister of the everlasting gospel. A short time after, he became the pastor of the Matthews Baptist Church; and in this relation he continued as long as he lived. Besides this, at their special and urgent request, he assumed the pastoral care of Zoar Church, in Middlesex County. In the discharge of these duties he was unblamable, notwithstanding which he was at one time the subject of persecution of a most aggravated nature. This all may expect who would live godly in Christ Jesus. Although constitutionally of a hasty temper, he bore the unmerited rebukes of those around him with Christian meekness, and lived in the constant exercise of those traits which are the chief ornament of the Christian character. There can be no lovelier object presented to the contemplation of man, than the child of God, living in the mortification of his selfish and carnal propensities, and bringing every thought into subjection to Christ.

Firmness and promptness in the performance of duty were characteristics of Elder Healy, and no one, perhaps, was more desirous to advance the cause he advocated. It pleased the Lord, however, to cut him off in the prime of life, and in the midst of his usefulness. He died in 1815, universally lamented. He was the father of several children, and his death was immediately followed by that of his wife; thus leaving a family of helpless orphans to lament their irreparable loss. There may have been men of more splendid abilities, but few who lived more in devotion to the duties of his office.

JOHN ASHCUM BILLINGSLEY.*

John A. Billingsley was born in St. Mary's County, Maryland, April 24th, 1770. He was the only son of Zachary Billingsley; his mother's maiden name was Ashcum. He removed to Virginia when about fourteen years old, and at an early age married Sally Duerson, daughter of Joseph Duerson, of Spottsylvania. He commenced the world in good circumstances, and though liberal to a fault, continued quite independent through life. In his youthful days he was a devotee to all the vain amusements of a giddy world. He was a very witty and agreeable young man, and uncommonly active; having a fine ear for music, and being an excellent performer on the violin, he was always a welcome visitor in the ball-room, and seldom lost an opportunity to gratify his fondness for this amusement. Horse-racing and card-playing also were with him favorite indulgences. Notwithstanding his zeal in his old master's service, (as he frequently called the devil,) he was never charged with any action that involved a compromise of honor.

In this round of folly and indiscretion, thoughts of a future state would sometimes be forced upon his attention; but by mighty efforts to resist the monitions of conscience, he lived in pleasure (falsely so called) till about the twenty-fourth year of his age, when an incident occurred, in the providence of God, that completely dissolved the charm of sinful indulgence by which he had been held. He happened to be present at a Baptist meeting, held by Elder Jeremiah Chandler, at Mine Road Meeting-house; after the services were over, Mr. Henry Pendleton, an aged member of the church, presented himself before the congregation, and begged an interest in the prayers of God's people. He had always looked upon Mr. Pendleton as one of the best of men, and concluded if *he* needed the supplications of God's people, that his own situation must be deplorable. He was brought down an humble penitent at the foot of the cross; and, leaving the gallery

* Prepared by Herndon Frazer.

where he was sitting, he fearlessly came up to the minister, and publicly besought the pious to remember him also in prayer. His distress of mind was sore indeed. Looking upon himself as a poor lost sinner, justly condemned by the law of God, he said he saw not how God could be just, and save such a rebel; and so strong was his regard for the character of God, that he could not desire his own salvation at the expense of the Divine honor. His anguish of heart continued until the next Lord's day, when he was enabled to believe in the Lord Jesus Christ; and so clear were his views of the character and offices of the Saviour, that he exclaimed, if he had ten thousand souls, he would resign them all into his hands.

From this moment he had impressions to preach the unsearchable riches of Christ to a dying world, but was prevented for a long time by a sense of unworthiness, and the fear of assuming a work for which he was not qualified. He was baptized in October, 1794, by Elder Absalom Waller, united with the church at Waller's, and became a very active and zealous member. He began to exercise his gift in exhortation on the 4th of July, 1808. In 1810 he was called to the pastoral care of the church at Zoar, Orange County, and was ordained in October of the same year. After the death of Elder A. Waller, he was chosen pastor of Waller's and Elk Creek Churches, and after the removal of Elder A. M. Lewis to the West, he became pastor of the churches at County Line and Bethany, having resigned his charge at Zoar and Elk Creek. It was also through his efficiency that the church at Mount Hermon, in the upper part of Spottsylvania, was planted, and by his ministrations it was watered as long as he was able to travel. The last time he visited this church, which was in the winter previous to his death, he was in very feeble health, but his physical energies appeared not to give way under a very long discourse. He was much emaciated by disease, his visage thin and pale, and his head covered with a cap. His words were regarded by all who heard him as the testimony of a dying man. He declared it to be his solemn conviction, that that would be the last time he should ever be permitted to address that church, and if he ever felt anxious to be faithful, he did then. He took as the foundation of his discourse, the letters to the seven churches in Asia, as contained in the second and third chapters of Revelations, warning the church against the errors of the times, among which he classed "The Views of Mr. Alexander Campbell," and exhorted them to continue in "the faith once delivered to the saints." Even after he was unable to travel, hearing that a few of the members of this church were rather inclined to subscribe to the views of Mr. Campbell, he wrote a long pastoral letter to the church, urging them to the prompt discharge of duty, and bearing his marked disapprobation to "the (miscalled) reformation."

Elder Billingsley discharged all the social duties incumbent upon him as husband, father, master, neighbor, etc., in a manner truly exemplary. He was a man of God; a firm believer in the efficacy of prayer; and oft engaged at the mercy-seat, in behalf of himself and others. His father, who was an Episcopalian by profession, was brought under conviction for sin, by overhearing him at prayer in secret for him. He was a popular, successful, and indefatigable preacher. Dr. Scott once told him, if he continued to travel and preach, it would certainly kill him. He replied he could not die in a better cause, and that he had much rather wear than rust out.

Elder Billingsley did not enjoy the benefits of classical learning, but possessed a good English education, which he greatly improved by subsequent reading and study. He was devoted to books, had a good library, and when not engaged in his duties from home, was generally found with a book in his hand. Among uninspired writers, Fuller and Newton were favorite authors with him. From this fact, the character of his preaching may be known. His labors were greatly blessed at various periods of his ministerial career—few men in modern times have been instrumental in the conversion of more sinners, or baptized more believing subjects. His praise was in all the churches in this region of country, as an evangelical preacher, a man of great humility, of deep-toned piety, and of considerable research in scriptural knowledge. Notwithstanding, he always had a very humble opinion of his own performances, particularly those of a religious character, often saying his *best* services had need to be washed in the blood of Christ, to cleanse them from sin. Elder

Billingsley suffered with ill-health for many years previous to his death, but continued to preach till a few months before his departure. His bodily strength at length failing him, he was compelled to take his bed. But after disease had wasted his body to a mere skeleton, his mental faculties existed in all their vigor, and his faith in the atoning blood of Christ produced joy inexpressible and full of glory. Christ and his cross were all his theme. A few days previous to his death, on perceiving his friends weeping around his bedside, he reached out his withered arms and put them around the neck of one of his daughters, clasped her to his breast, and said, "My dear, do not weep for me; do not grieve after me!" She replied, "We weep to see you suffer so much." He said, "Jesus suffered much more for me; it will soon be over." He clapped his hands and said, "Glory, glory! I shall soon be at home." On another occasion, when a singing-master, in company with some of his scholars, paid him a visit, he said, "I shall soon sing louder than any of you. I hope the Lord has a harp laid aside for me."

A day or two before his death, he observed to a daughter, who was watching by his bedside: "Oh, my child, I have been assaulted by some fiery darts from the enemy; he has been trying to tempt me to believe that if I were a child of God, he would not permit me to lie here and suffer so long. But it is the *enemy*, for it *is written*—yes, *it is written*, 'Man shall not live by bread alone, but by every word that proceedeth out of the mouth of God: and whom the Lord loveth he chasteneth, and scourgeth every son whom he receiveth.' No wonder the enemy should follow me down to the grave, for he contended for the body of Moses. But I shall yet come off conqueror. I believe my Saviour is now walking with me through the furnace, although I cannot see him." He often said he was a poor unworthy sinner, but trusted he had a kind intercessor and advocate with the Father, and through him he could be accepted. All his trust was in him. The morning he died, he said, "I feel very strange! Can this be death? Can I be dying?" One of his daughters said, "Father, you are not afraid to die?" "No, no!" he replied. He requested that all his children should be called to his bed; then, looking up, he said, "O death, where is thy sting? I hope death—" Here his voice failed him, but he clasped his hands, and was heard to articulate faintly, though distinctly, "Rest, rest, rest!" and closed his eyes on all earthly objects, on the first day of August, 1837, in the sixty-eighth year of his age. When he died, he was living at his plantation called Salem, in Spottsylvania, near Fredericksburg; he left a wife, and nine children who were married and comfortably settled in life, and all members of the Baptist church, save one.

As indicative of the state of Elder Billingsley's mind, during his long confinement, we append the following extract of a letter written to a physician of eminence, whom he had consulted concerning his case:—

"I have written you a long letter, and have scarcely hinted to you anything respecting the state of my mind, which is so much more important. I have reason to thank and bless God for the rich displays of his mercy, which have been mingled with my affliction. I may well abhor myself, and repent in dust and ashes, that my wretched state has not been more beneficially affected under the rod. Sometimes I have felt sweetly reconciled to God's will, then again restless and impatient. Sometimes I have been anxious to depart, and then fondly clinging to life. A thousand cords seem to be drawing and binding me to this world; but, thank God, he has not suffered any corroding fear to perplex my mind. I have had no particular manifestations of his love to my soul, but a firm, fixed reliance on the dear Friend of sinners, in whom alone we can be accepted, and by whom alone a sinner can be eternally saved. 'The time of my departure is at hand; I have fought the good fight!' At any rate, I have been fighting in a good cause, and under a good Captain. Oh that I had been a better soldier! I have, I trust, kept the faith; henceforth there is laid up for me a 'crown of righteousness.' I trust I love his appearing. I will hope for the crown, since it is freely given by Him who shall receive from the saved loud acclamations of praise. They will crown *him* Lord of all."

RICHARD CLAYBROOK.

HE was born October 18th, 1785, in King William County. In this county he remained until his twenty-fifth year, when he became a resident of Middlesex. Four years after his settlement in Middlesex, his heart was brought under the softening influence of the spirit of God. In the fall of 1814 he was baptized by Elder Philip T. Montague, and attached himself to the Hermitage Church, of which James Healy was pastor. Unlike many who name the name of Christ, he not only departed from iniquity, but engaged actively in every good word and work. A few years after this connection, Hermitage Church was left destitute by the death of her pastor. This circumstance was made of God the instrument of leading him to contemplate the great work of preaching publicly the gospel. The church encouraged him to exercise his talents, and, after a suitable trial, he was fully inducted into the ministerial office. This occurred in 1823.

He was called to the pastorate of Hermitage Church, and continued in this sphere of labor to the time of his death. Within the limits of this church he usually occupied two Lord's days in each month, one at the Upper Church and the other at Clark's Neck; he also preached one Sabbath at the Old Church at King and Queen, the other was generally occupied in attending protracted and other meetings in the adjacent counties. In the labors which were thus assumed, the time was most diligently employed. He became eminently popular among all classes of hearers, and by his brethren was much beloved. In the edification of Christians, his ministry was much blessed, as well as in the conversion of sinners.

In 1831 he was invited to the charge of Bruington Church, King and Queen County, which invitation he accepted. This church had enjoyed the personal labors of the venerated Semple for a series of years. To succeed such a man required no small share of talent and piety, and it is an evidence of the high estimation in which Elder Claybrook was held to be called to this station. He continued to preach for the church at Bruington as long as he lived. There was in many respects a striking similarity between himself and his predecessor, and he enjoyed to considerable extent the same confidence and regard.

It has been already stated that he employed a portion of his time in laboring for other churches. It was the joy of his heart to preach the gospel, and perhaps no man was ever more cordially received and heard in the several neighborhoods he visited. Nor was the favorable attention he received the mere empty praise which frequently follows the man of showy but superficial talents. He was not only admired, but loved, because, in simplicity and godly sincerity, he sought to do the people good. A brief survey of his character, as a Christian and a minister, will show how far the confidence reposed in him was merited.

He was pre-eminently "a good man." What he was in public, he was also in the retirement of domestic life. He loved his Divine Master, and served him with unfeigned faithfulness. It was evident, wherever he was seen, that he delighted in the law of the Lord. He was a regular and careful reader of the sacred volume, and particularly conscientious in regarding all its precepts. He was remarkable for his unaffected simplicity of manners and amiability of disposition. In his dress he was plain; his chief adornment was that of a meek and quiet spirit.

He was an able minister of the New Testament. With a mind naturally strong, he was capable of originating ideas and presenting them in an interesting shape. His education was slender, and although more than thirty-five years of age when he entered upon the ministry, he devoted himself diligently to a course of study, and acquired extensive information, especially on theological subjects. He was an interesting speaker. There was perhaps too much carelessness of style, but his sermons were full of thought. There were sometimes in his discourses a richness and sublimity which astonished all who heard him. On such occasions no one could listen to him without being convinced that the speaker was giving utterance to thoughts originating in the magnitude and importance of the subject itself. He was only giving vent to the fullness of a heart in which had been richly shed abroad the love of Christ. While he exhibited the doctrines of the gospel, illustrating them with clearness, his design was not to amuse, but to improve his hearers. He sought, by manifestation of the truth, to commend himself to every man's conscience in the sight of God. His appeals to the congregation were often of the most pungent character. He warned the wicked to flee the wrath to come, while he urged his brethren to engage in every good word and work.

He was a friend to every object that promised to be the means of doing good. His principles were drawn from the school of Christ, and the benevolence of those principles prompted him to rejoice in all plans which tended, in any measure, to advance the kingdom and glory of God. Though himself an uneducated man, he took a lively interest in the rise and progress of the Virginia Baptist Education Society. Liberal contributions were furnished by him, and all his influence was employed to sustain the rising seminary, located in the vicinity of Richmond. It afforded him the sincerest gratification to see others enjoying advantages which he had been denied.

The temperance cause found in him an active and able defender. The following anecdote, as related by a ministering brother, will illustrate the characteristic consistency of this man of God: "Passing through Middlesex, in the summer of 1827 or 1828, I was kindly invited by Brother C. to spend a night at his house. The temperance cause was then in its infancy in that region. The evening was mild and pleasant; we were sitting in the porch, in full view of a luxuriant orchard, that spread all around us in richness and beauty. This sight, together with the fact that the temperance question was then in some degree new, naturally led us to make the distillation and common use of brandy the subject of our conversation. In the course of our remarks, Elder C. observed to me, that he was at first not very friendly to the temperance cause, or at least not to the total abstinence principle; that he looked upon the proposed reformation, by means of societies, as altogether visionary. Many other good men were once of the same way of thinking. 'But,' said this man of God to me, 'I was recently cured of my opposition by this circumstance: there was a member of our church, who, though in other respects a good and orderly man, was in the habit of occasionally drinking *too much*. The deacons, and perhaps some other brethren, had talked with him on the sin and danger of his conduct, but without any permanently good result. His conduct was about to be made a matter of discipline. But I concluded that I would myself, as pastor of the church, make an effort to reclaim him, before the case was acted on publicly. I accordingly sought and obtained an interview with him. He confessed his fault, appeared penitent, and promised to do better; to *drink less* in future. I advised him to quit entirely, as the only hope of a permanent reformation. "But," said he to me, "Brother Claybrook, do you ever drink?" Very little, said I; I take a julep in the morning, with my family, and a little toddy before dinner. "Well, Brother Claybrook," said he, "how much do you drink a day on an average?" Why, I don't know, said I, perhaps I may use a half gill or so. "Well, really," said he, "that is more than I drink. If I were to drink that much I should be drunk all day long; your constitution may not be so easily affected by it; but, Brother Claybrook, you drink more than I do." I felt,' continued Elder C. to me, 'mortified and condemned, to think that I was censuring in him a course of conduct which I myself pursued, and that I was advising to do what I was not doing. From that moment I determined to use no more myself, nor allow its use in my family. I have there,' pointing to his orchard, 'fruit enough to make hundreds of gallons of brandy, and was about making some preparations to distil it; but I shall not make a drop. Though I have experienced no inconvenience myself from the use of it, yet I am determined, so far as my influence is concerned, utterly to discountenance the making, selling, or using it, unless purely for medical purposes.'

"His still, he told me, might sell to advantage, but as that would be indirectly to encourage the making of spirit, he intended to have it converted into culinary utensils."

The stand which he uniformly took in the cause of temperance evinced his sincerity in the determination he had formed. Comment is unnecessary. There may be, even at this late day, some brethren, yea, even some preachers, who would do themselves and the cause of truth no harm by taking a hint from this anecdote.

There is one particular in which, while the disinterestedness of Elder Claybrook is manifest, there is seen also a delicacy as injurious as it is unscriptural. This was an unwillingness to urge on his brethren the duty of ministerial support. He thought many of them remiss in this respect, and referred rather confidentially, to ministering brethren, to this defect. And yet, lest he should be thought to indulge improper motives, he never allowed himself to speak publicly on this subject. On one occasion, when a brother, who expected to preach within the limits of his pastoral labor, expressed his intention to advert to this duty, he was besought by Elder Claybrook to pass it by without notice. Such a course indeed exempted Elder Claybrook from the censure of men influenced by covetous motives, but was by no means consonant with the directions and example of the Apostle Paul. Some extenuation may indeed be found in the peculiar circumstances by which the early Baptists in Virginia were surrounded. But the minister of Christ should declare all the counsel of God, however unpopular it may render him. Since it is the ordination of God, that they who preach the gospel should live of the gospel, this subject in a proper spirit should be clearly preached to the churches. At the same time every pastor, by his whole life, should prove himself to be above the low principle of covetousness in discharging this duty.

The following allusion to this eminent servant of Christ, from the pen of Elder George Northam, of Middlesex County, will be interesting to all the readers of this memoir: "Having been well acquainted with Elder Claybrook, and much with him during his public ministry, I may say, he possessed naturally a vigorous and penetrating mind, a retentive memory, and an unusual share of good sense. His education was such as was generally obtained in the common country school during his youth; he made a very good use of it, and was the warm friend of an enlightened ministry. I have frequently heard him say, that many advocated it because they possessed it, and therefore knew its advantages; but he vindicated it because he knew the want of it. After he commenced preaching, few men perhaps studied more intensely than he did. But being far advanced in life, his studies were not so much directed toward the improvement of his education as toward acquiring a general knowledge of the sacred volume, in which he succeeded beyond many who far surpassed him in literary attainments. Being naturally fond of reading, and habitually industrious, he read much on theology to great advantage.

"Although his preaching was not with enticing words of man's wisdom, yet it was scriptural, spiritual, solemn, and impressive. His peculiar simplicity and earnestness so much engaged and riveted the attention of the audience, that they had but little time or disposition to attend to his style. They were constantly kept, either gazing at the humble man of God before their vision, or listening to his prominent descriptions of the wicked, and of the Christian character. He generally sustained his positions by plain and strong arguments, and by passages of Holy Writ. His illustrations, though sometimes, perhaps, a little offensive to the delicate ear, were nevertheless well applied. The responsibility of sinners; faith, repentance, salvation through the Saviour; a holy and pious life, and activity in every good work, were the themes on which he mostly dwelt in the pulpit; nor did he press one of these subjects so far as to lessen the claims or hide the necessity of another, but attached to each its respective importance. No persons, it is presumed, ever became better pleased with themselves and their own inherent goodness, by his preaching; but many, it is hoped and believed, have become more pleased with Christ and his merits.

"His unassuming manners, his uniform and exemplary piety, not only commended him to all with whom he was acquainted, but placed him above the reach of reproach by his enemies—if it were possible for such a man to have any. Perhaps no man, in his day, excelled him in prudence, candor, and punctuality. Bible, missionary, temperance, and education societies found in him a warm friend and advocate—not only in theory but in practice. The primary object at which he seemed constantly to aim was not to be great and splendid, but to be good and useful."

His ministerial career was comparatively short, but when summoned away by death he was not unprepared. He had indeed habitually lived with his "loins girt about," and his light burning. When in perfect health he would frequently speak in the most familiar and cheerful mannner of death and the future world. "If I am not called home, I may be with you," was a common reply, when pressed to attend distant meetings. He was attacked with pleurisy, November 23d, 1834, and from the first but little hope was entertained of his recovery. The subjoined letter from one of the members of his church was written shortly after his death: "It is with emotions of sincere regret that I have to apprise you of the death of our much beloved brother, Richard Claybrook. He closed his earthly pilgrimage on the fourth instant, at eight o'clock P.M., in the fiftieth year of his age, after an illness of eleven days, which he bore with great patience and resignation. He evinced from the first a strong preference to change worlds, if consistent with the will of God. He gave numerous evidences of his free and unshaken confidence in the Redeemer. A few hours before his dissolution he remarked to a member of one of the churches of which he was pastor, that he loved every member of the church, and if it was the will of God for him to remain, he had no objection; but for him to depart and be with Christ, would be far better. To another brother, he said that he had been running all his life for a sure prize, and that Jesus Christ could not tell a lie. He observed that no one knew the sufferings of a dying man, which he was then experiencing; at the same time appeared to draw comfort from the sentiment of the Apostle, that the sufferings of the present time are not worthy to be compared with the glory which should be revealed hereafter. When told that he was sinking, (in compliance with a wish expressed by him in the early stage of the disease,) and asked whether he felt any disposition to lengthen out his stay here, he promptly replied, 'No: not for one hour.' It was said by an irreligious gentleman, who was present, that amid the whole weeping group that surrounded him during his last hours, there seemed to be but one who was cheerful, and that was Mr. Claybrook. It was his special request that no funeral sermon be preached; that four of his brethren, whom he named, should carry his body to the grave; that two hymns, which he selected, be sung, one going to the grave, the other returning; and that the service be concluded by prayer. The first hymn was, 'Farewell, vain world, I'm going home;' and the second, 'While sorrows encompass me round.' He also requested, on his death-bed, that nothing relative to his death be published; but on being told by some friends present that something would be, he said, if you do, let it be nothing more than a poor sinner saved by grace."

Another minister in furnishing a tribute to his memory, when he heard of his death, says: "By a letter received from King and Queen I am informed of the recent death of our beloved brother, the Rev. Richard Claybrook. He fell a victim to his uniform zeal in the cause of Christ. By exposure to some of those inclement rains which fell on several Sabbaths in the fall, he contracted a pleurisy which resulted in his death. He was a plain, warm-hearted, old-fashioned, Virginia preacher, of strong native intellect; in the Scriptures well informed; of the most affectionate temper; of the most unobtrusive but steady and consistent zeal; an example to believers in word, in conversation, in charity, in spirit, in faith, in purity. He had a good report of them that are without, and was ardently loved by those that are within. The church in Bruington have thus, within a short time, been deprived of two invaluable men, Semple and Claybrook."

An interesting fact connected with the sad event of his removal may properly close this sketch. Two of the most influential brethren of the ministry, whose praise is now in all the churches, were, in a remarkable manner, brought into their present official position by the tidings of his death. One of them had, a short time previous, become a member of the church, and when it was announced, to his unspeakable sorrow, that Claybrook was dead, and that, in his death, was lost a standard-bearer among the hosts of Zion, the impression came with irresistible power, "I must take his place." He thought of the eloquent tongue now silent in death, and the question forced itself upon his heart, "Shall I not plead for Jesus?" He began to speak in the name of Christ, and now lives, well and worthily, to proclaim the great salvation. The other case was equally remarkable. A man of the world, loving pleasure and pursuing it, was, in the midst of it, arrested by an overwhelming concern for his soul by the announcement that Mr. Claybrook had been called away by death. He had been one of his admirers, regarding him as an earnest, consistent advocate of truth and righteousness, and now the desire sprung up in his heart to become not only a Christian, but a preacher of that gospel which had sounded out from the lips of his departed friend. The pleasures of sin were resigned; deep and painful sorrow in view of the past was cherished; and no rest was known until found in the atoning blood of Christ. Then he could speak experimentally of the value of spiritual things, and soon entered the ministry. Ever since, he has been a devoted and useful proclaimer of the gospel.

The Lord reigns. He calls men into his vineyard, and, when he pleases, dismisses them. Let all the churches trust and rejoice in him.

WILLIAM A. WOOD.*

ELDER WILLIAM A. WOOD was born in Fluvanna County, Virginia, February 8th, 1769. Before he was three years old his father died, leaving him and four other children, of whom he was the youngest, to the care of their widowed mother. Those who have attended to the prominent events connected with the history of our country, will remember that his youthful years embraced a period the circumstances of which form a very prominent link in the chain of events that terminated in the acknowledgment of American independence. To this the deceased attributed the almost necessary neglect of his early education. The rich patriot found it difficult to afford the advantages of education to his rising progeny, and the poor, though so disposed, found it utterly impossible. Among the latter was the mother of Mr. Wood; and he was consequently deprived of the means of acquiring the most ordinary education. A portion of his youthful energies were spent in the service of his country, and for three years, during the war of the Revolution, he was employed in guarding military stores in the vicinity of his mother's residence.

The scanty intervals of leisure which he could control, when, in maturer years, he was engaged as an apprentice to the shoe and boot making business, were directed to the pursuit of knowledge, and he thus succeeded in making himself acquainted with the rudiments of reading, writing, and plain arithmetic. In 1801 he married Frances Saunders, a native of the same county.

* By Elder William C. Ligon.

Fraternal affection bound him to the place of his nativity; nor did he relinquish the care of his widowed mother until her death. In 1810 he sold his patrimony, and moved, with his rising family, to the County of Kenawha, of which he was a resident at the time of his death. His moral deportment was highly commendable before he made any pretensions to vital godliness, having been influenced by the precept and example of a godly mother, who sustained the character of a pious member of the Baptist church for many years. In 1813 or 1814 the typhus fever prevailed to an alarming and fatal extent in the vicinity of his residence, and he was one of the comparatively few who survived an attack of that disease. This he afterwards recognized as the disciplinary Providence which admonished him of the necessity of immediate preparation for death and judgment. He saw that the slighted mercy of God had signally interposed in his behalf, and snatched him from the jaws of death, while others had fallen victims to the same disease. This reflection wrought in him deep and pungent convictions of his guilt; and an abiding sense of the ingratitude of his whole life so fastened upon his mind as not only to create bitter remorse and self-loathing for past offences, but took from him all hope of pardon, save from the superabounding goodness of God through the atoning merits of Jesus Christ.

Shortly after he had experienced a sense of pardon, he established the worship of God in his family, in which he steadily persisted. He is said to have labored under some difficulties on the subject of baptism, which were removed, as the result of a prayerful examination of the New Testament. Thus having the way of duty made plain, he presented himself as a candidate for this initiatory ordinance to the Baptist church which worshiped at the upper falls of Coal River, and was baptized in 1815. He was considered at the time a valuable accession to the church, and his subsequent usefulness proved the correctness of the opinion.

Immediately after his baptism he established neighborhood prayer-meetings, in which he would occasionally invite an aged and pious colored brother to participate. God owned and blessed his efforts, and in the course of a year many were hopefully converted and added to the church. He was licensed as a probationer for the gospel ministry in June, 1816, in which character he preached until August, 1819, and was then ordained by Elders Lee, Newman, and Young. His influence was extensively felt and profitably exercised within the bounds of the Teay's Valley Association, to which his labors were principally confined. Several of the churches of that body were brought into existence through his instrumentality, and perhaps not one of its constituent members failed to derive some benefit from his labors. Some time in January, 1833, he was confined from what was thought to be a rheumatic affection, located in one of his legs, and although the pain it produced was frequently excruciating, yet it was not attended with any alarming symptoms until a few hours before his death. On the 17th of February, 1833, while at breakfast with his family, he was taken suddenly ill, and for a short time deprived of the power of articulation. After having recovered a little he calmly advised the family of his approaching dissolution, gave suitable admonitions to his younger children; requested his two eldest sons to attend immediately to the equitable adjustment of his estate; and having thus briefly set his house in order, exclaimed, "God take my soul! my Lord and my God!" and calmly sunk to rest, having passed the sixty-fourth year of his age but nine days.

As a preacher, Elder Wood was plain and practical; his arguments and illustrations were deduced almost exclusively from the Bible, while his general deportment gave conclusive evidence that he drank deeply of the spirit of that inimitable book; the numerous quotations which he invariably employed in his sermons afforded evidence no less conclusive that he had successfully labored to imprint the word indelibly upon his memory. He not only possessed the confidence of his brethren, and as the result of their choice, officiated as Moderator of the Association for several years before his death, but no man had a better report from those that were without. His piety was steady and commanding, not breaking forth with occasional lustre, and then shining dimly for a season, but he held on the even tenor of his way. Elder Wood did not live to identify himself with either of the parties which have since existed in the Association, for and against the benevolent operations of the day; but he has left behind him a family who have warmly espoused the various institutions which have been signally blessed of God in the melioration of so many of our sinful race.

LUTHER RICE.

A MOURNFUL satisfaction is indulged by the biographer in surveying the history of him who forms the subject of this sketch. It has been thought suitable to place his name among those whose energies were devoted to the cause of Christ in Virginia, as he was deeply interested in all our institutions, and felt himself in a measure identified with them. Nothing like an extended biography will be attempted, as the limits of this work will not allow due justice to be done to his merits, and especially as it is superseded by a memoir in a separate volume which has been placed before the public. This volume contains a rich collection of facts deserving a place in the library of every American Baptist.*

Luther Rice was born in Northborough, Worcester County, Massachusetts. From earliest youth he was distinguished for love of study and the same indomitable perseverance in the prosecution of favorite objects which characterized him in all after life. It was soon discovered that he possessed a mind of no common order, and the best facilities were allowed by his parents for its cultivation. While prosecuting his preparatory studies, it pleased God to reveal his Son in him, and to make him an heir of eternal life. He became a member of the Congregational Church, and at once was recognized among the most exemplary and active of the Lord's servants. Whenever he could find an opportunity of meeting the people of God for prayer or conference it was embraced with joy, and soon he was invited to lead in

* A memoir of Mr. Rice was prepared several years ago by James B. Taylor, and published in a 12mo. volume of more than three hundred pages. Two editions have been issued.

public religious exercises. Feeling it to be an imperative duty to devote his life to the ministry, and desirous to obtain a thorough education, he entered William College in 1807. During his stay at this institution, he was not only a diligent and successful student, but specially devoted to God. A portion of his time was regularly employed in attending meetings for the benefit of persons in the vicinity of the college. It has been frequently stated by a member of the family in which he boarded, that he was regarded by all as an eminently holy man, maintaining habits of intimate communion with God, and giving promise of extended usefulness among his fellow-men. It was during his collegiate course, and indeed soon after his entrance into the college, that his attention was drawn to the subject of missions. Samuel G. Mills and he, with one or two other students, resolved to embrace the first opportunity of going to the heathen. At the same time, among the students at Andover, one of whom was Adoniram Judson, were three or four who were meditating the consecration of themselves to the cause of missions.

In 1810, Mr. Rice united with five of his brethren in addressing the General Association of Massachusetts, explaining their own views and feelings, and requesting the advice of their more experienced fathers. After the paper was prepared, his name with one other was withdrawn lest the churches should be deterred from action by the number who desired to be sent abroad. Their application at first excited among many the charge of rashness and fanaticism, and met decided repulse. But they had counted the cost and were not to be withstood in their purpose to preach among the heathen the unsearchable riches of Christ. After the delay of some months, they received an appointment to labor in Burmah, from the American Board of Commissioners for Foreign Missions, a society which had a few months before been organized. On the 6th of February, 1812, the subject of this memoir was ordained to the work of a missionary, in the Tabernacle Church in Salem. A few days after, in company with Mr. Hall, Mr. Nott and lady, he sailed from Philadelphia to Calcutta. On the next day Messrs. Judson and Newell, with their wives, sailed for the same place from Salem.

It will serve to present in a more striking light the circumstances attending Mr. Rice's consecration to the Foreign Mission work, by introducing a letter from Mr. Judson, in reply to some inquiries on the subject:—

"MY DEAR BROTHER RICE:—

"You ask me to give you some account of my first missionary impressions, and then of my early associates. Mine were occasioned by reading Buchanan's 'Star in the East,' in the year 1809, at the Andover Theological Seminary. Though I do not now consider that sermon as peculiarly excellent, it produced a very powerful effect on my mind. For some days, I was unable to attend to the studies of my class, and spent my time in wondering at my past stupidity, depicting the most romantic scenes in missionary life, and roving about the college rooms, declaiming on the subject of missions. My views were very incorrect, and my feelings extravagant; but yet I have always felt thankful to God for bringing me into a state of excitement, which was, perhaps, necessary in the first instance, to enable me to break the strong attachments I felt to home and country; and to endure the thought of abandoning all my wonted pursuits and animating prospects. That excitement soon passed away, but it left a strong desire to prosecute my inquiries, and to ascertain the path of duty.

"It was during a solitary walk in the woods, behind the college, while meditating and praying on the subject, and feeling half inclined to give it up, that the command of Christ, 'Go into all the world and preach the gospel to every creature,' was presented to my mind with such clearness and power, that I came to a full decision, and though great difficulties appeared in my way, resolved to obey the command at all events. But, at that period, no provision had been made in America for a Foreign Mission, and for several months after reading Buchanan, I found none among the students who viewed the subject as I did, and no minister in the place or neighborhood who gave me any encouragement; and I thought I should be under the necessity of going to England and placing myself under foreign patronage.

"My earliest missionary associate was Nott, who, though he had recently entered the seminary, (in the early part of 1810,) was a member of the same class with myself. He had considered the subject for several months, but had not fully made up his mind. About the same time, Mills, Richards, and others joined the seminary from William College, where they had for some time been in the habit of meeting for prayer and conversation on the subject of missions; but they entered the junior class, and had several years of theological study before them. You were of the same standing, but from some engagement (a school I believe) did not arrive so soon, though you ultimately finished your course before the others, and joined the first party that embarked. Newell was the next accession from my own class.

"As to Hall, he was preaching at Woodbury, Connecticut. I heard that he once thought favorably of missions, and wrote him a short letter. He had just received a call to settle in that place, and was deliberating whether it was his duty to accept it or not when the letter was put into his hand. He instantly came to a decision, and the next rising sun saw him on the way to Andover. I think that he arrived about the time of the meeting of the General Association of Ministers at Bradford, in the summer of 1810. I do not, however, recollect him present at that meeting, nor was his name attached to the paper which was presented to the Association, and which was originally signed by Nott, Newell, Mills, Rice, Richards, and myself; though, at the suggestion of Dr. Spring, your name and Richards's, which happened to stand last, were struck off, for fear of alarming the Association with too large a number.

"I have ever thought that the providence of God was conspicuously manifested in bringing us all together from different and distant parts. Some of us had been considering the subject of missions for a long time, and some but recently. Some, and indeed the greater part, had thought chiefly of domestic missions and efforts among the neighboring tribes of Indians, without contemplating abandonment of country and devotement for life. The reading and reflection of others had led them in a different way; and when we all met at the same seminary, and came to a mutual understanding on the ground of *foreign missions* and *missions for life*, the subject assumed in our minds such an overwhelming importance and awful solemnity as bound us to one another, and to our purpose more firmly than ever. How evident it is, that the spirit of God had been operating in different places and upon different individuals, preparing the way for those movements which have since pervaded the American churches, and will continue to increase until the kingdoms of this world become the kingdoms of our Lord and of his anointed."

Referring to this eventful period in a letter to a friend, Mr. Rice observes: "After the Society of Inquiry at Andover was well established, the views of the brethren were turned very much toward the East. Judson was the first, as far as I know, who mentioned Burmah. He had read Buchanan's 'Star in the East,' his 'Christian Researches in Asia,' and 'Captain Simon's Embassy to Ava.' He insisted that the east afforded much the widest and most promising field for missionary exertions, and that the path of duty led in that direction. Six months after Mills and Richards joined the Theological Institution at Andover, it occurred to me (always pushing forward) that by leaving half a year behind at college, and joining half a year in advance at Andover, I could save a year between the two; and yet, by diligent application, accomplish the studies, so as to sustain the requisite examinations with my classmates in both institutions, which, with the concurrence of the president and his recommendation, was carried into effect, and I became connected with those at Andover, who were a year before me at William College. Here I became acquainted with Judson, but chiefly in the meetings of the secret society, as he was but little at Andover after I entered that seminary.

"In June, 1810, Gordon Hall, who had been preaching for some time, and who had been invited to become the pastor of a church in Connecticut, came to Andover to consult with the professors, whether he ought not to hold himself devoted to missionary labor among the heathen. (Oh! how I love to trace important results to minute incidents!) It happened to be but a day or two before the meeting of the General Association of all the evangelical part of the ministers of Massachusetts, at Bradford, where the parents of Ann Haseltine lived, ten miles from the Institution, in Andover.

"The coming, and object of the coming of Hall, so enlivened the missionary sentiments and feelings, particularly in the bosoms of the members of the Society, that Judson immediately wrote the memorial which you see in the memoirs of Mrs. Judson, addressed to that body of ministers, which was subscribed, in the first instance, Adoniram Judson, Jr., Samuel Nott, Jr., Samuel J. Mills, Samuel Newell, James Richards, Luther Rice. The last two names were subsequently taken off, from a fear that the appearance of so many under such impressions of mind, when nothing had been previously known of this matter, not even by the professors, whose pupils thus suddenly burst forth in an attitude so peculiar, should create something of the nature of alarm, as if some kind of fanaticism had seized the minds all at once of the young ministers.

"The Association appointed a committee, to whom the memorial was referred, and who reported favorably; in consequence, nine commissioners were appointed by the same body, five of Massachusetts and four of Connecticut, who met in Connecticut in September of the same year, and formed the Constitution of the American Board of Commissioners for Foreign Missions. This body, which thus emanated from that little secret society of youth formed at Williams College, in 1807, (of which I esteem it the happiest point in all my life to have been one of the original members,) now embraces the entire Congregational and Presbyterian denomination, and employs from a hundred and fifty thousand to two hundred thousand dollars annually in their missionary exertions. From this arose the Baptist General Convention, formed in 1814; and since, more or less distinctly out of the same range of evangelical influence, the American Bible Society, the American Tract Society, the Columbian College, the Newton Theological Institution, and I know not how many other things of more or less importance. Glory be to God! attempt great things—expect great things."

An event will now be recorded, which, considered in all its singular coincidences and powerful results, was evidently under the special direction of the great Head of the church. We refer to the change of sentiment underwent by three of this noble band on the subject of baptism. All their early habits of thought and association, and every feeling of interest, uttered a voice in opposition to this step. They were entire strangers to the Baptist denomination, and as yet they could expect but little support from them in carrying on the missionary enterprise. But the mandate of their ascended Saviour was with them sufficient to determine their course. What in this circumstance was especially remarkable appears in the fact that, while Mr. Judson on his voyage was examining the subject of baptism, Mr. Rice, in another vessel without any previous concert, was engaged in the same process of investigation.

Referring to this circumstance, Dr. Carey remarks: "Brother Rice was, on the voyage, thought by our brethren to be the most obstinate friend of Pedobaptism of any of our missionaries. I cannot tell what has led to this change of sentiment, nor had I any suspicion of it, till one morning when he came, before I was up, to examine my Greek Testament; from some questions which he asked that morning I began to suspect that he was inquiring; but I yesterday heard that he was decidedly on the side of believers' baptism. I expect, therefore, that he will soon be baptized." On the first of November, he was buried with Christ by baptism, in the City of Calcutta, Mr. Judson and lady having previously taken the same step.

With respect to the change which was experienced by Mr. Rice, no doubt can be indulged that it was preceded by the same prayerful and protracted investigation. The struggle between the convictions of truth and prejudice was severe and desperate. He found himself exceedingly reluctant to break the denominational ties which bound him to so many of those in whose piety he had the fullest confidence, and to unite himself with a people to which he had been comparatively a stranger. He knew, too, that in the event of a change he should, with many, subject his character to reproach, and no longer be recognized as the authorized missionary of the Board. While all the means of support would thus be cut off, he was entirely uncertain as to the measure of countenance which would be given to missionary operations by the Baptists. There was no earthly motive in favor of the change; every selfish consideration was against it. Under these circumstances we might expect him to ponder well his steps, and to proceed no farther than the most solemn convictions of duty should require. During the progress of these investigations he appeared as the advocate of infant baptism whenever he conversed with Baptists, not allowing them to know the scruples which had taken possession of his mind until a short time previous to his requesting baptism.

The following extract from the pen of Mr. Judson will be read with interest, as it throws additional light on this part of the biography. "Mr. Rice arrived in Calcutta about six weeks' after those of us who sailed from Salem. At that time I was deeply involved in the subject of baptism, which I had begun to investigate on board ship, and I soon learned that some of the passengers from Philadelphia were in a similar position, and that Mr. Rice had rather distinguished himself by reading everything within his reach and manifesting uncommon obstinacy in defending the old system.

"Soon after my baptism he came to live with me, in order to enjoy better accommodations than he found elsewhere. At first he was disposed to give me fierce battle; but I held off, and recommended him to betake himself to the Bible and prayer. He did so, and lived much by himself, so that I seldom saw him, except at meals. But his inquiries, when we met, soon assumed that cool and solemn air which left me no doubt as to what would be the result of his investigation. His mind remained undecided throughout the month of September; so that, though perhaps he expected to become a Baptist, he signed the joint letter of the brethren which you allude to, as a thing of course, though that letter mentions my change of sentiment as a 'trying event,' and states the inexpediency of our laboring in the same missionary field. In the month of October, his mind became fully decided, and he was baptized on the first of November. In all this I discover not the slightest inconsistency, though persons at a distance, and not acquainted with the circumstances, might make the desired discovery.

"Both Mr. Rice and myself have been accused of changing our sentiments suddenly, prematurely, and, of course, through the influence of interested motives. The truth is, that a Pedobaptist examining the subject of baptism, though about convinced of the truth, is reluctant to communicate the real state of his mind, even to his nearest friends, lest he should finally resettle in his old sentiments, and be ashamed to have it known that he ever had a serious doubt on the subject. The consequence is, that when he can hold out no longer, and the unexpected fact is thrust perhaps unceremoniously into the faces of his friends, they all stand aghast, and are ready to ascribe his change to any other than an honest influence."

In a letter to his parents, dated November second, Mr. Rice says: "Whatever may be the consequence of this change, as it respects the Board of Commissioners and my numerous Christian friends in America, I cannot say, nor am I very anxious about it, though by no means indifferent to public opinion or insensible to the delicacy and serious responsibility of my situation; but let consequences be what they may, I hope nothing shall deprive me of the consolation resulting from a conscience void of offence. Yesterday, I was baptized by the Rev. Mr. Ward, and enjoyed the privilege of uniting with the Baptist church in Calcutta in celebrating the sacred ordinance of the Lord's Supper. It was a comfortable day to my soul!"

In a subsequent communication, addressed to his brother, he thus gives vent to his feelings on this subject: "Little did I think, dear brother, when conversing with you respecting Mr. G., that I should so soon belong to the same denomination with him—a denomination which I had thought, in no small degree, reprehensible for party feeling and sectarian conduct. I now believe that these things are not more justly chargeable to the Baptists than other denominations of professed Christians. It has, indeed, been no small trial to me to change my sentiments in a situation so conspicuous and delicate and so highly responsible, though I now conceive it to be a distinguished favor of Divine Providence."

These extracts furnish unequivocal evidence that the subject of this memoir was compelled to unite with the Baptists by the stern demands of duty. He knew not, as he remarked, what would be the consequence; but he was willing to trust in the Lord and do good, believing that necessary guidance and support would be bestowed. Too many instances are found among the professed followers of Christ in which worldly policy or convenience is allowed to control their minds, preventing, if not the performance of known duty, the investigation of its claims. A distinction is made between essentials and non-essentials, and if the former be complied with, it is considered quite pardonable to dispense with the latter. This spirit of compromise is far from being consistent with the devotion which should be cherished by a soul bought with the precious blood of Christ. It is the result of a selfishness which would say, I am willing to do what is essential to secure heavenly bliss, rather than inquire, How shall I best please and honor him who died for me and rose again? All must perceive that the latter question is that which should constantly press upon the conscience and interest the heart of one who justly contemplates his responsibilities to an infinitely gracious Redeemer.

Thus, for conscience' sake, they were separated from those on whom they were dependent for support, and it was determined that Mr. Rice should return to America for the purpose of bringing the interest of pagan nations before the attention of the Baptist denomination. He sailed for this country in March, 1813. Upon his arrival he visited a large number of churches, and succeeded in awakening a lively concern for the perishing heathen. Numerous missionary societies were organized, chiefly by his direct instrumentality; and in the spring of 1814 the Baptist General Convention was formed.

Although he, with Mr. and Mrs. Judson, were at once appointed by the Convention as their missionaries, it was deemed advisable that Mr. Rice should remain in the United States for the purpose of forming auxiliary societies and creating a permanent interest in the mission throughout the entire denomination. Accordingly he visited almost every part of the Union, and was successful beyond the most sanguine expectations of the Board. He continued to prosecute the duties of his agency for several years, and nothing could exceed his ardor and enterprise in this his favorite employ. No surmountable impediments were allowed to obstruct his course, no privations or sufferings were regarded, while he could in any way promote the cause of his Master.

The following extract from one of his annual reports will furnish a correct specimen of his feelings and habits while engaged in this agency:—

"Since the date of my letter of the 19th of June, 1816, I have traveled 6600 miles, in populous and in dreary portions of country, through wildernesses and over rivers, across mountains and valleys, in heat and cold, by day and by night, in weariness, and painfulness, and fastings, and loneliness; but not a moment has been lost for want of health; no painful calamity has fallen to my lot; no peril has closed upon me; nor has fear been permitted to prey on my spirits, nor even inquietude to disturb my peace. Indeed, constantly has the favorable countenance of society toward the great object of the mission animated my hopes, while thousands of condescending personal attentions and benefits to myself and the cause have awakened emotions which it is alike impossible to conceal, or to find terms sufficiently delicate and expressive to declare; and the fact that although so large a portion of the whole time has been unavoidably taken up in passing from place to place, I have, besides many other aids and liberalities, received for the missionary object, in cash and subscription, more than $4000, could not fail to create a confidence of success in the general concern, which nothing but a reverse, most unlikely to occur, can possibly destroy. This fact, too, is the more animating and sustaining, because, while the sum is but little larger than what passed through my hands last year, the time of collecting it has been considerably shorter, and a much smaller proportion of it consists of remittances from mission societies; remittances being this year made by the delegates to the convention. This, therefore, in conjunction with the multiplying of mission societies, especially considering some other things not necessary to be here mentioned, marks decisively a regularly growing increase of evangelic missionary zeal; and who can repress the exclamation, *the Lord hath done great things for us! blessed be the Lord God, who only doeth wondrous things; and let the whole earth be filled with his glory!*"

Among other objects which earlier engaged the attention of Mr. Rice was the cause of education. He saw the necessity of elevating the standard of ministerial improvement among the Baptists, and applied himself with unwearied diligence to this work. In 1821 the Columbian College was chartered, and commenced its operations under most favorable auspices. At that time but few colleges and seminaries of learning had been fostered among the Baptists. It was deemed by Mr. Rice an object of vital importance to rear a central institution of high literary character, which should collect the most promising talents of our country, and afford facilities for the education of those young men who might be licensed by the churches to preach the gospel. The history of this institution is well known. For its welfare he spent the best of his days. Although it has not answered all the expectations of its friends, it has been eminently useful. Many of the best and most talented of our ministry have been educated within its walls.

Some have been inclined to attribute all the reverses of the college to the mismanagement of its agent. That in some things he did wrong, it will not be denied, and it will also be conceded that as a financier he was not skilled; but there were others who equally with him were entitled to a share of the blame. In 1826 the college was separated from the Baptist General Convention, and after this period he ceased to be the authorized agent of the board. He however continued to employ his time and talents in endeavoring to relieve the institution from its heavy embarrassments. To the end of life this object engrossed his chief attention. Still he was not indifferent to the various other plans of exertion connected with the spread of the Redeemer's kingdom. His conversation in the social circle, his pulpit labors, and his addresses at associational and missionary meetings, were all powerfully influential in exciting the spirit of universal philanthropy. Although it may be doubted by some whether he did right in not ultimately joining his early coadjutors in the mission field, there is decided proof that the Baptists of this country owe more to him in regard to the education and mission cause than to any other man. It is questionable whether many other men among us have, with such unwearied assiduity and disinterested devotion, given themselves to the interest of truth and righteousness. In the Southern States, and especially Virginia, his influence will be felt while time endures. From his earliest labors as an agent he was exercising a power over men's minds, and giving them a holy direction. Eternity alone will develop the amount of good which has been effected by his instrumentality.

It will be gratifying to the reader to know that the first impulse to labor for the dying heathen which the devoted Kincaid received, was produced by one of Mr. Rice's sermons. In a letter from

Mr. Kincaid, dated February 12th, 1835, he thus writes: "It is impossible for me to forget the first, and the only time I have ever had the pleasure of seeing you. I heard you preach three times in the course of twenty-four hours, on the subject of carrying the gospel to benighted India. From that day onward I thought of the heathen world; an impression was made which time could not efface, and I began to pray for pagans of every land. Your preaching, which first led me to think of being a missionary among the heathen, is as fresh in my mind as though it was but yesterday."

The limits of this sketch will not permit us much farther to contemplate the labors of this devoted man. From the ample materials collected, the biographer has already, in a distinct volume, selected and arranged facts which cannot fail to interest the reader. A brief reference to the character of Mr. Rice will now be added from the pen of Dr. Jonathan Going: "He possessed a vigorous, discriminating, and comprehensive mind. There were in its constitution the stamina of mental greatness, and it had been well trained by a good education, and enriched by reading, acquaintance with society, and much reflection. He took enlarged and accurate views of all subjects which fell within the circle of his observation.

"He had great decision of character. Indeed this may be said to have been his distinguishing characteristic. He was naturally ardent and adventurous, and felt great confidence in his own powers, and the circumstances in which he was placed tended to fix and consolidate this trait of character. When he returned to this country, and entered on a course of efforts to sustain foreign missions, the enterprise was new to our people, and they were without the lights of experience; all turned their eyes to Mr. R. as a kind of oracle, and his opinions were almost of course adopted And as he became acquainted with those with whom he was associated, it is not improbable that he perceived that generally, however ardently attached to the cause of missions, they would not add much to him in conference, and, of course, that he must consult himself chiefly, in order to accomplish the object before him. Besides, he met with no small measure of opposition from many who should have strengthened his hands and aided his efforts;

and opposition tends greatly to strengthen the decided character. And again, he at length found himself deserted by many who had stricken hands with him, and from whom he seemed to have a right to expect better things; and desertion, too, more than almost any other thing, seems to strengthen such a mind, though it may break down one which is naturally feeble and irresolute.

"We have proof of this trait in his character, not only in his enterprise of awakening the denomination to missionary effort, and his perseverance in efforts to accomplish it amid discouragements, but especially in the pertinacity with which he clung to the college when it was nearly deserted by its friends, and apparently sinking under its misfortunes. And an illustration of it is afforded in an incident which occurred in 1832. While at Providence, Rhode Island, Mr. R. had a slight paralytical affection, and was informed, by the attending physician, that he would probably be soon visited by a recurrence of the shock, which would terminate his life. A friend asked him if he was ready to die. To the inquiry, he replied: 'Yes, though I should like to bring up the college first.' This is almost an instance of

'The ruling passion strong in death.'

It is not improbable that this attribute of character betrayed him into some imprudences, which were in the issue as much regretted by himself as they were by others.

"He was eminently *disinterested.* For twelve years he labored incessantly and laboriously for the small pittance of $400 per annum beyond his traveling expenses. We doubt whether there was an individual in the United States who endured so much exposure, who traveled so extensively, and who at the same time preached so much; and we doubt, also, whether there are more than a very few who could endure so much. To meet the wants of the college, he eventually relinquished all these small savings, together with some $2000 or $3000, which he inherited as a patrimony; so that in 1826 he was without a cent in the world. From that time till his death, he traveled almost constantly to preach and to collect for the college, without the least support from the college or salary from any other institution. Indeed, we believe that he, in a great measure, defrayed his traveling expenses from the sale of a few religious books, while the balance was borne by individual friends, who also furnished him with his wearing apparel. And, at his death, we suspect that his horse and sulky constituted all his earthly treasure, and these he directed to be forwarded to Washington, saying that all belonged to the college. And though some of his enemies maliciously accused him of embezzling funds committed to his charge, and though many doubted the wisdom of some of his plans, it is believed that no man acquainted with the facts even suspected him of speculation or dishonesty. In a word, if we have ever known a disinterested man, that man was Luther Rice.

"Mr. Rice was distinguished for great elasticity of mind, and an exuberant flow of animal feeling. He was apparently always cheerful and always buoyant with hope. We remember hearing his eldest brother say of him: 'Luther always looked for prosperity, and he always expected that to-morrow would be not only a fair day, but a little fairer than to day.' This cheerfulness of temper sometimes led him into slight improprieties, which were spoken of with regret by his friends, and seized on by the enemies of the great cause he advocated as an argument against his piety, though those who knew him best believed him a genuine Christian. For the last few years of his life, however, he was more solemn in his manner of conversation, and uniformly devout in his habits. His cheerfulness was evidently chastened into greater sobriety, and there is every reason to believe that his heart was more fully sanctified. We believe that he admitted and lamented his former levity; it seems to have been his temptation, as despondency, or fretfulness, or pride, is that of others.

"He was a sound divine and an able preacher. He was well-grounded in the great doctrines of the gospel, and exhibited its truths in the proportions they bear to each other in the Scriptures. His sermons were well digested and skillfully arranged. They were usually delivered with a good degree of unction and in an impressive manner. He preached at once to the understanding, the conscience, and the heart. Had he devoted himself to literary or theological studies, he would have shone as a scholar or a theologian. Had he entered exclusively on the ministerial office, he would have acquired distinction as a preacher and a pastor. Or had he returned (according to his intention when he left India) to the missionary field, he would have occupied a rank with the venerated Judson, to whom in very many respects he was in noways inferior. As it was, he did not live in vain. So far from it, that the Baptist denomination in the United States have had scarcely his equal among them, and to few are they more indebted. That he had faults, his friends admit, and he lamented; but he had redeeming qualities, which entitle his character to universal respect; and his memory will be cherished by all who knew him well, and most affectionately by those who knew him best and longest."

After an illness of three weeks, this laborious servant of the Redeemer closed his mortal career at the house of Dr. R. G. Mays, Edgefield District, South Carolina, on Saturday, September 25th, 1836. His remains were deposited near the Pine Pleasant Baptist Meeting-house. The South Carolina Baptist Convention have caused a large marble slab to be placed over his grave.

PETER NELSON.*

WE regret our inability to give more than a very imperfect sketch of ELDER PETER NELSON. It was expected that a memoir would be furnished by one who was well acquainted with the prominent incidents of his life, and admirably qualified to present those incidents in an interesting point of view. This memoir not having been received, and being unwilling to pass over in silence one who contributed much to elevate the character of man, we determined to insert the following hasty sketch. Virginia is much indebted to Elder Nelson, about forty years of his life having been devoted to the arduous and responsible duty of instructing youth; and he lived to see an evidence of the success of his efforts, in the elevated station and valuable services of

---

* Prepared by Thomas H. Fox.

many, the unfolding energies of whose minds received his fostering care.

We have a striking illustration of his high appreciation of intellectual attainments, and the extensive liberality of his heart, in the promptness with which he received, both into his family and school, those who possessed not the means of obtaining an education; and he received a rich reward in the brilliant career, the invaluable efforts in the cause of God and of fallen man, of some who were the recipients of his liberality, as recorded on the pages of this volume. Mr. Nelson, after completing his course of studies at William and Mary College, returned to Hanover, his native county, and entered on the duties of his profession. After a few years, he united himself with the Episcopal church, and was ordained to the work of the ministry. He soon located himself permanently at Wingfield, and established there an academy, whose recollection is intimately associated with some of the greatest men who have adorned the bar or councils of his native State.

About the year 1807, his companion became deeply concerned upon the subject of religion, and anxious to unite herself with the Baptists, a denomination held by Mr. Nelson in utter contempt. In his opposition, he prevented her from visiting their meetings, or even hearing what the "babblers might say." This, however, she never failed to do, whenever an opportunity offered; such was her very great anxiety upon the subject, and her sense of obligation to Jesus Christ. Mr. Nelson, no doubt anxious for the safety of his companion, and desirious to reclaim her from the errors of her way, searched daily the Scriptures for arguments to accomplish his purpose; and, after a very critical examination of them in the original text, (in a knowledge of which he was surpassed perhaps by no scholar of his day,) he became convinced of the necessity of immersion, and forthwith obeyed his Lord, by being buried with her in baptism, which ordinance he received at the hands of Elder Andrew Broaddus, about 1808 or 1809, after having been an Episcopal minister for upwards of twenty years. He died on the fifteenth of February, 1827, as says his physician, like a philosopher and Christian.

JAMES D. M'ALLISTER.

JAMES D. M'ALLISTER, between the years 1823 and 1834, was devotedly engaged in the ministry of reconciliation; most of the time in Eastern Virginia. It is to be regretted that very few particulars respecting his life have been furnished to the biographer, although considerable effort has been made to obtain them.

After he commenced his ministerial career in Pittsylvania, the county which gave him birth, he spent twelve months or more with that eminently devoted man of God, Abner W. Clopton. Being most of the time in the society of his talented instructor, and having the advantage of an excellent library, he greatly improved in general knowledge, and thus, to some extent, was supplied a deficiency occasioned by the want of early education.

During his residence in Charlotte County he assisted Mr. Clopton in the labors of the pulpit, and rapidly grew in the estimation of the people, as destined to become one of the most useful of Virginia's sons. He occupied his time for several years in itinerating, after which, with the advice of his instructor, he accepted the pastorate of the First Baptist Church in Lynchburg, at their special invitation. This position was occupied more than twelve months. Under rather discouraging circumstances he labored with much activity in pastoral employments, devoting his leisure time to study. To some extent he was successful in promoting the welfare of the church.

When the Virginia Baptist Education Society commenced its operations, he was induced to become one of its beneficiaries, for the purpose of still further improving his education. He entered the family of Elder Edward Baptist, under whose tuition the society had determined to place its young men. It is not thought he made much progress while with Mr. Baptist, as he had acquired, by frequent changes of location, such habits as were unfavorable to severe application. Besides, an interesting revival of religion commenced in Powhatan County, in which he was laboriously engaged; indeed he was one of its principal instruments. After having engaged for several months in preaching from house to house, and reaping the field, which was then white unto the harvest, at his request the Education Board were induced to give him an honorable dismission from their care that he might employ himself wholly in the duties of the ministry. He afterwards labored in Richmond and its vicinity, in Charlotte, Halifax, and Bedford, with much success. In the last-named county he closed his days, at the house of Captain B. Sydnor, in the year 1834.

These few allusions to the life of this estimable young man are mostly derived from the memory of the writer. The Lord honored him as the means of much good to many of his fellow-men, although he was removed by death when not more than thirty years of age. The style of his sermons partook of the florid; his language was grammatical, and quite appropriate; while his manner was animated and frequently impassioned. Usually he commanded the deeply interested attention of his auditors. By all who knew him intimately, he was regarded as a devotedly pious servant of Jesus Christ.

CRISPIN DICKENSON.

ALTHOUGH the name of this servant of God was enrolled with the ministry of reconciliation but for a brief season, it will be gratifying to many to preserve a memorial of his character and labors. He was born in Pittsylvania, November 19th, 1787. In his twenty-fifth year he was the subject of conversion, and joined a church in his native county. For several years he remained a private member, exercising a good influence, and adorning the doctrine of God his Saviour. But it was the will of his Master that he should not remain in obscurity. The field of ministerial labor was spread open before him, and he was invited to enter it. He was ordained March 24, 1827, and took charge of Locust Union Church, on Pig River, and Ararat, on Sandy River.

For these churches he labored with commendable fidelity, and was not left without tokens of Divine favor. The word preached was made the wisdom of God, and the power of God unto salvation. In both of these churches, within two years after his ordination, a revival of religion was experienced. The dormant powers of the saints were aroused. Their long-neglected harps were taken down from the willows, and a holy activity began to characterize all their exertions. As a necessary consequence, an interest in favor of eternal things was soon awakened among the unconverted. God's blessing descended, and the cry was heard, "what shall I do to be saved?" Numbers were brought to understand and rejoice in the plan of salvation through the atonement of Christ, and were added to the churches.

During this time of ingathering, ELDER DICKENSON, in season and out of season, labored in preaching the word, while his talents continued manifestly to improve. His influence among the churches over which he presided, and in the Roanoke Association, more and more enlarged. But he was not long allowed to retain his station in the field of labor. The Lord, in his inscrutable wisdom, determined to summon him to the world of spirits. How long he was sick is not known by the writer, but in his last hours he manifested much composure, willingly resigning himself into the hands of his Redeemer. He died October 28th, 1832.

JAMES O. ALDERSON.

JAMES O. ALDERSON, the youngest son of George and Sarah Alderson, and grandson of the Rev. John Alderson, was born in Kenhawa County, October, 1800. At four years of age his father died, leaving a wife and seven children; shortly after the death of his father, his mother removed to Monroe County, and settled on Greenbrier River; in this neighborhood he lived with his mother until he was about nineteen years of age. Possessing a weak constitution, and having by this time acquired a limited education, he left his mother in the care of an older brother, and commenced teaching school. During his earlier years he was much exercised on the subject of religion; but mingling with the world, these impressions would wear away, and he would again and again seem much carried away with its pleasures. Shortly after his marriage, which was in his twenty-fifth year, he again began to think seriously upon eternity. He was often awakened to a sense of his condition, and was at length brought deeply to feel the necessity of a change in his heart. In his twenty-seventh year he became a member of the Baptist church. Subject to melancholy, and often doubting his own acceptance, he still manifested the purpose of his heart to follow his Redeemer. From the first of his profession of religion he seemed much impressed with the condition of his fellow-sinners, and determined to devote himself to the great work of inviting them to Christ. Immediately after his baptism he commenced and continued exhorting sinners within the bounds of the church for twelve months, when he was licensed to preach, and was ordained at the Greenbrier Association, September, 1830.

From the period of his ordination he became a most zealous laborer in the vineyard of the Lord. He engaged as a missionary in the Geeenbrier Association, under the direction of the Central Committee, and never did any man more rapidly improve. During the year 1831 his efforts were attended with evident tokens of Divine approbation. Many seals were given to his ministry. Between eighty and one hundred were baptized by him in this year. Through the inclement season of the winter months he continued his indefatigable labors, though his constitution was evidently declining. He ceased not to preach until within about two weeks before his death, when he returned home scarcely able to sit up. He died of consumption, the 13th of April, 1832.

In the early part of his last illness he seemed to have the most humbling sense of the depravity of his heart and the infinite purity of God, which filled him with doubts and fears as to his state; these, however, gave way, after a day or two, to a calm serenity, and humble confidence in his Redeemer, which continued with him to the last. He left a wife and three children to mourn his death; and long will his removal be mourned and his memory cherished by the churches that enjoyed his short but useful labors.

RUFUS CHANDLER.

RUFUS CHANDLER was born in Pomfret, Windham County, Connecticut, May 26th, 1785, of parents who occupied a very respectable station in society. At an early age he gave evidence of possessing a vigorous mind, and an ardent desire to acquire useful knowledge. His father hailed these indications with delight, and determined to afford his son the means of gratifying his desire. He was sent to the best schools in his native town until he attained his sixteenth year, when he left the paternal roof for Plainfield Academy. In this institution he pursued his studies; and at the expiration of one year, his friends considering him prepared for an advantageous entrance into college, he removed to New Haven, and with credit entered the freshman class of Yale College in his seventeenth year. At the expiration of four years the degree of A.M. was conferred upon him, having previously obtained that of A.B.

In the spring of 1806 he was invited by several intelligent gentlemen to take charge of a school in Hanover County, Virginia; and having embraced the offer, continued in their immediate neighborhood for several years. In the summer of 1812 he became a Christian, and, recognizing his duty, he determined forthwith to obey his Lord, by being buried with him in baptism, which ordinance was administered by Elder Andrew Broaddus. Previous to descending into the water, Elder Chandler addressed a large assembly on the vital importance of religion, and gave his own views on the mode and design of baptism, as derived from a critical examination of the original text.

In the fall of this year he was united in marriage to Miss Nancy W. Trevillian, daughter of Mr. Thomas Trevillian, of Caroline County; and in the year 1815 he removed to that county, with a view to a permanent location. Here he prosecuted his profession for several years, receiving quite a liberal patronage; but, admonished by declining health, he abandoned it for the more active pursuits of agriculture. On the 13th of June, 1830, he was ordained to the gospel ministry, by Elders Spilsbe Woolfolk, Henry Keeling, and Eli Ball. It has been already observed that Elder Chandler's declining health had induced him to abandon a sedentary life for the more active pursuits of agriculture, and while we have every reason to believe that the change of his habits contributed to his stay among us, yet the seeds of disease were never entirely eradicated. At the time of his ordination he no doubt entertained the hope that he would be enabled to enter upon the arduous and responsible duties connected with the ministry. This hope was but partially realized: the church at Burruss', however, with which he had associated himself on his removal to Caroline, being at this time deprived of the services of a regular pastor, solicited his aid, and was regularly supplied by him, whenever his health would permit, until they obtained the services of a pastor. During the time Elder Chandler served the church at Burruss', a revival commenced which continued for some months, and in which sixty or eighty were added to their number.

Elder Chandler was not only a classical scholar, but a literary man; so far from supposing a collegiate course embraces everything necessary to be learned, he considered it only a foundation upon which to erect a superstructure of useful knowledge; and, possessing a talent for investigation, he made considerable attainments in science. He was very remarkable for neatness and order in all his business; the most casual observer could not fail to admire the systematic arrangement of everything around him. His attention, however, was more particularly directed to literary subjects. His library comprised some of the most valuable works, especially those connected with theology.

Much of Elder Chandler's time was devoted to the study and critical examination of the Scriptures; and, considering them as the only infallible standard of faith and practice, he never failed to urge on all around him the propriety of consulting them. His preaching was not very animated, but always instructive, and occasionally quite impressive. He was a warm advocate of benevolent effort, a liberal contributor to the different societies organized for that purpose, and earnest in his endeavors to interest others in their behalf. The temperance cause found in him an ardent supporter; and on all suitable occasions he feelingly portrayed the miseries resulting from intemperance, and forcibly sustained the views of the advocates of abstinence.

It is very certain that the last years of Elder Chandler's life were characterized by increased devotion to God, zeal in his cause, and anxious solicitude for the salvation of dying man; and as an evidence that this impression is not confined to the writer, he will here introduce a paragraph or two from the obituary notice written by Elder Andrew Broaddus, in which he says: "The latter part of his Christian profession shone with much more brilliance than the former part. But if the early stage appeared more dim and cloudy, how pleasant was it to find, that after a season of special revival, which he seems to have experienced, the light broke forth, and continued to shine on through the infirmities of nature, till death dismissed him to a brighter state! His retired habits, and his frequent bodily infirmities, seems to have circumscribed his ministerial operations, and confined them to narrow limits, but his preaching was of the intelligent and evangelical order, and by no means destitute of a degree of spiritual unction; while his zeal for the prosperity of religion manifested itself in more than verbal professions. Extracts from some of his letters would show how desirous he was to encourage his brethren in the work of faith and the labor of love, while bodily indisposition prevented his taking a part in active exercises. 'He was,' says an intimate friend of his, 'one of the most scrupulously exact persons, in all his transactions with men, I ever knew.' And along with this disposition, it may be added, there went a cordial sociability toward his particular friends, that naturally drew forth a return of affectionate esteem. Of this, the writer of this article, among others, may be allowed to bear witness."

During his last illness he frequently spoke of death with that composure of feeling, that serenity of mind, which can be experienced only by those who profess the blessed hope of a resurrection to life. To a particular friend, he said, "We have spent many happy moments together; I hope we shall spend many more in heaven." Just before his death, shaking hands with his eldest son, he uttered his last articulate words: "Farewell! I am going home." Thus died, at Little Yale, in the County of Caroline, on Tuesday, 18th of July, 1837, in the fifty-third year of his age, Elder Rufus Chandler, leaving behind him an afflicted wife and five children to mourn the bereaving stroke, and a circle of friends and brethren in whose recollections his name will be embalmed.

JOSEPH GOODE.

JOSEPH GOODE was the son of Elder John Goode, and was born in Chesterfield County, April 4th, 1776. He had serious impressions at the age of eight or ten years, and would often hold conversation with his brothers on the subject of religion. Resolutions to seek the salvation of his soul were made, but would relapse again into a state of unconcern. Being well brought up, he scarcely ever, if at all, committed an act known to any that would have placed him under the censure of a well-disciplined church.

In 1799 a revival commenced in the bounds of Skinquarter Church. He had long been waiting on the ministration of the Word without deep feeling, but about this time, at a night-meeting, the Spirit of the Lord reached his heart, and he was compelled to cry aloud with anguish. He extended his hand to a brother, with whom he had freely conversed on eternal things, and assured him he must turn or perish. His convictions were deeply pungent. In the fall of 1799, while securing his crop, deliverance was realized. His countenance bespoke the change, and constrained his friends to believe he had passed from death unto life. He soon made a public profession of religion, and was baptized by Elder Charles Forsee, attaching himself to Skinquarter Church. Shortly after he was chosen deacon of the church.

After some time he reached the conclusion that there was something required at his hands in warning his fellow-beings of their dangerous situation. He soon commenced the work of exhorting them in the name of his Master, and, after a few years, was ordained to the gospel ministry by Elders Forsee, Martin, and Leigh. Feeling the great responsibility of his station, he would sometimes, in the early part of his labors, desist, requesting others to take his place. His talents or acquirements were not such as to command the admiration of the highly cultivated. He was, however, gifted as an experimental preacher, and, at times, was exceedingly forcible in the elucidation of doctrinal subjects, and pungent in his appeals to the conscience. His countenance usually lighted up with a smile as he dwelt on the lovely character of Jesus and recommended him as the Saviour of the lost.

In his intercourse with men his uprightness of conduct gave evidence that he loved the law of God. He was much beloved by many and respected by all. Though his ministerial career was short, it was well spent. He seemed to have some presentiments of his approaching dissolution, and communicated them to his family before he was arrested by disease. On Friday, the 13th of October, 1823, he was confined by a sudden attack of sickness, and in little more than a week his spirit took its flight to a better world. On his dying bed he enjoyed much of the love of Jesus, and was confident of dwelling with him forever.

NOAH DAVIS.

How mysterious are the appointments of Him who worketh all things after the counsel of his own will! Verily, he is a God that hideth himself! His footsteps are in the great deep! Among the intricacies of Divine Providence is to be numbered the early removal by death of godly and useful ministers of Jesus Christ. If the wisest and best of human beings should be allowed to decide, it would be thought more conducive to the interest of man and the glory of God to retain able ministers of the New Testament until their physical natures were worn out, and there was no further capacity for efficient service. It would be one feature of the economy which they might devise, to "spare useful lives." So rarely is the cause of Christ advocated by men who unite eminent attainments in holiness with a high order of intellect, that it would be thought unwise soon to release them from their stewardship. But as the heavens are higher than the earth, so are God's ways higher than our ways, and his thoughts higher than our thoughts. He is himself the author of all those gifts which the church has received. He entertains an unchanging regard for her interests, and his wisdom is as perfect as his love. While therefore the precise design of such removals are unknown to us, we may still believe them right and rejoice that the Lord God omnipotent reigneth.

Momentary sadness came over many a heart when it was announced that Noah Davis was no more. The importance of the station he filled; the loveliness of his character and the extended influence which he had gained in our denomination, all rendered the bereavement deeply painful. But he has gone to his reward, and his Master, whom he served, can multiply laborers an hundred-fold and send them into the field. This mournful event will have resulted in good if it has, in any measure, begotten in the churches an humble dependence on the Lord of the harvest to supply the deficiency which everywhere prevails. It is believed, too, that the bright example of Davis will long exert its influence among men. He being dead, yet speaketh. In the brief record which this memoir will furnish, the desire is cherished to hold up, for the imitation of all, his heavenly spirit and self-denying activity.

The subject of this sketch was a native of Worcester County, Maryland. He was born July 28th, 1802. His parents were eminently pious members of the Baptist church. In their family arrangements they adopted that course which was most likely to result in the eternal welfare of their offspring. Noah, their first-born, was the object of special anxiety, and his infant mind received impressions which were never erased. Doubtless many a prayer ascended from her who watched over his childish years and who early taught him to think of spiritual realities. She, like Hannah, had given this child to God, and was strong in the faith, giving glory to Him. With unwavering confidence her heart rested on the assurance that when he was old he would not forget the instructions he had received. Happy is the man who is born of such parents. Though piety be not hereditary, the influence of pious counsels and example must be salutary. Such was the effect on him to whom reference is now made. He always considered it one of the richest blessings conferred on him to be the child of devout parents. In alluding to this subject he says: "I was the first child the Lord gave my parents, and my mother, who before my birth had dedicated me to Him, named me Noah, believing that I also should be made a preacher of righteousness. Of course, no pains were spared by my parents to instruct me in religious truth and bring me up in the fear of the Lord. Though they had the grief to see me, like others, taking the downward course and drinking in iniquity like water, yet my mother held fast her first impression, that I should be ransomed by electing love and made to preach the word of God to dying men."

When quite a child he gave indications of natural sprightliness of mind. His active, restless spirit sometimes caused painful fears to arise in the bosom of his pious parents concerning his spiritual welfare. They saw the influence of a depraved heart united with a warm temperament, and they dreaded the result when he should be brought in contact with the temptations of the world. As he advanced in years he was quite disposed to indulge in ambitious projects. He seemed eager to engage in great and difficult enterprises. He often thought and spoke of casting himself amid the perils of military life. The fires of patriotism burned in his youthful bosom and he panted for the field of battle. But He, in whose hands are the hearts of all men, was preparing him for other employments. It was to be his honorable lot to unfurl the banner of the Prince of peace. His was to be a bloodless warfare. "Thanks be to God," said he, after his conversion, "that I have undertaken, in his name, to fight for another kingdom than that of this world, and to serve under the High Captain of salvation."

From earliest childhood he manifested a fondness for reading, and would frequently separate himself from his youthful companions and spend hours in the perusal of some favorite book. At school he was studious. There was, however, at that time, but little promise of succeeding as a public speaker. "While at school," he remarks, "whether from diffidence or some other cause, I could at no time take a part in the exercise of public speaking, a proof that I was not then preparing for my present avocation." His education, while with his parents, was such as could be obtained in the common schools of the country.

He was not more than sixteen years of age when he was engaged as a merchant's clerk in the City of Philadelphia. The individuals by whom he was employed were pious men, and scrupulously guarded the morals of those placed under their charge. The parents of young Davis, in seeking a situation for their son, were not willing to disregard his spiritual good, but sought and found employers who feared the Lord. This is a subject concerning which all parents should be solicitous. On the connection in business which an inexperienced youth forms may depend his whole future destiny. Especially is it important, in this particular, to exercise caution when young men exchange the simple habits of a country life for those of towns. So numerous and fascinating are the temptations of a city that the unwary, without the restraints of some judicious guardian, are liable to be lured into the path of ruin.

Previous to his removal to Philadelphia, he was not the subject of any peculiar religious feeling. Notwithstanding the deep concern which his parents had always evinced for his salvation, he remained a thoughtless youth, without hope and without God in the world. But he had not long resided in Philadelphia before the influence of truth was felt. The gentleman with whom he lived insisted (much against his inclination) that he should regularly attend public worship. Almost imperceptibly was he led to the discovery of the exceeding sinfulness of sin. He thus describes some of the leading circumstances which resulted in his conversion. Speaking of his settlement in Philadelphia, he says: "Prior to this time I had no abiding impression of my state by nature, nor of the awfulness of my standing before God. It was in Philadelphia that my vile heart first revolted against attending strictly on the worship of the Sabbath day. I was now compelled to labor throughout the week, and surely, thought I, Sunday at least may be my own. But in vain were my murmurings. My respected employers knew the worth of immortal souls, and acted upon the good resolution that they and their's should serve the Lord."

The account of his first exercises in religion is thus given by himself: "I cannot remember any particular sermon that had a more than usual effect upon my mind. If my mind was ever operated upon by the Holy Spirit, it was in a manner silent and calm. The first material change of life, that I remember, took place in the winter of 1818–19, when I found myself almost imperceptibly led to the practice of daily prayer, and on Sabbath afternoons I spent my time in reading and prayer. Under this change of my views and habits, I began to hear the word of God with increased attention, and obtained a better comprehension than I had previously had of Divine things. I began to acquire a greater relish for the services of the sanctuary, and attended upon them more from choice than compulsion. The administration of the ordinance of baptism, in Sansom Street Church, had several times a very powerful effect upon my mind. Shortly after this I wrote to my parents, informing them of my religious exercises and of my desire to become a member of the church of Christ. They were the first to whom I made known my feelings and sentiments in relation to the concerns of my soul. I mentioned my exercises to Mr. Fassit, at the same time requesting him to state my case to Dr. Staughton, who was then pastor of the Baptist Church in Sansom Street. This he did, giving the doctor an account of my experience, with which he appeared to be satisfied. After examination, the church consented that I should be baptized at their next regular meeting, which took place July 4th, 1819. I had made known my intention to be baptized on that day, and to my surprise my father came from his distant residence to Philadelphia at that time almost purposely to witness this scene. Indeed it appeared to be one of a very affecting kind to him. In the afternoon of that day I was received into the visible church by the right hand of fellowship, presented by Dr. Staughton, the pastor, and for the first time partook of the Lord's Supper. Oh what a day to me! With what regret should I remember how poorly I have sustained the profession then assumed. In the church of which I became a member I found the interchange of religious affection most delightful; the services of the sanctuary became interesting, and I could sing—

'There my best friends, my kindred dwell.'"

Thus was he held by a way which he knew not. His subsequent history proves the reality of the change he professed when he was buried with Christ in baptism. Having recognized himself as saved by grace, he felt anxious to be employed in any way which might be conducive to the Divine honor. His soul was moved, too, with compassion for dying men. He saw them exposed to eternal burnings, and longed to warn them of their danger. Though his prospects in worldly things were encouraging, he could not be satisfied to remain in Philadelphia. Those with whom he lived cheerfully relinquished his services, and he returned to his father's house, resolved to embrace every opportunity of speaking in behalf of his Master's cause. By letter, he united with the church in Salisbury, Maryland. It was soon perceived that he possessed useful talents, and he was licensed to preach July 9th, 1820.

At the time he became a licentiate, he was only eighteen years of age. Although he had obtained from various sources much valuable information, he was impressed with the importance of still further improvement to qualify him thoroughly for the work of his ministry. In the following November he joined the Literary and Theological Institution under the care of Dr. Staughton and Professor Chase. When the Columbian College went into operation, in 1821, he removed to Washington, and there continued his studies. He did not remain until he completed his education. Although he was making commendable progress, and might have risen to eminence in scholastic attainments, yet his ardent desire to enter the field of labor prevailed over the love of literary distinction. He refers to this subject in the following language: "I entered the freshman class, and looked forward to the end of my course of study, when I should go forth to preach the gospel wherever my Master might send me. But as to preach the gospel was the leading motive of my heart, I began to look on the intervening years of study with some degree of uneasiness, especially as the directors of my education had determined to give me a thorough course, which would require four or five years more. I resolved, therefore, to leave college at the end of the current term, and to throw myself on the providence of God, with entire devotion to his work."

With reference to this particular circumstance, and the possibility that some students might be disposed injudiciously to imitate the example of Mr. Davis, Professor Knowles makes the following observations: "Soon after he entered the freshman class, he resolved to leave college. His health was not firm, and he feared that he could not prosecute, to the end, the course of study which he had commenced. He acccordingly left the institution in the summer of 1823. This measure, I may say with entire affection for his memory, did not meet with the approbation of many of his best friends. My dear brother acted conscientiously, but I thought, and still think, that he mistook, in that instance, the path of duty. I should not now allude to it, were I not fearful that his example might have some influence on other young men who may be impatient of study, and may rush into the field without his talents, piety, and zeal. It is no proof that he judged rightly, because he has been useful. Such a man could not fail to be useful in almost any circumstances. But how much more useful might he not have been, if his powerful mind had been thoroughly disciplined and amply furnished with good learning! That he has died young, is no argument. All students are liable to die before they complete their studies. Many have died in college, or at the theological seminary, or in a year or two after their settlement as pastors. Was it, therefore, unwise to spend any time in preparatory study? The plain rule of duty is, to aim at the greatest usefulness and to make the most thorough preparation which God's providence permits. The length of our lives is a point which God decides at his pleasure. It alters not our duty. We may live many years, and we must not disqualify ourselves for prolonged usefulness by calculating on a short course and making a stinted provision. If a man is to die young, there is so much the more need that he increase his power as much as possible, so as to do much in a little time. Life is not to be measured by years, but by the amount of useful labor done; and if a man can so multiply his talents as to do in one year more than he could otherwise accomplish in five, the church will be a gainer, though he should die early; and his education, we have reason to suppose, will make him a fitter instrument for his Master's use in the next world."

There is some reason to believe that Mr. Davis himself considered his abandonment of study premature, and regretted that he had taken this step. In 1825, he addressed a letter to one of his young brethren in the ministry, urging him to obtain an education before he made a permanent settlement. The following is a brief extract: "I have known some very eminent ministers to regret that, when young in the ministry, they preached so much, and devoted so little of their time to reading, meditation, etc., that their minds might be stored before they commenced dealing out so largely. The more I preach, the more I feel of the necessity of mental cultivation. We cannot expect a great abundance of fruit from ground which has not been well tilled, even though by nature it may be rich. Many young preachers start off as soon as commissioned, as if the world were to be taken by storm. They run well for a season, do good, I hope; but soon we find them, when the particular season for improvement has gone by, settled in some obscure corner, and having to contend with difficulties which keep them at one stage of knowledge and acceptance all their lives; if, indeed, they do not rather decline in these things. 'Tis obviously our duty then to endeavor to secure such a knowledge of our implements at the beginning, and the best way of using them, that we may become workmen that need not to be ashamed. I know that working only gives the power of doing it well, if the necessary qualifications be possessed; but still instruction is essential. He who works all and does not stop to take lessons of the master, cannot attain the art to perfection. We are authorized to covet earnestly the best gifts."

It will not be for a moment questioned that the leading motive which constrained him to leave college was the promotion of the Redeemer's glory. It was not mere indolence, nor was it a desire to enjoy the honors of the Christian ministry. His love to Christ and to immortal souls, like an overwhelming torrent, bore him away. From his earliest connection with the institution, while he applied himself to study, he could not rest unless he was engaged in some good work. The subjoined testimony of Professor Knowles, who was a fellow-student, and one of his most valued friends, deserves a place here. "The impression made by Mr. Davis on his fellow-students was rapid, deep, and complete. There was a transparency in his character which showed at once all its parts and proportions. There was in him no guile. The impression which he made at first was never changed. Respect for his understanding, entire confidence in his piety, and love for the virtues of his heart, were the immediate and permanent feelings of his fellow-students.

"His progress in study was rapid. His mind was strong, clear, and energetic. He was more distinguished for soundness of understanding than for activity of imagination or delicacy of taste. He possessed more aptitude for mathematics than for languages. He would have penetrated more easily the discriminations of metaphysics than the beauties of the classics. He would have grasped more eagerly and successfully the massive doctrines of theology than the refined graces of elegant literature. But the speedy interruption of his studies before he had fully acquired the habits of a student, has prevented a decided judgment respecting his intellectual character.

"While at Philadelphia his zeal and decision displayed themselves. He supplied for several months a destitute congregation in the neighborhood of the city. His mind and his hands were always busy in his Master's service.

"When the institution was removed to Washington City, in the autumn of 1821, he removed thither, and continued his studies preparatory to admission into the freshman class, it being the decided opinion of his most judicious friends that it was his duty to aim at a complete education.

"Here he manifested the same desire for usefulness, the same single-hearted surrender of himself and of all his powers, to the service of his Saviour. He preached frequently; he visited the poor families in the neighborhood of the college; he was punctual and devout at the prayer-meetings of the students; he was one of the most useful members of the Society for Missionary Inquiry. The writer had the pleasure of being associated with him in sustaining a Sabbath-school for blacks, where a considerable number of the poor slaves, of all ages, from childhood to threescore years, were taught to read the Scriptures."

Shortly after he left college, he united in marriage with Miss Mary Young, a lady in all respects qualified to assist in the toils of the Christian ministry. For a short time he labored in the County of Accomac, Virginia. The Lord was with him, and rendered his ministry greatly efficient in turning transgressors from their sins. He was also very useful among his brethren. The churches had become cold and barren under the withering influence of Antinomianism. Wherever he went, his scriptural exhibitions of truth, his simplicity and zeal, united with the most unaffected piety, commanded the attention and won the esteem of all who heard him.

From Accomac he removed to Norfolk, and became pastor of the Baptist church in that borough. His brief residence here was attended with evident marks of Divine approbation. With untiring diligence he applied himself to pastoral duties. But he could not circumscribe his influence within this narrow boundary. His benevolence prompted him, like his Divine Master, to go about doing good. There are some who are content to promote human happiness only when placed in the midst of exciting circumstances. They are not willing to lay aside their own convenience in showing kindness to others. No pains are taken to seek out the objects of wretchedness and to administer relief. Theirs is the charity which says to the sufferer, Be thou warmed and clothed, while it furnishes not the requisite relief. But the philanthropy of Davis was of a purer and more heavenly kind. He was ready to labor and to suffer for the good of his fellow-men. "The world needs," he said, "all the instrumentality that has ever been at any time in operation, or can possibly be brought to act upon it, to be continued until it shall attain the degree of knowledge, holiness, and happiness which will mark the state of the millennium. Let us not be weary in well-doing, for in due season we shall reap if we faint not."

He was the poor man's friend; among other objects to which he directed his attention was the improvement of seamen. His active spirit was not satisfied until he had awakened a sympathy in the public mind in behalf of this neglected class of men. His efforts resulted in the formation of the Seamen's Friends' Society. A very excellent selection of hymns for mariners was compiled and published by him. In all the plans of Christian benevolence he took an active part.

He became ardently attached to the church over which he exercised the pastoral rule. This affection was reciprocated. He cherished a deep concern for their advancement in knowledge and holiness, and for the conversion of sinners. During a season of general indifference, he writes: "Religion appears to pass along without much excitement. I pray the Lord to revive his work in my heart and the hearts of all his ministers and children. Then generally sinners begin to be alarmed. Here, however, hell appears not to terrify them, nor heaven to charm; they walk according to the course of this world; we are much too lukewarm; may the Lord pity us."

The following extracts from letters written during his residence in Norfolk, afford evidence of deep personal piety. They were addressed to his wife:—

"January 14th, 1826. Had one of the best times in preaching I have had for two months. I hope the Lord will make it useful. I am nothing; his grace must work, or it will be all in vain. But he will bless the faithful labors of those whom he sends, replenishes, and upholds. Oh that I might know the power of his grace on my heart more! Have had sore work in my soul for a day or two. If I am a child of God, 'tis strange, truly a wonder. My lusts rebel and bring my soul into bondage. O my dear, pray for a poor wretch, that I may not, after preaching to others, myself become a castaway! What grace it takes to save such a sinner! a brand *plucked* out of the fire. Let others depend on what they will, it will be great grace, nothing short of it, will save me. Oh that we could look more at Christ and his cross, and there become crucified ourselves! As Whitefield says, 'the old man dies hard, but die he must.' Amen."

"April 24, 1826. Have felt a good deal of late as if I should soon be called home to glory, but am willing to stay if I can be instrumental in promoting the cause of my Master. Have said little about it, knowing the thought gives you pain. But why, my dearest, why keep me a day or an hour from the enjoyment of supreme bliss and never-failing glory? To be with Christ is far better than to be toiling with an imperfect and sinful body. But his counsel shall stand. Neither of us shall go a day or moment before our work, which he means to do for, in, and by us, is done. Tarry his leisure then. My soul is almost in raptures at the thought of being forever with Jesus. Why not think and talk of heaven more? Surely it would make us more spiritually-minded, more diligent in filling up our short stay with service for God, and less appalled at the idea of change. But it must come. He that shall come, will come, and will not tarry. Even so, Lord Jesus, come quickly. This is the way to begin heaven, and the song of free, sovereign, everlasting, unchangeable love. There is my hope. Whom have I in heaven but thee, O Lord my Saviour, and who on earth is desirable besides thee, or in comparison of thee? Surely you are willing for me to love Christ above all. Yes, love him yourself, for he is altogether lovely. He deserves the first place in our hearts."

"July 28, 1827. It has probably occurred to you, my love, that this is my birth-day. It is now twenty-five years since I began to live on the earth. And for what, save a little that has been done in the last eight years, and that, not I, but the grace of God which has been with me, there is nothing on which I can look with any proper satisfaction. And how have these years been stained with sin. Yea, I daily deserve the lowest hell:

'The sins of one most righteous day
Might plunge us in despair.'

But having obtained the help of God, I continue to this day a monument of mercy and but a feeble advocate for the truth. My soul is under much darkness, or if there is light, there is want of heat, and, which is worse, darkness or coldness? I do desire to begin to live for God. I have begun to die, and the destroyer will be here. Days, and years, and lives pass away like a flood. Oh to be a Christian! By the death of Jesus, to conquer and rise to heaven!"

"July 28, 1829. Although I wrote to you yesterday, I feel like indulging in the same pleasure on my *birth-day*. Its occurrence reminds me that I am twenty-seven years old, and this month finds me *ten* years a professor of hope in Jesus; *nine* a minister of the glorious gospel, *six* years your affectionate husband, and my boy one year old. How many of the more important events of my pilgrimage have been crowded into this month! and where will another twenty seven years bring me? Most probably to the judgment-seat, and, I trust, though of all others most unworthy, to a dwelling-place at my Saviour's right hand.

'O glorious hour, O blest abode,
I shall be near and like my God,
And flesh and sense no more control
The sacred pleasures of the soul.'

Ten of my years I have been called a Christian. How unworthily I have lived, Jesus knows. On the arms and promise of his mercy I cast myself and mine. That he gives blessings to the undeserving and vile is the only reason we can have for hope. Oh that he may forgive all my sins! and do you, my love, forgive all my deficiencies of good conduct toward you. Too often have I offended God and the generation of his chosen, and I desire forgiveness, not only from him, but from all the world. What incentives should conscious deficiencies be to greater diligence in doing! His will, who so soon will bring us to judgment. I feel ashamed and grieved that with the Bible in my hands, and eternity before me, I have lived so negligently. And I dare not promise to do better for the time to come. Without Christ I can do nothing, and I have not fully proved the truth of the words, 'Through Christ which strengtheneth me, *I can do all things.* I have been praying for more grace to do his will as an heir of glory, that I may no longer grieve the Holy Spirit, and may not give any offence to the church of God. Lord help me, for thy help I need."

A short extract will be given from his diary: "January 3d. Expounded Matt. vii. 1–12, this evening. Very few at meeting. Had not much liberty in speaking. Fear my people (the church in Norfolk) see some defect in me which renders my labors useless to them. Lord help us to search and see. Oh search us thyself, and try us, and see if there be any evil way in us, and lead us in the way everlasting! I feel my very great deficiency, and instead of being surprised that so few come, I ought rather to be so, that any attend my ministry. Fear I shall be left to myself at some time, to mortify my pride and self-sufficiency. O thou whose compassions never fail, look in pity on my soul! Oh give me thy Spirit, and let it be poured out from on high on the people!"

"July 10th. A week ago from this completed the third year of my married life. I thank God for giving me such a companion. Our pathway has not been free from thorns, but these we must expect in the wilderness of this world. We have had some difficulties, and were bereaved of our first-born, but the Lord has shown us so much of his goodness and mercy amid all, that we have to account them as matters of thankfulness, instead of discontent; we have not learned as much as we probably ought and might from his corrections; but we hope they have not passed by as wholly unprofitable. No doubt we shall see the time when they shall be numbered among the greatest mercies of our lives.

'Ye fearful saints, fresh courage take;
The clouds ye so much dread
Are big with mercies, and will break
With blessings on your head.'"

It has been already intimated that Elder Davis's residence in Norfolk was of short duration. To his suggestions the Baptists are indebted for the existence of the Baptist General Tract Society. In a letter written to a brother in Washington, dated February 14th, 1824, he thus exhibits his sentiments on the subject: "I have been thinking for some time how a tract society can be gotten up in Washington, which shall hold the same place among Baptists that the American Tract Society does among Congregationalists. I now feel very much the necessity of having tracts to scatter in the waste places. It is a plan of doing good scarcely thought of among Baptists."

Such was the influence of his appeals, that a meeting was called, and on the 25th of February, 1824, the society was formed. Under the judicious management of Mr. George Wood, the society continued to advance until, at his suggestion and the advice of others, it was located in the City of Philadelphia, and Mr. Davis was invited to the management of its concerns. This office being accepted, there was now opened before him a new and interesting field of labor. The position was high and commanding. It afforded the opportunity of exerting a salutary influence over the whole denomination. Perhaps nowhere could he have found so wide a scope for the employment of his talents, and few men were as well qualified as he to occupy the station. He was pre-eminently fitted for the work. His mind was of that energetic cast, that he was able to grasp and control the weighty interests of a national institution. His views were enlarged, his aims lofty and noble. Had he been a mere worldling, he would have found himself in his proper element, when engaged in grand and important enterprises. But besides his natural talent for business, the heart of Davis had felt the expansive power of Christian benevelence. He knew how to sympathize with the woes of a guilty world, and he aimed to relieve them. For this he entered the agency of the Tract Society. "His heart," says Mr. Knowles, "was in the work; a qualification without which no man ever accomplished much. He possessed unusual talents for business. He was active, affable, and prompt. He spoke with fluency, and when excited, with much power and eloquence. His full, loud, and sonorous voice; his manly person; his simple, direct, and forcible diction, gave him great advantages in preaching, and especially in occasional addresses."

The following reference to his efforts and success in the agency is from the pen of Mr. William T. Brantley, who was intimately associated with him in the operations of the Tract Society: "The removal of our departed brother from Norfolk, and the transfer of the tract operations from Washington to Philadelphia, at his instance, were among the last important changes in his life. Here he entered the field of labor with all his might. The little interest, which had almost subsided into non-existence, began, in his hands, to gain strength and to assume a new character. He enlarged the plan, reduced to method its disjointed parts, roused our dormant energies, and infused into the whole concern a new spirit of action. His habits of good management and economy were carried into this service; his capacity and readiness in shaping into practicable dimensions a complex system were of admirable use in a business consisting of so many minor details. But the rapid growth of the society, the increasing demand for its publications, the extension of its operations to almost every part of this Union, will evince, with more force than we can command, the value of those labors bestowed upon it by its assiduous and intelligent agent. The estimate of his usefulness must not be restricted to the particular avocation which we are now considering. Besides his main business of preaching by means of tracts, he sounded the gospel abroad in many places where he traveled, and in others he preached more statedly, with great effect. He collected and published many useful facts connected with the statistics of our denomination. He was ready to aid by his presence and countenance every good proposition; and was always among the first to contribute such means as were at his disposal for the promotion of useful expedients.

"His mind was naturally capable of great research. He could divest difficult subjects of their obscurity; could see readily through the mazes of an intricate proposition; could arrange and methodize a multifarious business; and conduct doubtful plans to a good result. Many of his addresses from the pulpit—and on occasions connected with public objects—were distinguished by much force and discrimination. They will be long remembered by many whose hearts were deeply affected by his moving appeals."

In one respect Elder Davis was peculiarly well qualified for the office he filled. He entertained scriptural views of Christian benevolence. In all his correspondence and public addresses he urges the duty of ransomed sinners to work for God. He considered the church as belonging to Christ, and sought to rouse the denomination of which he was a member to regard their obligations. Referring to this subject, he says: "There is great responsibility resting on the Baptists of the United States; for 'to whomsoever much is given, of him shall be much required.' At least two millions of the population of this country are so connected with us that the work of preaching the gospel to them must be done mainly through our efforts. Many millions in other portions of the earth are accessible to the ministers of Christ, to whom men should be sent from us with the Word of Life. Are we exerting ourselves to fulfill our duty to these dying millions? Have we begun to do what we can and ought to do for them? Are our ministers engaged as they should be in the work of the Master? Are they striving not only to feed the people with knowledge and understanding, but also to provoke them to activity in promoting the prosperity of Zion? Much we know is done by many, but very much more remains to be effected

The Baptists of this land, because of their numbers and resources, are capable of doing great things. We profess purity of faith. Our holy lives and zealous endeavors to convert souls ought to show it. Is it then our duty, or is it not, to pray, and labor, and give of our substance, that the 'way of God may be known upon earth, and his saving health among all nations'?"

There is one interesting fact connected with the life of this worthy man which deserves a special record. In the early part of his Christian course he indulged a strong desire to spend his life in some part of the heathen world. An abiding confidence in the prophecies concerning the latter-day glory was cherished. Casting his eye over this apostate globe and recollecting what God had promised, his constant prayer was, "Lord, what wilt thou have me to do?" In the sincerity of his heart he said, "Speak, Lord, for thy servant heareth." The following references to his feelings on this subject furnish an indication of disinterested anxiety to do the will of God:—

Addressing his brethren in the early part of 1825, he says: "The spirit of missions is love to souls; therefore, by their value, we entreat you all to become missionaries at home—to your families and neighborhoods. This will afford the best proof that you are sincere in your professions of love to the Redeemer and his cause. Pray for, and exhort all around you, that they may seek an interest in the Saviour's merits; distribute Bibles, tracts, and other useful books. The Lord often blesses these means. And know, that whosoever converteth a sinner from the error of his ways shall save a soul from death, and shall shine as a star in the kingdom of Christ above."

In his diary for 1826 he thus writes: "I have had my mind much on the subject of missionary work among the heathen. Endeavored last night to move the spirit of it among my people. I read, at the prayer-meeting, Rev. Gordon Hall's Address to American Christians and ministers. Surely we wrong the souls of the perishing heathen by doing so little for them. The work of a missionary must be truly self-denying, trying, and laborious. It requires much of the spirit of Jesus, untiring zeal, and inextinguishable love. In meditating on this subject I have had some uncommon views of my own weakness and insignificance. The work appears so important that, if it be the will of God, and I can be assured of it, I will go anywhere among the dying nations to make known the Saviour's love. I dare not say that I have the necessary grace; but I know Christ can and will give it to me if he wills me to go into this department of labor."

"October 6th, 1826. How am I to know whether it is the will of Christ for me to go to any part of the heathen world? This, to me, is an important and interesting inquiry. I have, I trust, a love for Jesus; a delight in his work; a love of souls; and particularly a compassion for the miserable heathen. They are given to Christ for an inheritance, and he has promised to take possession and save a multitude of them. I should be glad to have the privilege of preaching Christ crucified to any of them. To one engaged in such a work the promises of Christ ought to be exceedingly precious. The effort has been made by hundreds; and why should not I do as much as others when my obligations are no less?"

Thus was our dear brother long agitating the question whether he should labor in foreign lands or remain in this country. But having been pressingly urged to engage in the tract agency, and finding in it a wide range for doing good, he considered it an indication of the Divine pleasure that he should occupy this field. But he did not therefore relinquish the views and feelings of a missionary. The labors upon which he entered, when he removed to Philadelphia, were arduous, and involving great responsibility; and his great object was to subserve the interest of Christ's kingdom and the salvation of souls. There never was a period to the close of his life when he would not joyfully have followed the leadings of Providence as a messenger of glad tidings to the most distant clime. The following record from his journal refers to this subject: "Yesterday completed my twenty-fifth year. The review of the past discovers the changing nature of life and its connections. I have changed my place of residence; given up a pastoral care; and, instead of being a missionary in some distant part of the world, am now, in Philadelphia, agent of the Baptist General Tract Society. It is an important station, and one in which, if the Lord will, I may be very useful. Anywhere or anyhow, dear Lord, only let me serve my generation according to thy will. I think I should feel no unwillingness to be a missionary and to embark in the toils and trials of such a work. But the Lord knows what is best for me, and he may see that I am not fit for that work, but has other labor for me to perform. I sometimes fear that I am not in the right place, because I have so little personal comfort in religion and communion with God in secret."

"*Anywhere, or anyhow, only let me serve my generation according to Thy will.*" This was the ruling desire of his heart. It was in perfect conformity to such a sentiment that he toiled in the tract cause. Expressions of the self-denying spirit which he habitually cherished, and which would have taken him anywhere. Mr. Brantley says: "Noah Davis possessed qualities of no common kind. His capacity for the transaction of business would have insured him wealth and respectability in any community. The patronage under which he could have entered upon commercial pursuits in Philadelphia was such as few young men could boast. Nor was his mind naturally so formed as to be indifferent to the inducements of secular advantage; but he had learned Christ in such a manner as to become willing to consecrate to him all the talents which he possessed. He was prepared to forego the comfort and accommodation of houses, lands, and kindred, to serve the blessed Jesus."

The following testimony to his disposition to seek not his own, but another's good, is furnished by Elder John L. Dagg: "The trait of Brother Davis's character which was least known, even to his intimate friends, was his *disinterestedness*. Though I was myself very intimate with him, my estimate of his character in this respect has undergone a great change by the perusal of his numerous letters of his most confidential correspondence with her who shared equally in all his secular interests. And yet I cannot make any extract which will exhibit the proof that these manuscripts furnish on this point; for it is not by any professions or positive declarations which these contain that this trait is discoverable, but by the absence of everything that would have proceeded from a mind not free, in an extraordinary degree, from worldly care. Every letter is religious; not one is secular. Scarcely an inquiry or suggestion respecting their private interests is to be found in the whole mass. Many an anxiety is expressed for the health and spiritual prosperity of his family, and many a calculation of dollars for the Tract Society is made, but not one for the replenishing of his purse, often nearly reduced to emptiness. His letters are full of affection for his wife and children, and of information, plans, hopes, and fears, respecting the Tract Society and other objects connected with the interests of religion; but, except the bare details of his journey, they contain nothing else. Of information, plans, hopes, and fears respecting the pecuniary interests of himself and family, they are absolute emptiness. Yet the great part of this correspondence was carried on at times when he was traveling in the services of the Tract Society, and when his income was barely sufficient for his family support. When he left Norfolk, to take the agency of the Tract Society, his income was $600; and a school, which his wife taught, with his occasional assistance, added about $1200. Instead of this, as she distinctly recollects, he stated to her that he expected, for the first years of his services as agent, to receive from $200 to $400 per annum, and to take a school in Philadelphia was neither designed nor attempted. Assuredly it was not, and any one who will read these letters will know that it was not, for the *salary* of the agency that he accepted the office.

"To the preceding remarks there is one exception that I have noticed, if exception it deserves to be called. It is found in a letter written on the way to Utica, August 16th, 1827. An allusion is here made to personal interest, but it is made in such a manner as evinces the caution and self-distrust with which he approached that subject: 'There is a time coming when, if I continue agent of the society, (as I presume I shall,) it will be necessary for me to remain almost constantly at home. The correspondence, etc. will be so much that I shall not be able to leave it and you long at a time. When that comes to pass, it will be in connection with such an increase of funds that I shall have no need, on account of personal interest, to take journeys. Though I speak of personal interest as having something to do in stimulating my exertions, I don't know how much effect it has; I will leave you to judge, who know perhaps quite as well as I do.'

"To evince his indifference or superiority to the praise of men, one extract will suffice. It alludes to some praises that our deceased brother, A. W. Clopton, had bestowed on him. I must premise that he had the greatest respect for Brother Clopton, and valued his judgment, honesty, piety, and zeal, very highly. The words are: 'Clopton's *puff superlative* will do us no good. None of us are doing what we might do for God's cause. All have occasion to be humbled on account of our shortcomings, and confess ourselves to be unprofitable servants. I never felt my deficiencies, as an agent, more than lately. He does not know how much others are doing, or he would not say so.'"

It would gratify his friends in Norfolk to read an extract of a letter written by him soon after his removal from that place, in which appears the deep interest that he felt in their spiritual welfare: "But Brother Hendren's letter—how many different sensations were excited in my mind in about half an hour! He says: 'They have heard from Brother Broaddus, and he cannot go. It is uncertain as to Brother Ball; he is to visit them next month. They have had no preaching for some time; but, in the midst of all, a revival has commenced. Brother D., I wish you were here; but, as you are not, do pray for us; intercede with the Lord to carry on his work here; it would do you good to see those weeping to whom you once preached.' This is good news, indeed! O Lord, revive thy work more and more. Oh revive it in our poor hearts!"

In the preceding extracts from his correspondence and journal enough is found to evince the ardor of his love to God, and the strength of his sympathy for dying men. His attainments in holiness were of no ordinary character. Nor could it be otherwise. He was much with God. In contemplating the Divine excellence, there will be felt a transforming influence. Beholding, as in a glass, the glory of the Lord, we are changed into the same image, from glory to glory, even as by the spirit of the Lord. Thus it was with our esteemed brother. He was a man of prayer. From the mount of communion with God he often came down, his heart burning with holy desire to diffuse abroad the heavenly influence he had received. The extract which follows, from the pen of Brainerd, was found in his pocket-book after his decease. He could experimentally adopt the sentiment as his own:—

Glory of God. "My heaven is to please God, to give all to him, to be wholly devoted to his glory; that is the heaven I long for; that is my religion; that is my happiness, and always was, ever since I suppose I had any true religion. I do not go to heaven to get honor, but to give all possible glory and praise. It is no matter where I shall be stationed in heaven, whether I have a high or a low seat there; but to love, and please, and glorify God, is all. Had I a thousand souls, (if they were worth anything,) I would give them all to him; but I have nothing to give, when all is done. My heart goes out to the burying-ground; it seems to me a desirable place; but, oh, to glorify God! that is it, that is above all! It is a great comfort for me to think that I have done a little for God in the world. Oh, it is a very small matter! yet I have done a little, and lament that I have not done more for him. There is nothing in this world worth living for, but doing good, living to God, pleasing him, and doing his whole will."

In one of his letters, he thus describes a season of special religious enjoyment: "I was alone in my room; I gave myself to prayer; the season was particularly comfortable; I felt an unusual reluctance to leave the delightful service. You had been borne before the Lord in supplication. In rising from my knees, in a sweet frame of mind, I began to pace the floor, when the love of Jesus appeared to be manifest to my soul, after the manner of increase of morning light. I was filled with gratitude at his mercy. My soul exulted in its God; I breathed forth its sensations; tears of joy flowed from my eyes. The Lord seemed indeed present. Never before did I feel such joy unspeakable and full of glory. I felt love to the children of the Saviour, and astonished at the fact that I was experiencing this without possessing any worthiness, and when I did not seem to look for it more than at other times. Then I regretted that so soon this foretaste would pass away. Oh, why not always weep tears of joy! why not always experience the love of God shed abroad in the soul! Then my thoughts turned to glory, where there will be no cessation or interruption of our bliss. I thought of our love, and rejoiced principally. I thanked God for it, that we were one in Christ. I asked myself the question, 'Would I prefer to go, to be with Jesus, to staying with you?' 'Yes,' said I, 'if it were God's will, even this night! She is Christ's, and will soon be there; and how shall we place earthly joys, which are transient, in competition with heavenly, which are eternal? How shall any one be preferred to the Lord our Redeemer?' Indeed, I felt that I would leave you in the Lord's hands, and felt assured that his favor and presence is of infinitely more consequence to you than I can possibly be in any way whatever. I thank my Master for this, and hope that many, many more such seasons may be mine. But I find that I am in the world yet, to serve my Master, I trust, and be perfected in fitness for his presence with exceeding joy."

A few days previous to the date of this letter, he thus writes in his diary, July 25th, 1829: "Ten years ago, I was baptized into Jesus Christ, and first partook of the Lord's Supper, in the Sansom Street Church, Philadelphia. Ten years! how soon have they gone forever! And how little have I done for the honor of my Master and the salvation of men! Blessed be his name, he has not forsaken me, nor allowed me to forsake him or his cause."

One who knew him best, thus speaks of his latter days: "For the last two months, I believe that the Lord was preparing him for that unutterable bliss which he is now enjoying. A spirit of meekness seemed to rule all his conduct. Seldom have I seen more of the spirit of Christ in any of his followers. A holy calmness seemed to have taken possession of his mind. He was sensibly alive to every relative claim; but these claims, closely as they were wound about his heart, were all subservient to his Master's cause."

In reference to his sudden death, Brother Brantley remarks: "His health was infirm; and though his application to the duties of his station was unremitting and efficient, yet he often groaned, being burdened under the frailties of a feeble constitution. Those of less decision and zeal than he possessed would have resigned themselves to supineness and inaction under such bodily infirmities as he endured. But he counted not his life dear in view of the weighty care which the interest of his fellow-men devolved upon him. We have seldom known an instance in which the spending and being spent for God were more in accordance with true Christian devotedness. Death could not come unexpected to him. His transit from us was sudden, but not confused. For a long time we had seen him reaching forth after the incorruptible inheritance, spreading his wings for flight, raised aloft on the summit of holy hope, and viewing with intense delight the distant scenes of the promised glory. All his matters were arranged, his house was in order, and he was awaiting his final discharge.

"It would have been grateful to have a dying testimony from the lips of such a Christian. It would have been grateful to bedew with the farewell tear of affection the conscious bosom of such a brother. But these small mitigations of our grief could not be allowed: the loss of sensation and consciousness were the fatal symptoms under which his manly form sunk almost without warning. The spirit that lingered a short time about him could not control its shattered and dismembered tenement. We were, therefore, left to witness, without the ability to relieve, the last struggles of a prostrate frame. The month of July, in which he was born, in which he was baptized, in which he was ordained to the work of the ministry, in which he was married, witnessed his passage from time to eternity. He died on Thursday morning, July 15th, a few days less than twenty-eight years."

The Tract Magazine, of which he was editor, contains an allusion to this affecting event: "This number closes the earthly labors of the late editor. It is a satisfaction to the writer of this, that he has been enabled to finish it thus far in the very words, and, as he believes, arranged exactly as the editor would have done it himself. Providence seems to have spared him just long enough to leave it so that it could be easily finished, and it is believed that he has left all his business in the same easy train of completion; so that it may be said of him, that he had finished the work that had been given him to do. Though taken apparently in the midst of his years, (being only twenty-eight years of age,) and in the midst of his usefulness, his Master accomplished by him his own wise purposes, and then relieved him from the pains and anxieties of this life, and took him to the enjoyment of himself."

On the thirteenth instant, in the afternoon, he felt a little indisposed, and took some medicine, supposing he would feel better after it. In the evening the physician was sent for. About twelve o'clock he became insensible, and continued so until six o'clock on the morning of the fifteenth, when he breathed his last. As he had no premonition of his approaching end, he had not any opportunity of leaving a dying experience. It was not necessary. His *life* was sufficient evidence of his state. The opportunity the writer of this had of seeing him devote his days and his nights to the service of his Master, leaves no doubt on his mind of his present situation.

Thus died one of the most talented, lovely, and useful servants of Christ, which the present century has known. In the vigor of life he was taken away. How unexpectedly did he surrender his stewardship!—

"Many fall as sudden, few as safe."

The following reference, made to his removal, and some other interesting circumstances, is from the pen of Mr. Dagg: "He has left a text-book of sixty-two pages, in which are regularly noted all the sermons that he preached during the last four and a half years of his ministry. The last sermon was preached at Haddonfield, New Jersey, July 4th, 1830, from the words, 'But of him are ye in Christ Jesus, who of God is made unto us wisdom, and righteousness, and sanctification, and redemption,' (1 Cor. i. 30.) The insertion of this text filled up the last page of the book, except a small space, in which he wrote the following lines, subscribing them with his name: 'I was baptized July 4th, 1819, and have been a preacher *ten* years. Have preached eight hundred and thirty-eight times, which is eighty-three and eight-tenths sermons a year. Can only subscribe myself an unprofitable servant, and beg for mercy to a sinner through the sufficient merit of Jesus.'

"Thus he filled up his book and his ministry precisely eleven years from the day of his baptism. Thus he subscribes his name; and casting himself upon the merits of his Redeemer, closed the account of his ministerial labors. Death, unseen, stood at his side as he executed the deed. But he was prepared, at any moment, to meet the ghastly messenger; and had he seen his terrific form, he would probably have closed the account just as he did. A few weeks before his death, I was cast low upon a bed of sickness, from which I expected never to rise. He visited me with brethren David Jones, Thomas Brown, and Joseph Cone, all able ministers of the New Testament, and among my most intimate friends, dearly beloved in the Lord. They all, I think, expected, as I did, that the time of our separation was near; but how little did any of us understand the inscrutable purposes of God! The time of separation was indeed near; for in a few short months all these brethren were taken to their rest, while I am still tossed on life's tempestuous sea, not knowing which wave is destined to receive me. To the affectionate attentions of Brother Davis, the restoration of my health was, in a great measure, attributable. As soon as I was able to take exercise in a carriage, he not only devised measures to procure that exercise for me, but, with assiduous care, accompanied me each day in the short excursions I was at first able to make. Afterwards, he projected a plan to take me with him on one of his tours in the service of the Tract Society, designing to bestow such attention to my slowly returning health as would tend to re-establish it. This plan his death frustrated. His solicitude for my recovery resulted not so much from personal attachment to me, as from love to the cause of Christ, in which he believed my life might be useful. The shock which I received from the sudden announcement is never to be forgotten. I had not heard of his illness. He vanished from us, as Brother Brantley has expressed it, like a winged dream. So, though by a less hasty flight, have Jones, and Brown, and Cone departed. Surely this life is all a dream. How unlooked for, how wonderful, how astonishing are its events! Great Author of my being, give me acquiescence in thy will, and help me to fill up the measure of my days in some useful service in thy cause; and when thou shalt call me hence, give me a place among those who have thus taught me how to live and how to die "

An extract from the pen of Professor Knowles will close this sketch: "I may say, with entire truth, that the death of Mr. Davis was a loss to our denomination, and to the Christian world. While his feelings were liberal toward all men, and he cordially prayed that grace, mercy, and peace might be multiplied to all who love our Lord Jesus Christ in sincerity, he felt a special concern for the welfare of our own churches. It was a desire for their benefit, which impelled him to exertion in the cause of tracts. It was because he was convinced that our churches would be more generally interested in tracts, if there were a society under our own control, that he advocated its cause, while toward that noble institution, the American Tract Society, he felt the utmost cordiality. He collected, with great labor, the statistics of the denomination, and his annual table of associations, published in the Tract Magazine, was the most accurate and complete account of our churches which has been published. Perhaps no young man among us was contributing more directly and powerfully to advance the interests of the Baptist denomination. His influence is not to be measured by the importance of the office which he filled, though that was a post of great usefulness. His office merely furnished a medium through which his energetic mind, and his warm love to God and man, were enabled to act on the Christian community. It was a kind of observatory, from which he could look abroad on the wants and interests of the churches, and from which, with telegraphic rapidity, he could spread among them the kindling emanations of his own and other minds. Though his immediate object was the distribution of tracts, yet there was no exclusiveness in his aims and efforts. He regarded the cause of the Saviour as one, combining, indeed, many interests, which may be advantageously separated and pursued individually, with concentrated force; yet he viewed that cause like the rainbow, in which the several rays of light are blended, and the prism through which he, in his official character, contemplated it, only presented its colors to his eye in a more beautiful and distinct relation to each other. Missions, education, Sabbath-schools, the distribution of the Bible, all modes of benevolent enterprise, held a place in his heart, and claimed a share of his efforts, while he was directly toiling in the great cause of tracts.

"He never sunk into a mere agent. In the pulpit he preached with the zeal of a missionary and the free-hearted affection of a pastor. At a missionary meeting he would plead for the heathen with an expansion of thought and feeling which stretched beyond the comparatively little space in which he was laboring, to the wide limits of the great field, the world. Those who attended the session of the Boston Association, in 1829, will not soon forget the spirit-stirring eloquence with which he urged the necessity of efforts to increase the number and the qualifications of our ministers. It is worth mentioning here, as an illustration of the zeal and liberality of his heart, that, at the Association, when a subscription was commenced to aid the Massachusetts Baptist Education Society, he rose and offered his watch as a contribution to the funds."

He is gone. Let us, who remain a while longer, gird ourselves for increased diligence, looking for that blessed hope, and the glorious appearing of the great God, and our Saviour Jesus Christ.

JOHN SPOTTS.*

ELDER SPOTTS was born 8th of October, 1784. His parents were of German origin, and resided in the Valley of Virginia. In the earlier part of his life he was employed for a number of years as a clerk in a store. He made a public profession of religion by connecting himself with the Presbyterian church, when about thirty years of age. His attention was immovably fixed on this all-important subject by an alarming *dream,* in which he thought the day of judgment had arrived and he was unprepared for its awful solemnities. While every intelligent person discards that superstitious belief in *dreams* that belongs only to the ignorant, there are but few who will not acknowledge that our heavenly Parent may convert to useful purposes the fanciful creations of the mind in our sleeping moments.

The subject of this memoir was an active elder in the church with which he stood connected for a number of years. More than twenty years of his life were devoted to teaching, during the greater part of which time he had the management of the English department in the Lewisburg Academy. The estimation in which he

* By L. A. Alderson.

was held as an instructor may be learned from the fact that his school was generally crowded to overflowing.

His usefulness as a Sunday-school superintendent cannot be fully developed on this side of eternity. He was among the first that engaged in this work of benevolence in Western Virginia; and during the space of sixteen years nothing but an unavoidable circumstance would induce him to be absent from his school. With melancholy pleasure does the writer look back upon those Sabbaths, when Brother Spotts, with feelings "too big to be uttered," would direct his pupils to Him who said, "Suffer little children to come unto me, and forbid them not, for of such is the kingdom of heaven." Nor were his efforts in vain, for many of his scholars became the humble followers of Jesus, *and more than* TWENTY *of them engaged in the gospel ministry, one of whom was a missionary in China.* "He being dead, yet speaketh," through those who were once taught by him.

He was among the first to engage in the cause of the temperance reformation. His influence was not confined to the Lewisburg Temperance Society, over which he presided, but by the distribution of tracts, and public addresses, he circulated information through the circumjacent country, and in various places formed new societies. Such was his opposition to intemperance, that he could not have full confidence in any professor of religion who would drink or sell spirituous liquors.

The mind of Brother Spotts having undergone a change on the subject of baptism, he connected himself with the Big Levels Baptist Church, which now worships in Lewisburg, on the 7th of August, 1831. Soon afterwards he engaged in the ministry; and on the 6th of May, 1832, he was ordained by a presbytery consisting of Elders V. M. Mason, A. Freeman, and E. W. Woodson. In the course of the subsequent year he was employed as a missionary, in which service he remained until October last. The Board had no laborer that was more persevering and untiring in his efforts than he.

He died of bilious pleurisy, on Tuesday, the tenth instant, after a short illness of eight days. Previous to his death he spoke of his departure with calmness and resignation. He said he did not fear to die. On one occasion, after prayer, he repeated the following appropriate lines:

"My suffering time will soon be o'er,
Then I shall weep and sigh no more;
My ransomed soul shall soar away
To sing God's praise in endless day."

His latest breath was spent in exhortation to those that surrounded his dying pillow. As the stars of night melt away in the light of the rising sun, so do the spirits of the just disappear—but they disappear that they may be drawn nearer to the sun of righteousness.

Elder Spotts, in his manner of preaching, inclined to be warm and animated rather than critical. He was possessed of much zeal, and, above all, of *ardent piety*—a qualification without which no minister of the gospel can gain any great success. Whatever might have been his errors, we feel convinced that they must have been errors of the head, and not of the heart. His great desire for the welfare of those among whom he ministered induced him to exercise self-denial and preach the gospel under most trying circumstances. But his labors are over. That voice, which to so many has spoken the truths of redeeming love, we firmly believe is still employed on the same theme, but in more glorious circumstances.

JOHN A. DAVIDSON.

THIS servant of Christ, the son of Elder Samuel Davidson, was a native of Campbell County, Virginia. He is said to have possessed a peculiarly amiable disposition. But this, he was enabled to perceive, was not sufficient to entitle him to the kingdom of heaven. In the eighteenth year of his age he was brought under the renovating influence of the Divine Spirit, and felt, in its energy, the whole force of the language of the Saviour, "Ye must be born again." He now saw the perishing nature of all earthly enjoyments, and that he could not be happy but in the favor of

God. He sought the salvation of his soul, and soon was enabled to testify that Jesus Christ hath power on earth to forgive sins. He attached himself to the Baptist church, and, from that time to the hour of his dissolution, he invariably sustained the character of a decided and uniform Christian.

Soon after his conversion he became impressed with the conviction that it was his duty to call sinners to repentance by preaching the unsearchable riches of Christ to a lost and ruined world. He conferred not with flesh and blood, but yielded to the heavenly mandate; and many a weeping penitent was by him pointed to the "Lamb of God that taketh away the sin of the world." Some of these will gratefully remember his ardent prayers for their conversion, long after nature has covered his grave with "its mantle of green." The silent bosom of earth has received his dust; his voice is hushed in death; but with him death and the grave were despoiled of their terror.

In his humble, meek, and holy life he exhibited "lucid proof" of the divinity of the gospel which he preached. Retiring and unobtrusive in his manners, he lived without reproach, possessing a conscience void of offence toward God and man. To all who saw him during his illness he gave the most indubitable evidence of a confidence firm and full of immortality. His affliction was of five or six weeks' continuance, and he bore it with patience and resignation. He had frequently been delirious until the morning of his dissolution, at which time he was perfectly in his senses and well aware that the cold hand of death was upon him. He met the grim monster without dismay, and was enabled to say, "I am perfectly happy and resigned," and then shouted, "Glory to God, hallelujah!" And continued, "Come, Jesus! come quickly! O Jesus, let me go! Why cannot I go now? Oh let me go!" He repeated, with peculiar emphasis, the following verse:—

"Jesus can make a dying bed
Feel soft as downy pillows are;
While on his breast I lean my head,
And breathe my life out sweetly there."

He feelingly exhorted those around him to seek the salvation of their souls and to meet him in heaven. Just before he expired he applied to his own case the words of the Apostle: "I have fought a good fight, I have finished my course, I have kept the faith. Henceforth there is laid up for me a crown of righteousness, which the Lord, the righteous judge, shall give me at that day." His declining sun set without a cloud. The weary wheels of life gently ceased to move; his exit was so easy that it was not exactly known when the spirit took its flight.

END OF FIRST SERIES.

www.ingramcontent.com/pod-product-compliance
Lightning Source LLC
LaVergne TN
LVHW021318110826
845150LV00003B/604